kids   on   the   street

kids   on

the street

Queer Kinship and Religion in San Francisco's Tenderloin

JOSEPH PLASTER

DUKE UNIVERSITY PRESS
Durham and London
2023

Designed by A. Mattson Gallagher
Typeset in Untitled Serif and Univers LT Standard
by Copperline Book Services

Library of Congress Cataloging-in-Publication Data
Names: Plaster, Joseph, [date] author.
Title: Kids on the street : queer kinship and religion in
San Francisco's Tenderloin / Joseph Plaster.
Description: Durham : Duke University Press, 2023. |
Includes bibliographical references and index.
Identifiers: LCCN 2022029358 (print)
LCCN 2022029359 (ebook)
ISBN 9781478018957 (paperback)
ISBN 9781478016311 (hardcover)
ISBN 9781478023586 (ebook)
Subjects: LCSH: Sexual minority youth—Social networks—
California—San Francisco. | Street youth—Social networks—
California—San Francisco. | Street youth—Religious
life—California—San Francisco. | Marginality, Social—
California—San Francisco. | Sociology, Urban—California—
San Francisco. | Tenderloin (San Francisco, Calif.)—Social
conditions—20th century. | BISAC: SOCIAL SCIENCE / LGBTQ
Studies / Gay Studies | SOCIAL SCIENCE / Sociology / Urban
Classification: LCC HV1426 .P53 2023 (print) | LCC HV1426 (ebook) |
DDC 362.709794/61—dc23/eng/20220902
LC record available at https://lccn.loc.gov/2022029358
LC ebook record available at https://lccn.loc.gov/2022029359

Cover art: Rob Bennett and friends at a phone booth
at Polk and Geary, San Francisco, ca. early 1980s.
Photograph courtesy of Rob Bennett.

CONTENTS

ACKNOWLEDGMENTS

First and foremost, I thank the more than eighty people who recorded stories with me along Polk Street and in the Tenderloin. My informants challenged and transformed me; in many cases they became my kin. A special thanks to Coy Ellison, Alexis Miranda, River Sims, Cecilia Chung, and Megan Rohrer, who became key interlocutors and co-conspirators.

I owe a great debt to San Francisco's Gay, Lesbian, Bisexual, Transgender Historical Society, where I began this project as an independent public historian. The activists, artists, and academics who animated this organization shaped my work from the very beginning. I am especially grateful for Dr. Martin Meeker, who helped me win grants and assisted with virtually every aspect of my early research, including exhibit development, archival research, intellectual and emotional support—the list goes on. Thanks also to GLBT Historical Society archivist Rebekah Kim, who gave me considerable freedom to commune with the archive's ghosts, as well as Gerard Koskovich, the late (and great) Willie Walker, Don Romesburg, Marjorie Bryer, Ramón Sylveste, Daniel Bao, Kelsi Evans, Isaac Fellman, and many others. I was also inspired by scholars who came before me at the GLBT Historical Society—including Susan Stryker, Nan Alamilla Boyd, and Allan Bérubé—who often operated outside the academy and mobilized research to animate their social justice commitments. Finally, I am indebted to the many people who volunteered at the GLBT Historical Society to transcribe my oral histories, including Yasmin Golan, Marika Cifor, Virginia Lenander, Lauren Richards, and Michael Thomas Angelo.

Throughout graduate school in the Program in American Studies at Yale University, I was fortunate to have a supportive and brilliant group of mentors. It is impossible to imagine a more thoughtful and engaged advisor than Kathryn Dudley. The shape of this book is in large part the result of her careful guidance. Performance studies legend Joseph Roach was also a revelation: when I first met him at a Performance Studies Working Group reception, he held out his arms, embraced me, and said, more than a bit dramatically, "We welcome you with open arms!" I've felt that embrace ever since—during private readings, through his guidance as a committee chair, and since receiving my PhD. Thanks also to Jean-Christophe Agnew, whose encyclopedic knowledge and interdisciplinary creativity continue to inspire. I learned a great deal through George Chauncey's and Joanne Meyerowitz's courses, our frenzied preparation for oral examinations, and their Yale Research Initiative on the History of Sexualities. I also thank Joseph Fischel, Andrew Dowe, Emily Johnson, and Heather Vermeulen of the Women's, Gender, and Sexuality Studies Graduate Colloquium and Working Group. I am grateful for the support provided by the Performance Studies Working Group, including Elise Morrison, Tina Post, and Paige McGinley, as well as Public Humanities Working Group members Najwa Mayer and Lauren Tilton. My collaborators in the Ethnography and Oral History Initiative kept me going, especially Rebecca Jacobs, Alison Kanosky, and Karilyn Crockett, as did fellow graduate students madison moore, Megan Asaka, Michelle Morgan, Devin McGeehan Muchmore, and Michael Amico. Finally, I was fortunate to learn from incredible colleagues and students as a lecturer in the American Studies Program.

At Johns Hopkins University, I benefit from the support of many individuals, programs, and institutions. I completed this book—during the early months of the COVID-19 pandemic—while serving as curator in public humanities and director of the Winston Tabb Special Collections Research Center. I thank my colleagues for the opportunity to finish this manuscript, including faculty and staff in the Program in Museums and Society; the Alexander Grass Humanities Institute; the Program for the Study of Women, Gender, and Sexuality; and the Engaged Scholar Program. Thanks especially to Jennifer Kingsley, François Furstenberg, Todd Shepard, William Egginton, Shane Butler, and Shawntay Stocks for supporting my work. I am also grateful for the brilliant students in my queer history and public humanities courses. Many thanks also go to my Duke University Press editor Joshua Gutterman Tranen, who has been essential to making this book possible. I am also indebted for his selection of two extremely helpful readers whose comments substantially improved this manuscript, as well as to Liz Smith for her assistance during the production process.

I also recognize the foundations and institutions who provided the economic resources that made this book possible. Funders include the California Council for the Humanities, the National Endowment for the Arts, the San Francisco Foundation, the Human Rights Campaign Religion and Faith Program, the St. Francis Foundation, the E. Rhodes and Leona B. Carpenter Foundation, the Horizons Foundation, and many individual donors. I benefited from an OutHistory fellowship through the Center for Lesbian and Gay Studies at the City University of New York; a Martin Duberman Visiting Scholar award at the New York Public Library; and Yale University's Fund for Lesbian and Gay Studies. This project could not have come to fruition without the support of these institutions.

Finally, I couldn't have completed this work without a huge network of friends and collaborators. I am grateful for support from members of Groundswell Oral History and Social Justice, including Amy Starecheski and Sarah Loose, as well as Concordia University oral historian Steven High. I am indebted to Gabriela Hasbun for her carefully staged photographs of Polk Street denizens, many of which are reprinted in this book. Thanks also to the staff at the Sylvia's Place homeless youth shelter, the congregation of the Metropolitan Community Church of New York, and the San Francisco Night Ministry. I am beyond grateful for the friends who have sustained me in so many vital ways, especially Jeremy Melius, Timothy Stewart-Winter, Paul VanDeCarr, Shannon O'Malley, Noah Miller, Rosalie Zdzienicka Fanshel, Jonathan Ned Katz, Jonas Meckling, and madison moore. Thanks for dancing with me at Divas, biking to the orchards, joining my pandemic pod, housing me, mentoring me, and otherwise teaching me about the importance of mutual aid.

Introduction

SAN FRANCISCO'S POLK STREET was a whole world to itself: about ten blocks of old-stock rooming houses, dive bars, coffeehouses, and nightclubs sandwiched between the downtown Tenderloin "vice" district, City Hall, and the affluent, residential Nob Hill. The city's premiere gay business corridor in the 1960s and 1970s, Polk Street later became a national destination for runaway and "throwaway" youth, many surviving through sex work, and an older, paternal social world of survivors, caregivers, and clients. When I started hanging out there in 2007, a diverse group of trans women, johns, social workers, drag queens, and tourists cruised and caroused on the heavily trafficked thoroughfare.

One of the first people I met there was the Reverend River Sims, a squat, queer man in his fifties. The self-described "punk priest of Polk Street" worked independently, his ministerial garb a leather jacket festooned with Misfits patches. I got to know River over the course of a year, serving free dinners together in an alleyway during a weekly needle exchange and handing out condoms and insulin syringes to his congregation of the previous fifteen years: the "kids" on Polk Street, many of them runaways, most of them hustlers and addicts. I recorded oral histories with the kids in River's single-room occupancy (SRO) apartment, a tiny space saturated with religious statues and icons. One wall featured a motley collection of handmade crucifixes and a painting of a nude man, pocked with Kaposi's sarcoma, titled *Man of Sorrows: Christ with AIDS*. Another showcased a painting of hypodermic syringes in the shape of a skull and crossbones. Most strikingly, the wall near River's door was covered with more than fifty framed photos of boys he had known—most of them, he said, long since dead.

When we first met, the Reverend was playful—even flirty. "i'll have to watch you," he emailed in 2007, "because the johns will be trying to steal you from me, which they can for the right price. Ha." Introducing me to another queer independent minister on the street, River laughed and said I was "just like one of the boys," probably referring to my age and appearance. A skinny, white queer kid in my late twenties, I may have sometimes passed as one of the boys. (One day, as I was crossing the street, a wiry, middle-aged man shouted out: "I'll give you two hundred dollars!") River may have also sensed other similarities. For decades, Polk Street had been a destination for runaways seeking sanctuary in the "gay mecca." While I enjoyed much greater educational and economic privilege as a recent college graduate, I also came to San Francisco in search of a home and family. If outsiders maligned the corridor as a dangerous marketplace—the *Wall Street Journal* called it "San Francisco's worst neighborhood" in 2006, a "gathering point for pimps, drug addicts and transvestites"—I romanticized it as a refuge for castaways.[1] "I think I'm interested in Polk Street," I told an informant during an oral history, "because it's a place where people who don't fit in in other parts of the country can find a home."

This was all changing in the late 2000s, as the infusion of Silicon Valley capital drove up rental prices and radically reshaped the corridor. Luxury condos and upscale "mixed" bars began replacing SRO hotels and gay taverns. New business associations pressured the police to sweep away the homeless. People said gentrification was pricing queer people out of the neighborhood—and the city—as business interests ate away at the downtown. The conflicts were often dramatic. When a new business association strong-armed a hustler bar off the street, activists plastered the district with "wanted" posters featuring a photograph of the association president. Queer activists held anti-gentrification protests, holding signs that read "Don't Erase Our Past." Drag queens led "Take Back the Polk" marches. The press chimed in: some called gentrification a death, some a renaissance.

It felt to me like an enormous loss. Gentrification was erasing a history I had come to San Francisco to claim and become a part of. I became obsessed with "saving" the street's history before it was swept away. As an independent public historian, I partnered with San Francisco's Gay, Lesbian, Bisexual, Transgender (GLBT) Historical Society—a nonprofit hub of queer academics, artists, and activists—and began recording oral histories in the SRO hotels, churches, bars, and alleyways.

River agreed to record his story and connect me with informants because he was excited about documenting a history being erased by the "white, upper-middle-class older people" new to the street, but our relationship was also highly transactional. River told me he'd arrange oral histories with the boys in exchange for my volunteer work with his ministry. We established a routine: River said I should be at his apartment at 3 p.m. every Thursday, at which time I would record an hour-long interview with him. We would then prepare a meal and drive it to Hemlock Alley, where I would help him unload his car and serve a meal to the kids. River would ask one of the boys to give an interview, which I would conduct after unloading the meal at his apartment. "I am counting on your help," River said, "not having other people who help." River insisted that I pay the boys ten dollars per interview. He would give the kids clean socks before they left his apartment.

River also warned me to not be "taken in" by the boys. They sometimes threatened him when he refused to give them cash or didn't let them stay at his apartment overnight. Some of the kids assaulted and robbed a former volunteer. "These guys look for every angle," River said, "and so know that beneath the sweetness and the niceness there is the possibility for violence and anger. They are trying to survive, and so to survive for them means to get what they can." Finally, River warned me that the interviews would be emotionally draining. "It is obvious that you feel for people," he said, "and this will tear you up. The suffering you will hear will tear your heart out."

One Thursday night, after pouring cups of Kool-Aid in Hemlock Alley, River introduced me to Richard, a boyish twenty-one-year-old sporting a pink mohawk and goofy smile.[2] We packed River's car and drove a few blocks to his apartment. After unloading the meal, Richard and I sat on River's futon and I began recording. Richard told me he'd been on Polk Street since he was fifteen. "I was molested when I was a child by my stepfather," he said. "When my parents kicked me out, it was one of the reasons why I came up here. Because I figure that if I'm up here then he can't get to me anymore." A friend dropped him off in front of a trans club called Divas. Trans women quickly took him into their hotel rooms and shared food and money. "They all just reached out to me," Richard said. "Maybe it was just because I was really, really young, but they just felt the need to take me under their wing and show me what they thought was the right way."

Polk Street "is like family," Richard said. "Even though the people out here will give you drugs, they'll also give you money for food if you need it. They've always made sure that if I need a place to stay that I'm inside for the night. And that if I need a shower that I can wash myself. Or if I need clean clothes, they'll take me shopping at Goodwill." Richard was "one of the Polk Street kids. I was fifteen when I came here, but I was pretty much raised by Polk Street. All of my adult life I've lived here." When we finished, I gave Richard ten dollars. River handed him a pair of clean socks.

When I started recording, I worried that these transactions—cash for interviews, volunteer work for informants—would cheapen the "authenticity" of the historical narrative I hoped to write. I came in time to realize that these transactions were instead at the heart of the story I needed to tell. As a young researcher, I was becoming another link in the reciprocities and mutual obligations that comprised people's everyday survival on Polk Street. In the process, I was being drawn into the kinship networks my informants called "street families" and the religious formations I call "street churches."

Over the course of five years, from 2007 to 2011, I recorded oral histories with more than seventy people in the Tenderloin's alleyways, hotels, and churches. At the same time, I explored the archives of the GLBT Historical Society. I would go there late at night and sit cross-legged on the carpeted floor between the stacks. Pulling archival boxes, I encountered the traces of figures uncannily similar to River and the kids: people who, as early as the 1960s, established their own congregations in the Tenderloin; ordained street youth, themselves, and others; and banded together in loosely structured street families. I developed a kind of "archive fever": a desire to collapse time, to bring the past closer, to cross what Saidiya Hartman calls the "barricade between *then* and *now*."[3]

This queer desire for history led me to more than a dozen archives across the country as well as the published archive of surveys, sociological studies, reportage, and memoirs. I found that the Tenderloin was once one of many similar red-light districts—often called "tenderloins"—in cities across the United States. By the late nineteenth century, cities constructed these districts as zones of abandonment where the degradation and immorality associated with the poor, sexual and gender deviants, and racialized populations could be contained and cordoned off from respectable white families and homes.[4] These seemingly abject, antidomestic, transactional, and profane districts were at the same time incubators for rich kinship networks, syncretic religious practices, and oppositional politics. Street kids, sustaining themselves through prostitution and other criminalized economies, created in these districts a counterpublic complete with rituals for renaming new members, conventions for collective housing, and networks for pooling resources to increase the chances of mutual survival. From the early twentieth century through the 2010s, kids traveled from "tenderloin" to "tenderloin," often in sync with festival and seasonal patterns, creating a web of familiar places and kin.

Performative Economies

Kids on the Street is an exploration of the informal networks of economic and social support that enabled street kids to survive in tenderloin districts across the United States, and in San Francisco's Tenderloin in particular, over the past century. I combine archival, ethnographic, oral history, and public humanities research to explore the social trauma inflicted on street youth and the ways they have worked, collectively and creatively, to reframe those brutal realities. This book focuses on four world-making practices: queer kinship networks my informants call "street families," which resemble the moral economies common among people with severely limited resources; syncretic religious formations I call "street churches," which are often based on a streetwise, gothic Catholicism bent toward the redemptive power of abjection; performative storytelling, narrative strategies that enabled youth to secure employment in the district's vice and bar economies and, at times, to reinterpret the abuse from which they were running; and migratory circuits that connected far-flung tenderloin districts across the country and the people who traversed them, all the while fostering alternative socialities, cooperative economies, and novel forms of mutual aid.

These rituals and kinship networks comprise what I call a performative economy: a shared repertoire of creative strategies for managing the affective and economic impacts of abandonment. More precisely, a performative economy references the reciprocities, obligations, and moral norms shared by a population and the ways they are materialized and transmitted intergenerationally via performance, broadly defined to include religious ritual, storytelling, kinship, and gesture—"in short, all those acts usually thought of as ephemeral."[5] Basing my analysis on the concept of moral economy, queer studies of affect, and performance studies, I show that street kids developed morally inflected conventions around resource sharing, mutual protection, self-policing, and other survival strategies that they instantiated through a variety of ritualizations and performative enactments. They were in turn "taken in" by an older, paternal community of survivors, intermediaries, and long-term caregivers (for example, bartenders, bouncers, ministers, johns, and patrons) for whom the kids remained, after all, the principal draw for the formal vice economies. I experienced the traces of this social world when I recorded stories and walked the streets of San Francisco's Tenderloin.

The kids often referred to their migratory world as "the scene," a phrase that suggests a degree of self-conscious theatricality—of characters playing roles and an urban stage on which to play them. They could recognize the scene in each city by its material environment: the rooming houses, diners, dive bars, theaters, all-night coffee shops, and heavily trafficked boulevards. They could identify it by the stock characters of the queen, the hustler, and the urban cowboy, and the poses and gestures that indicated sexual availability. In his classic 1963 novel *City of Night*, for example, John Rechy instantly recognized "the scene" in downtown Los Angeles by "the vagrant youngmen dotting those places: the motorcyclists without bikes, the cowboys without horses, awol servicemen or on leave."[6] More intangibly, migrants could identify the scene by its affective intensity. "When you cross over into [San Francisco's] Tenderloin," a hustler wrote in 1967, "it's like walking into another room. The change in atmosphere is obvious."[7] My informants indexed this intensity when they referred to the Tenderloin as a "magnet," a "vortex," or a "whirlpool"—metaphors suggesting an attractive, spiraling force. As such, I approach the scene—a phrase I use interchangeably with "performative economy"—as an assemblage that includes humans and their (social, performative, and narrative) constructions as well as the nonhumans that shaped those performances: the "vice and amusement" economies; the material environment; and the districts themselves, in their aggregate form.[8]

My interest in the kids' world-making practices is more than academic; it is for me, as it is for my informants, a matter of survival in spaces widely regarded by outsiders as dirty, dangerous, and duplicitous marketplaces. The stories, the dramas, and the scenes I document played a central role in the development of one of the country's earliest and most visible queer public cultures.

At the heart of this book is also a methodological question: how to best represent the history of a migratory culture that left few archival traces.

Studies of queer affect and urban history have relied heavily on literature, archival evidence, and oral history interviews from settled urban communities. By relying on these forms of evidence, researchers risk privileging the histories of housed populations and occluding the experiences of people living on the economic margins. Particularly for subaltern groups, Dwight Conquergood argues, "texts are often inaccessible, or threatening, charged with the regulatory powers of the state."[9] I instead insist on an interdisciplinary approach, drawing on my own ethnographic research, based on more than seventy oral history interviews, and research at more than a dozen archives throughout the country. I build on methods from performance studies, which ask that researchers rethink our method of analysis from a wholly text-based approach to one that approaches performance as a system for transmitting cultural memory, and rethink the site-bound ways that we have often written urban histories of sexuality by focusing on the reciprocities, moral norms, and performance practices created through migration. These interdisciplinary methods enable me to broaden the queer studies archive and create an alternative mapping of queer life, one in which class, migration, and economy are as central as sexuality.

Centering the experiences of street kids enables me to articulate—indeed excavate—a history of queer sociality that has been overshadowed by major narratives of gay progress and pride. I represent a politics where the marginal position of street youth—the self-defined "kids on the street," hair fairies, hustlers, queens, and "undesirables"—is the basis for a moral economy of reciprocity and mutual aid. Tarnished as criminal and immoral, as undesirable blights on downtowns ripe for reinvestment, street kids developed a flexible and fraternal accumulation of obligations and reciprocities by which they could "watch each other's backs." Many insisted on the value of sociality and sexuality untethered from the nuclear family, reproduction, and the gender binary and dramatized their moral vision on the streets and boulevards in spectacular fashion.

This said, I am not ultimately writing a redemptive narrative. It is important to guard against the impulse to revise or romanticize history—to insist on liberation where there may have been only survival. Where the kids' cooperative relationships worked, they were not always a product of altruism but a necessity for mutual survival.[10] I instead document what Elizabeth Povinelli calls the "immanent dependencies that emerge in actual life."[11] In spaces of abandonment, everyday survival can be a minor miracle and the development of an alternative politics a major achievement.

Scope and Bearings

Because a study of the scene is beyond the scope of this book, I have settled on an exploration of the performative economy as it manifested in San Francisco's Tenderloin and on Polk Street, primarily from the 1960s through the 2020s. Viewed on a map, the Tenderloin is a triangular piece of land in the heart of downtown. It borders Market Street, the city's main thoroughfare, and is situated between some of the wealthiest and most powerful neighborhoods in San Francisco, including the upscale Union Square shopping district to the northeast; the retail corridor of Powell to the east and south; the seat of government at Civic Center to the southwest; the wealthy, residential Nob Hill on one of the sloping hills to the north; and big-name tech offices, including Twitter, on the Mid-Market corridor to the east. West of the Tenderloin is the Western Addition, a historically black neighborhood that is gentrifying and whitening along with the rest of San Francisco.

With roughly thirty thousand people in forty square blocks, the Tenderloin is one of the most densely packed districts in the city; at the time of this writing, it retains its function as a haven and containment zone for migrants and the poor. Located in the flatlands, the "red-light" district is saturated with old-stock housing dating to the early twentieth century; "Rescue Missions"; porn theaters and dive bars; nonprofit organizations that house residents on public assistance, the formerly homeless, people living with AIDS, the elderly, and many low-income queer and gender-variant people.

I open this book with a genealogy of the kids' performative economy, surveying the "main stems"—downtown lodging house districts—through which runaway and "throwaway" youth regularly circulated from the early twentieth century through the 2010s. I then focus on the scene as it took shape in San Francisco's Tenderloin, from the 1950s to the 1960s, concentrating on the ways street kids formalized the performative economy via the street youth organization Vanguard. I follow the scene, after it was displaced by redevelopment and police sweeps in the 1970s, to the nearby Polk Street corridor and outline the forms of masquerade and storytelling that kids developed in the district's alleyways, taverns, and hotels. I then look to the disintegration of the performative economy in the 2010s, as the combined pressures of rising rents, aggressive policing, and the politics of respectability transformed central cities across the country and drove the kids out of the Polk Street corridor in San Francisco. Finally, I examine the ways in which the City of San Francisco, developers, and activists are remembering

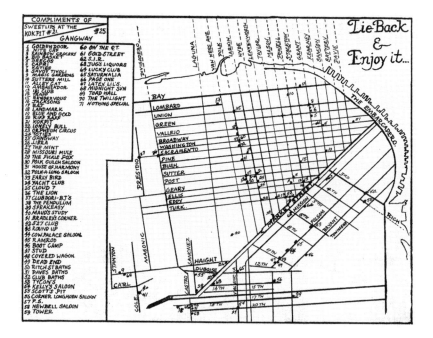

FIGURE I.1.

Map of San Francisco gay bars, baths, and hotels compiled by Sweet Lips, a.k.a. Richard Walters, ca. early 1970s. Note especially the businesses along Polk Street and the Market Street meat rack at the intersection of Turk and Market Streets. Courtesy of GLBT Historical Society.

(and forgetting) the performative economy in the 2010s and early 2020s. I interrupt this chronological narrative with two "interventions" that showcase public humanities projects I developed to intervene in debates about gentrification, policing, and displacement.

I focus on performance to show how the kids, their patrons, and their protectors elaborated new social worlds in vice and amusement districts across the country. Tenderloin districts were carnivalesque spaces in which people became, for better or worse, what they ordinarily were not.[12] Through performance, people displaced by social trauma—often severe physical and emotional abuse in their families of birth—could play with new identities, new forms of embodiment and style, and new strategies for survival.[13] I document activities such as religious ordinations, communions, and christenings; kinship terms and practices; collective theatricality and "flaunting" of gender norms; reform work, hustling poses, migration, and my own oral history encounters and public humanities projects. I position these performances as embodied practices that structured and were structured by material environments: the transient hotels and all-night coffeehouses; the downtown streets and boulevards; and the "vice" districts themselves, in their aggregate form.

Through such performances, street kids collectively reframed and reinterpreted the social trauma many experienced throughout their lives: namely, the experience of being perceived as and experiencing the self as "trash." Woven into the tissue of their performances is a shared moral universe, a common notion of what is just.

Kids on the Street

This interdisciplinary approach enables me to represent social worlds created by self-described "boys," "girls," "kids," and "kids on the street"— phrases people circulated in central city districts as early as the 1920s and continued to circulate when I walked Polk Street in the 2010s.[14] While kids were usually teenagers through their early twenties, the term did not necessarily refer to chronological age. "In common parlance," a gay bar rag clarified in 1966, the phrase "kids on the street" can "mean of any age, from 16 to 60."[15] According to a reporter writing the same year, "'kid' is the generic name for a habitue of the Tenderloin, regardless of age."[16] River Sims told me around 2009 about "thirty-year-old guys [on Polk Street] who call themselves 'kids.'" In other words, people in tenderloin districts approach age identity categories not as fixed but as relational and performative. Instead of chronological age, "kid on the street" refers to a person's role in the tenderloins' intergenerational sexual economies and kinship networks. The kids are those, regardless of chronological age, who perform "youth" to stimulate desire in potential clients and are cared for, materially and emotionally, by people who identify as mothers, fathers, aunts, and uncles.

The term *kid* may have originated in the early twentieth century with the white male wageworkers, known as hoboes, who migrated between the downtown "main stems" in cities across the country.[17] Since the turn of the century, intergenerational same-sex encounters were considered a defining characteristic of the public culture they created in these districts, known as "hobohemia," and the most typical "on-the-road" relationship paired an adult with a youth.[18] Nels Anderson's studies of hoboes in the early 1920s described in detail the relationships between older men known as "wolves" or "jockers" and younger men or adolescents referred to as "chickens," "punks," "lambs," or "kids."[19] Historians show that the erotic system of wolves and kids was widespread among seamen and prisoners in US cities in the early twentieth century.[20] It also appears to have animated the tenderloin street scene. In 1941 the Times Square john and amateur ethnographer Thomas Painter, in a letter to Alfred Kinsey, claimed that "a great factor in homosexual prostitution" was "the road, by which is meant the vagrant world: hitch-hiking and railroad hoboing." Boys who "hobo it . . . often become hustlers because of their introduction . . . into homosexual practice at the hands of older fellow-tramps."[21] The "punks" who "served their apprenticeship among tramps may later become hustlers to homosexuals and wolves in cities."[22]

The word *kid* also references a person's role in the central city's intergenerational sexual economies. Hustlers often made great efforts to appear or "act" young, regardless of chronological age. Rechy wrote in 1963 that he learned to play a "variety of roles" designed to perform "youth" and thus arouse desire in potential clients: "young man out of a job, the 'drifting' boy, the young man lost in the city 'pleasehelpmesir.'"[23] Joel Roberts, an informant who hustled San Francisco's Tenderloin in the 1960s, told me that "youth was what we were selling." You "saw yourself as younger and you made more money if you were younger, so the word *kid* works." Tamara Ching, a trans woman of color who hustled the Tenderloin in the late 1960s, told me she adapted her performance of age and gender to the needs of potential clients. "I could go ahead and morph from male to female, [and] back to male," she said. "I could morph my age, and I could be a little child, or I could be a teenager. Or I could be a full-grown adult going into bars and picking up men." The term *kid* also references a person's role in the central city's intergenerational kinship systems. The kids are those who were cared for and initiated by an older, paternal community of survivors who identified as mothers, fathers, uncles, brothers, sisters, and "social workers," which a 1964 "Lavender Lexicon" dictionary defined as a "homosexual who cruises among the unemployed and destitute. Can be a slightly mocking term applied to those who assume a fatherly or motherly role."[24]

Being a "kid on the street" references behavior associated with the "storm and stress" of adolescence. From its construction in the late nineteenth century, adolescence has been understood as "a sexually tempestuous period," Jeffrey Moran argues, marked by an emotional rebelliousness that "demanded careful and sustained external control."[25] The kids on the street were known for drug use, sexual experimentation, "flaunting" of gender conventions, and a "wanderlust" figuratively connected with unrestrained sexuality.[26] In his 1963 account of a peripatetic hustler, Rechy wrote about "the frantic running that, for me, was Youth."[27] Many kids "flaunted" nonnormative gender identities on the downtown streets and were known, during different historical periods, as belles, street queens, or hair fairies. "When I am in the group," a Chicago street queen told a sociologist in the 1930s, "I holler and scream to have people look at me and make remarks. I do it because the rest of the kids do it."[28] A psychologist wrote in 1957 about young "gays" who "submerge themselves in a herd," adopt "common jargon like teenagers' . . . 'jive' talk," and "find a welcome outlet for their resentments and hostilities toward a world which rejects them." These street kids, the psychologist felt, should be considered "homosexuals in adolescent rebellion."[29]

Street kids often identified as "butch," "femme," or "trade," sexual regimes that historians associate with working-class queer publics in the early and mid-twentieth century.[30] While second-wave feminists often derided these formations as recapitulating patriarchal divisions or imitating heterosexuality, queer theorists argue that butch/femme "both drew on and transformed the dominant society's male supremacist and heterosexual uses of gender."[31] Men known as "trade"—usually conventionally masculine adolescents from working-class backgrounds—could engage in homosexual acts without assuming the identity of a homosexual, so long as they maintained a masculine demeanor and limited themselves, at least in principle, to a penetrative role.[32] While historians often assumed that a homosexual/heterosexual binary constituted the dominant way people in the United States thought about sex by the mid-twentieth century, scholars such as Regina Kunzel show that this binary was "remarkably uneven and considerably less hegemonic and less coherent than historians have often assumed."[33] Multiple understandings of sex and gender overlapped in time and space and continue to do so.[34] Indeed, a Polk Street hustler told me around 2009 that he identified as straight and had sex with men only for cash. Street kids' declaration of sexual identity—then and now—was often performative, depending on the perceived desires of a potential client.

I build on the work of Cathy Cohen and Kwame Holmes to show that the kids on the street deprivilege a binary opposition between queer and nonqueer subjects, a binary that occludes the interplay of race, gender, "economic exploitation," and "class structure."[35] The kids did not always define group belonging based on a shared sexual or gender identity—for example, a common gay, lesbian, homosexual, or transgender identity—but might identify as trade, queens, heterosexual, straight, butch, femme, transsexual, or any number of other performative identities.[36] Moreover, there were (and continue to be) profound class and cultural differences—and reciprocal hostilities—separating street kids and "respectable," settled homosexuals. The kids instead defined group belonging based on a shared way of life characterized by casual lodging; temporary labor; frequent migration; participation in the "street" economies of prostitution, narcotics, and panhandling; and, perhaps most importantly, what Holmes calls a "disruptive relation to normativity" along lines of racialization, class, and respectability.[37] The struggles street youth waged rarely looked like the activism of the homophile or gay rights movements but instead took the form of mutual aid, kinship, and collective actions such as needle exchanges that, Cohen argues, "challenge dominant constructions of who should be allowed and who deserved care."[38]

An Ethics of Reciprocity and Mutual Aid

While the kids' scene took a number of historically and geographically specific forms, an ethics of reciprocity appears to have crossed the decades and therefore indicates some continuity in the history of the scene. For this reason, we can begin to understand the kids' sense of justice and exploitation by examining the principle of reciprocity, a principle based on the simple idea that people should help those who have helped them. More specifically, according to James Scott, it means "that a gift or service received creates, for the recipient, a reciprocal obligation to return a gift or service of at least comparable value at some future date."[39] Anthropologists argue that the norm of reciprocity is steeped in morality: by giving, receiving, and returning gifts, a moral bond is created between people exchanging them. Reciprocity thus contributes to social cohesion.[40]

As early as the 1920s and well through the 2010s, kids in tenderloin districts developed conventions for collective housing, self-policing mechanisms, and networks for pooling resources. They were motivated to help one another—to pool funds and "watch each other's backs"—because they themselves would need assistance at a later date. In their own interest, they cooperated in order to survive in environments that challenged their existence. The norm of reciprocity also applied to relationships between kids and those who animated the meat rack "vice" economies, among them bartenders, bouncers, and johns, as well as the management of coffeehouses, pinball arcades, and hotels that benefited from the trade in sex. These actors developed a collective vision of the proper economic functions and performances of those who animated the downtown "vice" economies.

While these informal networks based on reciprocal exchange were vital strategies of survival, they were also critical components of a counterdiscourse that enabled kids to critique the dominant culture and develop an alternative set of values against which the worth of individual lives could be measured. Because the kids existed toward the bottom of the moral and economic structure, they were in a position to see the discrepancies between the ideals of American culture and their actions—between respectable "fronts" and the deviant and exploitative behavior that "front" sometimes covers over.[41] Many developed an irreverent attitude toward society's "morality" and rejected as hypocritical the "respectable" world that condemned them while simultaneously purchasing their sexual services. Through collective performance and ritual, many creatively exploited the epistemological gaps, fractures, and contradictions of the social fabric and, in doing so, subverted the authority that establishes normative assumptions about sexuality, gender, and ability.

Kinship and religion—the very cardinal forms of sociality that are often placed in opposition to queer world making—are common frames through which street kids expressed mutual obligations and reciprocities. The social formations my informants call "street families" resemble the moral economies common among marginalized people with limited resources. People living at bare subsistence create patterns of reciprocity, pool resources, and create extensive networks of kin to ensure mutual survival. Carol Stack showed how African American families living at bare subsistence in central city districts establish "socially recognized kin ties" with people not related by blood to "maintain a stable number of people who share reciprocal obligations."[42] They are adaptive institutions developed for coping with poverty.[43] Street families served a similar function—but with a queer twist. The kids sexualized their kin relations, producing what Lauren Berlant and Michael Warner call "criminal intimacies": relations and narratives "that are only recognized as intimate in queer culture," including "girlfriends, galpals, fuckbuddies, tricks."[44] Drawing on my research, I would add, more incestuously, daddy, uncle, son, and mother—and, not least, the "Holy Father."

People in the scene drew on these relations to elaborate a world of belonging and transformation.

The syncretic religious formations I call "street churches" are essential sources of housing, food, and other material resources for abandoned youth in the central city. As such, they are part of the accumulation of obligations that comprised the performative economy. But religion was not simply a source of economic support or a form of solace in a precarious life. It offered a powerful critique of the moral order that cast street youth as unclean, damaged, and deserving of abandonment. The religions of subordinate classes, Scott argues, can represent "an alternative moral universe in embryo—a dissident subculture, an existentially true and just one, which helps unite its members as a human community and as a community of values."[45] Drawing on Christian scripture and ritual, queer ministers mobilized a gothic Christianity to devalue the rich and powerful and ascribe the greatest worth to the "least of these." They oversaw rituals that reconstituted the street scene and materialized its moral vision. Many ministers used scripture to reinterpret experiences of abandonment as collective sources of power, fueling their pathbreaking activism.

Street kids formalized the performative economy by establishing explicitly activist organizations, including Vanguard, founded in San Francisco's Tenderloin in 1966; Street Transvestite Action Revolutionaries (STAR), founded in Times Square in 1970; and the Lavender Panthers, founded in San Francisco's Tenderloin in 1974. Young organizers worked to meet street kids' needs—pooling resources for food, housing, and medical care—while also building shared political analyses of the structural inequalities that produced those needs in the first place. Organizers built on the preexisting web of reciprocities, kinship networks, and performance practices to forge a politics of mutual aid: a voluntary reciprocal exchange of resources and services for mutual benefit done in conjunction with social movements demanding transformative change.[46] At its best, Dean Spade argues, mutual aid produces "new ways of living" and "systems of care."[47]

While the scene was animated by an ethics of reciprocity, there were as many exploitative dynamics operating within this world as threatening it from without. As a general rule, the kids considered relationships to be exploitative when they violated the norm of reciprocity. Business owners and johns were in a position to supply resources that street kids often desperately needed for their survival. These differences allowed them to potentially take advantage of the needs of street youth and thus violate the norm of reciprocity, leading to situations that the kids considered "exploitative." I show throughout the book that economic and social changes—including the redevelopment and policing of downtown districts in the 1950s and 1960s, the HIV/AIDS and methamphetamine epidemics in the 1980s, and the economic and social transformations associated with urban neoliberalism from the 1990s through the 2020s—could radically undermine the mutual obligations, networks of mutual support, rate structures, and conventions by which the kids "had each other's backs." These changes could permit johns, police, and business owners to violate the performative economy, and often provided the indignation that fueled countless riots and rebellions.

Turn to Affect

My analysis of the scene grows out of my experiences with San Francisco queer politics in the first decade of the twenty-first century, when activists and academics were increasingly dissatisfied with a gay rights movement intent on state recognition, privatized family life, and individual economic interests: a politics often glossed as "homonormativity."[48] I organized with Gay Shame, a direct-action group that "shamed" the city's gay political establishment for its support of consumerism and gentrification. During the annual pride celebrations, we organized alternative events that brought together musical acts, speakers, and food to build an "anti-capitalist" space. I also devoured academic studies animated by longings for utopian queer futures and disappointment with a neoliberal political agenda, as Ann Cvetkovich wrote in her 2003 book *An Archive of Feelings*, based on "assimilation, inclusion, and normalcy."[49]

These political longings animated a "turn to affect" in the academy. Critics argued that affective experience, including the "negative" affects associated with shame and abjection, could serve as the grounds for forging new collectives and the basis for alternative models of queer politics. Queer scholars explored the counterintuitive power of shame (Eve Kosofsky Sedgwick, Jack Halberstam, Michael Warner); *sinvergüencería* (Lawrence La Fountain-Stokes); abjection (David Halperin, Darieck Scott); trauma (Ann Cvetkovich, Judith Butler); and "backward feelings" (Heather Love).[50] Eve Kosofsky Sedgwick coined the evocative phrase *queer performativity* to refer to strategies for refiguring affects associated with shame and developing from them particular structures of creativity, power, and struggle.[51] This affective turn reoriented the study of queer subjectivity to the conditions of a history marked by injury. Scholars examined "shameful" figures from the pre-Stonewall past, exploring negative affects, David Halperin and Valerie Traub wrote, "that have not totally disappeared from the lives of queer people with the allegedly newfound possibilities of gay pride."[52] Critics were more willing to "investigate the darker aspects of queer representation and experience," Heather Love wrote, "and to attend to the social, psychic, and corporeal effects of homophobia."[53]

These academic and activist currents animated my work on Polk Street and in the Tenderloin. In the 1960s, before a wide range of people began publicly proclaiming their sexual identities during the gay liberation movement, the Tenderloin was the epicenter of San Francisco's public queer life and the kids who gathered there were among the most visible manifestations of gender and sexual dissidence. A 1964 *Life* magazine article described the district as a "bleak agglomeration" of hamburger stands, cheap hotels, pornography shops, and "bottom-of-the-barrel bars" where one found "the stereotypes of effeminate males—the 'queens,' with orange coiffures, plucked eyebrows, [and] silver nail polish." One found "dope pushers and users, male and female hustlers . . . a few Lesbians, some 'gay' prostitutes, drunks and cheap con men."[54] Street kids embodied the stereotypes the gay rights movement would work to scrub clean over the following decades: that is, homosexuals as criminal, mentally ill, degenerate, and incapable of "responsible" participation in public life, their wanderlust figuratively connected with unrestrained sexuality.[55]

Since the 1960s, there has been a dramatic transition in the United States from rhetoric linking homosexuality with vice and criminality to the more recent articulation of the homosexual as a respectable form of sexual nonnormativity, one dissociated from the crime and vice of the city.[56] This transition is reflected in historical narratives that trace a monolithic "gay community" from the ghetto to respectable citizenship; from shame to pride; "from abjection to glorious community."[57]

These progress narratives render retrograde the queer and trans people who continued to make a home in the Tenderloin. In contrast to narratives that circulated widely of dramatic progress in the lives of queer people, I found a remarkably similar social world when I walked the streets of the Tenderloin in the 2010s and 2020s. The vice economies and material infrastructure— lodging houses, cheap restaurants, and coffee shops—continued to call to runaway and "throwaway" youth, trans women, immigrants, and sex workers and continued to serve as a containment zone for the formerly incarcerated or people suffering from addiction and mental illnesses. Many outsiders saw the kids on the street as anachronisms—vestiges of a shadowy past when homosexuality was associated with poverty, crime, and addiction—to the extent that they were seen at all.

By researching the Tenderloin's history, I sought to join scholars like Love, who asked that "rather than disavowing the history of marginalization and abjection," we "embrace it, exploring the ways it continues to structure queer experience in the present."[58] I set out to explore the transformative impulses that spring from abandonment and document them as political resources.

I documented a local past rich in street-level queer solidarities and kinship networks, but instead of recording a simple story of home lost and found, I archived alliances that were far more ambivalent, contradictory, and ultimately more breathtakingly creative than I could have originally imagined. On the one hand, my informants described Polk Street and the larger Tenderloin as a space of abandonment in which low-income, immigrant, and "throwaway" populations—particularly queer and transgender youth—are corralled, policed out of other parts of the city, and left to die. At the same time, they described it as offering a space where they could form queer solidarities, share resources, and develop a sense of "self-worth" they did not find in their families of birth.[59]

I hung out at the trans nightclub Divas and talked with the club's manager and self-described female impersonator Alexis Miranda. Polk Street "will make or break you," she told me. "I've seen a lot die on Polk Street, chased down by a car and hit, get into fights and just bash their head and die right there." It "can be the worst place. But if you know all of those things and you overcome it, that creates a strength and a power for you—and it did exactly that for me." I recorded stories with Cecilia Chung, who told me she began fashioning a transgender identity in the early 1990s while dancing at a Tenderloin dive bar called the Motherlode. "It was one of the seediest bars in the city," she said. "You know that there was a lot of wheeling and dealing in and outside of the bar. And I felt that I found paradise." The Motherlode "would come to life at night, when the girls start to show up and their followers and their admirers show up. There was a little stage at the corner of the club where the girls would just go up and parade themselves, dancing as if they were angelfish in a fishbowl." Cecilia transformed herself through these performative encounters. "I was able to see my true self," she said, "through other people's eyes." There was an "element of extreme freedom and extreme despair, and definitely violence," Cecilia told me. "That's how to define Polk Street. It's a big paradox. And at the same time, people find validation, people find their connection to their own sexuality, to their own self-discovery, and to a community that's forgotten by most people outside."

This paradoxical dynamic has long defined San Francisco's queer Tenderloin. One of the most common stories I heard on the street and read in the archive was the story of the young person sapped of life and vitality. To enter the Tenderloin is to be "immediately caught up in its whirlpool," a hustler wrote in 1967. "Once they get caught, they become too weak to fight and are drawn down to the bottom." Their eyes are "cloudy" and their bodies "emaciated."[60] My informants told similar stories. "The world and the lifestyle, the culture—it tries to kill you," a genderqueer informant named Lala Yantes told me of Polk Street in the 1990s. "People in general love youth and vitality, but it gets sucked out of you so quickly." I focus on a less well-known story—one that relies on but creatively reframes the first—about street kids who metabolized social trauma into novel public cultures and collective action. They drew on the counterintuitive power of abjection through a variety of performative vernaculars and approached the streets and boulevards as "sites for nurturing counter-hegemonic affects, emotions, and norms about emotional display."[61] The subversive possibilities of repetition with a difference, via butch/femme, drag, street families, and religious ritual, provided the basis for restorative rituals and new forms of solidarity and kinship.

Moral Economy

While queer studies of affect show how people reinterpret the affective impacts of abandonment, they have little to say about how people manage the economic impacts of abandonment—an issue that was critically important to the kids on the street. For example, in one of the SRO hotels that lined Polk Street, I talked with Shane Gibson, also known as Yoyo, who told me they ran away from a sexually abusive home in the 1980s. "Back when I was first here, we watched each other's backs," Yoyo told me. "Like somebody needed to get well, we helped out with that. A couple would go to a needle exchange or get carryout back for us from different places to eat. Make sure our blankets and gear was watched. . . . We were a big family. We'd share expenses, camping and watching out for each other." Yoyo felt that an increasingly affluent and respectable gay community, working to construct a proud heritage, would rather leave this history behind. "Like it or not," Yoyo said, "Polk Street is a part of our history. When we usually hear about Polk Street, we think of male prostitution and gay sex and . . . all those stereotypes and labeling." Yoyo instead highlighted histories of kinship and mutual support. "It was about family and friends—not so much as what *you* can do for *me* as to what *we* can do for each other. . . . That's what Polk Street taught me: it's not all about just *me* all the time."

I analyze the kids' strategies for managing the economic consequences of abandonment by building on the concept of moral economy, which shows that people living at bare subsistence often create patterns of reciprocity, pool resources, and create extensive networks of kin in order to increase the chances of survival. Without mutual support, fluctuations in the flow of available goods could destroy a community's ability to survive.[62] A moral economy references two related concepts: (1) a set of moral or values-based beliefs concerning economic agents, practices, or structures that are shared by a population; and (2) the actualization of these attitudes in specific social practices.[63] The advantage of the concept of moral economy is that it allows researchers to fold cultural values into political economy and thereby dramatize the moral debates over social change.

I borrow the concept from E. P. Thompson, who originated the term *moral economy* to refer to norms governing economic exchange among English peasants in the eighteenth century, and James Scott, who brought the concept to the attention of anthropology with his analyses of rural resistance to exploitation in Southeast Asia during the 1930s.[64] Instead of seeing food riots as irrational and instinctive reactions to hunger, Thompson argued that they "operated within a popular consensus as to what were legitimate and what were illegitimate practices in marketing, milling, [and] baking," and "a consistent traditional view of social norms and obligations, of the proper economic functions of several parties within the community." This "delicate tissue of social norms and reciprocities" constituted the "moral economy of the poor."[65] An emerging capitalist market economy violated these norms and practices, leading to violent outbreaks of class conflict.[66] James Scott similarly argued that the economic and political transformations of the colonial era systematically violated the peasantry's vision of social equity, sparking major riots and rebellions. If we can understand the "indignation and rage" that prompted these actions, he argued, we can grasp what he calls their moral economy: "their notion of economic justice and their working definition of exploitation—their view of which claims on their product were tolerable and which intolerable."[67]

Anthropologists have more recently built on the moral economy literature to explore the ways market forces shape seemingly private relationships and kinship practices. In her study of contemporary commerce in Bangkok, Ara Wilson proposes the term *intimate economies* to denote interactions between economic systems and social life, particularly gender, sexuality, and ethnicity. Global economies interact with local systems to create new social identities, including "tomboys," corporate tycoons, and sex workers.[68] Noelle Stout, in her research on male sex workers in Cuba as the island opened to foreign tourism, proposes the phrase *affective kin economies* to illuminate connections between the economic realm and the arena of familial bonds. Queer kinship terms offered a common frame through which gay male foreigners and Cuban sexual laborers solicit ongoing forms of affection, mutual obligation, and care. These kinship practices, while subverting dominant notions of biological kin, are "inextricably tied to forms of market capitalism."[69]

I show that the kids' performative economy developed through racialized sex tourism economies. In the late nineteenth century, for example, San Francisco located its vice zones in the racialized districts of Chinatown and the Barbary Coast. Social arrangements in these spaces opened up opportunities for life outside the norms of respectable Anglo-Saxon, middle-class, heterosexual marriage, producing what historian Nyan Shah calls "queer domesticity": female-dominated households, groups of Chinese "bachelors" cohabiting, and interracial relationships.[70] In the early 1900s, San Francisco's business and shopping districts expanded westward, cutting into the southern part of the red-light districts, and the city passed new laws that forced sex workers and venues for entertainment southward to the Tenderloin. By the 1920s, the Tenderloin had become San Francisco's de facto red-light district and the epicenter of queer life.[71] Nan Alamilla Boyd shows that the city's material interests in promoting sex tourism in the early twentieth century were a primary factor in the emergence of queer public cultures in districts like the Tenderloin. "As sexualized entertainments became part of San Francisco's allure," Boyd argues, "tourist industry dollars cast a thin veneer of protection around the city's queer entertainments."[72] By the late 1960s, redevelopment and police sweeps again forced the scene from the Tenderloin to the Polk Street corridor. My informants described Polk Street in the 1980s and '90s as a sexual marketplace in which clients—primarily white men—could fulfill sexual and often racialized fantasies.

My informants presented commercialized sex not as inevitably exploitative but as an often dangerous means of survival that enabled them to escape even worse dangers in their families of birth. Tamara Ching told me that sex work enabled her to develop a sense of self-worth. "Out of sex work I got esteem," she said. "I knew that people couldn't make fun of me because they couldn't *afford* me. Being one of the few Asian and Pacific Islander hookers back in the sixties and seventies, I was at a premium." Commercialized sex, in an ideal situation, is one component of the kids' performative economy, one that operates according to different values than those enforced by the dominant culture but which nonetheless serves to shore up the self-worth of the kids on the street.

Street kids often took pride in the fact that they were at the center of local vice economies. A twenty-five-year-old named Mathew, who made money by cleaning apartments and turning tricks on Polk Street when I met him around 2009, told me merchants might not always like him and other hustlers on the street, "but I think some of them are smart enough to know that a lot of the lure of Polk Street is *that*," he said. "That's why a lot of people come to Polk Street. So, you know, I mean a lot of them, if they feel like they want to keep their business, and make as much money as they do, then they tend to leave us alone." The cruel paradox for young sex workers was that the very qualities for which they were shunned and sometimes punished—the danger and abjection that was supposed to attend them—were also part of their allure. This paradox, too, became part of their performances.

Materials and Methods

My interdisciplinary approach cuts across disciplinary boundaries and the periodizations within them. As such, I must be explicit about the materials and methods I have employed.

My methods grow in large part out of my political and ethical commitments. I was not motivated by a need to "extract" information from informants or act as a dispassionate, academic observer. I felt an ethical responsibility to respond to the dehumanization and displacement of the people whose stories I was recording. Before writing up my oral history and archival research, I interpreted it through two public humanities projects designed to intervene in debates about gentrification, public safety, and the criminalization of homelessness. In collaboration with my informants on Polk Street and the Tenderloin, I developed what Cvetkovich calls "an engaged public history that connects the past with the present to create a history of the present."[73]

From 2007 to 2009, "Polk Street: Lives in Transition" challenged gentrifiers' claims to be promoting "safety" and "family" by circulating alternative understandings of both concepts, alternatives drawn from oral histories I conducted with queer and trans people on Polk Street. I broadcast these stories through "listening parties," neighborhood dialogues, a multimedia exhibit, and radio documentaries. The project enabled my informants to assert their identities and insist on the existence of a collective history, fostered dialogue among groups competing for urban space, and forced developers and public officials to acknowledge the history of those people they were displacing. From 2010 to 2011, I directed "Vanguard Revisited," a historical reenactment project that introduced the history of Vanguard, a direct-action organization founded by Tenderloin street youth in 1966, to marginally housed youth in the Tenderloin. The project enlisted contemporary youth in interpreting the Tenderloin's history in relation to their own lives—to enter into conversation with and position themselves as part of a historical lineage. They drew genealogical connections between themselves and original Vanguard organizers, illuminating continuities and discontinuities in the lives of street kids over the previous fifty years. Contemporary youth ultimately staged a reenactment of the Vanguard rebellion that turned a street-level countermemory of trauma and resistance into a call for economic justice against the forces of gentrification and homonormativity.

These projects—which nurtured performative connections between past and present, the archive and the street, historical research and social activism—shaped my approach to this book, which often registers flashes of resemblance across temporalities. It is less an account of "how it really was" than it is an exploration of the social trauma and survival strategies that span the decades and therefore suggest some historical continuity in what my informants called the scene. I structure the book as a dialogue between the archive and the street—between ethnographic and historical methods—rather than a strict account of change over time. The historian who takes up this approach, Walter Benjamin argues, "stops telling the sequence of events like the beads of a rosary" and instead "grasps the constellation which his own era has formed with a definite earlier one."[74]

I also draw on methods from performance historiography, as developed by Joseph Roach, Shannon Jackson, and Rebecca Bernstein, which broad-

ens the scope of historical inquiry by approaching embodied memory, gestures, and ritual as systems for learning, storing, and transmitting cultural
knowledge.[75] A powerful current in performance studies contrasts "archival"
memory—written and material texts that can be housed in an archive—with
what Diana Taylor calls the "repertoire"—embodied memory and traditions
of performance, including "gestures, orality, movement, dance, singing—in
short, all those acts usually thought of as ephemeral."[76]

An overreliance on "archival" memory can devalue the memory practices
of marginalized publics. For Taylor, the political implications of this argument are clear. "If performance did not transmit knowledge," she argues,
"only the literate and powerful could claim social memory and identity."[77]
This does not mean we should align texts with domination and performance
with subversion.[78] The "pursuit of performance," Roach argues, "doesn't
require that historians abandon the archive" but does encourage them to
"spend more time in the streets."[79]

Scholars show that cultural memory does not need to be actively written
or archived. It can be remembered every day by those who practice ritualized
traditions. Many street kids had a keen sense that they were performing roles
that existed before they themselves came onto the scene. Rechy's fictional
character in *City of Night* migrated through Times Square, New Orleans,
Hollywood Boulevard, and the Tenderloin, all the while learning from other
kids "the stance, the jivetalk—a mixture of jazz, joint, junk sounds—the
almost-disdainful, disinterested, but, at the same time, inviting look; the
casual way of dress."[80] He learned to play a role. "Certainly the hustler knows
he hasnt created the legend of what he is in our world. Like other legends,
it's already there, made by the world, waiting for him to fit it. And he tries
to live up to what hes supposed to be."[81] The kids created and re-created the
scene through attempts to "live up to" what came before them.

In this passage, Rechy succinctly expresses the concepts of "surrogation" and "effigies," as developed by performance studies theorist Joseph
Roach. Roach argues that common definitions of performance—"repetition
with a difference" or "restored behavior"—assume that it offers a substitute for something that preexists it. The rituals we perform—whether a
religious sacrament, an everyday habit like tying one's shoes, or the rituals
that constitute "gender"—have already been structured and given meaning by a culture. A performing body stands in for something it is not but
must vainly aspire to replace. This practice of standing-in defines what
Roach calls "surrogation." A performer's body is an "effigy" as it bears and

brings forth collectively remembered, meaningful gestures and surrogates for that which a community has lost, providing communities with a method of perpetuating themselves.[82] Street kids often had a self-consciousness about surrogation that could sometimes pass for reflexivity. Many embraced "role-playing," theatricality, and camp—the notion of "life as theater." By performatively blurring the lines between artifice and "reality," they called into question the moral order that cast them as damaged, deviant, and deserving of abandonment.

At the intersection of commerce and vice, tenderloin districts are examples of what Roach calls "vortices of behavior," spaces whose function "is to canalize specified needs, desires, and habits in order to reproduce them." Roach shows how architectural invention and social organization create spaces whose gravitational pull brings audiences together and produces candidates for surrogation.[83] Performers develop effigies by improvising within a scenario provided by the "behavioral vortex" of the setting itself.[84]

Street kids improvised within the scenario or on the "stage" of the central city. They adapted cultural forms specific to these districts—theater, advertising, and celebrity culture, especially—and developed from them three primary effigies: the queen, the hustler, and the minister. The street queen or hair fairy modeled their personas on the movie star and female prostitute, cultivating forms of inverted glamour through collective theatricality on the streets and boulevards. The hustler promoted himself as part of the central city's advertising culture, transmitting a masculine glamour by embodying three homoerotic icons of working-class American masculinity: the cowboy, the soldier, and the sailor. The minister forged kinship through reference to a suffering Christ, staging religious rituals that revalued the abject and the sacred. The kids created and re-created the scene through these archetypal queer figures that continue to exert influence on the queer cultural imaginary.

I ultimately produce a performance genealogy of the kids' scene—an exploration of what Roach calls "the transmission and dissemination of cultural practices through collective representations."[85] In constructing genealogies, the task is to note patterns in the transmission of these practices through time and to show how contemporary practices emerged out of specific struggles and exercises of power. It is not always motivated by a historical concern to understand the past—though any historical claims must be valid—but by a critical concern to understand the present.[86] I show how people in motion, with few material resources, developed a public culture and transmitted it intergenerationally via performance.

Performance genealogies can leave their traces in a variety of places, including archives, the streets, literature, and the rituals practiced by contemporary actors. Accordingly, I draw on and juxtapose a diverse set of sources to represent the performative economy: oral histories and archival research; newspaper and magazine articles; pulp novels, memoirs, and fiction; pornography and homophile newspapers; and the published archive of surveys and sociological studies. I draw on materials from LGBTQ-specific archives as well as labor, church, and theater archives; records held by social service organizations; and personal collections compiled by bartenders, johns, street kids, and sociologists. I ultimately built my own queer archive by collecting materials from my informants in the Tenderloin, most of which I donated to the GLBT Historical Society.[87]

Finally, I approach San Francisco's Tenderloin itself as an archive of performance and storytelling practices. Most cities have demolished or radically transformed their rooming-house districts. San Francisco's Tenderloin is one of the few central city rooming-house districts that remains largely intact, if under threat from gentrification.[88] I approach the district as one port on a migratory circuit that once connected tenderloin districts across the country. I show how the memories of particular times and places are embodied in the performances of people I met in the Tenderloin.[89] My encounters in the hotels and bars may not tell us what queer actors did in the past or in other tenderloin districts, but they do help clarify what kind of survival strategies these spaces of abandonment encouraged and what kind of challenges to normative thought they made possible.

Oral History and Performative Storytelling

The people I encountered in the Tenderloin were masterful storytellers. I met informants by hanging out at the bars, clubs, social service agencies, and churches, and through word of mouth. I conducted most interviews in apartment buildings, bars, churches, and some at the GLBT Historical Society, where the recordings and transcripts are currently archived. The people whose stories appear in this book range in age from their early twenties through their early eighties, though a preponderance were in their early forties to their early fifties. Roughly eight were from people who identified, at the time of the interview, as "street youth" or street hustlers. Many of the people I interviewed entered the Tenderloin as young runaways—surviving through prostitution or under-the-table work—and later climbed employment ladders to become bartenders, bouncers, hotel managers, social workers, ministers, and caregivers. They joined others to form the backbone of a distinct counterpublic with its own history, mythology, moral values, and economic norms.

My experiences in the Tenderloin transformed my approach to oral history methods. I came to the district devoted to social history, which assumes that researchers can produce a history "from below" by gathering data from the "underside," inserting it into a chronological narrative, and making "visible" that which had been hidden.[90] I found that this approach was not well suited to representing the subversive and performative aspects of Tenderloin narratives. My informants related intense stories—vivid accounts of childhood abuse and mystical experiences—that seemed to exceed historical analysis. When I opened the door of the GLBT Historical Society to greet one informant, he literally danced his way into the archive, contorting his body into the angular shapes characteristic of modern dance. Another responded to my request for data with poetic language that seemed designed to deliberately obfuscate. Others seemed to creatively stretch the truth. I talked with hustlers who told fantastic tales that strained credulity. I met bartenders who spun yarns about secret tunnels that once ran under Tenderloin bars—stories they likely knew were untrue.

I found that researchers before me recorded stories they felt were intentionally deceptive. In 1964, reporters writing about Toronto's "Trade Beat" listened to a group of street kids tell "remarkable" stories "of easy pickings and good times" before realizing that none of them actually "believed a word of these wild and wonderful stories."[91] Thomas Painter wrote in 1941 that sociologists visiting Times Square, plying their subjects with cash, may record stories, but they will be as "false" as the confidence men and "clip-artists" who populated the central city. "The man who buys 'French pictures' from a furtive sidewalk peddler," Painter wrote, "probably deserves to find, as he will, that he has purchased a small packet of neatly folded toilet paper." The stories hustlers tell are just as "phony." If one is looking for "color and allure," Painter wrote, "one will get color and information for one's book or to shock and delight one's pretty lady companion, but it will be adapted to the informant's or inquirer's mood, and by no chance will a syllable of it be true."[92]

I came in time to understand that stories in tenderloin districts are not so much "phony" as they are "performative": they construct or affect reality rather than merely describing it.[93] The function of a story in tenderloin districts is not always to describe an objective reality but to act on it—to call forth and create a social world of fantasy and belonging. My informants told stories to reinvent themselves and manage the emotional impact of abandonment. Like the working-class lesbians interviewed by Elizabeth Lapovsky Kennedy and Madeline Davis, street kids were "constantly creating their lives" and developing "new guidelines for living" through the process of storytelling.[94] The stories they told were more than individual life preservers; they were distinctively communicative devices in the creation and re-creation of a shared performative economy.

For example, I spent months hanging out and recording stories with Coy Ellison, a bartender on Polk Street. Coy told me he fled an abusive home as a teenager in the 1970s and hitchhiked to Polk Street, where he changed his name, affected an Irish accent, and began passing himself off, more or less convincingly, as an "illegal Irish immigrant." The persona, as I show in chapter 4, endeared him to bartenders and business owners who secured him under-the-table work. It was also part of the labor that won him entrance into a street family composed of runaways, hustlers, and "lost kids." Most importantly, the masquerade—which Coy developed over twenty years, first as a street kid and later as a bouncer, bartender, and caretaker—enabled him to creatively reinterpret the abuse from which he was running. This drama took on meaning within a scene that embraced the paradox of masquerade: a social "truth" told through the form of deception.

I am ultimately less interested in whether a particular story is "true" than I am in what that story does in the world, how it ushers in a new state of affairs—how, in other words, it is a communicative device in the creation and re-creation of the performative economy. I build on the work of E. Patrick Johnson to approach life stories as "narrative performances" that offer insight into identity formation. Framing oral history as a "co-performance" between narrator and researcher "destabilizes notions of the truth and focuses more on 'truth' as experienced in the moment of the storytelling event." This not only means acknowledging that "both the researcher and the narrators are performing for one another" but also entails "paying attention" in a way that "engages the bodily presence of both the researcher and the researched in the moment of the narrative event."[95] Oral history "creates its own space of play in which we meet the other, and in which we see ourselves in the other." It is "a valuable tool for engaging the lives of the other, the self, and the self and other in each other's eyes."[96] I test oral history against the documentary record with the knowledge that both can mislead and that each works best in critical dialogue with the other.

I build on Cvetkovich's work by showing how oral history can produce "a vast archive of feelings, the many forms of love, rage, intimacy, grief, shame, and more that are part of the vibrancy of queer cultures."[97] After we conducted oral histories, many about his history of sexual abuse, Coy Ellison could probably tell I was agitated and tense. He would tell me to "breathe." Oral history encounters often brought back to emotional life the feelings associated with abuse and abandonment. They also traumatized me in listening. Crucially, oral history encounters taught me that the affects associated with abandonment are at the heart of street families and street churches.

Because affective experience does not always take the form of language but is also expressed through the life of the body, I find meaning in nonverbal forms of expression, including dance, poetic language, and body language. Attention to the embodied, performative nature of oral history encounters is key to representing queer cultures. Oral history can produce a version of history "but also an archive of the emotions, which is one of trauma's most important, but most difficult to preserve, legacies."[98]

Finally, I follow oral historian Marie-Françoise Chanfrault-Duchet by showing that the most crucial information in an oral history is not always the answers to specific questions but "the narrative organization itself."[99] I pay close attention to the structure of my informants' oral narratives, which dramatize their sense of self and the shared politics of a public culture.

The structures of the narratives I recorded were strikingly different from those that generally mark gay and lesbian life stories. Narrators participating in queer oral history projects often justify their historical value by mapping their memories onto what Boyd calls the "intelligible gay/lesbian narrative structure" of the coming-out story.[100] The coming-out narrative, developed by gay liberation organizers in the late 1960s, seeks to resolve the conflict of stigmatized sexual identity by narrating a movement from the "closet" to awareness, from shame to pride, "from abjection to glorious community."[101] Actors who have taken this stereotypical trajectory are those most likely to tell their stories to historians, who in turn aggregate these narratives to construct what John Howard calls "history's 'coming out' narrative writ large": a story of invisible, isolated, and abject individuals transforming—usually after the 1969 Stonewall riots—into a visible, politicized, and "proud" community.[102] This movement from abjection to glorious community—the structure of the coming-out story—continues to inform both personal and collective histories of liberation.

The stories I recorded trouble the hegemonic status of "coming out" as the primary framework through which we narrate queer history. Almost all the personal stories I recorded open with a recollection of abuse, rejection, and banishment by the families into which they had been born. Many sought sanctuary in tenderloin districts, but in these spaces of abandonment, scenes of childhood violence were restaged through social scenes that reenacted the "moral drama" of familial abuse: police violence, exclusion from sites of consumption, and, perhaps perceived as self-inflicted, slow deaths through drug abuse and diseases of poverty. While there are critical differences across space and time, the social trauma many experienced lay in the ongoing experience of a specific kind of social scene: throughout their lives, figures who stood in for the moral order—parents, police, psychiatrists, business owners, and juvenile detention authorities—made them feel that they were worthless and undesirable, unworthy of care and deserving of abandonment.[103] This dynamic continued to manifest in the 2010s, with the transformation of the Tenderloin from a queer working-class district to a gentrified entertainment destination. The most vulnerable and fugitive members of street families, such as homeless and transgender people of color, fought a losing battle against the neoliberal, homonormative neighborhood boosters who wanted them gone, "sweeping the streets clean" of trash.

The underlying structure of my informants' narratives was not the linear movement from abjection to liberation that defines the coming-out story. It was most often a cyclical return to scenes of childhood violence, reframing and reinterpreting those scenes to produce particular "structures of expression, creativity, [and] pleasure."[104] This narrative structure took many performative forms: florid, often gothic Christianity, especially Catholic narratives of a suffering Christ; allusion to the white masculinist Beat poets, who found the highest spirituality among the dispossessed; and collective theatricality on the streets and boulevards. My informants' primal memories of betrayal, abandonment, and abjection became in one way or another the touchstone—at once the password and magic armor—in the reconstitution of family via street families. Performativity is a matter of a different kind of reiteration of the norms by which one is constituted. I show throughout this book that street kids developed a shared repertoire of creative strategies for refiguring the affects and economics associated with social trauma into particular structures of power and kinship.

A final note on terminology: in most cases I depend on my informants to designate their own identifiers, which include historically specific terms such as female impersonator, transsexual, hair fairy, homosexual, kids, and kids on the street. In some cases, I take the liberty to use the categories "transgender" and "queer" for groups of people as a shorthand for a wide range of gender and sexual identities specific to historical periods before these words were popularized. Scholars show that the term *transgender* is a category of identity popularized in the 1990s that incorporates a diverse array of gender-variant people who had previously been understood as, and understood themselves to be, distinct kinds of people—including transsexuals, drag queens, butches, hermaphrodites, cross-dressers, and hair fairies.[105] I use the term to refer broadly to people who move away from the gender they were assigned at birth. I use the term *queer* in two somewhat contradictory ways: as a term that approaches sexual identity categories (such as "gay" and "heterosexual") as socially and historically constructed, and as a cross-historical umbrella term that encompasses a number of people who might identify as gay, lesbian, transgender, butch, femme, and otherwise sexually dissident.[106] I sometimes use the anachronistic term *they* to refer to people who are no longer living and whose gender identity is unknown. I use the terms *meat rack*, *the scene*, and *performative economy* throughout the book to reference the same concept: the kids' flexible and fraternal view of social norms and the proper economic functions of actors in the vice and amusement economies.

Organization and Chapter Outlines

Chapters 1 and 2 examine the kids' performative economy in central city districts across the United States, from the late nineteenth century through the 2010s. In chapter 1, "A Performance Genealogy of US Tenderloins," I draw on oral histories, archival research, and the published archive of surveys, sociological studies, and memoirs to survey the central city "stems" and amusement districts in and through which runaway and "throwaway" kids regularly circulated, usually in sync with the seasons or the local political climates. In chapter 2, "Street Churches," I juxtapose archival and ethnographic research to outline the crucial role that extra-ecclesiastic "street churches" have played within the networks of mutual obligation that comprise the kids' performative economy, exploring the ministries of River Sims (Polk Street, 2000s), Raymond Broshears (San Francisco's Tenderloin, 1960s–1980s), Michael Itkin (Times Square and the Tenderloin, 1960s–1980s), and Sylvia Rivera (Times Square, 1960s–1970s).

The remaining chapters focus on San Francisco's Tenderloin and Polk Street, from the 1960s through the 2020s. Chapter 3, "Urban Reformers and Vanguard's Mutual Aid," examines the history of Vanguard, a direct-action organization founded in 1966 by street kids, hustlers, and young adults in the Tenderloin. I turn to original oral histories and archival research to show how Vanguard formalized the web of reciprocities, obligations, and religious practices I refer to as the kids' performative economy. In a brief "intervention" after chapter 3, I analyze Vanguard Revisited, a historical reenactment project I launched in 2010. In chapter 4, "The Urban Cowboy and the Irish Immigrant," I tell the stories of two migrants who fled abusive homes for Polk Street in the 1970s and 1980s. I first give an account of Coy Ellison, who reinvented himself on Polk Street as an "illegal Irish immigrant." I then tell the story of Corey Longseeker, a once iconic "urban cowboy" of the Tenderloin in the 1980s who, by the time I met him, was a destitute thirty-nine-year SRO resident. Their performances dramatize the promises and perils of the kids' performative economy.

In chapter 5, "Polk Street's Moral Economies," I draw on ethnographic and archival research to focus on the transformation of Polk Street from a working-class queer commercial corridor to a gentrified entertainment destination in the first decade of the twenty-first century. I show that the economic and social transformations associated with urban neoliberalism radically undermined the social patterns that constituted the street kids' performative economy. A second "intervention" reflects on my experience as director of "Polk Street Stories," which drew on life stories to shape debates about gentrification and displacement in this highly polarized setting. A conclusion examines efforts in the 2010s and early 2020s to memorialize queer and trans histories on Polk Street and the Tenderloin Mid-Market corridor, two sites where the kids' performative economy took shape.

Throughout the book, I center the kids on the street—those who live at the intersections of economic precarity, racialized surveillance, and sexual respectability politics—to highlight an ethics of reciprocity and mutual aid. Enacting dramas of survival on the margins of mainstream life, street kids received and provided care to survive in environments that challenged their very existence.

1.   A   Performance   Genealogy
of   US   Tenderloins

I MET ONE OF MY FIRST ethnographic informants, in 2007, through a trick. I was in my late twenties when I messaged a boy around my age online, probably via Craigslist m4m, and caught a bus to his San Francisco apartment. I remember lying on his bed and watching a terrible horror movie called *The Mist* while we talked and made out. A few weeks later, I was walking up Polk Street from City Hall—past the Mitchell Brothers O'Farrell Theater, a massive striptease club adorned with an enormous rainforest mural; past a crowd gathered in front of the Sophia Spa, a twenty-four-hour massage and private hot bath; past the Polk Gulch, a gay porn arcade featuring a large photo of a bare-chested man and sign screaming "COMMITTED TO PLEASURE!"— and on the corner of Polk and Post, I ran into the boy standing under a neon "DIVAS" sign advertising a three-story trans nightclub of the same name.

He introduced me to his friend Kelly Michaels and told me she'd just performed in the club as a Madonna impersonator. I could see the resemblance: a white woman with bleached-blonde hair and Tammy Faye mascara, she wore a neon-green mesh top and faux-leather jacket. With hints of a southern drawl, she introduced herself as "the Godmother of Polk Street." Over the past two decades, she'd been a sex worker, a porn star, and "a mom to

FIGURE 1.1.   Kelly Michaels, 2007. Photograph by Charles Russo.

the kids on the streets—a caretaker." Kelly told me she'd be happy to record her story and gave me her phone number.

A few days later, I followed Kelly into a single-room-occupancy apartment near Divas. Her friend, a Latinx trans woman named Alejandra, lounged on a lofted bed above a sewing machine and pile of fabric scraps—for drag shows, they told me. A middle-aged black man wearing a green polo shirt sat on a chair in the corner. He looked at the recorder I was toting and, probably ribbing me for playing the part of anthropologist, introduced himself as Terri, a "viewer of local culture." Kelly quickly cut him off. "He's one of the fans of the transgendered," she told me, "and he's got a Jurassic cock." I sat on the carpeted floor. Alejandra and Terri were quiet as I turned on my recorder and Kelly began what sounded like a well-rehearsed story.

Kelly said she was following the "San Francisco dream" when she escaped her small Alabama hometown at seventeen and hitchhiked west. It was 1989. "I had stars in my eyes. When you're sixteen or seventeen and have dreams of being famous, you come to California. And you probably end up on Polk Street in drag." Kelly said her dad was embarrassed by her "overflamboyancy" and didn't want her around. She dropped out of high school and fled to New Orleans, where she worked as a stripper before hitchhiking to San Francisco. A trucker dropped her off on Polk Street. "They'll take you over there," she remembers him saying. "That's where all the youngins go." With little more than blue jeans, a bra, and "rubber falsies," she started a new life.

Kelly romanticized Polk Street as a kind of queer Wild West frontier. The taverns were populated with characters like a "big, tall, black Egyptian transsexual hell-raiser" known to pack a gun. Scores of hustlers "coming in daily from the Greyhound station" made money stripping in the bars. Polk Street had a "Barbary Coast feel," Kelly said, referencing San Francisco's vice and amusement district from the Gold Rush through the 1910s. She began claiming a transsexual identity in a sexual economy that valued gender-nonconforming women in particular. "The gay bars [in the Castro], they hated us. The hustler boys, they loved the transsexuals." Terri interjected: "The bars were the churches, the sanctuaries," he said. "You weren't really going to be hassled there."

At the end of each night, Kelly's new "street family" pooled the money they earned through sex work and stripping to buy food and rent a hotel room for thirty dollars a night. They would often pile eight or nine people into one hotel room. "The queens," Alejandra said, "were more united then." The "seedy" corridor wasn't what Kelly was hoping for when she fled Alabama. "It's so evil, so dark, full of drugs and despair," she told me. "You're trapped once you're here. I'm almost forty years old, and I keep coming back. This is a vortex. Everyone calls it a vortex. But this is my home and this is my family. I can't go back to Alabama where I grew up. My dad doesn't want me to come because the neighbors will talk. I don't know where else to go. I've made my own personal family. I have brothers, sisters, more than one mom, more than one dad."

Kelly told me it was increasingly difficult to survive on the corridor. The hotels were getting more expensive. Many were requiring credit cards to keep out the "undesirables." The bars were closing, or going straight, and sex work was moving to the internet. "Polk Street is dead," Kelly said. "Dead as fuck now." Business associations were trying to "clean up" Polk Street, Kelly said, "but there's more pain now than ever. The people left here are going to fight for their home. Some people have been here forever. Their whole life is here." Moreover, gentrification was transforming the city's character and reputation as a wide-open town. "People come to San Francisco to look at the hookers. If you run everything out of here, what are you going to have? One big Disney World? They're taking the sparkle out of San Francisco."

Overview and Methods

In this chapter, I juxtapose ethnographic and archival evidence to produce a performance genealogy of the social formations Kelly called "street family" and I refer to as the kids' performative economy. Because the kids' social worlds are occluded when we imagine cultures to be static or place based, I offer a broad, synthetic overview by panning out from San Francisco's Tenderloin and surveying the central city "stems" and vice districts across the United States through which street kids circulated, usually in sync with the seasons or the local political climates, from the late nineteenth century through the early twenty-first.[1] Instead of offering a conventional account of change over time, I focus on the world-making strategies that appear to cross the decades and therefore indicate some continuity in what my informants often called "the scene." The result is a portrait painted in broad brushstrokes rather than great detail, a representation of the scene that underscores broad patterns across space and time. Because this approach is less effective in providing an analysis of change over time, I also outline key moments of transition in the development of the performative economy, including changes in transportation technologies, policing practices, and processes of racialization.

I juxtapose a diverse set of sources to create a portrait of the migratory scene: oral histories and archival research; newspaper and magazine articles; the published archive of sociological studies; pulp novels, memoirs, and fiction; and secondary sources. These sources were produced by a wide range of actors, some sympathetic insiders, some outsiders interested in diagnosis, and therefore call for reading with and against the grain. Sociological studies, for example, often presented street kids as social problems to be rehabilitated through welfare or medical interventions. Like Saidiya Hartman, I read these sources against the grain to "untether waywardness, refusal, mutual aid, and free love from their identification as deviance, criminality, and pathology."[2] Each source, regardless of its author and intended purpose, includes fragments of information about the kids' public performances and social worlds. In the same way that an archaeologist pieces together shards of artifacts to construct stories about an early civilization, I take fragments of information from each source and combine them together to create a portrait of the migratory scene, drawing on what Jack Halberstam calls a "scavenger methodology" to collect, deconstruct, and recombine cross-disciplinary methods that refuse "the academic compulsion toward disciplinary coherence."[3]

This interdisciplinary approach enables me to challenge surface descriptions that often imagined street kids as isolated and unattached, corrupted by the urban environment, and hopelessly arrested in their psychosexual development. The archive I compiled shows that many were instead socially enmeshed. They developed a counterpublic complete with rituals for renaming new members, conventions for collective housing, and networks for pooling resources. They established self-policing mechanisms, warned each other about abusive clients, and developed shared moral values.[4] While popular opinion holds that the "ghetto" is a place of immobility, I found that kids traveled from tenderloin to tenderloin, connecting far-flung districts through migratory circuits, all the while fostering novel forms of kinship and mutual aid. They ultimately developed a flexible view of social norms and obligations, a moral vision that they constituted and reconstituted through performance.

The performative economy developed through sex tourism economies in "vice and amusement" districts across the United States. These "tenderloin" districts emerged after the 1850s, as new zoning and policing practices created an unprecedented geographical divide between the urban poor and the elite.[5] Politicians and anti-vice reformers felt that complete eradication of prostitution, alcohol, drugs, and gambling was impossible.[6] They instead used zoning laws, policing practices, and housing discrimination to confine and regulate disreputable pleasure in red-light districts, which were often located in racially and ethnically mixed areas, contributing to cultural associations between poverty, racialized minorities, and deviant sexualities.[7] They became zones of abandonment where the immorality associated with the poor, sexual deviants, immigrants, and racialized populations could be contained and cordoned off from respectable white families and homes.[8] By making the "tolerated tenderloin" part of the urban landscape, cities were at the same time delimiting the boundaries between the licit and the illicit, the family and the nonfamily, the respectable and the abject, those functional to societal value and those to be swept away.[9]

The sheer commerciality of these districts gave them an identity distinct from other "immoral" neighborhoods.[10] As epicenters of a new consumer culture, they housed department stores, movie theaters, burlesque shows, slot machines, and arcades. By the 1920s, the advertising industry perfected people's desires to own and consume goods and created a "staggering machine of desire" in these commercial districts.[11] Prostitution was an integral component of amusement economies. Historian Timothy Gilfoyle shows that sexual pleasure for men was "frequently treated as a commodity, bought and sold in the urban marketplace." Brothels and theaters, concert saloons, restaurants, and cigar stores introduced, protected, and profited from commercialized erotic activity.[12] The appellation "tenderloin" references these transactions. The first district named "Tenderloin" was New York City's entertainment and red-light district in the final decades of the nineteenth century.[13] According to one origin story, "tenderloin" was originally a police nickname signifying a juicy or "choice" cut of police duty, full of opportunities to fatten one's pay through graft and blackmail. A "tenderloin" soon became a generic term designating vice districts known for police corruption and saturated with rooming houses, brothels, and theaters.

The early twentieth century was a watershed in the development of tenderloin districts. From the early twentieth century through World War I, Progressive reformers throughout the United States launched successful campaigns to suppress red-light districts. Politicians, police, and reformers, horrified by the commercialization of prostitution, criminalized brothels, opium dens, and saloons and "cleaned up" dance halls, movie theaters, and amusement parks. They succeeded by the late 1910s in shutting down red-light districts in most cities and, in so doing, ending the era of controlled toleration.[14] Those condemned by new moral regulations, historian Mara L. Keire shows, were banished "into a criminal urban underclass."[15] Throughout the twentieth century, public opinion and political action continued to confine "immorality" in spaces with the least political clout: low-income, mixed-race "ghettos" where police could contain vice without fear of opposition.[16] Congregating in these spaces were immigrants, prostitutes, and racialized populations, as well as tourists who—crossing moral and physical boundaries—slummed for sex and entertainment.[17]

Outside observers often understood working-class and racialized populations as an unfortunate but inevitable part of the urban landscape, situated in their "natural" environment of slums and ghettos. These racialized populations around the turn of the twentieth century included groups now widely understood to be "white," such as the Irish, Italians, and Jews, and immigrants from Slavic and southern European countries, which were at the time seen as racial inferiors to white Protestants with northern European ancestries.[18] Thomas Painter wrote in the late 1930s that most Times Square hustlers were from the "immoral countries" of Italy, Ireland, and Poland. Their lack of "moral training" and "lax" sexual mores contributed to their immoral livelihoods.[19] The period from 1890 to 1945 saw the ascent of a monolithic whiteness, as southern and eastern European groups went from racial-outsider status to entrance into the white mainstream.[20] As they graduated out of "slum" neighborhoods, Kwame Holmes notes, African Americans replaced them and inherited not only their dwellings but the association between poverty, vice, and homosexuality.[21] In 1966 Painter noted that most Times Square "delinquents" were Puerto Rican and black.[22] He fetishized black hustlers as "tough, depraved, [and] sensual," invoking fantasies of black sexual potency.[23]

Tenderloin districts were the center of the best-known homosexual public cultures because they were also centers of other commercialized vice.[24] Hustlers and street queens gathered on "meat racks" or "meat markets," colloquial phrases that referred to young sex workers displaying themselves like products in a food market and the bars, hotels, theaters, and arcades in which they socialized and met clients. The "traffic" in male prostitution, a homophile organizer said in 1964, took place "in the tenderloins, the Pershing Squares, and the Main Streets" around the country, in "the streets, theaters, gay bars, sailor hangouts, pinball palaces, hotdog stands, and the parks and street corners of the 'meat blocks' of some of the main thoroughfares."[25] Surface descriptions in the mid-twentieth century often imagined street kids as corrupted by the urban environment. A 1948 newspaper story on Times Square bemoaned the "nauseating spectacle of a small boy who has learned to negotiate the sale of his body" under "the glaring movie marquees, in the gawdy [sic] fun palaces, subway arcades and jammed bus terminals." Lacking "normal home and family life," he was "demoralized, unhappy, roaming the trackless sands between childhood and maturity."[26]

The boundaries of meat rack districts fluctuated over the decades as the result of police persecution and urban renewal. Vice districts serve a need in the city and are tolerated within limits—limits that are usually reached when transgressive sexual or gender expression threatens to spill across boundaries, or when land becomes too valuable for developers to ignore.[27] In New York City, redevelopment and policing forced the scene from the Bowery and Tenderloin in the late nineteenth century to Times Square by the 1920s. "As the theatrical and amusement district, and the people with money, moved uptown; so did the homosexual area," the Times Square john and Alfred Kinsey informant Thomas Painter wrote in 1941.[28] In San Francisco, redevelopment and policing forced the scene from the Barbary Coast in the late nineteenth century to the Tenderloin in the 1920s and the Polk Street corridor in the late 1960s. This pattern—in which policing and redevelopment force sex economies to neighboring districts to develop "undervalued" land—would repeat countless times in cities across the United States.

An Extended Experience of Social Trauma

The kids on the street often shared stories with one another and outside observers about abusive families of birth or violence in orphanages and juvenile detention centers. In the 1930s, a nineteen-year-old hustler on Chicago's State Street told sociologists he fled his aunt's home, where he was regularly beaten, and an "orphan asylum" that had constructed a machine, complete with mechanical paddles, to punish the kids "because too many

FIGURES 1.2 AND 1.3. Photographs of the San Francisco Tenderloin meat rack, ca. 1962. From "What to Do about Market Street: A Prospectus for a Market Street Development Project, an Affiliate of SPUR: The San Francisco Planning and Urban Renewal Organization," 1962.

of us were running away."[29] The artist Thomas Lanigan-Schmidt, who lived with other street youth in Manhattan rooming houses in the 1960s, recalled the "queen [who] had an enormous burn-scar covering her face and most of her body. Her mother didn't want men to be 'tempted' by her son's beauty."[30] In 1964 a twenty-year-old hustler said he escaped an alcoholic father in Salt Lake City who "ripped him up with knives" for being homosexual and a Mormon boys' home where he was told "that I was going to hell if I didn't change my ways."[31] Many of my ethnographic informants recounted similar stories of physical and often sexual abuse in their families of origin.

The kids may have sought to leave their pasts behind by fleeing to large cities; many instead found themselves policed and corralled into zones of social abandonment. There was a "tacit understanding with the police," a sociologist wrote of San Francisco's Tenderloin in the late 1960s, "that [transsexuals] would not be picked up for impersonation as long as they stayed in the Tenderloin." If they "strayed outside," they were "liable to be, and frequently were, arrested."[32] A process of abjection ejected "undesirables" outside the moral community and into zones of abuse and abandonment. Into this "dumping ground," a reformer wrote about San Francisco's Tenderloin in 1968, "have been moved all the people and problems our society . . . decided it would ignore; the older person, the homosexual, the alcoholic, the dope user, the black . . . the immigrant, the uneducated, the dislocated alienated youth."[33] Street kids were often represented from the outside as dirty and dangerous blights on downtowns, in need of arrest, punishment, or reform.

Scenes of childhood abuse were restaged through police violence, which functioned to punish and humiliate those who transgressed gender and sexual norms. In 1950 a cop told a young man waiting outside a Times Square bar to "move on." When the youth refused to do so, the cop beat the boy, who was "so severely injured that he lost vision in one eye and partial sight of the other." He justified the action by claiming that the young man "looked like a queer and was loitering in a place where homosexuals are known to congregate."[34] For street queens, the experience of being detained, according to a sociologist writing in 1969, included "having one's feminine clothing and possessions confiscated and laughed at, being required to submit to the indignity of a haircut, [and] being placed in a 'tank'—where one will certainly experience ridicule from guards and from . . . male prisoners."[35]

Starting in the late nineteenth century, kids were arrested along with other migrants via vagrancy laws, often defined as peddling, begging, prostitution, petty thievery, and any other "disorderly" activity that threatened the moneymaking potential of urban real estate. These broadly defined laws gave police a great deal of leverage in dispensing "sidewalk justice" and set the stage for police payoffs.[36] A 1967 study claimed that Chicago hustlers avoided police not only because they'd be arrested "but because they are going to get shaken down by the cops for part of their profit."[37] A butch lesbian recalled of San Francisco's Tenderloin in the 1960s that the "Tax Squad," that is, the police, "allowed the queers to prostitute as long as they stayed in the gay ghetto" and also "cracked a lot of heads and made big bucks shaking down the homos, hustlers, hookers, and dealers."[38]

Reform movements and juvenile detention centers subjected working-class and sexually nonnormative kids in particular to humiliating punishments.[39] Because adolescence was constructed in the late nineteenth century as a period of sexual maturity and a phase of development wherein youths had not yet matured, reformers argued that migrants required instruction in middle-class moral and sexual values.[40] This belief fueled the development of juvenile courts, truancy officers, social workers, psychologists, and counseling programs in the early twentieth century to "save" young people from the moral dangers of the urban environment.[41] The so-called child savers movement did not so much humanize the criminal justice system; if anything, historian Anthony M. Platt argues, it helped create a system that subjected working-class urban adolescents "to arbitrary and degrading punishments."[42] San Francisco homophile organizer Guy Strait wrote in 1967 that the juvenile detention centers "are nothing short of jails"; they are "the most vicious system that has ever been devised by the American public."[43] Street kids were also subject to "status" offenses, actions that are only violations for minors, such as violating curfew, running away, and truancy.[44]

From the late 1950s through the 1960s, growing numbers of white "runaways," often from middle-class suburban homes, set the stage for a dramatic change in the public representation and policing of street kids. White runaways were often viewed by politicians and reformers as a social crisis: good, middle-class kids sucked into the depravity and immorality of city life, as socially needy "victims" in need of help rather than "criminals" in need of incarceration.[45] With the reproduction of the white middle class at issue, public support began to mount.[46] Congressional hearings were held in the early 1970s, culminating with the enactment of the Runaway Youth Act of 1974, which decriminalized runaways by requiring states to separate services to runaway youth from the law enforcement, and required that states provide runaway youth with shelter, food, counseling, and other necessities.[47]

A 1974 Federal Juvenile Delinquency Act emphasized "deinstitutionalizing" status offenses such as running away, but critics argued that its application was erratic.[48] Indeed, many of my informants who fled abusive families in the 1980s and 1990s told me they were arrested, held at juvenile hall, and often returned to abusive families of birth.

Migratory Circuits

From the late nineteenth century through the 2000s, many young people "voted with their feet" and pursued lives that deviated from ideals of conformist adolescence.[49] They traveled frequently from meat rack to meat rack, sustaining themselves through prostitution and other criminalized economies. "Many hustlers make a roundabout tour of the entire country once a year," Painter wrote in 1941. "Simply crossing the continent from east to west or vice versa is the merest routine with them." They can "describe the bars and public squares and 'main stems' of most of the cities and towns of the country, and will often launch into detailed accounts of their adventures."[50] A San Francisco homophile organizer referred in 1966 to the "large number of young persons who travel from city to city, tenderloin to tenderloin, sustaining themselves by prostitution and attendant criminal activity."[51] In 1983 a sociological study noted a "transcontinental movement [of hustlers] from East to West," including an eastern circuit, through Chicago, Denver, and Las Vegas; a southern circuit, through Florida, New Orleans, Houston, and Phoenix; and a western circuit, through Los Angeles, San Francisco, and Portland. "Some hustlers," the sociologist noted, "shuttle frequently between these cities several times during their careers."[52]

One of the primary reasons for new mobility in the late nineteenth century was the expansion of the nation's railroad network in the years following the Civil War.[53] A queen in Seattle's central city recalled that "a lot of queens traveled by boxcar" in the 1930s. "Seattle queens would bunch up and travel to San Francisco on boxcars and stay for three or four months. Then the queens in San Francisco would come up and stay in Seattle for three or four months. . . . Sometimes we'd meet each other in between cities on the rails. That was a wild time, lots of hot stories and carrying on and we shared our food over a campfire along the tracks."[54] The advent of the automobile in the 1920s signaled the end of railroads as the predominant transportation and began a new era of mobility in the United States.[55] Many boys, Painter claimed in 1941, first learned about hustling when they were hitchhiking. "A homosexual," Painter wrote, "knows that usually a boy on the road is 'wise,' broke, and willing to make a dollar or two, and get a lift."[56] Two sociologists in 1969 "talked with a 12-year-old boy" in Times Square; two weeks later, in San Francisco, "we met the same 12-year-old soliciting on Market Street. A man had picked him up in New York as a travelling companion for an auto trip across the country and dropped him off in San Francisco."[57] By the midcentury, street kids took interstate buses, especially Greyhound Lines.[58] Downtown bus stations attracted mobile populations to tenderloin districts, which were often located between the business district and transport terminals.

Changing seasons often dictated migratory routes, as kids traveled to the most hospitable locations. Painter wrote in 1941 that kids congregated in "New York in the Spring and Fall, Miami in the winter, [and in] general travel in the summer."[59] During the winter, "hustlers flock to Florida from all over the nation to cater to . . . the hundreds of wealthy homosexuals who go South for the winter season to loll on the beach and enjoy life generally."[60] Cold weather during the winter in New York City, Painter wrote in 1966, "discourages all but the hardy or desperate." They migrate to "Los Angeles, San Francisco (mild winters), New Orleans, or Miami."[61] A San Francisco pornographer noted in the mid-1960s the "summer migration" of hustlers "with hitch-hikers who may be heading north or south from Seattle or Los Angeles" to Los Angeles, San Francisco, and New Orleans.[62] In the 1980s, an informant named Coy Ellison told me he was aware of a "hustler family" that migrated from Los Angeles to San Francisco and Denver: "In Denver, the couple times I'd leave off there, the hustlers there in the bar would always talk about 'when it's winter in Denver, summer in San Francisco.' So there was this big migration back and forth."

Annual fairs, conventions, and national festivals dictated movement. One of the most important festivals was New Orleans's Mardi Gras.[63] Tennessee Williams wrote in the late 1940s about a "vagrant" hustler who traveled through "the underworld that seethes around Times Square" and, "when summer had passed," joined "the southern migration" to Miami and New Orleans during "the Mardi Gras season."[64] In 1963 John Rechy fictionalized the annual "exodus" from Times Square, San Francisco's Market Street, and other "darkcities" when "the vagrants of America's blackcities are washed into New Orleans" for Mardi Gras.[65] Migration was above all an economic strategy, as frequent travel to fairs, conventions, and vacation spots increased the pool of new johns. "They migrate," Painter wrote in 1966, "which is only sensible, as so do the clients with money."[66] Moreover, young hustlers and queens were among many criminalized populations who found it profitable to migrate with weather and festival patterns over the decades, including hoboes, female streetwalkers, and migrant workers.[67]

The "heat" applied by police during periodic crackdowns also stimulated movement. When police cracked down on street kids in one city, the kids might travel to cities where policing was more lenient. In 1963 Guy Strait argued that "totalitarian" policing in Los Angeles had led to "an unusual gain in prostitutes in San Francisco."[68] Painter noted in 1941 that the authorities might round up the hustlers known to the police or state troopers, the latter of which have met while on "the road," take them to the city limits, and force them to leave.[69] Police raids "do little more than shift the scene of his action temporarily," read a 1941 sociological study. "When the authorities close one homosexual rendezvous another springs up overnight and word of its location is passed from one client to another."[70] Support networks in tenderloin districts and frequent movement between them enabled kids to avoid detection by authorities who might incarcerate them or return them to abusive families of origin. In 1983 a hustler told a sociologist, "When the local pigs start to hassle you or something . . . you can just use the next town as a hiding place for a short while."[71]

The kids' cyclical migratory patterns stand in contrast to studies of homosexual migration that follow subjects from the oppression of rural or suburban conformity to urban liberation. Historians argue that this mass migration from rural to urban spaces contributed to the development of "homosexual" identities and a settled "gay community."[72] Street kids' cyclical migration instead produced what Nyan Shah calls "stranger intimacies"— fleeting encounters that can result in "alternative socialities, experimental intimacy, [and] cooperative economies."[73] Frequent travel could be an implicit rejection of developmental paths conducted in a linear progression— birth, childhood, adolescence, early adulthood, marriage, reproduction, child-rearing, and retirement—a progression often marked with weddings, christenings, and other rituals.[74] The circuit's seasonal and festival rhythms instead "bound" bodies to cyclical patterns set against the linear, teleological time of normative (or homonormative) developmental paths and fostered novel forms of solidarity.[75]

The Norm of Reciprocity: Pooling Resources
and Protection from Violence

While the kids' performative economy took historically and geographically specific forms, the ethic of reciprocity appears to have permeated the scene across the decades. For this reason, we can begin to understand the kids' sense of justice and exploitation by examining reciprocity, which is based on the idea that one should help those who help you, or at least not harm one another.

From the late nineteenth century through the 2000s, kids pooled their funds to obtain housing in the cheap rooming houses dotting the central city. In these spaces, veterans initiated newcomers and taught them how to hustle, avoid the police, and share resources. A queen in Seattle's Pioneer Square recalled housing up to a dozen kids at a time in the 1930s. "It was like kids together, fellows, comrades," she recalled in an oral history. "The gay kids looked out for each other. We had to. We had to protect ourselves."[76] The trans Puerto Rican actress Holly Woodlawn, in her memoir *A Low Life in High Heels*, recalls hitchhiking from Miami to Manhattan in 1962, at the age of sixteen, and hustling Times Square. "One afternoon, I met a Puerto Rican queen who empathized with my situation and took me under his wing," she wrote. "Then I met some queens from Miami who were living in a seedy hotel on 72nd Street and Broadway. They were all crammed into one room, and made their living on the street, hustling their young virile bodies for 20 dollars a pop. At the end of the day, they'd pool their funds to make ends meet."[77] According to my informant Michael Norton, who hustled San Francisco's Tenderloin in the 1960s, kids "watched out for each other. If one had a place to live, then three or four or five others would be living there. Each one would pitch in. None of us went hungry."

The transient hotels were attractive to those seeking to remain anonymous or evade the police, as the frequent change of address (and often accompanying changes in name) helped keep them hidden.[78] Esther Newton noted in her 1968 dissertation (which later became *Mother Camp*) that street queens in New York, Chicago, and Kansas City allowed "'husbands,' 'tricks,' and numerous acquaintances from the street life [to] come in and out [of the hotel rooms] constantly." The hotels were not "homes" in the middle-class sense of a private domestic sphere; they were extensions of the street scene. A friend "who needs a place to rest, recover from a 'high,' or get a new one can generally 'fall by' and stay for a couple of hours or a couple of weeks."[79] A 1964 sociological study tells the story of a twenty-three-year-old male who preferred to "keep it on the move" by hustling in "three or four cities on the Coast, Tucson, Kansas City, St. Louis, Chicago, Philadelphia, New York, [and] Boston." He had few expenses because queens housed him. "When I hit town," he said, "I find me a queen . . . to shack up with, and a queen will always look after you if she can."[80]

The kids renamed themselves or were renamed by others as they assumed a new identity and life. The activist Sylvia Rivera, named Ray at birth, said that she "became" Sylvia and formally entered the Times Square scene in the early 1960s after meeting an "old butch dyke" and an "old queen" known as "the godfather and godmother of Forty-Second [Street]."[81] Among the godparents' tasks was renaming young people who "came on the scene."[82] Street names enabled kids to generate some amount of glamour in spaces of abandonment and abjection. A queen recalled in 1974 that kids on San Francisco's Market Street in the late 1920s took on "stage names," including "'Miss' Applegate, the Countess Leamington, Bubbles, and the Mystery Woman."[83] The trans activist Felicia Flames Elizondo told me she often named kids new to the scene in relation to their physical attributes: one girl who "looked like a rat" became "Rachel the Rat Woman," she said. A chubby Latino girl became "Cupid." Street names enabled hustlers to protect their anonymity and functioned to elevate aspects of their identity as sex workers. In the early 1980s, a hustler told a researcher that he chose the name "Butch" because "it means I'm a top." Another said he chose "Angel" because he looked "like I'm an innocent type, harmless and stuff."[84] These anecdotes suggest that the formation of individual subjectivity in tenderloin districts was part of a collective process and tied to economic imperatives.

Street kids often banded together to generate protection from physical violence. A 1959 study of Chicago hustlers noted that "cliques" often include "husky 'studs' and pimps who provide physical protection for the bar and its inhabitants." In return, the "studs" receive the "highest status in hustling society."[85] A sociologist in Times Square wrote in 1994 that one hustler receives respect and status in the scene because he serves as a "protector" for other hustlers in the area.[86] Hustlers, according to a 1959 study, "settle grievances between hustlers . . . and mutually assist each other in such crisis as evictions, raids by the 'heat,' and 'pinches.'"[87] Robert "Birdie" Rivera, a Puerto Rican queen in Times Square, said that in 1965 she and other young people formed their own "gang" called the Commando Queens. Part of their "code of ethics," Birdie recalled, was that each member "had to protect somebody who was getting beat up, someone who was queer."[88] An observer described in San Francisco's Tenderloin in 1968 a "violent exchange between saleswoman and customer. . . . A crowd moves in and she moves out, protected by her 'sisters.' The camaraderie is amazing! I am surprised that no union exists for prostitutes."[89] An informant named Rob Bennett told me that "there was quite a few really hot, buff prostitutes" on Polk Street in the 1980s. When a few men attempted to mug Bennett, two hustlers "beat the crap" out of his attackers. "I think the camaraderie [was] like a brotherhood. The hookers all looked out for each other. It was pretty safe."

The kids helped each other obtain and share state and welfare benefits and coached each other about the stories they should tell in order to obtain them. Writing in 1923 about "juveniles" on Chicago's State Street, Nels Anderson noted that "some boys make a practice of going from city to city 'working' the welfare agencies." They were so familiar with the organizations "that they usually know beforehand what questions they will be asked and how best to answer."[90] A sociologist on Polk Street in the late 1970s noted that "youths coming into the area are immediately oriented by peers on how to obtain social benefits—housing allowances, food stamps and medical benefits."[91]

This informal web of reciprocities and obligations continued to animate queer scenes in San Francisco's Tenderloin from the 1980s through the 2010s. Kevin "Kiko" Lobo told me that in the early 1980s, his street family would hustle Polk Street and pool money for expenses, including hotel guest fees, food, drugs, and liquor. "We all needed each other," he told me. "We would go out and hustle, and we would all pool our money together and get hotel rooms and there'd be four or five of us in a hotel [room]. Everything was family." Lala Yantes, who identified as genderqueer and hustled Polk Street and Los Angeles's Santa Monica Boulevard in the 1990s, contrasted the "culture [of] the kids" with what she called "mainstream society." The latter, Lala said, "likes normal, routine, safe, middle-of-the-road stuff. If you're anywhere outside that you can be looked at as a threat, or something that's unsafe or potentially dangerous." In opposition is "this whole other culture—these 'kids,' and these little families that we make up out here . . . that just accept you for who you are and what you do." The kids "looked out for each other. When one of us was sick the other one made sure that fuckin' they had what they needed. When one of them went to jail we made sure that we kept up the room, 'cause we were always living in hotels. We just did what we had to do for each other. Like a family, except there was none of the hang-ups that comes along with a bloodline."

While these examples show us the importance of the kids' mutual obligations, we must guard against the impulse to idealize or romanticize the forms of reciprocity that animated the scene. The kids were motivated to help one another—to pool funds and "watch each other's backs"—not always out of altruism but because they themselves would need the same assistance at a later date. In their own self-interest, abandoned people must cooperate in order to survive.

Additionally, the kids' scene was divided along racial and class lines. As a general rule, white sex workers recognized that their skin color entitled them to charge more than sex workers of color.[92] In the mid-1960s, for example, San Francisco's meat rack was known for "trade," or heterosexual-identified, masculine young men, and hair fairies, many of them people of color, who received lower fees for sex work. An eighteen-year-old Mexican hustler told a reporter in 1966 that "Americans think all Mexicans are drunks and dirty and all they are good for is sex."[93] In contrast, the primarily white, gay-identified hustlers, many with some college education, worked outside Union Square's upscale St. Francis Hotel and could obtain higher fees or live with a sugar daddy for extended periods of time. "A competition exists between the devotees of each location," a sociologist wrote in the late 1960s. "The Hustlers of Market Street view those of the St. Francis as snobs and conversely the Hustlers of St. Francis view those on the meat rack as trade and dirty."[94]

Counterdiscourses and Moral Visions

"Street families" were important forms of sociability and strategies of survival, but they were also critical components of a counterdiscourse that aimed to legitimize street life and reject as hypocritical the world that cast them aside. Because the kids existed toward the bottom of the moral and economic structure, they were in a position to see the discrepancies between the ideals of the dominant culture and its realities. Sex workers saw that the authorities who condemned them—judges, priests, and politicians— also purchased their sexual services.[95] "The people who put me down in the daytime for being a male prostitute and a pill pusher," a kid in San Francisco's Tenderloin said in 1966, "are the same people who buy my drugs and go to bed with me at night."[96] Many rejected as hypocritical the respectable world and developed an irreverent attitude toward its morality. A 1959 study claimed that Chicago hustlers "paint the non-hustling world as a world of hypocrites."[97] Esther Newton wrote in 1968 that queens in New York, Chicago, and Kansas City "made little distinction between the working class or middle class." From their perspective, "all of 'respectable' society seems very distant, very square, and above all, very hypocritical."[98]

A shared "hatred of the powerful" can be a generative source of moral values. Many street kids appear to have rhetorically inverted the dominant moral order by rejecting the "respectable" and ascribing the highest value to the "lowly" and morally despised. "If you stay a while," a street kid in San Francisco's Tenderloin wrote in 1967, "you scuffle around and hustle up some money to help with the rent and food. You have acquired friends; they too have been forced into these circumstances. You have a common bond of destitution." You are "somebody society doesn't like—a homosexual, ex-convict or a member of a minority group."[99] In time, "you look at the people on the street, hating what they are (good citizens) and revel in the secret knowledge that they hate what you are (dope fiend). The dope fiend is one of the lowest things that our society can conceive of, so, if you care for our society's esteem, you don't want to be a dope fiend. What happens though when you are a person with a reverse estimation of who is a low person? The leaders or 'great men' look to you like the lowest beings."[100] The kids developed a public culture that found value in a variety of criminalized and morally despised behavior, including the use of narcotics, commercialized and intergenerational sex, and public displays of eroticism and gender nonnormativity. Many kids found value in people and things deemed worthless and embraced the "gaudy" and "vulgar." The homosexual world of Times Square, Painter wrote in 1941, is "gay" and exciting with "all the trappings of amusement even if to the outsider it all seems very grim and tawdry indeed."[101]

Hustlers in particular often argued that all people in a capitalist economy "sell themselves." A Chicago hustler told a sociologist in 1958 that bankers, advertisers, politicians, and wives all "sell themselves." They "hustle just like we do—the advertiser spends all his time conning you out of your money; the politician is a whore." Hustlers often argued they were morally superior because they were "honest" about their hustle. We "know what we are and we admit it," he said. "I like the people here because they're real people."[102] According to a 1969 study, most hustlers "regard most of the other members of society as being much like themselves. Their motto is, 'Everyone is for sale. Wall Street bankers sell themselves one way, others another.'"[103] I heard versions of this maxim—that the central city is authentic and "real"—from many of my informants. "A lot of people call it the gutter," Coy Ellison told me of Polk Street. "Well, you know, call it what you want—it's honest."

Many nonhustling homosexuals were attracted to and adopted the kids' moral vision as their own. The poet Hart Crane, visiting Los Angeles in the late 1920s, found a thriving sexual culture on the downtown streets. "Just walk down Hollywood Boulevard someday," he wrote in 1928. "Here are little fairies who can quote Rimbaud before they are 18."[104] A 1941 study followed a Times Square john who "lessened the intensity and the pain of this conflict [with his sexuality] by gravitation to the society of male prostitutes." He began to "challenge polite society to show that what they may choose to call his moral degeneracy is any less desirable than their pretense and hypocrisy."[105] Mark Forrester, a homophile organizer in San Francisco's Tenderloin, saw an explicitly political critique in the kids' scene. "It's seeing behind the power structure," he said in 1966, "when you watch a lovely big Cadillac drive up, pick up a boy and a businessman goes off and the boy's back an hour later with $20 in his possession. And this man may have been a judge or an important politician or a high placed lawyer." The kids see "adults saying on the one hand, this is the ideal way of doing it and they see all the crap which is the actual way business is conducted in this country."[106]

Performed Effigy: The Queen

The kids materialized this moral vision through performances that spoke back to power. They improvised within the scenario of the central city, adapting cultural forms specific to tenderloin districts—theater, advertising, and celebrity culture, especially—and developing from them particular stock characters, structures of power, and novel forms of solidarity.

Modeling their personas on the movie star and female prostitute, the "fairy," "street queen," or "hair fairy" cultivated forms of inverted glamour through collective theatricality. Fairies were among the most visible manifestations of homosexuality in cities across the United States as early as the late nineteenth century. The subculture of the "flamboyant effeminate 'fairies'" in New York's Bowery, George Chauncey notes, "was not the only gay subculture in [New York City], but it established the dominant public images of male sexual abnormality."[107] Adopting mannerisms such as plucked eyebrows, powdered face, and dyed hair was "a deliberate cultural strategy" to publicly declare a nonnormative sexual/gender identity.[108] The term *fairy* was adopted by a diverse group of people: those who considered themselves women or otherwise not conforming to a gender binary, those who identified as men who inhabited diverse forms of male femininity, and people who adopted the "stylistic repertoire of fairies" to make their desire for men intelligible to others.[109]

This performed effigy changed over time as those new to the scene attempted to live up to the performances of those who came before them. A nineteen-year-old queen in Chicago who left home in 1935 and lived on the North Side of Chicago told a sociologist they "did every possible thing to imitate the effeminacy of the queers that I had come in contact with." They "began to wear flashy and obvious clothes, and use cosmetics to a greater extent. I did this just to get into the swing of the thing. . . . The gayity [*sic*] was what I was looking for."[110] A street queen in San Francisco's Tenderloin told a sociologist in the 1960s that "you watch other queens and learn from them. . . . I watched other queens, how they moved, acted, and spoke."[111] The paradox of restored behavior, Joseph Roach argues, resides in the phenomenon of repetition itself: "No action or sequence of actions may be performed exactly the same way twice; they must be reinvented or recreated at each appearance." Performance is not merely the recapitulation but also "the transformation of experience through the displacement of its cultural forms."[112] Through repetition with a difference, this stock character changed from the "fairies" of the late nineteenth century to the "belles" of the 1920s to the "hair fairies" and "transsexuals" of the 1960s. While there are crucial differences, each variant features a public theatricality that speaks back to normative conceptions of gender and respectability.

Street queens survived not by rejecting the abject status they were culturally assigned but by reinterpreting the agonizing effects of social abandonment as forms of glorification and celebrity. They often found power in what David Halperin calls the "paradox" of abjection: "the more people despise you, the less you owe them, and the freer and more powerful you are." Abjection endows subjects with "an inverted glamour, an antisocial prestige," while opening up opportunities for solidarity with other outcasts.[113] Consider the hair fairy quoted in a 1962 sociological study of London's central city: "My hair is blonde now instead of 'mouse,'" she said. "They can't go on saying 'You'll end up in the gutter'; I am in the gutter. They can't touch me now. People can stare at me if they want to. I quite enjoy it. It's as good a way of being stared at as being a celebrity or a pop-singer."[114] This street queen's performance of inverted glamour, signified by dyed blonde hair, found a counterintuitive power in abjection through celebrity culture and an embrace of "the gutter."

Street queens could claim social status by performing an "infamous" personality. Historian Warren Susman argues that as growing numbers lived in crowded urban environments in the late nineteenth century, success became a matter of displaying one's poise among a crowd and being perceived as unique.[115] A queen on Chicago's State Street told a sociologist in the 1930s, "If I think anybody is looking at me or talking about me, I say, 'Take a good look at me. It is not every day you can see a person like me.' And at times when people are staring at me, I will walk up to them and ask them why they are looking at me, and they will say, 'You have a striking personality.'"[116] Many homosexuals associated this "flaunting" with adolescence. "It is quite easy," a gay man in San Francisco wrote in 1965, "to understand why some, when young, go through a freakish, flamboyant era in their lives. It is the first feeling of being defiant and angry (and hurt) when encountering rejection and ridicule."[117]

Fairies rhetorically inverted the moral order that cast them as abject. In *Autobiography of an Androgyne*, published in 1918, Earl Lind (also known as Ralph Werther and Jennie June) wrote that as a young person, assigned male at birth, they regarded their "feminine predilections" as "the most heinous of sins."[118] Feeling as "an outcast from society," with "a deformed nature, and despicable in the eyes of all people," Lind "suffered from shame and remorse."[119] After Lind's father caught them dressing in women's clothes and beat them, Lind fled to the Bowery. Their reason for doing so was ingenious: Lind's father said that "taking the part of a girl was the very lowest thing a boy could descend to," and Lind read in the newspapers that the Bowery was the "lowest" place in New York City.[120] Therefore, Lind decided to explore the "lowest of dives." Lind found among "the most criminal-faced of the Bowery boys . . . a hearty welcome."[121] After exploring New York's "Underworld," Lind traveled to central cities across the country and socialized with the fairies who "throng the red-light districts."[122] Lind's involvement likely enabled them to became one of the earliest people in the United States to publish a defense of what they called "androgynes," people who did not fit into a culturally prescribed gender binary, via books including *The Au-*

tobiography of an Androgyne (1918), *The Female-Impersonators* (1922), and *The Riddle of the Underworld* (1921).

Street queens became part of the "spectacle" associated with tenderloin districts—performers and advertisers in their own right.[123] San Francisco's Market Street, for example, was a "fashionable promenade," one observer wrote in 1912. The wide sidewalks were crowded "from curb to house line with a leisurely moving throng" after theater performances. Shoppers were drawn to the large department stores offering attractions in "brilliantly illuminated show windows."[124] By the 1920s, street queens socialized and paraded on Market Street.[125] It was "the focal point of all the action," Toto le Grand (a.k.a. Lou Rand Hogan) recalled in 1974.[126] "Local belles all had to make the scene each evening the 'promenade' was marvelous to behold." Queens would gather on Market Street to "show off new 'outfits,' hair-do's, jewels, or the like. One might latch on to a trick; quite often one who would pay."[127]

Hair fairies in the 1960s walked the downtown in large groups and "flaunted" a highly effeminate embodiment. A sociologist observed in the late 1960s that "most 'hair-fairies' (also referred to as 'street queens') use feminine pronouns and terms of reference among themselves (e.g., 'she,' 'her,' 'that bitch,' etc.)." They "often can be seen in large 'packs' walking down the main street in the central shopping district of San Francisco." While not dressing in female attire, they "use heavy facial makeup, wear bouffant hairdos, and exhibit many feminine characteristic (e.g., swiveling the hips, falsetto voices, holding cigarettes with bent wrists, etc.). They are perhaps the most openly rebellious and defiant of all homosexuals, wearing their sexual orientations like a lavender badge of courage."[128] A sociologist writing about San Francisco's Tenderloin in the 1960s noted that the "hair fairies" had "what seems to be almost a uniform: a little makeup, a bulky sweater and tight trousers—as tight as possible." Their dress, he felt, was "intended to startle and to attract attention," he wrote, "and it did. Frankly, they could not have looked more like whores if they tried, and they seemed to get some kind of perverse pleasure out of this."[129]

Queens approached the boulevards, alleyways, and transient hotels of the central city as sites for nurturing counterhegemonic affects and reframing the emotional impacts of abandonment.[130] One queen, talking with a Chicago sociologist in the 1930s, said she "had a very unhappy childhood, because people made fun of me at times." Collective theatricality enabled her to revalue those feelings. "When I am alone, I do not holler and scream," she

FIGURE 1.4.   Queens in front of Times Square's Hotel Astor, 1965. Photograph
                   by I. C. Rapoport.

said, "but when I am in the group, I holler and scream to have people look
at me and make remarks. I do it because the rest of the kids do it. That way
I get out of the dumps. I begin to think that there is something to look forward to in a few years."[131] Jean Genet perhaps put it best when he described
street queens in his 1949 novel *The Thief's Journal*: "their shrill voices,
their cries, their extravagant gestures," he wrote, "seemed to me to have
no other aim than to try to pierce the shell of the world's contempt."[132] A
street queen told a Chicago sociologist in the 1930s that people called her a
sissy growing up. As a sex worker, she embraced the attention she received
from men on the street. Prostitution was "gay and brilliant," she told the
sociologist. "I just fell into it and made myself to be a good prostitute. I was
not shy in the prostitute role. My self-confidence goes up and down. I am
elated with my future and depressed with my future, exalted and morose.
Praise and encouragement makes my emotions go up."[133]

   There were profound class and cultural differences—and reciprocal
hostilities—separating "overt" street kids and "covert" homosexuals. Because homosexuality was defined legally as a criminal and immoral prac-

tice, public recognition was a threat to a person's social status and economic position. The "orderly homosexual," according to a 1938 study, "constantly seeks to conceal his homosexuality from outsiders." They are "haunted by the constant fear of the police and the blackmailer" and "must protect their small jobs or their tiny incomes at all costs, in order to safeguard themselves from the terrifying consequences of exposure."[134] These "covert" homosexuals, fearing loss of status, often shunned street queens because of their high degree of public disclosure. The "obvious ones" are "looked down upon by the run of the mill" homosexuals, a homophile organizer wrote in 1962, and "represent the greatest extreme of variance and are probably less than 1% of the total."[135] Street queens' "open display while strangers are looking on is what so infuriates the socially trained homosexual," a homophile magazine noted in 1964. "The queens, as if noticing this discomfort, seem compelled to outrage their spectators."[136]

Street queens often denounced "covert" homosexuals as hypocrites and claimed moral superiority because they "honestly" proclaimed their sexual deviance. "Misguided though you may believe us to be," a queen in Pershing Square said in 1964, "we at least stand on our own two feet proclaiming exactly what we are." The "masculine homosexuals" instead "shrink and hide." She wrote that she gravitated toward Pershing Square because it was "the haven of the delivered; that is, it is the meeting place of all those who have somehow emancipated themselves from the straight-jacket of conventional behavior."[137] A twenty-two-year-old hair fairy in San Francisco's Tenderloin wrote in 1963 that they were "not ashamed of being an obvious social variant. If I were ashamed, I'm sure that I would be like many I see who glance furtively as they walk by. When people see me on the street they might think that I am connected with the theater, because of the makeup. But those in the know, think differently."[138] If "covert" homosexuals attempted to conceal their sexual identities, the hair fairy or street queen responded to social stigma by performatively refiguring it.

Felicia Flames Elizondo told me that her sugar daddy introduced her to San Francisco's Tenderloin when she was a teenager in the 1960s. She recalled being exhilarated to see hair fairies with "ratted hair, makeup, skin-tight pants, angora sweaters, [and] tennis shoes. . . . I said, 'Oh my God, there's this place there's a whole bunch of us.'" Felicia was electrified by "the anxiety and excitement of a whole bunch of people like us in one place." She and her friend Frankie would skip school in San Jose and take the Greyhound to the Tenderloin. One day an older hair fairy took them to her hotel room and taught them how to apply makeup: "He explained [that] he couldn't dress as a woman because it was illegal, and [police] would throw him in jail. And that was the closest to being a female that he thought would be okay." The Tenderloin "wasn't a pretty place. There was a scary feeling surrounding you about you're going to get killed, raped, thrown in jail, murdered or beaten up." She explained that "it was the most horrible place in San Francisco, but yet it was the most beautiful place. For the simple reason is you could be who you were meant to be. It was a place where we did not know how long we were gonna survive, but we were gonna survive somehow."

Performed Effigy: The Hustler

If street queens developed a highly stylized femininity, the rough trade hustler cultivated a hard masculinity. He promoted himself as part of the central city's advertising culture, transmitting a "masculine glamor" by performing as urban cowboys, soldiers, and sailors.

Illustrative of these performances is a 1941 account by Thomas Painter. As a teenager bedridden with a heart condition in the 1910s, Painter entertained himself by playing with collectable cigarette cards. Cigarette companies enclosed a pasteboard card in each carton, Painter wrote, which ran in a series of "cowboys, prize fighters, Indians, explorers, athletes, etc." The object was to collect the cards until one had a complete set. Painter invented stories about the bare-chested prizefighters and cowboys depicted on the cards. They became "characters in a long and complex history . . . of war, intrigue, [and] politics." Bedridden, he would imagine he was a prizefighter, "longing to be as free and daring and unconventional as they." He also erotized the characters depicted on the slick cards, using a crayon to cover the bodies of the bare-chested prizefighters and cowboys with clothes, and "then with a knife, slowly and in various ways, remove the crayon covering [and] exposing the nude torso again."[139] He "gained sexual thrill from dressing and undressing pictures on cigarette cards. . . . Since the cards were slick," he wrote, "this could be done countless times, and was."[140]

The cigarette cards seemed to come to life when Painter entered Times Square in the 1930s. In his late twenties, he saw hustlers wearing "white sailor caps, riding breeches, cowboy outfits, wide metal-studded motorcycling belts, [and] riding boots," clothing that transmitted a "masculine glamor" and suggested the "virile occupations" of seamen, cowboys, soldiers, sailors, and laborers.[141] One twenty-five-year-old, Painter wrote in

1944, "affect[ed] a costume which gained him the nickname of 'cowboy.'"[142] He met kids on the streets, and in the cheap eateries, peep shows, penny arcades, and dime museums. A twenty-year-old "wore dungarees and a sailor cap, and claimed he was a seaman, and so became known as 'Matey.'" When another "seaman" came into the scene, "Captain Eddie," the two fell in love and lived together before Eddie returned back home with a wife and child.[143] Painter saw in the rough trade "independence, a physical courage or boldness, utter unconventionality, strength, hardness, vitality and an ebulence [sic] of spirit."[144]

Performing the white masculinity associated with the sailor, soldier, and cowboy was a canny economic strategy to attract potential clients. The sailor, soldier, and cowboy are iconic points of reference for American identity—masculine, heroic, independent—and represent enduring objects of queer fantasy. The cowboy, as developed through movies, comics, and advertising campaigns, was represented as a virile Anglo-Saxon facing off against a wild frontier populated by savage Indians.[145] The "queer" cowboy imaginatively expands and reinterprets this narrative but does not divest it of its white supremacist underpinnings. Hiram Pérez shows how the sailor, soldier, and cowboy have been desired for their masculinity while also functioning as "extensions of the U.S. nation-state and as agents for the expansion of its borders and neocolonial zones of influence."[146] Investigating the circulation of homosexual desire within the erotic economies of capitalism and the nation, Pérez refers to these iconic figures as "the rough trade of U.S. imperialism."[147]

Hustlers designed their performances to fulfill the perceived desires of potential clients. "According to the person," a Chicago hustler reported in the 1930s, "I had to act very sweet and to others I had to be very forward and bold, because that kind you had to give the treatment to in order to make a profit."[148] Another Chicago hustler said in the 1930s, "I play the man. I have a deep voice which helps quite a bit."[149] In the mid-1960s, hustlers on San Francisco's meat rack "resort[ed] to masquerading as seafood" (homosexual argot for sailors) to increase their hustling rates.[150] These performances were fraudulent only in light of dominant moral standards. "That's what they want is fake," a hustler in downtown San Diego said in 1983. "That's what they're buying. They want a superman or something for their fantasies and that's what you give them. Or you're not hustling right."[151] Hustlers knew that the clothes we wear, the conversations we hold, and our gestures all are signal systems to others of our social location.[152]

The kids' dramas took on meaning within a social world that embraced the paradox of masquerade: a performance that tells a social "truth" in the form of deception. It is not an accident that Mardi Gras was an important destination on the migratory circuits. In 1963 John Rechy wrote about the street queens, hustlers, and "vagrants" who were "washed into New Orleans" each year for Mardi Gras.[153] A fictionalized queen participating in the festivities pointed to the paradox of masquerade: "Im gonna tell you The Real Truth. People wear masks three hundred and sixty-four days a year. Mardi Gras, they wear their own faces!"[154] According to a 1968 account in a homophile magazine, San Francisco's Tenderloin was a space of authenticity "where we find out what people really are." Not that "phoniness is absent," they noted, but the "masquerade is so apparent that it is comparable to Chinese opera. Half the fun lies in stripping off the masks to find out who is hiding beneath, and the hustlers are as good at this game as the visiting psychologists."[155]

Those new to the scene imitated poses that indicated sexual availability. In the 1930s, a Chicago hustler recalled that he learned how to hustle after meeting "a fellow [who] said if you ever want to make money come down to Randolph and State [Streets] in your uniform, and stand with your arms crossed. That was a sign that you could and wanted to be picked up."[156] Hustlers constructed performances from particular features of the built environment. A letter to the editor of a San Francisco bar rag in 1963 pointed out "the ones [on Market Street] who pose against doorways and lamp posts, taking advantage of lighting and posing and Clorox to show off their supposed prowess."[157]

The kids devised public performances that were subtle enough to evade the detection of police but powerful enough to communicate their commercial availability. A hustler made himself known by various "stigmata," Painter wrote in 1941, "many of them subtle and only apparent to an experienced eye."[158] He cultivates a "facial expression," he wrote in a long passage, "not only by their steadiness or furtive motion but by the wide openness or suggestive half-closing of the eyelids, or by their fluttering; and also by the angle at which the head is held and the resultant obliquity or directness of the gaze, and the way in which the mouth is held—intently closed, lasciviously drooping—and even by open gestures of invitation with the eyes and head, the head being snapped to the side and back while the eyes steadily meet those of the invitee." This expression is "heavy with furtive obscenity." A "slow sexual air of sensuality—a lewd look" was combined with "cold calculation and sultry suggestion."[159] As such, the hustler developed a world of ocular communication that was largely invisible to the dense crowds pouring past.

The Norm of Reciprocity: Meat Rack
Businesses and Clients

It is critical to understand that the obligation of reciprocity is a moral principle that applies as strongly to relationships between unequals as between equals. Meat rack businesses—hustler bars, arcades, transient hotels, adult bookstores and theaters, all-night coffeehouses, and pornographic studios—knew the kids were the main attraction; they often allowed them to congregate because they knew they would draw paying customers. The kids claimed space in these businesses to socialize, advertise their services as sex workers, and discuss prices with potential clients.

Painter described the numerous bars harboring hustlers in Times Square in the late 1930s: "The management knew the boys were the attraction[,] so they allowed them to stand around, not buying anything frequently."[160] A 1959 sociological study noted that bars that "harbor hustlers . . . provide a social center as well as a place for the hustler to advertise his services to prospective clients."[161] Bar employees devised stratagems to protect themselves, by paying off the local patrolmen and negotiating informal limits on the conduct of patrons.[162] I show in chapters 4 and 5 that bartenders at Polk Street hustler bars, in the 1980s and 1990s, introduced and facilitated transactions between sex workers and clients and were tipped for this service. The kids benefited by having a relatively safe space to meet and discuss prices with clients, avoid police, and socialize. "They had peanuts and finger foods and people would just go in there and make a day of it," one informant told me. "A lot of the kids, especially if you didn't have money, could always go in there and get snacks."

The all-night coffee shops and diners often allowed hustlers and street kids to congregate and benefited from their patronage, especially at night, when respectable people were in their homes or apartments. In the 1920s and 1930s, George Chauncey shows, the cafeterias in the Childs restaurant chain could become astonishingly open, especially late in the evening, when managers tolerated a wide range of behavior. Several cafeterias assumed that they could attract slummers and sightseers by allowing "campy" queens to gather; the kids also attracted johns who were paying customers.[163] Painter wrote that those who couldn't find housing could stay the night at a coffeehouse: "with a nickel one can stay in an all-night cafeteria, nursing a cup of coffee."[164] Philadelphia coffeehouses in the 1940s and 1950s were "late night hangouts," one person recalled. "People would just go in there and try to make eye contact and then maybe get talking to one another or meet out on the street."[165] In late-night Los Angeles, Rechy wrote in the early 1960s, the coffee shops were the "meeting and exhibition place for the nightworld."[166] The "scores," or clients, will "offer a cigarette, a cup of coffee, a drink in a bar: anything to give them the time in which to decide whether to trust you during those interludes in which there is always a suggestion of violence."[167]

Transient hotels often rented rooms by the hour or charged an extra fee to allow clients into rooms. Mara L. Keire shows that prostitution kept many Progressive Era hotels running in the black. In a time when hotels had permanent residents, some prostitutes lived in these quarters, paying extra to rent rooms "with privileges." Others took their tricks to hotels that catered to the "transient trade." Johns rented rooms directly from desk clerks and paid the prostitutes separately, a highly profitable arrangement. One owner confessed that in a new hotel, he planned to "put his permanent guests on the upper floor and reserve at least 75 rooms [out of 170] for transient trade."[168] Real estate speculators often supported the centralization of vice districts at the edges of the central business district, basing their investment on the eventual expansion of the business district. When leasing to tenants engaged in illicit but profitable activities, landlords demanded higher rents from disreputable tenants than they could ask of respectable ones. The owners raked in exorbitant sums while they awaited the development of vice districts.[169] Similar transactions took place in midcentury tenderloin districts. According to a sociologist writing in the late 1960s, San Francisco's El Rosa hotel, in the heart of the Tenderloin, charged residents to bring clients to their rooms. A sign at the hotel "announces that an additional guest may be registered for the night for three dollars."[170]

The managers of amusement arcades and pornographic movie emporiums sometimes welcomed hustlers, who drew paying customers. According to a 1969 article, the "amusement arcades" on San Francisco's Market Street contained cubicles that hustlers used for rendezvous with clients.[171] In 1963 Rechy wrote about "Buzz," a "youngish score" who made his pickups at the arcade on San Francisco's Market Street: "On weekends he would be at the arcade playing the machines with the young vagrants."[172] Pornography studios were often located in tenderloin districts. Painter noted that the Athletic Model Guild had its "source" of models in Pershing Square and Hollywood Boulevard. Bob Anthony, who provided images for *Butch* and *Tiger*, had a studio in Times Square.[173] David K. Johnson shows that Bob Mizer socialized in Los Angeles's Pershing Square before founding *Physique Pictorial* in 1951.[174] *Physique Pictorial* tended to display its models in traditionally heterosexual masculinity honed by hustlers, dressing them up in the garb of cowboys, construction workers, bikers, and sailors.[175] Johnson notes that Anthony Guyther photographed male models, often kids in Times Square, in his Upper East Side apartment.[176]

As in other markets, the rates for sex work on the "meat market" fluctuated according to the laws of supply and demand. The rate structure in "meat racks," Guy Strait wrote in 1966, "is just exactly like buying used merchandise anywhere—the price depends on the expressed desire of the buyer and the need to sell of the seller."[177] When large numbers of navy men began hustling on San Francisco's meat rack in the mid-1960s, they flooded the market and lowered the going rate. Hustlers "say the sailors hurt their business" and "break the rate structure," claimed a 1965 radio documentary.[178] Guy Strait noted in 1966 that the number of "part-time entrees into the market . . . declined the value of professional seller as to disrupt the entire economic structure of the market."[179]

Due to the variability in the market, hustlers enforced control over pricing through shared moral codes based on the principle of reciprocity. A 1959 study in Chicago noted that "cliques" of hustlers "have control over the informal minimum price scale for tricks." Within the clique, "competition for Johns is restrained by the rule that, once a hustler has a mark [client] in tow, other hustlers will make no approaches to the mark."[180] A 1994 study in Times Square similarly noted that "once a hustler and a client begin a conversation, another hustler should never intervene."[181] There is a "certain amount of honor" among hustlers, Guy Strait wrote about San Francisco's Tenderloin in 1966. Among hustlers, it is "unwritten but understood that you don't 'burn' your good friends."[182]

The kids took collective action to eject outsiders, avoid police detection, and develop spaces that were conducive to business. In 1947 Painter wrote about a Times Square hustler who was "complaining about a bunch of very obvious, flaming young (entirely too young) faggot boys who were *accosting* people on the street, on the Square. This was very bad, made things 'hot,' roused complaints. So he and a number of older hustlers got together and warned them to go elsewhere—and gained their point."[183] A sociologist in 1967 attempted to go native, "donn[ing] the typical hustler togs, Levi's and heavy jacket; no doubt his age, twenty-four, aided his initial acceptance." The sociologist was accepted by the hustlers as one of them until he walked away from a potential client: "A hustler standing nearby noticed this; he moved over to several other hustlers and said something in a low voice. It here must have been apparent to some members of the hustling community that I was, in fact, not one of them. Antagonism, directed toward me by a small core of the more hostile hustlers, effectively closed the door to further communication."[184]

Sex workers developed shared conventions to garner respect from clients. One cardinal rule, according to a 1995 study of Times Square, "is to never allow a client to publicly humiliate or insult them in front of their peers." This can lead to loss of status among peers and sends a message to clients that public humiliation is acceptable.[185] The kids compared information about clients and shunned those who did not pay a high enough rate or did not treat them with respect. A 1947 study of high school and college-aged prostitutes in "the square of a large city" notes that the "regulars . . . know each other and compare notes. A customer who becomes known for demands that are considered unreasonable or for payments that are too small has difficulty getting a boy."[186] Because covert homosexuals needed to conceal their nonconformity, hustlers could also supplement their earnings by robbery, extortion, and blackmail without danger of arrest.[187] Clients were compelled to treat the kids with respect because the kids "had each other's backs."

In an ideal situation, actors in meat rack economies—bartenders, business owners, clients, and street kids—developed a flexible system of shared moral rules and conventions to compel equal exchange. Hustlers took steps to collectively set pricing and limit competition; they generated access to protection from physical violence and assisted one another in evictions and raids. There were, in other words, shared expectations about the behavior of others in the scene, grounded on a flexible view of social norms and obligations, of the proper economic functions and performances within the meat rack. This tissue of social norms and reciprocities motivated reciprocity as an exchange pattern and served to inhibit "exploitative" relations that would undermine the meat rack economy.[188]

Exploitation, Riots, and Rebellions

Street kids often made distinctions between relationships they understood as offering forms of mutual reciprocity and those they characterized as abusive and exploitative. As a general rule, the kids considered relationships to be exploitative when they violated the norm of reciprocity.

The kids might consider a john to be exploitative if they refused to pay or did not pay an agreed-upon fee. "Today, what people think is exploitation is just having sex with somebody young," Joel Roberts, who hustled San Francisco's Tenderloin in the 1960s, told me. "I don't think we felt exploited by the john unless he didn't pay you what he said he was gonna pay you." Michael Norton, who hustled the Tenderloin in the late 1960s, explained, "The ones who were willing to give you money were the ones who actually cared. They wanted to make sure that you were inside, that you had some food money. . . . The ones who didn't dish out the money, you were just another cog in that assembly line." Lala Yantes told me she "jacked" her first trick because he violated her sense of self-worth: "I got into his car and he goes around the block and he offered me fucking forty dollars to give him a blowjob. So I said, 'Sure.' And I took his forty dollars and at the next red stoplight I got out. I said, 'That, sweetie, is for your disrespect.' I was offended! I was like, 'Forty dollars. Is that what you think I'm worth?'"

Kids nearly always considered police to be exploitative—if not simply abusive—because they made money by "shaking down" hustlers, claiming sex workers' resources without returning a service of comparable value. The kids might consider businesses to be exploitative when they benefited financially from the trade in sex but mistreated them, for example by imposing service fees, installing security, or calling police. In a 1991 interview with a sociologist on Polk Street, a sex worker named Ariel argued for his right to remain in a "dirty" bookstore after he was "harassed" and kicked out by the manager. "It infuriates me that those fuckers would treat us like that when they know that's what's producing the fucking money," Ariel said. "Let's be real. Who do you think brings in the revenue here?"[189] Police persecution and urban renewal, two intertwined exercises of spatial power, could produce environments many considered exploitative.

I show throughout this book that a variety of historically specific forces—including urban redevelopment, health crises such as HIV/AIDS, and new policing strategies—could undermine the mutual obligations, networks of support, rate structures, and conventions by which the kids "had each other's backs." These changes could lead to an environment that kids considered exploitative—that is, one in which there was an unfair distribution of effort and rewards.

Consider the example of the redevelopment and policing of downtown districts during the 1950s and 1960s. The Housing Act of 1949 allowed the federal government to finance the cost of buying and bulldozing urban blighted properties, clearing the way for wholesale conversion of downtown districts.[190] Urban reform campaigns focused attention on the dilapidated and morally degenerate condition of the downtown districts and the "undesirables" who gathered there. Entire sections of downtown cores were acquired, razed, and rebuilt. With the aim of luring upscale shoppers back downtown, for example, urban renewal in Los Angeles proceeded in conjunction with vigorous policing of prostitution and homosexuality in Pershing Square.[191] In 1966 Painter noted that the newly elected New York mayor was "determined to clean up 42nd St and Times Square in general. For the tourists, largely."[192] Coffee shops and diners—many of which had previously allowed kids to congregate and benefited from the trade in sex—began imposing service fines, installing security, calling police, or otherwise excluding street kids.

These structural changes upended the moral norms and practices that comprised the performative economy, providing the indignation that fueled countless food riots and sit-ins. In 1959, according to Rechy, kids rioted at Los Angeles's Coopers Doughnuts, a twenty-four-hour downtown coffee shop patronized by queens and hustlers, many of them Latinx and black, after police ordered two hustlers into their squad car.[193] "First people started throwing the doughnuts they were eating at the cops," Rechy recalled. "Then paper cups started flying. . . . Then coffee-stirring sticks and other things started flying at them."[194] In April 1965, a Philadelphia coffeehouse called Dewey's began claiming that the "gay kids" were "driving away business" and started refusing to serve customers who wore nonconforming clothing.[195] After more than 150 people were denied service, three teenagers refused to leave the restaurant and staged a sit-in.[196] In June 1966, a street kid in the Tenderloin wrote that "a store owner who was notorious for his mistreatment of the street-kids had his place broken into and many on the street ate that night." The same month, the organization Vanguard threatened the boycott and picket of three coffee shops in response to what one organizer called "open harassment of young homosexuals."[197] Later that summer, street queens rioted at Compton's Cafeteria after it imposed a service fee and hired security to exclude street kids.

Historians, in accounting for these acts of resistance, have focused on the influence of 1960s movement culture and political protest, including the civil rights movement, the New Left, the counterculture, and an increasingly militant homophile movement; the impact of urban redevelopment and police raids; the ways in which the rights of consumers took on political significance during this period; and the sudden availability of a transsexual identity in the mid-1960s, which enabled many gender nonnormative people to insist on the value of their lives.[198] While these influences are vital, we cannot fully appreciate the rage and indignation that led to these rebellions without understanding the moral values shared by those who took collective action: the kids on the street who migrated from tenderloin to tenderloin, connecting them through migratory circuits. We must understand the kids' notion of economic justice and their working definition of exploitation and the ways in which urban development and policing violated these moral norms and practices. Riots and pickets operated within a popular consensus as to the proper economic functions and performances of the bartenders, street kids, clients, and many others within meat rack districts.

Urban Neoliberalism

Cities across the country began dismantling their central city vice districts from the 1970s through the 2000s, dramatically impacting the kids' scene. Urban neoliberalism—a set of practices including governmental tax breaks for large corporations, public-private partnerships, and "quality of life" policing strategies designed to drive perceived sources of disorder from public spaces—undermined the networks of mutual support, rate structures, and moral codes that functioned to limit competition and control pricing.[199] The evidence indicates that these structural changes permitted clients, police, and businesses to increasingly violate the kids' performative economy, leading to an environment that many street kids considered unsafe and exploitative.

During the redevelopment or "Disneyfication" of Times Square in the 1990s, for example, the state condemned land parcels, evicted and razed businesses, and offered developers property tax abatements to build luxury skyscrapers and shopping malls.[200] Mayor Rudolph Giuliani introduced zoning policies to restrict strip clubs, erotic video stores, and theaters, which forced many to close.[201] A sixteen-year-old hustler named Paco pointed out the unintended consequences of redevelopment in an interview with a sociologist in the early 1990s. "What little hustlin' is left is gonna be *real* competitive," he said. If sex businesses were closed, and there were fewer places to hustle, sex work would become far more competitive. If this happened, "all the rules is out the fuckin' window. It's everybody for themselves. Ain't gonna be no, 'Oh, I'll watch your back for you,' or 'I won't interrupt you when you with a trick.' All that shit is gone. It's gonna be everybody for themselves and fuck everybody else."[202] Paco predicted, correctly, that redevelopment would undermine the kids' ability to collectively set pricing, limit competition, and maintain shared moral codes.

I experienced similar dynamics on San Francisco's Polk Street, one of the country's last meat racks. The hustlers I talked with told me about the collapse of "street family" and the resultant lack of safety and respect. In years past, a thirty-six-year-old hustler told me, "we used to stick together, look out for one another. If one of us was dope sick one would help the other out. If there was a john on the street that was rough, we would tell each other." The kids cared for one another and "got more respect." Redevelopment decimated these networks of reciprocity. Now, "we don't stick up for one another like we used to. And the johns notice that." While gentrification radically undermined the local scene, I experienced the vestiges of this social world when I recorded stories with Kelly Michaels in her friend's single-room-occupancy apartment. I experienced the traces of this migratory public when I served meals with the Reverend River Sims. In talking with people on the street and exploring the archive, I found that religion had long played an important role in the kids' performative economy, a subject I explore in the following chapter.

2.　　　S t r e e t　　　　　　　　C h u r c h e s

But God hath chosen the foolish things of the world to confound the wise; and God hath chosen the weak things of the
world to confound the things which are mighty.

—1 Corinthians 1:27

THE REVEREND RIVER SIMS set up a hot stove and cooked a meal of rice
and beans in his single-room-occupancy apartment. It was a Thursday night
in 2008. "Every Thursday night I fix a meal and serve in Hemlock Alley to
the people who come for needle exchange," he told me. "I've done this for
ten years." Before serving meals during the exchange, which operated off
Polk Street to stem the spread of HIV and hepatitis C, "I'd take a meal and
take it out on the street, so I've always provided some kind of hot meal once
or twice a week."

River said he modeled his ministry on the anarchist Catholic Worker
movement, devoted to nonviolence, voluntary poverty, and serving people
on the margins; and the Old Catholics, a religious underground that claims
ecclesiastical authority through an unbroken chain of ordinations stemming
from the apostles. He called his ministry the "Temenos Catholic Worker,"

using the Greek word *temenos*, a piece of land marked off from common uses and dedicated as a holy precinct—or, as River interpreted it, "the area outside the walls of a city to which social outcasts such as prostitutes were exiled." River approached street kids as sacred figures and the Tenderloin as a sacred space. Taking as his inspiration the life of Christ, he "sought out the most loathsome and unclean" and created a ministry identified with those "who find themselves abandoned and isolated in their suffering." Each year, using the Tenderloin as a stand-in for ancient Jerusalem, he made the Stations of the Cross, reenacting the journey of suffering that marked Christ's last hours. "People think about the crucifixion in terms of the past, something that's *back there* two thousand years ago," he said. "But to me, Christ is right here. I see him being crucified every day on the streets of this city."

As we finished recording, a white trans woman named Jennie showed up to volunteer. Jennie and I prepared a box of plates and plastic forks as River finished the meal. River began to recite scripture as we worked. After a few lines, I was startled to realize that the three of us were in the middle of communion. It was a standard liturgy, familiar from my staid Presbyterian upbringing, though River substituted the word *Mother* for *Father*. (For example: "The Mother, the Son, and the Holy Ghost.") River gave Jennie and me a flavorless wafer and told us it was the body of Christ. He handed us a cup of wine and told us it was Christ's blood. I wasn't sure what to think about the ritual, but Jennie was excited. "That's the first communion I've had 'out,'" she told me. "That's the first communion I've had as Jennie."

The three of us then walked out onto Polk Street, pushing a baby stroller saddled with a hot pot of rice and beans, and handing out food on paper plates to the kids on the street. River was in high spirits, ribbing me—with Jennie as his audience—about being a "yuppie" and a "Castro queen" and making up stories about my sexual exploits at a local hustler bar. He seemed to relish nothing more than perversely fusing the sacred and the profane on the urban stage of the Tenderloin.

Overview and Methods

While a commonplace understanding of queerness and religion paints the relationship in stark opposition, I found that seemingly abject and profane tenderloin districts were at the same time incubators for syncretic religious practices and institutions. A Polk Street john told me he'd been dating a hustler who was a "total religious fanatic." There was "alotta religion on this street," he said. "Peculiar religion. People who swore they were one of the Four Horsemen of the Apocalypse." I encountered at the GLBT Historical Society the records of Tenderloin street ministers who, as early as the 1960s, established their own extra-ecclesiastic congregations; ordained street youth, themselves, and others; dressed in clerical costume; and staged public rituals of inclusion and healing. I traveled to archives throughout the country and read about gender and sexual nonconformists who created ministries in central city districts as early as the 1930s. I wanted to know why queer and trans solidarities so often took religious form in spaces of abandonment.

In this chapter, I juxtapose ethnographic and archival evidence to explore the crucial role that extra-ecclesiastic "street churches" have played within the networks of mutual obligation and reciprocity that comprise the kids' performative economy. These churches were essential sources of food, housing, and other resources for abandoned youth and, as such, were part of the accumulation of obligations, mutualities, and reciprocities that characterized the scene. But religion was not simply a source of economic support or a form of solace in a precarious life. It also offered a powerful critique of the moral order that cast street kids as unclean, damaged, and deserving of abandonment. Drawing on Christian scripture and ritual, ministers established the supremacy of weakness over strength, the superiority of the poor and "lowly" over the wealthy and powerful.[1] They fashioned a philosophy of life that affirmed that which had been rejected by ascribing the highest value to the "least of these." These figures ultimately developed a symbolic refuge that James Scott refers to as "an alternative moral universe in embryo—a dissident subculture, an existentially true and just one, which helps unite its members as a human community and as a community of values."[2]

I focus on four religious leaders who established their own congregations in tenderloin districts; claimed religious titles; ordained street kids, themselves, and others; and engaged in a politics of mutual aid and care: the Reverend River Sims (Polk Street, 2000s); the Reverend Raymond Broshears (San Francisco's Tenderloin, 1960s–1980s); the Reverend Michael Itkin (Times Square and San Francisco's Tenderloin, 1960s–1980s); and Sylvia Rivera (Times Square, 1960s–1990s), as well as the congregants who today remember and venerate Rivera as a queer saint (Times Square, 2010s). The ministers and saints I follow did not seek to condemn, rehabilitate, or "save" kids from a way of life characterized by migration and commercialized sex. They were often former sex workers themselves and/or lived their lives in tenderloin districts, outside the bounds of middle-class respectability. Many denounced the respectable world as immoral and elevated the outsider to the realm of the sacred. These religious figures, in other words, were part of "the scene."

I ultimately produce a performance genealogy of these street churches, focusing on the ways in which they materialized the kids' performative economy and transmitted it intergenerationally through ritual. For many anthropologists, ritual is where culture—as a shared normative orientation—expresses and reconstitutes itself most densely. The point of ritual in this literature, Elizabeth Povinelli writes, is "the generation and reconstitution of community by stimulating desires and feelings towards components of the moral and social orders through concentrated references to symbolic phenomena and processes."[3] Through ritual, street churches reinterpreted the agonizing effects of social trauma as forms of glorification by drawing on Catholicism's gothic language of abjection. Ministers oversaw rituals—ordinations, faith-healing ceremonies, communions, and christenings—that united abandoned people as "brothers," "sisters," and "Holy Fathers." Woven into the tissue of these performances is a shared moral universe, a common notion of what is just.

The Old Catholics

Many of the queer ministers I follow were part of an ecclesiastical subculture called the Old Catholics, Independent Catholics, or "episcopi vagantes"—literally "vagrant bishops." The Old Catholic Church began as part of a reform movement in Europe in the early eighteenth century and arrived in the United States by the nineteenth century.[4] These priests formed religious orders that emphasized the doctrine of apostolic succession—the belief that Christ's twelve apostles passed on their authority through their ecclesial successors to the current church authorities—and ritualized their authority with grand titles and vestments. Many Old Catholic churches in the United States formed to assert ethnic or racial independence for marginalized people who rarely headed their own churches. The Polish National Catholic Church and the African Orthodox Church, for example, formed to stress independence from primarily Irish and white churches, respectively.[5] Founded in 1959, the Church of Antioch ordained women as priests at a time when no large Catholic bodies were doing so.[6] The fringe nature of this underground also attracted confidence men who founded Old Catholic churches as welfare scams.

This ecclesiastic underworld became a haven for homosexuals. In the 1950s, George Hyde founded the first known Old Catholic Church serving homosexuals, tracing his line of succession to the African Orthodox Church.[7] Hyde's interracial ministry reportedly included female prostitutes, homosexuals, heterosexuals, black, white, Catholic, and Protestant members. "The group welcomed known prostitutes and other outcasts," a former congregant recalled, "and always black and white sat together in equality."[8] Another congregant remembered meeting in a rented hotel lounge with a small group in the 1950s. They gathered before a makeshift altar made of two cocktail tables.[9] By 1964 Hyde opened a church in New York City and outlined a plan to train youth as nurses and yardmen at a local hospital. This would be an effort to "save a vocation and a soul," he wrote, and render a "service—as Religious—to the community."[10] Old Catholic Churches headed by homosexuals often highlighted service to the "least of these" cited in Matthew 25:40.

Many Old Catholic ministers gravitated toward the seemingly abject and profane tenderloin districts. In 1963 the twenty-two-year-old Brother Marion Gerard Greeley told a reporter that he chose to work with "derelicts" because "God lives in the lowest person on earth."[11] In a May 1966 church newsletter, after a "pilgrimage to New York," he reported that the police department "is trying to clean up Greenwich Village and Times Square & 42nd Street" of "perverts, alcoholics, and derelicts." They are "Children of God," he wrote, "and should be treated as such."[12] Greeley then traveled to San Francisco's Haight-Ashbury neighborhood by the late 1960s, where he worked with street kids and operated a church out of his SRO apartment.[13] He asked mainline churches for donations of altars and other paraphernalia, presenting himself to a researcher in 1974 "as a religious scavenger who is preserving the old ways of the church." According to the researcher, "countless religious statues, icons, altars, mementos, and vestments . . . crowd the tiny apartment."[14]

The number of Old Catholic ministers exploded during the early gay liberation movement. In 1970 a gay organizer in San Francisco gave up on attempts to clarify the "confusion" over "bishops, priests, ministers, etc." He complained in the monthly newsletter for the homophile organization Society for Individual Rights (SIR), which had opened a community center in the "skid row" South of Market: "There are so many people around S.I.R. Center these days with clerical collars and titles that we haven't time to figure it all out."[15] In 1971 the twenty-six-year-old Joseph Feldhausen founded an Old Catholic congregation that met in the living room of a parish house in Milwaukee and, he said, "functioned like an inner-city mission for gay people." His congregation operated counseling and referral services to help people with medical and legal problems, visited gay men in prisons, and performed a Mass that was "theatrical, mystical, and highly personal."[16] *Jet* magazine featured Feldhausen in 1971 when he officiated the marriage of a black female couple. Feldhausen told the magazine that "the Orthodox Church is supposed to be one where oppressed people can come and worship in peace."[17]

By the early 1970s, the Church of the Beloved Disciple in New York City was the largest of the independent Catholic churches, proclaiming in every Sunday bulletin, "Gay People this is Your Church," and fusing ancient liturgies with gay liberation symbols.[18] Their pastor, Robert Clement, was ordained in the Polish National Catholic Church and served for a decade as a parish priest before founding a church serving homosexuals. The church worked with queer people in prisons, sponsored a gay Alcoholics Anonymous group, and performed "Holy Unions."[19] George Hyde worked with Clement to nurture the parish and, by the mid-1970s, passed along to Clement the original vestments his church used at the first 1940s liturgy. Hyde named Clement as his successor, using material culture to draw ecclesiastic lineages from the 1940s through the 1970s.[20]

Mainline congregations often condemned Old Catholic ministers for their lack of establishment credentials, aligning their religious performances with fraud and "role-playing." Many painted Old Catholic ministers as theatrical, immature, and fraudulent—attributes often wielded in homophobic attacks. "Instead of playing at queens and princesses like little girls, or cowboys and Indians like little boys," a 1964 theological journal read, "they play at being bishops, archbishops and patriarchs. They amuse themselves with collecting lines of episcopal succession, by undergoing repeated acts of consecration in back streets. They assume fantastic secular titles [and] worthless degrees from so-called universities."[21] These "paper priests," as the *San Francisco Examiner* referred to them in 1971, received their accreditations from mail-order "diploma mills" that ordained anyone for a fee, and were part of "a growing number of homosexuals who play church in the grand manner, creating occasional havoc."[22] If outsiders aligned their religious performances with fraud, street ministers took advantage of the culture-creating capacities of performance. Many understood that symbolic actions have the potential to create or undermine social reality and oversaw elaborate rituals to forge solidarities and oppositional politics among the abandoned and dispossessed.

The street churches I follow in this chapter were affiliated with highly sexualized homosexual undergrounds. According to an Old Catholic minister writing in 1962, one Old Catholic church posted notices in homoerotic "physique" publications alongside "advertisements for jock-straps, body-oils and leather trousers."[23] In the late 1950s, a London-based Old Catholic ministry advertised their monthly mass in the *Grecian Guild Pictorial*, a popular physique magazine.[24] At least some street ministers engaged in sexual relationships with the kids who made up their congregations. Some appear to have perversely melded Catholic ritual and sadomasochistic sex. A 1976 sociological study, for example, mentioned an Old Catholic bishop, "ordained by one of those mail-order organizations," who celebrated communion with Times Square hustlers: "The high point of the Communion was when the bishop would lie on a crucifix on the floor . . . arms outstretched . . . and the boys would file past and fellate him."[25]

While it is sometimes difficult to tell when kids considered sexual relationships with ministers to be exploitative and when they understood them as offering forms of mutual reciprocity, it is possible to make a distinction between the contemporary abuse of boys and girls by mainline Catholic priests and the queer ministers who maintained sexual relationships with street kids. In the former, an adult's power vis-à-vis the powerlessness of children acts as a method for forcing obedience and maintaining silence. In the latter, relationships operated as part of a performative economy based around intergenerational sex in which the kids often exercised a certain amount of agency and sexual relationships were a matter of public knowledge. For many street kids, the "Holy Father" was one of the sexualized kin relations that comprised the social formations they called street families.

The Reverend River Sims

I experienced the traces of this religious counterpublic when I volunteered with River Sims in the late 2000s. One Thursday night, I helped River pack up a pot of heavily salted rice and beans at his SRO apartment. We drove to Hemlock Alley to serve people leaving the weekly needle exchange. I got out and set up a table with a few other volunteers as River attempted, unsuccessfully, to parallel park. After a few failed attempts, he cursed and hit the horn. "I think he's getting frustrated," a volunteer whispered. River gave up and parked at a perpendicular angle; cars could barely squeeze by in the narrow alley. He emerged with a mischievous grin, pleased with his parking job, and began unloading the rice and beans from his trunk.

One of the boys—a hustler with long brown hair—looked at River's car and laughed. "The yuppies are afraid to drive around your car!" River laughed and greeted him. The kid handed River a *Lord of the Rings* fanny pack. River took a cautious look around and slipped him some cash through his sleeve. I wasn't sure what was happening. I asked River how he thought the boy got the fanny pack. "I never know," he told me, grinning. "I have a Bible up in my room that was stolen by one of the guys. It's *nice*. Priced at 120 dollars. I would have bought it myself if I had the money." He was relishing this juxtaposition of Christianity and criminality. The volunteers and I finished setting up the table and preparing the meal. I poured cups of Kool-Aid to people leaving the needle exchange at the end of the alley.

River introduced me to Matthew, a twenty-five-year-old who had been hustling Polk Street for a year. We drove back to River's place and sat down on his futon for an interview. I asked Matthew what he did for money. "I DJ, I clean people's houses that are on Section 8 disability, and I suck dick." I asked him about the johns. "You kinda gotta play the game a little bit," he said. "You know, you gotta figure them out, and figure out what kinda person that they want. And if you can do that, then you can kinda fit in. They feed you and take you out and they treat you very nice. You get treated really well. It's kind of a replacement for, like, you know, when you were growing up and your parents or whatever didn't treat you like they should have. And then you come across some fat old guy and he's all happy to see you and he treats you very nice." River took out his camera. "River's taking a picture of us for posterity," I said. "Yeah," Matthew said, "to jack off." River shot back: "You know that my dick goes limp when I think about you." Matthew let out a long guffaw.

Another day, River introduced me to a thirty-six-year-old who moved out of the house at age thirteen. He told me his mother sent him to Florida to live with his dad, but his father wasn't there when he arrived. "I started eating out of dumpsters, and eventually I started to prostitute myself." He made his way to San Francisco because it's the "gay capital," and gravitated to Polk Street. "We're basically just a bunch of people, kids, who grew up on the street who never really had a chance to have a real life," he said. "We're kids who were kicked out when we were young, we don't have any future, 'cause we got strung out on drugs when we were young." Most of the guys are hooked on heroin or speed; "it's kind of hard to stay off drugs when you're getting paid to use."

I also conducted oral histories with River. Over the course of several interviews, River told me he was born in southeast Missouri, ordained as a minister in the United Methodist Church, and then drummed out of the church and blacklisted for jobs when church fathers discovered he was queer. River turned to sex work in the early 1990s, on Polk Street and Los Angeles's Hollywood Boulevard. When he first came to Polk Street around 1990, it "had at least seven gay bars, and . . . was constantly filled with hustlers. . . . The average age was about seventeen. And it was a street where a mixture of people on the margins and gay men would be here drinking and partying. The people who came lived more on the margins, the poorer gays." Sex work "was a very spiritual experience," River told me. "It helped me work through my own 'coming-out' process. It helped me get in touch with my sexuality [and] find out who the hell I was." As a hustler, River often talked with older clients about their struggles with their sexual identities. "I used to joke that I was a counselor for older men," River told me. "In fact, when I did my résumé with that period of gap in there, I put in there that I had done counseling with older men struggling with their sexuality issues."

River told me he left Polk Street in the early 1990s, finished a master's degree in counseling, and became a therapist before returning to Polk Street around 1994 as head of an independent ministry. "I could never stay away from the streets," he said, "but I've come back and learned to do the streets *appropriately*," he said, grinning. "'Cause I mean there's a romance, to me, to the streets." He told me his ministry was devoted to "living simply, working with people where they are, nonviolence, and practicing the works of mercy, which is feeding the hungry, and taking care of people basically. Providing their basic needs." His years as a sex worker "taught me that sex workers were the ones who are the most disenfranchised in the Church. The Church they experienced was a Church that was very judgmental, always judgmental." He differentiated himself from other evangelists on Polk Street who attempt to "convert people and tell them that Jesus will take care of all of their problems. They tell people that 'homosexuality is a sin'" and "give them false hope. Because their false hope is the middle-class lifestyle 'that can come if you know Jesus, and that Jesus will take care of all of your problems.'" Unlike church groups that attempt to "change" people, River told me he was simply providing care: handing out condoms, blankets, food, and

River Sims, 2008. Photograph by Gabriela Hasbun.

information on safer sex. "The fulfillment I get is just *in the moment*," he said, "it's just being there for someone."

As we were recording an interview one day, I asked River about the more than fifty framed photos of the boys covering the wall by his door. River motioned to a photo, indistinguishable from the rest, and told me it was his son. He said his story needed to be recorded but it would be difficult for him to tell it. We should record it in one sitting, at some point in the future, and never revisit it.

After serving a meal off Polk Street another night, we drove back to River's apartment, and River pulled out a photobook to tell a few stories about the young people he's worked with. He pointed to a photo of one kid, a fifteen-year-old from Mexico who worked Polk Street and sent money back to his parents. He pointed to a photo of another kid who was using heroin. "Josh here is—this is ten years ago—I saw him yesterday doing the same thing, using heroin. I probably have the same conversation with him ten years ago as I had yesterday. About the same thing around drugs and sex, and whatever else is going on with him. The same drama." He turned the page and pointed to a photo of a boy who was raised fundamentalist and was overwhelmed by guilt about his sexuality. "Danny is twenty-eight now—I've known him since he was fifteen—still out there using drugs, and still doing the same thing." There was a photo of River and a young man at Yosemite National Park. The kid was sexually abused as a teenager, River said, and he's been shooting up on the street for years now, "like he always has. My guess is he's running from his demons, around the sexual abuse."

River pointed to a photo of Anthony, taken when he was seventeen, who had since aged into the general homeless population. Another kid was still shooting up. He's "trying to get clean," but it's "the same thing, over and over, he has repeated since I have known him." River felt the root cause of his drug use was that he "never faced being gay." River turned to me. "I mean, you want stories? I have stories about my relationship with them, but it's the same story over and over. It's the story that I mean that they all 'try,' but they repeat their own same life cycle. In their minds, they're still kids. And they're not. And the world's passed them by." River saw the ravages of homophobia on the streets of the Tenderloin. Religion and sexuality are the "two most powerful forces in the world. And you either come to terms with those in your own life, or it will be destructive to your life," he said. "If you're not open about [sexuality], if you don't deal with it, if you don't respect it, it will destroy you."

Another night River introduced me to Richard, the skinny, mohawked twenty-one-year-old I mention in the book's introduction. Richard was cheerful when we began the interview. He told me that he'd just been to New York to "get clean" off meth; he wanted to get involved with the needle exchange and help other kids addicted to speed. But his body tensed when I asked him how he came to identify his sexual orientation. "I am bisexual," he said. "I've worked as I guess they call them 'the Polk Street hustlers.' I've worked pretty much turning tricks to survive when I was younger. And my sexual orientation . . ." He paused. "It wasn't right how it was brought about. I was molested when I was a child by my stepfather, and I think that's one of the things that brought me towards being bisexual was that interaction because at that young age I thought it was right." I interjected, "You don't have to tell me anything you don't want." I said this partly for his benefit but also because I found it difficult to hear this story. I found that it was a commonly told story on Polk Street.

Abused by his family of birth, Richard told me that he formed a street family on Polk Street. Among the most important members of his family were

Kelly Michaels, the trans woman I interviewed earlier, who taught him "you can't love somebody else unless you love yourself," Richard said, "because my self-esteem used to be *way* down in the gutter." Richard also considered River to be part of his family. "I can tell whether a person is kindhearted or not when I first meet them, and I like kindhearted people. And I like to surround myself with those people because I'm extremely kindhearted. I'll give somebody the shirt off my back." People on Polk Street "got all these little tight-knit groups of really good friends."

Richard said he tried to bring other young people into his family. A few months before we talked, Richard saw "this *young* kid" walking toward Polk Street. "And I felt so bad for him because I saw him when he first came to the city three years ago, and he was in the same boat that I was in. I offered to take him under my wing and pull him into my little group that I had. And he turned me down. I saw him a week ago and he's got abscesses all over his arms and just looked like he weighed eighty pounds soaking wet. And I just felt so bad. I cried for him." He paused. "What people don't realize is they think it's cool to come out here and run the streets, but these streets will eat you. See, I was raised tough, so I guess that has something to do with why I've survived out here as long as I have."

As River gave Richard some clean socks, I asked him what he wanted to do with his future. "I want to open a skate shop somewhere," he said. "And I also want to open up my own youth center. Because the state of California keeps building all these prisons, getting them ready for the youth; why don't they get smart and build more youth programs? And that's what I want to do is I want to pull the government grants and use it for something good." When we finished talking, I turned my audio recorder off. Later that night, River emailed me and asked me to "take care of yourself emotionally" after interviews. The oral history interviews did take a toll on my mental health; they also helped me understand the ways in which abandonment was at the heart of the kinship networks people called "street families" and the religious solidarities I call "street churches."

I also got to know River Sims well enough to witness his mood swings. Some days he wore a mischievous grin and cracked crude jokes. Other days he was morose and withdrawn. One night, after we unloaded pots and pans at his place, he answered my questions with one-word answers: "Fine." "Yeah." I left, unsure what was affecting him. A week later, as we were driving to set up a meal at Hemlock Alley, he told me that he was feeling pessimistic because this is "just a project" for me. The interviews had been emotionally and physically draining. "That is what you saw last week," he said, "and one of the reasons I was not as forthcoming. I cried when I was alone. There's a lot of pain on the streets." His driving was erratic. Two cars nearly hit us as he weaved through traffic. River lay on the car horn, yelling, "Come on people, let me in!" Then he was quiet. He said we shouldn't joke at meals anymore. "You need to feel their pain." River told me he'd been sick, that he hadn't felt right lately, but he still wanted to record the story about his son. "To interview me about Zach is going to be very painful," he said, "and I need to have plans to do something afterward."

River's Son

In early 2008, River called me and said he was ready to tell his son's story. One night at his apartment, I unpacked my digital recorder and took the clock off River's wall so the recorder wouldn't pick up the ticking. "Joey the perfectionist," River teased. We sat down on his pullout bed. "I think we should record the story about your son," I said, "but are there other things you want to talk about first?" River let out a sigh. "I think . . . let me tell that story, and then you can ask questions if you want, but . . ." I said, "Okay, I'll let you tell it and I won't interrupt." River shot back: "That'd be a miracle from God." He lay down on the futon and closed his eyes as he began telling his story.

"When I was fifteen," he began, "my initial experience with sex was having sex with this girl under the altar of the church. She got pregnant. And a boy was born, and he was adopted to a fairly wealthy family in Portland. And his name was Zach." River's story immediately had the cadence of a biblical story or a Greek myth. A boy was conceived under the altar, a table used for making offerings to a deity. River too would have to make a sacrifice. The Methodist Church fathers grooming River to become a minister told him that, because the pregnancy was out of wedlock, he would have to keep it secret and give up his son for adoption. River accepted this sacrifice, he told me, as "a consequence of my sin." His son was also adopted out with the provision that his son would not know he was adopted, or who his biological parents were, until he turned twenty-one.

River said he felt tremendous guilt for giving up his son. When he was in his late twenties, he decided to find him. River told me Zach was about twelve at the time. River discovered through his son's adoptive parents that Zach was out on the streets, in San Francisco and in Portland, and was heavily involved in drugs. River set off to search for a son who did not know he existed. He traveled to San Francisco's Polk Street as a street minister, serving the kids who flocked there. Zach's adoptive parents sent River pictures so he'd be able to recognize his son. "And so I came out here to San Francisco. And I knew he'd be around, because he's out here hustling. And I intentionally looked for him." River recognized Zach the first time he saw him. "I remember he came skating up and asked me for some food," he said. "That's the first time I saw him."

Zach came to know River as his "friend" who gave him special attention. River said he never told Zach he was his father. He told me he didn't want Zach's parents to sue him. "That was part of the agreement of the adoption was, until he was twenty-one—and he wasn't twenty-one—so I didn't, I never violated that. I couldn't take a chance on them suing me." River also felt that telling Zach he was his father "would just add to his own psychological stuff. 'Cause they had never told him he was adopted." They developed a close relationship. "I remember one time," River said, "he came over to me and he'd been on speed for days, and he wanted to lay down, somewhere he could lay down, because every time he laid down at someone else's house he'd get raped or something. Usually raped. I remember he fell asleep, and for five days I'd have to move him around when I would have people in and out, because he was so sound asleep. And he trusted me that much. And I remember that. I remember that was . . ." River's voice trailed off. "And he loved me, like a lot of these guys."

River watched his son age, traveling between Portland and San Francisco and getting deeply into speed. "As the years moved on, I watched him go from being about twelve or so, thirteen, on the streets, to being like the typical street kid: pretty unworkable, and pretty needy. And we had this relationship I have with most of the guys out here—they trusted me, they depended on me. And you know it was hard—watching it, watching what happened with him. But," River said, "you know, I also took care of him. And I did the best I could with him. But I had my chance with him."

The two became so close that Zach used River as his emergency contact and carried River's business card and phone number in his pocket. In 2002, five years before we recorded the interview, River got a call from the Portland police. "I got this phone call . . ." River sighed, his eyes still closed. "From the police in Portland, where he had been murdered . . . in some kind of drug deal. He had apparently tried to steal or cheat the guy with drugs, so they gave him an overdose of speed—a 'powerpack,' they call it. And in the end, what happened is I had his body cremated, and scattered his ashes in Pioneer Square, where he skated. And I had a service down here."

Three years before our oral history, River said he got a call from a hospital in San Francisco. "And it was a guy who was dying that asked for me, to hear his confession." River didn't know who he was, but the person requested him in particular. "And he was the person who had killed Zach. He wanted to tell me that." I asked him how this impacted him.

I remember I became, like . . . I was, like I'd drifted out of my body, like I was another person looking down, dealing with this person, when he started telling me what had happened. I mean, the details was very painful. I mean, it was the whole description of how he died. And I think what I remember most was this guy's pain, and his fear of death, and fear what was going to happen, as he told me not only about what happened to Zach, but a lot of other things. And at that time, my anger just went. I thought all I could do was hear his confession, give him the last rites and then I—buried him. I paid for his funeral.

River explained, "The thing with Zach would have eaten me up. And I think at the time, for some reason or whatever, I asked him to let go, and I realized that." He paused. "I was a priest, and that's what I do." As a "priest," River not only hears confessions and forgives but also fashions a philosophy of life that affirms that which has been rejected. "I see the very worst in people here," River said of the Tenderloin.

I see evil face-to-face. I've seen people murdered, I've seen people brutally raped, I've heard the worst stories, and yet, on the other hand, I've experienced the best. And I mean I think that's part of the mystery of life: there's no answers to why good happens, or bad happens. And I can find both the good and bad in anyone. I mean, that's part of one of my gifts, is I will see what I call "the face of Jesus" in each person I meet, even if they've been violent towards me, even when they killed my son. And that's think that's what, that's basically what I've learned.

River opened his eyes and stood up. He opened a drawer at his desk and showed me a small wooden box his son used to store his drugs and other belongings. A few of Zach's rings were still inside. River also showed me a pamphlet for his ministry that read, "A Sacramental Ministry of Presence & Harm Reduction for Sex Workers & Homeless Youth Adults." On the cover is a photo of Zach, grinning for the camera. There is an undeniable genetic

FIGURE 2.2.   A photo of River Sims's son, Zach, on his Temenos Catholic Worker informational pamphlet.

resemblance. River's search for his lost son reverses the more common narrative on Polk Street of the innocent son fleeing the abusive father. River is instead the surrogate Holy Father to the "lost boys" on Polk Street and they are his sons.

The Reverend Raymond Broshears

While I was out on the streets with River, I was also exploring archival records at the GLBT Historical Society. I was drawn especially to the papers of the Reverend Raymond Broshears, an Old Catholic minister working in San Francisco's Tenderloin from the 1960s to the 1980s. When I encountered the collection, it was an unprocessed hodgepodge of disparate time periods and subjects: I found newspaper clippings about a gay priest filed with photos of men in bikini bottoms competing in a gay bar's "Groovy Guys Finals"; an advertisement for the "tender touch" of a Swedish massage "in the privacy of your home" was filed with a poster for a faith-healing ceremony. Identified in a 1969 Federal Bureau of Investigation (FBI) memorandum as "a homosexual, hippie minister, with a history of mental illness," Broshears was an instrumental part of San Francisco's early gay liberation movement.[26] He advised the Tenderloin street youth organization Vanguard in 1966, founded the Gay Activists Alliance in 1971, and organized San Francisco's first officially recognized gay freedom march in 1972. He may have received the most publicity—in magazines like *Time*, *Rolling Stone*, and newspapers as far away as Texas—when in 1973 he founded the Lavender Panthers, a vigilante group of Tenderloin street kids who patrolled the city with sawed-off pool cues and shotguns.[27]

It is difficult to piece together a reliable account of Broshears's life because of his incredible talent for fabricating an often-contradictory personal mythology and because of the many aliases he used: Raymond Broshears, Ray Allen, Raymond E. Allen, and Earl Raymond Allen. A reporter wrote in 1973 that it was hard to "accept Ray Broshears at face value" because "there are so many faces."[28] Broshears himself noted in 1968 that performative storytelling was a feature of queer counterpublics. "In the homosexual underworld," he said, "everybody likes to make themselves out to be something more than what they are. You know, real important, especially the more they're hitting the skids." The "deeper down, the more important they like to make themselves."[29] As such, I am ultimately less interested in whether a particular story Broshears told was "true" than I am in what that story did in the world, how it created a new state of affairs—in other words, how his storytelling and performances functioned as part of the kids' performative economy. I piece together evidence from court cases, archival records, FBI investigations, and oral histories to show how Broshears deployed narrative and ritual to forge kinship among the kids on the street.

Broshears appears to have been born Earl Raymond Allen in 1935, in either Missouri or Illinois.[30] At the age of five, his name appeared as Raymond Broshears in the 1940 Census.[31] He moved frequently with his mother and stepfather between various navy bases, and at the age of seventeen, in 1952 or 1953, he appears to have enrolled in the US Navy.[32] Three years later, in 1954, he was honorably discharged due to medical conditions.[33] Broshears claimed that he began treatment in 1955 at Veterans Affairs (VA) hospital facilities "due to the seizures and the strong emotional disabilities" he "incurred while in the United States military."[34] According to files compiled by the FBI, Broshears was treated at VA hospitals for "chronic brain syndrome associated with convulsive disorder" and "a schizophrenic reaction," likely occurring after a traumatic experience.[35] He began living off a navy disability check, his main source of income for the rest of his life.[36]

Broshears joined the Pentecostal church, which had grown from a marginal group in the early twentieth century to a movement that, by the 1950s, was starting to capture the attention of mainline theologians and national news magazines.[37] He joined the Church of God, one of the most significant Pentecostal denominations to emerge in the southeastern United States in the early twentieth century.[38] Often from lower socioeconomic strata, Church of God members were ridiculed as ignorant by mainline denominations and stigmatized for their passionate displays of worship, including casting out demons, laying on of hands in healing services, and taking up venomous serpents.[39] Broshears claimed that he became a Church of God minister by the early 1960s and led "evangelical crusades" across the South.[40] He later recalled that he was active in the American Crusade Against Communism and, according to one reporter, was "as anti-homosexual as any clergyman in the 1950s and early '60s."[41]

This all changed in 1964, when, at twenty-nine years old, Broshears was arrested on charges of sexual relations with a seventeen-year-old male in Belleview, Illinois.[42] The *St. Louis Post-Dispatch* reported the conviction, adding that Broshears "plead[ed] guilty to a morals offense involving a 17-year-old boy."[43] The *Chicago Tribune* reported that Broshears was sentenced to six months in the state penal farm at Vandalia.[44] His extended family disowned him. "When all that hit the newspapers," Broshears wrote in 1976, "all my relatives became my 'ex-relatives' right down to the last second cousin. They didn't want no faggot in the family!"[45] The charges also haunted him after he was released from prison and fled to New Orleans.[46] "I didn't know which way to turn," he said in 1968. "I had lost the church, I lost the family, everything over it."[47] He worked at a New Orleans carnival under the name Raymond Allen and the nickname "Corky."[48] He "could not find any other employment," a 1968 report read, "as a result of his prior arrest and incarceration."[49]

The Tenderloin and Broshears's Orthodox Episcopal Church of God

Broshears reported that in 1965, at age thirty, he fled to San Francisco and took up residence in a downtown SRO hotel in the Tenderloin, at the center of the city's meat rack.[50] He might appear to have made a complete break with his rural Pentecostal past by taking up residence amid the cheap hotels, pornography shops, and adult bookstores in a district the press called the "City's Sin Jungle."[51] Broshears's former congregations would have likely experienced the district as a modern-day Sodom. But as before, Broshears continued to draw on Christianity's language of power and abjection. "Sometimes we wonder," he wrote in 1968, "why God in His infinite mercy reached down and saved us, for we are so unworthy. The Bible says 'God hath chosen the foolish things of the world to confound the things which are mighty.' So, the more unworthy we feel, the more He can use us. The more lowly we are, the greater winners we are for God."[52] In Broshears's description of his love for God, we can hear an implicit reproach against a dominant moral order. It was only in the Tenderloin, Broshears wrote in 1976, "that I would even admit that I was a homosexual."[53]

Broshears drew on scripture to reinvent himself as a righteous crusader for the street kids and hair fairies in the Tenderloin. He ordained himself through the Universal Life Church, a religious organization that offered ordination papers through the mail, and made contacts with Old Catholic ministers. In 1965 he founded the Orthodox Episcopal Church of God. He raised money through donations from the gay bars, businesses, and individuals in the Tenderloin and held late-night organizational meetings in its all-night Foster Cafeteria, a well-known hangout for bohemians, gay men, artists, and sex workers. He connected street kids with housing and social

FIGURE 2.3.   Raymond Broshears and young adults at a demonstration, ca. 1968. The protest sign on the left reads: "The draft board recognizes the Roman Catholic Church, Council of Churches members! They have money, we don't! Draft the poor people was the policy, now it has become, in addition, draft the poor churches ministers!" Courtesy of GLBT Historical Society.

services and "advocate[d] the works as outlined by Jesus of Nazareth," he wrote in 1979, "that being, that we are to assist the sick and the lame, to assist the poor, to sacrifice whatever we can to bring about a better world for all on this earth plain. Thus, many of the Clergy of the Church are considered 'Social and Spiritual Activists.'"[54]

Broshears rejected medical models of disability and the designation of homosexuality as a mental illness by aligning himself with the Old Catholic movement, which presented itself as the "true" and "original" church, the church of Jesus Christ and his disciples. "In the day of Jesus and the Apostles," he wrote in 1968, "there was not such a word as homosexual, for it was not considered evil, for no one thought of it as such. Only since the advent of Mr. Freud has the world, and especially the people with 'hangups' has sex become sinful. . . . In Jesus Christ, God identified himself not with the respectable, but the 'outsider.'"[55] The world "in its more peaceful days," he wrote in 1967, "practiced homosexuality without anything being said, for it was not considered abnormal."[56] If queer street kids in the Tenderloin internalized narratives casting them as unclean, sinful, and mentally ill, Broshears encouraged youth to "accept" their sexuality. "If you believe the act is evil it will be evil," he said in a 1967 interview. "To try and fight it will end up causing you a nervous breakdown or psychotic disorder from which there may be no return."[57]

Broshears sought to cleanse the abject through Pentecostal "faith healing" ceremonies—ritualistic practices of communal prayer that are claimed to solicit divine intervention in initiating healing—which he held on Monday evenings on the fifth floor of a building at Market and Seventh in the Tenderloin meat rack.[58] Broshears claimed in 1970 that his "healing service" was "quite similar" to that of the Pentecostal preacher Oral Roberts.[59] People who are "jobless, or . . . sick, or . . . have lost their families," he wrote in 1969, may be the result of someone having "cast a curse upon them." The "ONLY way to get rid of the evil possessions" is to ask that the "blood of Jesus" "cast out . . . all evil that has come to me . . . into the depths of eternal darkness."[60] We can imagine Broshears as a performer and showman during these rituals. Broshears's speech patterns, according to a reporter writing in 1973, "reflect[ed] the dramatics of the revival tent, his voice drooping to a low whisper then soaring out at full sonic boom when he wishes to make a particularly telling point."[61]

Broshears organized a seminary through which he trained and ordained ministers, many of them Tenderloin street kids. The seminary combined Christian traditions with New Age practices popular in California. The ministerial tests he administered in his seminary touched on the New and Old Testaments—as well as subjects like telekinesis, auras, astral projection, Buddhism, and the zodiac.[62] Broshears wrote in 1974 that the priests of his church may use the gifts of "prophecy, dreams (clairvoyance), etc., and the Gift of Healing through Faith by the laying on of hands."[63] He ordained many members of Vanguard, an activist organization created by street kids in 1966, as I outline in the following chapter, and drew on Christian scripture to call for mutual aid among the kids on the street. "He who liveth in his own cares and associations shall surely drown in the waters of self-pity," he wrote in 1968. "For, it is in doing for others that we truly find God, for then . . . you are letting others see by your good deeds the beauty of brotherhood."[64] By 1968 Broshears proclaimed himself bishop and counted thirty-one ministers, most of whom appear to have been street youth.[65] He claimed in 1969 that he had six churches in the Bay Area and a membership of nine hundred people.[66]

Broshears just as quickly unordained those people who displeased him. In the late 1960s, for example, a young person reported that Broshears moved into a house in which he and other youth lived. "There has been nothing but hostility in the house since," he wrote. "The person I love was ordained Sunday night in Ray's Church. A few hours later he was un-ordained because he was sleeping with me. Ray liked me, but he knew it wasn't possible. He hates us for being together." Broshears's "hostility" was "frightening."[67]

It is unclear whether street kids considered Broshears to be exploitative or whether they understood him as offering forms of mutual aid and support. Two letters from a hustler who went by the name "Macho Mouse" in the early 1980s suggest that some kids may have considered him to be both. "I just can't wait until I get back to SF and sit on your face," Macho Mouse wrote Broshears in a letter from jail. "Did I say that?"[68] Sometime later, Macho Mouse sent a more hostile letter, claiming that he was going to make Broshears's life "miserable" when he got out of jail. "You are really degrading person," the letter reads. "You are no Reverend—it's just your front. Also, you will no longer be a Reverend after I get you put away for molesting children under 18. Do you recall 16 year old Steven. That's right. I've got evidence."[69] Broshears's friend Elisa Rleigh recalled that "Ray could be a real letch" and "could really take advantage" of people. She said Broshears would occasionally offer food, legal services, and shelter in exchange for sex, though she didn't know of an instance in which he physically forced himself on anyone.[70] Broshears's photobook, archived at the GLBT Historical Society, is teeming with photos of nude young men that appear to have been taken in his apartment.

Broshears's Helping Hands and Lavender Panthers

Broshears was one of the few activists who organized hustlers and street queens in the Tenderloin. In 1971 he founded San Francisco's chapter of the Gay Activists Alliance, which he called a "'street peoples' gay organization."[71] The alliance organized "brunches and other activities to aid the Tenderloin's large population of indigent elderly."[72] In 1971 they marched in an antiwar demonstration and stopped traffic in the meat rack. The meat rack "is the front porch of gay people—transvestites and transsexuals," Broshears said. "It is time we . . . have an anti-war demonstration against

FIGURES 2.4 AND 2.5. Two pages from Raymond Broshears's photo album. Courtesy of GLBT Historical Society.

the war we have to fight with police here every day."[73] Broshears supported and organized people we might now identify as transgender, who in the late 1960s and 1970s often referred to themselves as transsexuals, drag queens, hair fairies, or "the girls." In 1971 he called a meeting to protest the arrests of "46 persons, mostly transsexuals," in a sweep of the Tenderloin and led a picket line to protest housing discrimination after a hotel evicted thirty-three "drag queens" in 1973. The same year, the trans activist Sandy Green called Broshears one of only a few activists who "consistently stood up and fought battles for the drag queens of San Francisco."[74]

Broshears also provided material resources to impoverished people in the Tenderloin. In 1973 he opened a Helping Hands Community Center in the heart of the meat rack, at 225 Turk Street. Helping Hands was a drop-in center, Broshears wrote in 1974, open for "those who need legal assistance, those who need housing, those seeking roommates, those seeking employment, those just wanting a place where they can set down and have a cup of coffee or tea (free), and merely rest." The center was staffed by members of the Gay Activists Alliance and sponsored by Broshears's Orthodox Episcopal Church of God. "But religious trips are not laid on people using the Center," he wrote, "as the Church feels that the Center should serve and assist the people first above all."[75] For those "new to town," the center provided "maps, guides, directories, and other resource materials. . . . We will assist you in housing, legal matters, and whatever else."[76] The center hosted a weekly "Rap and Social" and urged "all transsexuals, and transvestites and drag queens and their friends" to attend.[77] "Drag queens find themselves at home as does the hustler," read a 1973 article, "or super businessman types. It is a true melting pot. All colors of Gaypeoples are found there, as well as political spectrums."[78]

Helping Hands also operated as a clearinghouse for jobs. There are "plenty of people who are quite anxious to work," read a 1974 advertisement in Broshears's newspaper. "You pay what you feel is reasonable, remembering that It says in the Bible, 'a laborer is worthy of his/her hire!'"[79] Michael Norton told me that Broshears connected him with work at the center in the 1970s. "I had left San Francisco for a while and came back with some friend of mine that I had met on my travels," Norton said. He learned about "a little drop-in center for people, mostly gay but not exclusively," and went in "because he was serving free coffee and food and you didn't have many places like that in those days. And it was clean." Besides offering food and drink, "it also acted as a clearinghouse for trying to get you jobs; you'd get in contact with local gay men around the city who had a place to live who would be willing to open their doors to other people staying there." He recalled talking with Broshears. "And he asked, 'Ya lookin' for work?' I said, 'I always am.'" Broshears called the *P.S. Bar and Restaurant, on Polk Street, "and said 'congratulations, you got a job.' . . . I was washing dishes, emptying garbage, doing a little bit of bussing. All the waiters were like in their twenties—of course always having to be young and good-looking but very well-mannered, very professional."

In 1973 Broshears founded the Lavender Panthers, a vigilante group of Tenderloin street kids who patrolled the city with sawed-off pool cues and shotguns.[80] According to a *Berkeley Barb* article, the Panthers were the Gay Activists Alliance's "militant youth arm."[81] The basic band numbered "21 homosexuals, including two lesbians," and formed "from the 'street people' of the Tenderloin."[82] They were mostly "poor kids," according to another report, "who are just beginning with Ray's help to get their feet on the ground."[83] Their purpose, Broshears told *Time* magazine in 1973, was to strike terror in the hearts of "all those young punks who have been beating up my faggots."[84] Norton told me he saw the Panthers filming police harassment in the city. "They used to ride around in cars," Norton told me. "They'd film the police harassing people, arresting people. They'd go chasing after the gay bashers, making sure that the police arrested them. . . . 'Cause [Broshears] realized, like I did, a gay person's number one priority in life should be survival. That means more than just eating, it means more than just sleeping, finding shelter. It means not giving into physical violence [and] police brutality." A photo in the *San Francisco Examiner* shows Broshears at a press conference at his Helping Hands Community Center in clerical collar, a cross around his neck, holding a sawed-off pool cue and shotgun. Flanking him are two fey youth identified as "drag queens," Woody and Finis, one in a bouffant hairdo and displaying a handgun.[85]

Not surprisingly, Broshears had an adversarial relationship with the city's more respectable homophile organizations. The Tavern Guild, a gay business association, dismissed the Gay Activists Alliance as a group of "ex-convicts, prostitutes, and mental patients."[86] A coalition of twelve homophile groups "flatly disavowed any support for the 'Lavender Panthers.'"[87] Broshears in turn condemned the "'gays' that denounce the street gays of the Tenderloin everyday . . . but yet 'sneak' down to the 'meatrack' to 'pickup' a trick when they think no one is looking."[88] In 1974 Broshears conducted demonstrations against Pacific Telephone (he "crucified" one of his team members to

San Francisco Examiner

U`1-2424 ☆☆☆☆ SATURDAY, JULY 7, 1973 34 PAGES

"LAVENDER PANTHERS" WOODY AND FINIS FLANK REV. RAY BROSHEARS
Patrol armaments will include guns and sawed-off pool cue displayed at press conference
—Examiner photo by Bob Bryant

Gay Vigilantes to Fight Back

You won't have gay people to kick around any more, the Rev. Ray Broshears proclaimed at a press conference yesterday marking the formation of the Lavender Panthers, a gay vigilante group.

Although the San Francisco gay community deplores violence, said Broshears, chairperson of the Gay Alliance, gays are going to adopt a tough new law-and-order-outside-the-law response to harassment of their ranks.

Broshears sat flanked by two drag queens — Woody and Finis — armed with rifles. Woody smiled a lot. Finis did not.

Attack

Not coincidentally, the announcement of the Lavender Panther patrols — which will scour Polk Street, the Tenderloin, and Eureka Valley at night — followed by two days an attack on Broshears himself.

Citing a long list of unsolved homosexual murders and 38 beatings of gays in the last two months, Broshears urged his gay brethren to stock rifles and pistols in their homes and stores.

He also urged them to carry small aerosol cans of red paint to spray on attackers in the streets. "Of course (the assailant) will lose his eyesight," Broshears said, "but he will remember he attacked a lavender peron."

Insignia

Initially, three-person Lavender Panther patrols will carry sawed-off pool cues, but Broshears admitted the police are reviewing the legality of this. Patrols will be identified by a silkscreen Lavender Panther insigne and red and lavender armbands.

Broshears admitted the lavender gangs are not totally supported by all elements with the Gay Alliance. He said the patrols were made necessary by the indifferent hostility of police toward gay beatings, and the intolerance of the age.

"The youth of America," he said, "is devoid of any moral responsibility toward their fellow man."

Among the paraphernalia cluttering the walls at the Helping Hand Community Center on Turk Street where the press conference happened was a large red panic button which stared Broshears in the face throughout his speech.

FIGURE 2.6.   The Lavender Panthers as pictured in the *San Francisco Examiner*, July 7, 1973.

a telephone pole in front of their employment offices), taxicab companies (he threatened to "smash the windows of cabs if any gay drivers were dismissed"), and the police department. He "aligned himself with the poor and is incensed by gay churches that cater to the middle class" and venerated the Tenderloin.[89] "No Tenderloin fag is going to take any jive off any straights, like the Castro queens of today," he wrote in 1976. "The Tenderloin today is just as ruff and tuff as it was when I moved there ten years ago. People are a lot more real in the Tenderloin than they are anywhere else in the city."[90]

Broshears died of a cerebral hemorrhage in January 1982. His friend Elmer Wilhelm removed his belongings and, when Wilhelm died in 1985, they were donated to the GLBT Historical Society. "Because Ray Broshears had made many enemies in his years as a gay activist and as editor of *Gay Crusader*," a 1986 GLBT Historical Society report read, "an agreement was made between all parties to keep the existence of this collection a secret for the foreseeable future."[91] An undeniably controversial figure, Broshears defies easy categorization. He attempted to reframe the abandonment and abuse he experienced through religion, but he may have also restaged this abuse via his relationships with the kids who made up his congregation. "There is no telling how many people he has arrested from the tombs of the City and County jails," a gay activist wrote in 1972. "Perhaps I wouldn't be too concerned with him if he didn't wear that collar and those black clothes. What bothers me really is that I can't make up my mind whether he does more good than bad, or more bad than good. He is the most vicious individual I know, yet one of the most dedicated workers in the community."[92]

The Reverend Michael Itkin

The Reverend Michael (a.k.a. Mikhail) Itkin was among the many queer Old Catholics in Raymond Broshears's orbit. From the 1950s to the 1980s, Itkin ministered to "alienated" youth through social outreach, counseling, shelter, and mutual aid, but just as important to him were creative arts. "Let us recognize," he wrote in the 1970s, "that a striving for self-realization, for poetry and play, is basic to man once his needs for food, clothing and shelter have been met."[93] Itkin wrote in the early 1970s that "true Christianity" was synonymous with "the Creative Life."[94] His theatrical approach to religion enabled him to blur the lines between "reality" and artifice, thereby calling into question a moral order that devalued him and other marginalized people.[95]

Born to Jewish parents in the Bronx in 1936, Itkin was introduced to left-wing politics through former vice president Henry Wallace's Progressive Party and the Communist Party. At age fourteen, he became a Dianetics auditor. In 1952, at the age of sixteen, he appears to have been ordained by the far-left People's Institute of Applied Religion, which organized rural farmers, youth groups, and industrial workers by reaching workers through their Christian beliefs.[96] In 1955, at the age of nineteen, Itkin was arrested on a "petit larceny charge." He wrote in 1958 that he was placed on probation "with the conditions that I make restitution and take psychiatric treatment." His "emotional problem was and is such that I cannot hold a job."[97] Itkin later wrote that he was on disability for epilepsy, a nervous system disorder that causes seizures.[98] Itkin's mind, according to one of his friends, seemed "overloaded [and] jumpy." He had a famously short attention span.[99] Throughout his life, Itkin quoted Corinthians 1 to contest normative assumptions about his mental health and ability: "God hath chosen the foolish things of the world to confound the wise; and God hath chosen the weak things of the world to confound the things which are mighty."

Itkin founded his own Old Catholic ministry in the late 1950s after he learned about George Hyde's church through an advertisement in *ONE Magazine*, a homophile publication.[100] Hyde wrote that he ordained Itkin in New York City in 1957, when Itkin was twenty-one years old.[101] Unsubstantiated but plausible rumors suggest that Itkin supported his ministry through the money he made as a hustler.[102] According to one Old Catholic minister, "Hyde told me that his investigations showed [Itkin] to be a male prostitute who went around bars picking up people to support him in his ministry."[103] In 1961 Old Catholic ministers uncovered Itkin's police record. "I will never rest until I see Itkin behind bars," wrote one minister. "Itkin is a crazy liar and according to his police record also a thief."[104] Itkin responded in a 1961 letter: "I am what I am. I care not at all what mankind bathing in its depraved western morality may think of me."[105]

Itkin claimed that he started his ministry as a "mission" at the Living Theatre, one of the oldest experimental theater groups in the United States. His ministry, he wrote in the 1970s, "met at the building of the Living Theatre until we opened our own mission building."[106] I interviewed Living Theatre cofounder Judith Malina, who confirmed that Itkin was part of the theater's "extended family" in the late 1950s and early 1960s. He may have acted in some of their productions, she told me. Regardless, he was "fundamentally" theatrical. "I would say, like me, he was acting all the time. He never didn't act." She felt that his church was a form of "religious theater."

Itkin and the Living Theatre shared a commitment to anarchist and pacifist political organizing. Itkin and Julian Beck, the theater's cofounder, served together on the steering committee for the New York City League for Sexual Freedom, which sought to extend "full sexual freedom" by demonstrating for legalized prostitution, protesting raids on sexually explicit avant-garde films, and defending the rights of homosexuals. Itkin claimed that Malina and Beck wrote an introduction to his church's first informational pamphlet in the early 1960s.[107] The "worth of the world is proclaimed," it read, in "the underground" and "wherever change is initiated." In the "invisible lofts where the anarchists and pacifists defy money and the structures of society, where the lies are being examined and reversed, lies which are the allies of death, in these places is the poetry which is the language of God."[108] It was "to those in these places," Itkin wrote, "the unchurched and the alienated, that we seek to minister in this ecumenical mission."[109]

Itkin's religious commitments animated his work in leftist movements. "My work for peace and my work in the non-violent revolutionary movement," he wrote in 1962, "traces from my acceptance of the saving grace of our Lord Christ and of his Gospel."[110] In 1960 Itkin demonstrated, along with a group of teenagers and trade unions, against segregated lunch counters in the South. The group marched at entrances to the Woolworth variety store at Thirty-Fourth Street and Seventh Avenue. Itkin was in clerical garb. The group believed it was wrong for Woolworth to segregate its lunch counters in the South.[111] The same year, according to one article, Itkin led a group of twenty-two marchers on a 150-mile "peace walk" in protest over the United States' Polaris missile submarine program.[112] Itkin served on the New York Committee for the General Strike for Peace, which Living Theatre cofounders Beck and Malina organized in 1961. In 1962 Itkin was arrested at an antinuclear demonstration in New York. He was associated with the Western Orthodox Communion of the Old Catholic Church.[113]

Itkin and the Living Theatre also shared a commitment to ritual as a means of cultural transformation. By the late 1950s, the Living Theatre was devoted to creating ritualistic theater that removed the "fourth wall," negated hierarchal relationships between performer and audience, and enacted the "anarchist revolution." In the early 1960s, they narrowed the gulf between everyday life and politics, staging performances and actions in public spaces rather than theaters or museums, in ways characteristic of the New Left and the counterculture.[114] In the 1960s, speech act theory and performance art shared the insight that symbolic actions—performative actions in everyday life as well as artistic performances—have the potential to create or undermine social reality. Groups reconceived the relationship between politics and culture, using performance to express their politics. While their political objectives varied, these groups shared the impulse to stage their performances in public spaces, eschewing museums and theaters. This allowed groups like the Living Theatre and the Diggers "to narrow the gulf between everyday life and politics," the scholar Bradford Martin writes, "broadening the definition of politics in a way characteristic of both the New Left and the counterculture of the sixties, and redefining the uses of the public space."[115]

In Itkin's constant creation of new churches, his only continuing spiritual practice appears to have been his almost daily celebration of the Eucharist, a ritual reenactment of the last meal Jesus shared with his followers on the night before he was arrested and killed.[116] The ritual commemorates his suffering, death, and resurrection. Bread and wine are ritually transformed into the body and blood of Christ, offered up by the priest as a sacrifice, and shared by the assembled believers in a communal meal. The meal establishes kinship among the congregants through collective identification with a suffering Christ. In a pamphlet outlining his observation of the Eucharist—an elaborate affair incorporating hymns, censers, and costume—Itkin wrote that the ritual encapsulated "the entire Work of the Community for spiritual renewal, consecration and transformation of Humanity." Itkin's celebration began with a processional hymn, after which the priest notes that Christ is the "Brother/Sister" overcoming "sin, sickness and death." Christ unites the world, "binding in covenant faithful people of all races, sexes and tongues."[117] The effects of the sacraments, Itkin wrote, is to "purify the imperfect" and "illuminate and initiate those whom it has purified."[118] Judith Malina told me she celebrated the Eucharist with Itkin in the late 1950s. Itkin maintained "certain aspects of the traditional, and at the same time [flew] off into sheer madness." He integrated these contradictions, she said, "in a way that we liked to think our theater represents."

Itkin drew on Christianity to rhetorically invert the schemes used to distinguish between people who can be made functional to the societal order and those who should be left to die. "If we believe in Christ," he wrote in 1959, "we cannot believe in a value system which places property above humanity, enslaved to material cares the divine within Man." Christianity enabled Itkin to reject "social traditions, mores, and moral systems which are outgrown, repressive, and immoral." He approached Jesus's teachings as "the revolutionary catalyst needed by society in our time" that would value humanity above property, the "divine within Man" above materiality, and a release from "all taboos and restrictions."[119] His independent ministry was devoted, he wrote in 1961, to the "Social Gospel of Christ Jesus: nonviolence, love, mutual aid, voluntary poverty, sharing, [and] a cooperative social order."[120] Itkin combined social justice activism and religious commitments. "The Christ that we serve is not the Christ of quiet withdrawal from the sphere of social action," he wrote in 1963, "but the vigorous Christ of rebellion against all vested bureaucracies." It is the Christ of "nonviolent revolution, who sweated and bled and understood the smell of sin."[121]

Itkin's religious commitments animated his social activism. In 1969 Itkin "performed an exorcism to drive the demons of violence and exploita-

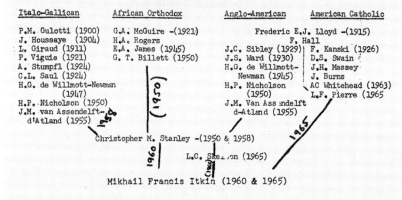

FIGURE 2.7.   Michael Itkin traces lines of apostolic succession from the apostles of Jesus Christ to his own ministry, date unknown. Courtesy of ONE Archives at the USC Libraries.

tion from the Federal slab" at San Francisco's Federal Building.[122] Itkin wrote and presented the Resolution on Homosexual Rights adopted by the American Sociological Association, the first such resolution adopted by an American scholarly or professional society. The following year, he and other San Francisco Gay Liberation Front activists famously disrupted the 1970 American Psychiatric Convention held in that city. Dr. Irving Bieber "was a magnet for protesters, and the Gay Liberation Front decided to be there too. . . . Michael Itkin, among others, haunted the APA sessions, disrupting them with displays of guerilla theater and angry protests from the floor."[123] In 1972 Itkin ordained residents of the Gay Liberation Front House in Washington, DC, and inspired them to form an Old Catholic congregation.[124] As one member recalled, some residents found his Catholic denomination "could be useful for propagating the GLF message." By "combin[ing] Marxist ideology with Catholic ideology," they "appealed to a more radical element in our gay society." The commune's front room became "the Chapel of St. Francis and St. John" every Sunday, holding a generic Mass. "Anybody brought up in a Catholic or Episcopal tradition would have been comfortable with it."[125]

By the 1970s, independent ministers like Itkin faced charges of "role playing" from gay congregations associated with the gay liberation movement, like the Metropolitan Community Church. After detailing the genealogy of his church in 1972, Itkin responded to one gay Protestant challenger: "all of us are into the same type of role playing; buttress up your own glass walls, honey, before you throw stones."[126] Itkin often presented himself as a trickster: foolish and weak given his affinity with storytelling and fantasizing; and yet rebellious, syncretic, and potentially undermining of larger cultural structures. There was a flair of the theatrical when, in 1971, he "officiated at a wedding held in the Glide Memorial Church . . . in which the Bride and Groom were dressed and painted like Clowns, with the wedding procession being led by a Llama" with "exhibitions by tumblers, people carrying live serpents, women doing the hoochy koochy (belly) dance, and so on."[127] According to a researcher writing in the early 1970s, one of Itkin's priests related wild tales about Itkin's ministry "that are repeated from bar to bar." For example, "in Minnesota Itkin was asked to dedicate a chapel, but after arriving, reportedly held an orgy in the sanctuary instead."[128]

Itkin argued that the problems of "alienation" were "particularly acute" in the "gay ghettos" of New York, San Francisco, and other major cities. Street kids "arrive daily in the cities—and are to be found on the streets of every gay ghetto in America," Itkin said in a 1969 Christmas sermon in San Francisco. Without money or marketable skills, they often resort to prostitution and theft. In the Haight-Ashbury and Tenderloin, the people he met—street youth and homosexuals, hippies and draft resisters, racial minorities and immigrants—point to the "alienation of an entire cross-section of our population." Despite their alienation—or perhaps because of it—they are "young and potentially creative," part of a "new community we see emerging." Therefore, "in the midst of this desperation, there also lies our most creative hope."[129] These districts "abound with runaways and castaways, the 'weak . . . of the world,' the despised and rejected of God's children: our common brothers in Christ."[130] In these spaces, and he was clearly inspired by the counterculture, "the new situation of urban man, with his rebellion against cultural poverty, [and] economic oppression . . . is now coming to a head: shaping new structures, new patterns, alternative forms of human life."[131]

In the early 1970s, Itkin's "Community of the Love of Christ" consecrated a "Bishop to the People of the Tenderloin" in an SRO hotel at the heart of the San Francisco meat rack, a hotel that also housed a gay adult theater featuring live strip shows.[132] We can imagine the scene: a small group gathered in the spare room on the ground floor, some in clerical collars, Itkin likely wearing the purple shirt and ornamental headdress of a bishop. Itkin's own title was so excessive that it may qualify as camp: "President and Metropolitan Bishop-Abbot of the Holy Orthodox Catholic Synod of the Syro-Chaldean Rite: Evangelical Catholic Communion Brotherhood of the Love of Christ, Incorporated."[133] Itkin oversaw the "episcopal consecration and installation" of the "most Reverend Mar James Abdul Mikhaelovitch Dennis."[134] Broshears wrote in 1981 that "Jim Dennis whom Bishop Itkin named 'Bishop of the Tenderloin' has been roaming Polk Street in his collar."[135] Itkin died in 1989 of complications from HIV/AIDS and his ashes were scattered in the garden of an Episcopal church in the city. After his death, Itkin's acolytes continued to provide and receive care on the streets of the Tenderloin and other cities across the country.[136]

Saint Sylvia Rivera

A final example of street churches animated by street kids centers the trans activist Sylvia Rivera. We remember Sylvia today for her role in the 1969 Stonewall riots and as cofounder, in 1970, of Street Transvestite Action Revolutionaries (STAR). We often associate Sylvia with a gay liberation movement that is figured as hostile to religion. Throughout her life, however, Sylvia drew on religious commitments to animate her activism and forge solidarities among street kids. She was devoted from childhood to Santería—Spanish for "the way of the saints"—a religious practice that syncretizes Roman Catholic saints and West African orishas, or divinized ancestors, and focuses on communication with the spirits and saints.[137] She claimed that she entered the Times Square scene and "became" Sylvia through a Pentecostal christening ceremony, and, in the 1970s, she prayed to the saints at her STAR House. Drawing on oral history and archival evidence, I show how Sylvia drew on religious commitments to animate her activism. I also examine how congregants at the Metropolitan Community Church of New York remembered and venerated her as "Saint Sylvia" in the 2010s.

When recounting her life, Sylvia highlighted stories of abandonment and rejection. "I basically grew up without love," she wrote in the early 2000s.[138] Born Ray Rivera on July 2, 1951, in the Bronx, she was three years old when her mother mixed rat poison into a glass of milk, swallowed it, and forced Ray to drink it. "I believe the brand was J.R. Rat Poison," Sylvia recalled, "and it came in a light reddish orange tin." The paramedics saved Ray. "When they took me off to get my stomach pumped was the last time I saw my mother alive, because after being in the hospital three days, she died."[139] Ray's grandmother adopted her, but, as Sylvia recalled, she wanted a white Venezuelan girl, not an effeminate mixed-race Puerto Rican / Venezuelan boy. Ray's grandmother "knew I was going to have a hard life," Sylvia wrote. "And she pinpointed it, because it has not been an easy road."[140]

Ray may have been attracted to Santería at an early age because the religion is based on the development of relationships between practitioners of the religion and the *orishas*, who provide devotees with protection and guide them in times of crisis.[141] The religion is also an alternative kinship network that transcends blood relations. The religion of West African orishas, historian Miguel Barnet shows, is "linked to the notion of a family—of an extended and numerous family," originating with one ancestor and encompassing the living and the dead. Out of this system of lineage emerges a "religious brotherhood," involving godfather and godchildren, in a kinship that "transcends blood connections to form an all-inclusive and compact horizontal lineage." This "family system" has been one of the most genuine characteristics of Santería.[142]

Ray would become Sylvia and join a street family when she left home for Times Square. "Ray Rivera left home at the age of 10 to become Sylvia," she wrote in the early 2000s. "And that's who I am."[143] A few queens "adopted" her, housed her, and taught her how to survive through prostitution and panhandling. Sylvia recalled that she met an "old butch dyke" and an "old queen" known as "the godfather and godmother of Forty-Second [Street]."[144] Among their tasks was renaming young people who "came on the scene." They decided "what name fit you properly," Sylvia said in 1990. They told her there was "no Sylvia around at this realm" and declared that she would "be Sylvia."[145] Perhaps the most important member of her new family was Marsha P. Johnson, an eighteen-year-old African American queen who taught Ray how to apply face makeup, got her a part-time job at a Childs restaurant, showed her how to pick up tricks, and instilled the rules of the street: "Don't mess with anyone's lover; don't rip off anyone's dope or money."[146] Marsha was well known for her remarkable generosity. Agosto Machado, a longtime friend, compared her to "Jesus with the loaves and fishes," explaining that "Marsha always had something to share."[147] Being in Times Square was frightening, Sylvia recalled. "It was dangerous on 42nd Street. We all stuck together."[148]

Sylvia recalled that Ray "became" Sylvia—and formally entered the street scene—through a Pentecostal "christening" ceremony held at the godfather of Forty-Second Street's apartment and overseen by a preacher from a "Pentecostal Spanish Church." Sylvia claimed that she arrived at the christening wearing a white ceremonial gown. Roughly fifty people from Times Square, nearly all of them Latino or African American, gathered at the apartment: "And I remember [the preacher] saying when he put the water on my head . . . 'Now don't forget that this is going to be a *hard* life.' And it sure was."[149] The christening enabled Sylvia to transition into a new street family and congregation. "Everybody was gay and it was beautiful just to be around all these people," she recalled. "It was like being reborn and having a new life." In the 1950s and 1960s, historian Arlene M. Sánchez Walsh notes, many Puerto Rican Pentecostals founded churches in New York City to work with street youth.[150] Historian Eldin Villafañe believes that this work signifies a "Hispanic Pentecostal social ethic," or a quest for community, as Puerto Rican migration spiked in the 1950s and 1960s and people sought to counter the discrimination and homesickness they found on arrival.[151] Sylvia's account suggests that religious actors who composed street churches also christened the kids on the street and brought them into new street families.

Stonewall and Street Transvestite Action Revolutionaries

By the late 1960s, the women's, black power, and Chicano movements provided Sylvia and other kids frameworks for understanding their abandonment as the result of structural forces rather than individual moral failures. Her street family began considering possibilities for political change. "Even back in the days of pre-Stonewall," Sylvia recalled, "we would sit on 44th Street, a lot of us girls like Marsha and Vanessa, Miss Edwina, Miss Josie, a whole bunch of us. . . . We'd be getting high or something and we'd start talking about politics. We'd start talking politics and about when things were going to change for us as human beings."[152] Sylvia claimed that she threw the second "Molotov cocktail" at the 1969 Stonewall riots and gave countless interviews about her experiences.[153] "I wanted to do every destructive thing that I could think of at that time to hurt anyone that had hurt us through the years," she said in 1989.[154] "Cars are being turned over, windows are being broken, fires are being set all over the place. Blood was shed," she recounted, but the "most impressive" thing about Stonewall "was that the more that they beat us, the more we went back for."[155]

In 1970 Sylvia and Marsha founded Street Transvestite Action Revolution-aries (STAR), which helped meet street youths' elemental needs, including food, housing, protection, and family, while also organizing pickets, visiting prisons and mental institutions, and developing a voice for what they called the "drag queens" and "transvestites" in the gay liberation movement and revolutionary left.[156] "STAR was for the street gay people, the street home-less people, and anybody that needed help at that time," Sylvia stated in 1998. The group also rented a building in the primarily Puerto Rican neigh-borhood known as Loisaida and dubbed it STAR House. Sylvia explained, "Marsha and I decided that it was just time to help each other and help our other kids. We fed people and clothed people. We kept the building going. We went out and hustled the streets. We paid the rent."[157] Sylvia and other Times Square veterans hustled to make money so that the kids would not have to hustle themselves. "For us, we knew we could make it," she recalled, "but we were thinking about the young kids. . . . Whenever daybreak broke, whatever money we'd have we'd combine, and we'd get everybody something to eat, and wake everybody up and feed them."[158]

Shared spiritual practices helped sustain STAR House. "Before Sylvia went out" to hustle, STAR member Bebe Scarpinato told me, "she prayed every night and the queens who were with her in STAR prayed every night. They had their candles, their saints, they prayed to make money, they prayed to be safe, they prayed to make it back to the house." The residents practiced their own version of Santería complete with a personalized lit-urgy. As Sylvia recalled, "A majority of the queens [at STAR House] were Latin and we believe in an emotional, spiritualist religion." Every night af-ter they cooked dinner, residents "worked with the saints" before leaving to hustle.

We had our own saints: Saint Barbara, the patron saint of homosexual-ity, St. Michael, the Archangel; La Caridad del Cobre, the Madonna of gold; and Saint Martha, the saint of transformation. . . . St. Martha had once transformed herself into a snake, so to her we'd pray: "Please don't let them see through the mask. Let us pass as women and save us from harm." And to the other three we'd kneel before our altar of candles and pray: "St. Barbara, St. Michael, La Caridad del Cobre: We know we are doing wrong, but we got to live and we got to survive, so please help us, bring us money tonight, protect us, and keep evil away." We kept the sword of St. Michael at the back door to ward off evil.[159]

"We *were* watched over, though Marsha came close to getting killed by tricks a number of times, and I looked down the barrel of many a gun. . . . But my saints protected me."[160]

In the 1980s and 1990s, Sylvia remained a mother and provider for street youth, mostly black and Latino, displaced by redevelopment and police sweeps from Times Square to the West Village piers.[161] In a 1999 interview, Sylvia said she was "the typical mother to all the children living out there. I guess it comes from not having a mother or not having any love when you were a child and always being told that no one wanted you. When I see someone that's alone, and the person is hurting and they need some comfort, my heart opens up. I can't say no if they need a little help."[162]

Sylvia's Ashes and Urn

In 2001 Sylvia joined the Metropolitan Community Church of New York (MCCNY), a three-story brick building at Thirty-Sixth Street, a fifteen-minute walk from Times Square. She was baptized, appointed head of the church's food pantry, and recognized by the congregation as a pioneer. Later that year, she fell ill with liver cancer and her health quickly deteriorated. According to MCCNY congregants I interviewed, Sylvia demanded on her deathbed that the church serve homeless youth and that they cremate her body, scatter some of her ashes in front of the Stonewall Inn and some in the Hudson River, and preserve the remaining ashes in an urn in the church sanctuary. Sylvia died of liver failure on February 19, 2002. The next year, the church founded Sylvia's Place, a homeless shelter located in the basement of MCCNY. Congregants also began doing the work of preserving Sylvia's memory. A funeral home that provided low-cost memorials during the early years of the AIDS crisis donated an urn. The congregation "blessed and enshrined" it through a special ceremony and placed her urn in the second-floor worship space on a pedestal behind the altar.[163] They venerated her relics as saintly relics, a practice that dates to the sixth and seventh centuries, when a body or some part of the "special dead"—a saint—was housed in a church, "protecting all the other bodies with its aura."[164]

In 2011 I visited the church to talk with congregants and shelter staff, many of whom told me they experienced Sylvia as a spiritual presence. Inspired by what she knew of Sylvia's difficult childhood, Rev. Moshay Moses, a black transgender minister, told me she sang the spiritual "Soon Will Be Done with Troubles" at the dedication. At the church, "we honor those who have pulled up stones before us," Moses said. "They inspire you to pick up your own stones." Every Sunday morning before services, a congregant enters the minister's third-floor office, walks to an elaborate altar, and carries the red reliquary urn to the second-floor pedestal. They are careful to place it decorative side forward, one congregant told me, so Sylvia can "see what's going on." The church's reverend explained that a church member built a pedestal on the back wall "so [Sylvia] would always have a view." When the lights flicker in the sanctuary, "people say, 'That's Sylvia, you know, letting us know she's around,'" another congregant told me. When a pot drops in the food pantry downstairs, a volunteer explained, "We'll say, 'It's Sylvia. Sylvia's angry about something.'"

Sylvia's Place shelter staff told me they remember Sylvia by caring for homeless youth. The shelter's director, a thirty-year-old white trans activist named Lucky Michaels, told me she never met Sylvia in person but feels an intense connection to her memory. "I *did* what Sylvia would have done," she told me. "I'm living in her memory." It was "Sylvia's dream to house and feed homeless queer youth." The shelter's director of HIV prevention, a thirty-four-year-old black trans woman named Kristen Lovell, told me she had developed an intense relationship with the memory of Sylvia and Marsha. "I *felt* everything that they went through," she told me, including homelessness, drug abuse, and the power of social justice work. "So I feel *spiritually* connected to Sylvia and Marsha. Our stories were so closely knit." Kristen felt she was continuing Sylvia's legacy by "doing the work that she wanted." Kristen and Lucky also shared Sylvia's story with young people at the shelter. Especially when kids "were showing their internal transphobia, or they're down and out on themselves or their ability to do anything." Lucky would use Sylvia's story as a "rebuttal." It was "just this little Puerto Rican drag queen," Lucky tells them, that "started this for all of us, and if she could do it . . . they could do it." Kristen told me she passes down Sylvia's story through "history lessons" at the shelter. "A lot of people fought, died, a lot of blood was shed for you to be where you're today," she tells young people. "You need to pay homage to your elders."

Sylvia's urn seemed to spark with electricity when I first saw it in 2011. The urn, for me, was a visceral, material manifestation of a dynamic I follow throughout this chapter: queer revaluations of the abject through religious ritual and iconography.

The Sacred and the Abject

Anthropologists from Émile Durkheim to Mary Douglas demonstrate that religions often sacralize those abject things that have been rejected with abhorrence.[165] For example, a religious leader approaches the corpse—the utmost in abjection—and though ritual practices transforms it into a sacred relic. The street churches I follow throughout this chapter sacralize people and things constructed as abject: the urban poor, sexual deviants, racialized populations, and tenderloin districts themselves. These ministers draw on the florid religiosity associated with Catholicism and Santería—their gothic language of abjection and martyrdom, theatrical rituals, and often-sadomasochistic imagery—to reframe and refigure the affective and economic impacts of abandonment. For this reason, street churches played a central if under-documented role in early movements animated by sexual and gender dissidents. These include the street youth organization Vanguard, founded in San Francisco's Tenderloin in 1966—the subject of the following chapter.

3. Urban Reformers and Vanguard's Mutual Aid

We know that you want us to fit your mold and tear us to shreds and pieces and put us together again looking like you. We say screw you let us do what we have to ourselves, help us if you wish but don't tell us what we need. You don't live in this forest of glass and plastic of powders and liquids of steel shine-dusted and of garbage all designed to help us escape you.

—"impression of the Tenderloin written by a 22 year old while he was high on Methedrine," 1967

IN THE LATE 1950s, a sixteen-year-old named Joseph fled his abusive father, cut ties with his Italian Catholic family in Upstate New York, and "hit the road," he told me in 2009, "kind of like Kerouac—to see America." At a time when homosexuality was criminalized, Joseph said he gravitated to the "seedy" districts in large cities where criminality was a given. Hitching a ride to Times Square, he found among the dirty bookstores, pinball arcades, and rooming houses other young people like himself: abandoned by their families, disinherited, "kids who had been editors of high school newspapers, wrote poetry, and were slightly crazy. And they were living on the streets, selling their bodies, sometimes being petty criminals." There was no sense of "coming out" for these kids, he explained. "There was a sense of getting the shit beat out of you and hitting the streets."

Street kids in Times Square quickly initiated Joseph into their social world. A queen, Miss Maynes, gave Joseph a new name—"Blaze," because of his inexhaustible energy—and invited him to sleep in her hotel room with a half dozen others. Joseph also adopted the name Joel Roberts, which he continued to use for the rest of his life, and at the time of our interview. The kids taught Joel to hustle, pool resources, and share information about abusive police and clients. Kids were living "day to day," Joel told me, sneaking into "stinky hotel rooms," shacking up with tricks, or spending the night in coffee shops. Suicide and drug overdoses were common, but it was better than home. "It was an incredibly horrible time," Joel explained, "and yet it was an incredibly wonderful time. Because I had the family I never had. . . . There was just this underground where you could make it. You were ashamed to be there, at least I know I was, but I was happy to be with these other kids. That's what the street meant. There were people that would immediately help you survive."

Joel learned "early in the game" that hustlers and street queens traveled from tenderloin to tenderloin, often following seasonal patterns. "Kids in the summertime would be in cities like New York City, and then move down to Miami or San Francisco in the wintertime because those were more livable places." In the winter of 1965, Joel hitched a ride to San Francisco and found on the Market Street meat rack—the string of hotdog stands, bars, and transient hotels—an extension of the world he had left behind. "I instantly saw this is where the cheap hotels are, this is where cheap food is, and I know I can turn a trick." He also had his street family. Walking on the streets a few weeks after arriving, "I hear somebody shouting 'Blaze!' [I thought,] 'God, who's calling me Blaze?' And there was Miss Maynes, God bless her." Hearing her voice "was like coming home."

Joel and other street youth found themselves under intense pressure in the mid-1960s as San Francisco began redeveloping the Tenderloin and sweeping away its undesirables. Police abuse, which became more pervasive, targeted those who transgressed gender and sexual norms. Businesses that had relied on the revenue sex workers generated put into effect service charges, hired security, or otherwise excluded street kids. Inspired by the civil rights movement, the New Left, and the counterculture, young people seized the chance to tell a different story about their lives and worth. Forming a direct-action organization called Vanguard, from 1966 to 1967 they picketed discriminatory businesses and protested police harassment; served free meals; held fundraising dances; and, according to a contemporary account, promoted "self-help and protection" among "the hair-fairies, hustlers, lost kids, and all the other varied types that frequent Market Street."[1]

Overview and Methods

In this chapter, I outline efforts to organize the kids on the street from the 1950s to the late 1960s, focusing on Vanguard's pathbreaking activism. I turn to original oral histories and archival research to show how Vanguard organizers built on the preexisting web of reciprocities, kinship networks, and religious practices that composed the kids' performative economy to cultivate a politics of mutual aid: a reciprocal exchange of resources for mutual benefit done in conjunction with social movements demanding transformative change.[2] Vanguard worked to meet survival needs—providing free meals, emergency housing, and medical aid to street kids in the Tenderloin—while developing a shared political understanding of the structural inequalities that produced those needs in the first place. Above all, the organization argued that the kids migrating between tenderloin districts were not criminals or unsightly blights to be swept away through urban development projects but young adults with value who were "exploited" by police, meat rack business owners, landlords, redevelopers, and a broadly defined "middle class." Vanguard organized to change those conditions through pickets, protest, mutual aid, and, not least, religious ritual.

I found that many Vanguard organizers joined counterculture seminaries and were ordained as activist-ministers in the street churches I analyze in the previous chapter. They approached Christianity as a radical political practice at a time when the civil rights movement, Catholic Worker movement, Beats, and counterculture were fusing activism and religion. Roaming the Tenderloin in clerical collars, activist-ministers oversaw marriages, engaged in faith-healing rituals, and, according to one account, found "emergency housing, satisfy[ied] bail, and offer[ed] needed counseling" to the kids on the street.[3] Through a variety of performances—street theater, protest, dance, and religious ritual—they responded to and creatively reframed the social trauma many kids experienced throughout their lives: namely, the shame of being perceived as and experiencing the self as "trash."

A crucial part of this story is the coalition of Tenderloin reformers—social workers, sociologists, homophile organizers, and mainline Protestant ministers—who began intervening in the lives of migratory youth as early as the 1950s, a history that reveals the profound class and cultural differences separating street kids and housed adults. Emphasizing the need for local leadership, reformers felt they could inculcate street kids with mainstream—or what we would today call "homonormative" values—by democratically involving them in the implementation of their own uplift activities. Reformers developed indigenous leadership initiatives, "halfway houses," counseling programs, and other programming to settle transient youth, "free" them from their "play-acting" and "theatricality," impose a hetero/homosexual binary, and integrate them into the formal economy. By 1964 reformers fostered youth-led activism to fulfill the federal War on Poverty's guidelines calling for the "maximum feasible participation of the poor," enabling them to establish, in May 1966, the Central City Target Area, an antipoverty program covering the Tenderloin and South of Market. Vanguard worked in collaboration—and in tension—with these reformers.

Oral histories with three Vanguard veterans—Adrian Ravarour, Keith St. Clare, and Joel Roberts—enable me to show how affect, including "negative" affects associated with abandonment, served as the basis for their pathbreaking activism. My informants related intense stories of childhood abuse, of fathers who beat them for being "sissies" or "incorrigible." While we often regard experiences of abuse as shameful secrets rather than stories to tell, an oppositional queer politics "cleaves" to the childhood scene of shame, Eve Kosofsky Sedgwick argues, drawing on it "as a near-inexhaustible source of transformational energy."[4] This said, it is important to note that Vanguard was composed of a relatively privileged subset of the street scene: young white men in their early twenties, many with some college education. Vanguard is in many ways a story about queer white men reclaiming the power that had been culturally reserved for them. My informants cultivated forms of counterculture authority by styling themselves after African American civil rights ministers; identifying with the white masculinist Beats who, Joel told me, were "beaten into becoming beatitude"; and maintaining, as Adrian did, that as artists they were "rugged individualists."[5]

While I organize this chapter as a more or less chronological narrative, there are moments when the felt and traumatic dimensions of Vanguard's activism seem to erupt into the ethnographic present. My informants confessed the anguish of losing friends on the street and seethed with anger at their abusive parents. They leapt up and danced during our encounters and used poetic language. Conflict erupted when two narrators demanded that I recognize them as the sole founder of Vanguard. They were not satisfied with my response—that I did not plan to name a founder—and responded with surprising emotional intensity. I approach our oral histories as archives of feeling that have much to tell us about Vanguard's activism. Like the genre of "survivor testimonies," oral history excels not only in providing "positivist history" but also in recording "the psychological and emotional milieu of the struggle for survival, not only then, but also now."[6] The moments that seem closest to offering access to the unspeakable essence of trauma and its continuity in the present are often the moments where speech fails and the distance between past and present seems to collapse.[7]

Homophile Organizers, Protestant Ministers, and Social Workers

While accounts of social justice movements often center one heroic founder or a few charismatic individuals, Vanguard grew out of countless interactions on San Francisco's meat rack between people and institutions with intersecting and often divergent goals: Protestant minsters, homophile organizers, social workers, young adults, hustlers, and other self-described "undesirables." I begin with an account of the homophile organizers, Protestant ministers, and social workers across the United States, and in San Francisco in particular, who began intervening in the lives of street youth as early as the 1950s—a time when the front end of the postwar baby boom generation entered adolescence, leading to a sharp increase in the number of kids "on the road."

In the 1950s, a fledgling homophile movement established itself to address the needs of people marginalized because of their sexual and gender identities. The best-known organizations were the Mattachine Society, based in Los Angeles, and the Daughters of Bilitis, based in San Francisco.[8] They organized at a time, in the two decades following World War II, when US culture idealized the white, patriarchal, heterosexual, middle-class family. Those whose sexual desires and gender presentation fell outside rigid norms confronted charges that they were sick, criminal, and deviant.[9] Male homosexuals in particular were represented as villains who "seduced" youth away from settled family life into lives of irresponsible freedom.[10] Many homophiles rejected elements of the street scene that did not conform to their view of white, middle-class respectability, including sex work, butch/femme "role-playing," and the camp theatrics of street queens. A psychologist working with the Daughters of Bilitis, for example, wrote in 1957 that homosexuals "shudder at the vulgar mannerisms of 'gays' and 'Nellies' as much as 'straight' people."[11] The anxiety over "overtness" and "flamboyance," anthropologist David Valentine notes, indexed conflicts over racial identification, class difference, public displays of sexuality, and "antagonism to white, middle-class norms."[12]

Homophile organizers hoped to settle transient street kids and integrate them into the formal economy. In 1954 Mattachine Society organizer Chuck Rowland proposed the development of a "halfway house" to serve migrants in downtown Los Angeles. His prospectus describes "3,000 young men and women with *special* problems [who] arrive in our midst annually." With homosexuality criminalized and no social agency serving these "social outcasts," thousands "become wards of State, County or City or drift into criminal or at least anti-social activities." It would operate as a "social welfare institution" endorsed by clergy, psychiatrists, teachers, social workers, and probation officers.[13] Because the house would involve cooperation with mainline institutions, it would "prove to be our first, big step in rallying the heterosexual majority to—at the very least—a recognition of our problem."[14] According to a 1955 letter by Mattachine organizer Jim Kepner, Rowland proposed that Mattachine "lease a house as a sort of home for the lost ones from Main Street."[15] Kepner later recalled how Rowland "eloquently described the scores of young Gays arriving daily" in downtown Los Angeles "and quickly falling prey to vice cops, hustlers or selfish johns."[16] The house did not materialize, he recalled, because homosexuals could not associate with minors without opening themselves up to criminal charges of "contributing to the delinquency of a minor." Mattachine members and their lawyer, Kepner said, were scared off by "what some would interpret as recruiting."[17]

In 1957 the Mattachine Society moved its national headquarters to San Francisco and opened an office in the South of Market "skid row," a few blocks from the Mason and Market Street meat rack, where it quietly met the needs of street kids, skid row residents, and others experiencing marginalization. A newspaper article described the meat rack as a "bleak agglomeration" of hamburger stands, cheap hotels, pornography shops, and "bottom-of-the-barrel bars" around which gathered "the stereotypes of effeminate males—the 'queens,' with orange coiffures, plucked eyebrows, silver nail polish and lipstick."[18] The residents of "skid row" were mostly impoverished, single elderly white men surviving on the meager proceeds of Social Security benefits.[19] The Mattachine Society's president, Don Lucas, remembers quietly counseling the "hustlers, transvestites, transsexuals, ex-prisoners, and mental patients" in the downtown coffee shops and reaching out to the unemployed longshoremen in the "skid row" flophouses.[20] Lucas characterized street queens as rebels in need of love and assistance. "Those who tend to flaunt their sexuality in public and therefore are seen as 'homosexual' are actually rebelling against society," he wrote, and need "extra help and understanding."[21] But in 1962 the Mattachine Society was still discussing the "eternal problem" of the "teenager," according to one internal report, "who is too young for us to deal with, and yet is at the only time to deal with if any worthwhile help is to be given."[22]

Help would soon come from an unexpected source: mainline Protestant leaders who, in the 1950s and 1960s, were undergoing a revolution in the ministry. As racial minorities and young adults migrated to central cities, and white flight claimed urban congregations, churches scrambled to develop new forms of ministry and activism. According to a 1965 article, "the picket line, the poolroom, the house of iniquity, the police station or the legislative hearing are becoming almost as common setting for ministers' work as is the pulpit on Sunday."[23] Heather White shows that a generation of left-leaning clergy cast their lot with urban churches "as a sign of God's preferential option for the poor and disenfranchised." Through a network of urban training centers, they gained skills in grassroots organizing and developed experimental programs that focused on the needs of disenfranchised people.[24] These included ministries targeting gang members, through which they advocated for the deployment of social services instead of incarceration. In 1959 a church in Toronto's central city created an "experimental program" for gang members. They sponsored dances and organized meetings to bridge barriers between warring gangs, mitigate tensions with the police, and, as one gang leader recalled, help youth "develop a sense of responsibility."[25]

An important precursor to Tenderloin-based reform work were several "consultations" organized by the National Headquarters of the Methodist Church in the 1950s and early 1960s to grapple with the social problem of migrant youth. "Many young persons who are migrating are 'on the road,'" a 1962 internal report read, "to escape ties because they either do not know how to form relationships or are uncertain as to whom they can trust."[26] The National Headquarters formed the Young Adult Project in 1962 and began organizing "action-research" missions across the country to encourage young adults to "assum[e] the productive role of the adult."[27] They located one of their projects at San Francisco's Glide Methodist Church, located in the heart of the meat rack, and in 1963 hired a young minister named Ted McIlvenna to manage the program. He spent his first six months observing kids in the meat rack's homosexual "sub-rosa world," he wrote in 1966, composed of "dozens of apartment houses which rent exclusively to homosexuals," Turkish baths, and "gay bars."[28] McIlvenna "found immediately" that youth were struggling with "problem[s] of sexual identification."[29] On the streets around Glide, he wrote in 1965, he saw "young men wearing make-up and beauty parlor hairdos, conversing with young women sporting short, cropped hair, leather boots and jackets."[30]

McIlvenna insisted that the Methodist Church confront the needs of street kids by allowing a methodology that accepted sexuality as a legitimate area of concern and action, which threw the Church into dealing with homosexuality, and, more broadly, human sexuality. McIlvenna formed working relationships with homophile leaders and hired Phyllis Lyon, cofounder of the Daughters of Bilitis, as his assistant at Glide Methodist. By late 1964, McIlvenna reported to National Headquarters, "significant penetration and communication with the young adult in the city [was] being accomplished" and he had made "extensive contacts with the homosexual community."[31]

A final antecedent to Tenderloin reform work were the San Francisco social workers who began experimenting with community-driven responses to youth delinquency in the 1950s. Historian Christopher Agee notes that many drew inspiration from the Chicago Area Project, a pioneering program founded in 1934 by University of Chicago sociologists.[32] The project stressed the inevitability of delinquency in "slum" areas and the need to channel the energies of gangs into "legitimate" neighborhood groups that could apply pressure on municipal and state welfare bureaucracies.[33] The best-publicized form of this work was the one-to-one interaction between gang members and "street workers," who served as a concerned, knowledgeable older sibling to youth running afoul of the law.[34] The assumption behind street worker programs was that gangs generated "natural" leaders who wielded influence on other gang members. Gang leaders could be employed, once rehabilitated themselves, to transform the behavior of other gang members.[35]

Among the organizations inspired by the Chicago Area Project was San Francisco's Youth for Service, founded in 1957, which recruited gang members (primarily youth of color) through street worker programs, helped them find employment, and encouraged them to participate in community service projects like construction, painting houses, or tending gardens.[36] Supported by the Ford Foundation and the President's Committee on Juvenile Delinquency and Youth Crime, the organization threw dances and created a youth-led "council" to address conflicts between gangs "before they blew up into rumbles."[37] Their director, a black social worker named Orville Luster, hoped to "[mold] promising gang leaders into street workers" and hire them as project staff.[38] By 1965, according to one article, Luster hired gang leaders "to help fight juvenile delinquency and street violence in San Francisco." The racially diverse group included "two Negroes, a Chinese, a Caucasian and a Latin." According to Luster, quoted in the article, "These boys are natural leaders."[39]

Protestant ministers, social workers, and homophiles began working together by 1964 to intervene in the lives of Tenderloin street youth. Searching for organizing models, urban ministers and homophile organizers reached out to Luster. The San Francisco chapter of the Daughters of Bilitis (DOB) wrote in January 1964 to the national DOB governing board that homophile organizers met with McIlvenna and Luster "to explore the possibility of such a representative group . . . participating in a round table discussion with religious leaders in an off-the-cuff exploration of homosexual life."[40] Del Martin, cofounder of DOB, wrote in February 1964 that Luster "felt that his staff" should "have some knowledge and understanding about homosexuality."[41]

As a result of these conversations, McIlvenna convened a group of thirteen homophile organizers, sixteen Protestant clergy, and social workers—including Luster—for a weekend-long "consultation" on the topic of homosexuality and the church, from May 30 to June 2, 1964.[42] McIlvenna's goal, he wrote in 1965, was to forge a "new ethic" for solving the problems of youth "who virtually become lost in our large cities."[43] Presentations and group discussions addressed topics like homosexuality and the law, theological issues, and, not insignificantly, the plight of street kids.[44] Billie Talmij, a DOB representative, referred to the young people who feel "so separated" from mainstream society that "they band together in packs for mutual protection."[45] One of the "main problems needing attention," a consultation summary noted, was "the young teenage homosexual." It "was impossible for homophile organizations to work with them due to legal implications" and was felt that the clergy should serve as the public face of their work with street kids.[46] They formalized this partnership by founding the Council on

Religion and the Homosexual (CRH), the nation's first mainstream ecumenical organization devoted to the issue of homosexuality.

Historians recognize San Francisco's Tenderloin as a major flash point of homophile activism between 1964 and 1966—years, according to D'Emilio, when the movement entered a "qualitatively new stage in its evolution." Despite the persistence of rhetoric casting homosexuals as sinful, mentally ill, and criminal, a cohesive "gay community" began to form around shared sexual orientation, and San Francisco became known as the country's "gay capital."[47] An underdocumented aspect of this history is reform work targeting the kids on the street. The migratory street scene was a foil against which reformers crafted a new vision of the responsible, settled "gay community." By creating programming to settle transient youth and integrate them into the economic mainstream, they were popularizing a figure the public considered a contradiction: the mature, settled, "responsible" homosexual citizen deserving of the benefits and responsibilities of the welfare state.

Redevelopment and Police Sweeps

We cannot appreciate the significance of reformers' work without understanding the moral values and economic norms shared by the people they targeted: the kids who migrated from tenderloin to tenderloin and created a distinct social world in the rooming houses, coffee shops, and streets. We must understand the kids' vision of the proper economic functions of actors within the meat rack economy, their notion of economic justice, and their working definitions of exploitation.

Meat rack businesses benefited financially from the kids' trade in sex and, in return, often allowed kids to meet, socialize, and discuss prices with potential clients. Hustlers, street queens, and homosexuals met at the Chuckkers (often spelled Chukkers), an afterhours coffee shop owned by a hair fairy named Carlos (or Carlo) Lara, and congregated at an all-night Gene Compton's Cafeteria at the crossroads of Turk and Taylor.[48] They met at the Plush Doggy (often spelled Plush Doggie), an all-night coffeehouse, which made money off "the gay trade," homophile organizer Guy Strait wrote in 1964, "otherwise they would have had to close their doors many months ago."[49] The kids held each other and danced to slow music at the Lettermen Club (often spelled Letterman) or used fake IDs to get into Pearl's, an afterhours club, Joel told me, populated by "underage teenage boys and older guys that were mad for us."[50] Hustlers also played pinball machines in the "amusement arcades" while they waited for clients to approach them. "You do the pinball machine," Joel explained, "and a guy comes up and starts talking to you. There were a lot of these little cheapo places." On a typical night, according to a 1965 radio program transcribed in one of Guy Strait's newspapers, one could see "homosexuals standing by the Plush Doggie, Cavalier Restaurant, or up at Chukker's, or Comptons, introducing themselves, or being introduced by others to other clients that they wish to make an acquaintance of."[51]

By the early 1960s, urban redevelopment and police street sweeps began undermining the accumulation of obligations, mutualities, and reciprocities among hustlers and hair fairies, leading to a more competitive environment that many street kids considered exploitative and abusive.

San Francisco government and business organizations, taking Manhattan as their model, began transforming the city into the West Coast's corporate and banking capital. The San Francisco Redevelopment Agency acquired "blighted" land and reimagined the Mid-Market thoroughfare as a site for tourism and hotel construction.[52] In 1964 Mayor John Shelley promised that Market Street was "about to undergo changes which involve many millions of dollars of public and private investment." These infusions of cash would result in "the creation of a great thoroughfare."[53] A 1962 redevelopment plan aimed to "rid Market Street of its shabby atmosphere" by revitalizing it "as a center of Bay Area business, shopping, and entertainment." Among the elements depreciating real estate value, the report read, were the "gaudy storefronts, chaotic jumbles of signs, festoons of overhead wires, conglomerations of street furniture, [and] trash and litter."[54] Hustlers and street queens, while not mentioned in the report, were clearly among the "trash" to be swept away. "The newspapers and the Board of Supervisors were screaming about the trash on Market Street," Raymond Broshears recalled of the mid-1960s. "Well, let me tell you, they were not talking about paper . . . they were talking about the homosexuals, faggots, hustlers, [and] drags."[55]

The city ordered police sweeps to "clean up" the Tenderloin and crack down on street kids' use of public space. In March 1965, the San Francisco Police Department Sex Detail Inspector announced a crackdown on the "between 200 and 300 male prostitutes in feminine attire" who "infest the downtown area." They "frequently lure homosexuals and the unwary in general to hotel and rooming houses where their pickups are beaten, robbed, or both."[56] That month, police arrested fifty-six patrons at the Chuckkers and charged them with municipal ordinance 440 (wearing apparel of opposite sex with intent to deceive) and California penal code 650 (openly outrages public decency).[57] An observer in 1965 noted that the "hustler activity has not been as prevalent since the first of the year due to a police crack-down. . . . The Plush Doggie has glassed in the front, closes earlier and has made an effort to keep the hustler out."[58] A Glide employee who transcribed tape recordings made by victims of police brutality recalled being "in shock as one person after another described being stopped by police in the Tenderloin and beaten with nightsticks."[59] Mayor Shelley defended the sweeps. As long as homosexuals "keep their affairs private," he told reporters in 1965, "they have no reason to fear our police." If there was "increased display and arrogance and promiscuity," he would "exercise whatever law is necessary . . . to eliminate such activities."[60]

Once arrested, youth were often confined in the city's overcrowded juvenile detention center, where they ostensibly waited for foster homes. Built to house 195 youth, the Youth Guidance Center grew from an average of 242 in 1960 to 341 in 1963.[61] According to a 1963 investigation, the detention center was used "as a dumping ground" for unwanted youth.[62] A minister recalled that police "would drive the kid around the City and scare the hell out of them and put them off in a different part of the City and tell them to go home. . . . But they had no place to send them."[63] Gender-nonconforming youth in particular were rarely adopted by foster parents and became "institutional babies," according to a 1966 report by Tenderloin reformers, "whose only home becomes a series of impersonal, inadequate pseudo jails in which they are treated as special problem cases, [and] often isolated from the other children."[64] An informant named Davida Ashton, who frequented the Tenderloin as a teenager, told me police would often arrest kids, hold them overnight at the Youth Guidance Center, release them, "and then they'd do it again the next day." Kids "just had enough of it," Davida told me. "I could just see the anger in all of us coming."

A "Homosexual Halfway House" and the War on Poverty

The Council on Religion and the Homosexual began proposing alternatives to the arrest and incarceration of street youth. The council appears to have taken up Chuck Rowland's original prospectus by proposing, in late 1964, a "homosexual halfway house" in the Tenderloin to assist "the so-called 'rejects' of society, the unloved, the unwanted, those who do not seem to fit into society's general idea of productive citizenship."[65] In contrast to the city's approach to growing numbers of young migrants arriving downtown—police raids and incarceration in juvenile detention centers—reformers envisioned a surrogate family and "house" at which street kids could access psychiatric care and counseling and find employment, a place where the "young and confused could discuss their problems [and] a place where the old and useless could feel wanted." In the context of Great Society liberalism, during which service programs often served as vehicles for community mobilization, reformers imagined the house as a base from which they would organize a "homosexual voting bloc," guide street kids into a nascent "gay community," and advocate for the homosexual's integration into the American polity: "This is a Half Way House to help the homosexual take care of his own, the first step he must take if he is ever going to reaffirm his place in society."[66]

The campaign to establish a halfway house soon expanded into a push for new funding sources for antidelinquency work, which became available in late 1964, when President Lyndon Johnson signed the Economic Opportunity Act, initiating the federal War on Poverty. Instead of relocating the urban poor through urban redevelopment projects, War on Poverty architects hoped to organize impoverished communities and assist them in "uplifting" themselves while preserving their sense of cultural and neighborhood identity. The main effort of the Economic Opportunity Act was to provide localities with the resources to develop their own antipoverty campaigns under the Community Action Program, which fed millions of dollars to communities to address poverty at a grassroots level, often bypassing traditional federal, state, and local bureaucracies. By requiring "maximum feasible participation" of the poor in Community Action Agencies, the War on Poverty mobilized the poor into a political instrument to restructure and reform community institutions.

The War on Poverty descended directly from the federal government's interest in juvenile delinquency and the popular sociological theories government actors used to explain it.[67] Among them was the "culture of poverty" thesis, as developed by sociologist Oscar Lewis, to refer to what he called a subcultural adaptation to poverty, a way of life and value system handed from generation to generation along family lines. One of the best ways to lift the poor out of a culture of poverty, he argued, was to organize the poor. "Any movement," he argued in 1966, "be it religious, pacifist or revolutionary, which organizes and gives hope to the poor and effectively promotes solidarity and a sense of identification with larger groups, destroys the psychological and social core of the culture of poverty."[68] War on Poverty architects often assumed that the "powerlessness" of the poor perpetuated poverty. Only as low-income persons were mobilized as a pressure group could they take control of their own neighborhoods and begin to influence city hall, the schools, and the welfare and housing bureaucracy.[69] This concept was absorbed into official Community Action Program guidelines requiring "maximum feasible participation" of the poor, which many approached as a kind of collective therapy to awaken the poor from their supposed apathy.[70]

Community action began in San Francisco in September 1964, when Mayor John Shelley created the San Francisco Economic Opportunity Council as the city's Community Action Program, which organized itself around "target area" neighborhoods suffering from concentrated levels of poverty.[71] The four neighborhoods initially designated as target areas were the city's widely recognized racialized "ghettos": Hunters Point, Chinatown, Western Addition, and the Mission district.[72] The central city, by contrast, was almost entirely white and did not fit within the reigning racial definition of poverty.[73] Homophile organizers attributed the central city's exclusion to antihomosexual stigma. "Homosexuals pay the taxes that fund the EOC," one homophile organizer wrote in 1965, but are "in-eligible to receive any of these funds or to be on the paid staff." He noted that more than $650,000 could be made available to fund health clinics, a halfway house, and vocational programs.[74] A coalition of ministers, social workers, and homophile organizers worked tirelessly from late 1964 to the summer of 1966 to fight what they perceived to be a gross injustice.

Tenderloin-based reformers began organizing street youth to fulfill the War on Poverty's "maximum feasible participation" requirement and qualify for funding. In late 1964, McIlvenna outlined a proposal to select forty to fifty young adults to "identify and articulate [their] own needs and concerns" and "design their own vehicle (or even movement) for fulfilling" them. He planned to bring in representatives from the Congress for Racial Equality and the Student Nonviolent Coordinating Committee, among a cadre of new "militant" and radical black activist organizations, to speak with young people in the Tenderloin.[75] McIlvenna hoped that the kids' enthusiasm, with adult direction, could "be tapped for constructive growth into real community action and progress."[76] In 1965 Glide founded Intersection for the Arts, a coffeehouse ministry located in the heart of the meat rack, to attract and organize street kids. The space was a hothouse for new music, theater, poetry, improvisational theater, painting, and other creative arts.[77] It was one of hundreds of coffeehouse ministries across the country, according to a 1965 article, "helping thousands of confused, probing, often rebellious young [people] to find new meanings and new directions."[78]

By the mid-1960s, homophile organizer Mark Forrester had distinguished himself as one of the most effective organizers of street kids in the central city. Forrester arrived in San Francisco in 1961, at twenty-seven years old, after traveling the United States as a prostitute, "pimp," and, as he later put it, "other strange things."[79] He took up residence in a South of Market "skid row" hotel and organized with the Mattachine Society. In May 1964 he cofounded a new homophile organization, the Society for Individual Rights, which historian Nan Alamilla Boyd argues was significantly different from earlier homophile organizations because of its bold language of social activism and open democratic structure.[80] Inspired by Saul Alinksy and enabled by what he later called the "absolute freedom of no income," Forrester became an organizing powerhouse in the central city.[81]

By the fall of 1965, Glide Methodist directed its Young Adult Program intern, a twenty-five-year-old named Ed Hansen, to work with Forrester to organize youth and qualify for antipoverty funds. Hansen felt he was often "the front person for what Mark was doing," since Forrester "was a person off the street and struggling to survive financially" and "didn't have the legitimacy that I did as a minister serving at Glide."[82] Forrester and Hansen began interviewing street kids and consulting with hospitals, psychiatric clinics, public health associations, churches, and university sociologists to write a report on Tenderloin youth.[83] They led medical experts, psychologists, and youth groups on tours of the Tenderloin, the Lettermen Club, and the Chuckkers.[84] Forrester noticed pronounced generational differences in responses. "Most of the adults we took down there," he told CRH in February 1966, offered suggestions for "immediately cleaning the place up and helping rehabilitate these people to a nice heterosexual middle-class existence." Young adults instead "perceived that there were no easy solutions, there were no easy programs, there were no dramatic changes to occur here."[85]

Ed Hansen and his wife hosted weekly gatherings for young adults in their North Beach apartment through 1965. It was in this context that a kid told Hansen he should visit the South Side Hotel, a "skid row" hotel populated primarily by hustlers and street queens, and meet Joel Roberts.[86] Hansen remembered wearing a clerical collar and going to the South Side one night in 1965. "I was excited but afraid, fearful," he recalled. He met

Joel—"a real radical activist"—who invited him to his room to tape-record an interview. Joel "described how in New York, how the police harassment was really bad," Hansen recalled. Police would raid the bars, "and he said the patrons would scatter and would run. And he said the police, instead of yelling, 'Stop that man,' would yell, 'Stop that queer.' And then he said, 'It seems like our very existence is illegal.' And that phrase . . . just stuck with me and I thought, 'It's not right when people have to feel like their very existence is illegal.'" When Hansen walked downstairs, he found that police were raiding the hotel, "and there's a group of guys lined up and the police are . . . checking the ID of all these people in the lobby." Hansen took out his business card and gave it to the kids "and said, 'If you need something, give me a call.'" Hansen later played Joel's taped story to educate people about the "prejudice gay people . . . confronted."[87]

Hansen responded by organizing free meals at the South Side in late 1965, he told me, part of his efforts to organize youth and therefore "qualify for the antipoverty campaign that didn't at that time include the Central City." Guy Strait also noted that Hansen organized a Thanksgiving dinner at the South Side and a Christmas meal at Glide Methodist in 1965.[88] According to Hansen, "We ordered lots of turkeys and food and invited the hustlers and their friends to come and have a celebration dinner meal." The kids "put on their own little drag show for some entertainment."[89] The meal and drag show "created a stir among the church members," Glide pastor John Moore recalled. "The movement of young white families to the suburbs or suburban churches has been hastened by our involvement with homosexuals."[90] Hansen felt that Vanguard grew out of these events. "We were already thinking about it at Thanksgiving and Christmas," he recalled. "I thought it would be good for them to have a little organization and invited them to do that."[91] It is unclear if Hansen was accurately recalling Vanguard's formation. Regardless, he and Forrester were bringing street kids together, providing services, and inviting them to organize around common needs.

"I Am Called Joel Roberts"

I met Joel Roberts at a train station in Palo Alto in 2009 after reaching out and scheduling an oral history. In his late sixties, he was trim and still recognizable from photos I had seen of him as a Vanguard organizer. We took a bus to Joel's church, where the minister lent us his office to conduct several oral histories. The interviews themselves took on a ministerial dynamic as

Joel confessed the anguish he felt at losing so many friends to drug abuse and suicide in the Tenderloin. He told me during our second interview that he'd been crying at night thinking about the kids. "I've had a hard life," he said, "but whatever happened to them? I know what happened to a lot of them. They were dead. And I never got to grieve for them. I didn't have time. I had to just keep surviving."

A consummate storyteller, Joel began our first oral history interview by alluding to the restlessness that would characterize his life. "I am called Joel Roberts," he told me. "It's not really my name. I was born in Western New York on a farm. I was born August 28, 1941. I popped out two weeks early, anxious to get away, I guess." Born "Joseph" and raised by an Italian Catholic family that owned hundreds of acres of farm property, Joel worked the fields, from sunrise to sundown during the farming season, growing berries, beans, and other crops.

Joel highlighted stories of an abusive father, vividly describing scenes of domination that had an enormous impact on his life and politics. "If you know anything about Italian Catholic families," he explained, "it's really oppressive, it's very Dark Ages. My father would physically beat my mother with his fists. I remember very early, maybe three years old, screaming for him to stop and him flinging me across the room." After one beating left him bloody, Joel told me, his parents kept him home from school and told his teacher he was sick. He called his father a "tyrant" and his home "like a cult." In our oral history interviews, Joel still seethed with anger. "My father was always beating me, and he would say if you try to fight back, I will beat you harder. And I know it sounds pathetic, but I know I will never forgive my father for what he did. Never."

Access to Christianity at a young age offered Joel resources for managing and reinterpreting the abuse he experienced. "I don't have happy memories of my family," he said, "but while I was living it, I made it happy. I think that's part of why religion attracts me, because you get all of these religious stories of people turning something good out of something really bad. Catholicism was a story about a man who was persecuted, beaten, and crucified and somehow ended up being the winner." The Church became his "alternative reality." As an altar boy at the Italian Sacred Heart Church, he learned Latin, wore religious garb, and participated in esoteric rituals. Being an altar boy, Joel told me, "was a chance to become special when your father was so abusive." He felt at the time "that I better be a priest because they don't have to get married or do anything normal."

Joseph enrolled at the University of Buffalo, where he met homosexual professors and began to identify as gay. He dropped out at the end of his freshman year, around 1957, and came out to his father. "He had been so brutal all my life," Joel said, "and then when I finally came out—he just walked out of the room. He really looked like he had been defeated." His father disinherited him. A gay professor drove Joel to New York and dropped him off in Times Square. "I guess he knew that there was a scene that somehow I would blend in," Joel said. "When homosexuality was illegal, unless you want to slice your wrists and spend a lot of time in psychotherapy, where did you go? You went to these sleazy places of town, where being illegal was a given."

Joel found other kids in Times Square who pooled their resources, "which meant you at least had a hotel room, you had food, and for them you had drugs—I have to say almost all of them were on drugs." The street scene was Joel's "social security," he told me. "I would look to the people on the street because there's a reason why they were there and there was a reason why I was there. And that was because no one else would have us, basically. You've got no money, you got no resources, no career, no family, what have you got? You've got your fellow freak on the street." At the same time, there was "bitchiness going on, there's competition. There were definitely kids who would steal from you." Street kids were "the dregs of society," Joel said. "Nobody wanted you. You were outlaws. Homosexual prostitute drug addicts. I know I wasn't but most everybody was taking drugs—pills, uppers, downers." The street queens called each other Miss Thing, "Miss That, Miss Texas, and I think the word *queen* really applied. Now it means just anything almost. But *queen* actually meant princess. It meant everyone else doesn't want me but I know that I'm beautiful."

Joel turned tricks and briefly worked for a florist; he lived with sex work clients for short periods of time before cycling back through the hotels. Joel approached hustling as a means of reframing childhood abuse. "I was clear when I was doing it, I never got love from my father; now if a man wants to pay attention to me he's gonna pay for it. I remember other kids saying the same thing." The kids "said it and we felt it, and it was healing. Well, you have a father that treats you like nothing, like dirt, and suddenly, you have guys paying, I won't say, they did things they maybe should be ashamed of, and they paid to do it. In a weird, upside-down way, we were getting our love."

Joel ultimately fashioned a politics out of abandonment. "I felt hurt," he told me, "so of course I identify with the people who are wounded, not with the person who does the wounding. I don't identify with America and suddenly I got all these Beat writers who also don't. And I've got the gospel. You know Jesus again is a big loser—and that's his appeal." Joel explored the bohemian, activist, and gay scenes in the West Village. He learned about gay artists like Andy Warhol, which "gave gay kids an identity more than being a prostitute and an outcast," Joel said, laughing. "'I'm a prostitute, outcast, but I'm an artist.'" He volunteered with the Catholic Workers, an anarchist religious movement, serving soup and working on their publication. He was also inspired by the Beats, a white, male movement that romanticized skid row as a refuge from postwar suburban domesticity. The reason "the beat movement was called the beat movement," Joel told me, "is that they were beaten into becoming beatitude." By being "so broken, they were now seeing visions."

Even before movements emerge, stories that circulate in subaltern worlds provide counterpoints to powerful myths. Joel told me the kids "shared our stories in West Greenwich Village, and we shared our stories in the Tenderloin in particular. . . . You paid a price for being gay," Joel explained, "and I don't think my family story is that unusual. Because when I hit the streets, I heard the same story—heard worse stories." Circulating stories may have enabled abandoned youth to approach abandonment as systemic rather than a result of individual moral failures.

As winter approached in late 1965, Joel hitched a ride to Berkeley with a friend from the scene before taking the Greyhound bus to San Francisco. He disembarked in the heart of the Tenderloin meat rack. Soon after he arrived,

I'm walking on Market [Street] on the right side going towards the financial district. And on the right, I see a young kid crying and holding his ribs. . . . I think he was about thirteen, a young boy, wearing false eyelashes and makeup, crying and bleeding. And I rushed over to him, and he said his ribs were broken. . . . And I stupidly said—I thought he had been jumped by somebody—"Well, we should call the cops." And he said, "No, the cops did this to me." And he said they regularly did it to him. . . . That was the spark that eventually made me want to do Vanguard. It was just—somehow—I couldn't stand it, the way people were being treated. And I think because of my background with Catholic Worker and the civil rights movement was influencing all of us, understanding how religion and nonviolence can really uplift people.

Joel explained, "People who are abandoned don't always die quickly or dramatically; they also die of diseases of poverty, drug overdoses, trauma inflicted by the criminal justice system, and other causes they might see as self-inflicted. These kids were my friends, and they were dying like flies, overdosing." Joel told me about "Rosie Cheeks," one of the "prettiest boys I'd ever seen," who was arrested for some petty charge and sent to jail, where he was raped, had his teeth broken, and, when Joel ran into him years later, "was carrying a doll, so he was definitely out of his mind now." In the course of a few years, he "went from being a kid who looked underage to looking like a beat-up old wino." Rosie Cheeks "had been through the mill, man, and I think a lot of kids knew that ten years from now that's who I'm going to be. I am grateful that I read gay writers and I had a little bit of university education and I had my religious background. So that's the pain I carry with me."

Adrian Ravarour and Billy Garrison at the El Rosa Hotel

While Joel was out on the street, other young people were migrating to the Tenderloin and organizing their peers, among them a young adult named Adrian Ravarour. In 2009 Adrian traveled by bus from Los Angeles to record an oral history at San Francisco's GLBT Historical Society. Our oral history encounter was highly performative. When I opened the door to greet him, he danced his way into the archive, contorting his body into angular shapes characteristic of modern dance. The name Vanguard, he said, derived from the dance form: "avant-dance, avant-garde, and Vanguard—all of the same thing." Adrian's narrative was also highly performative, establishing at the outset the persona he was crafting for the archive. At the age of five, he told me, he wanted to "be Moses, to lead people, to free them." His "social activism," he said, "was a spiritual activism."

Like Joel, Adrian highlighted scenes of childhood violence during our oral history recordings. "I have to give my father credit for beating me," he said, "because when he beat me, it triggered, I guess, psychological reactions or intuitive reactions, or some people would say mystical experiences." After months of beatings as a five- and six-year-old, Adrian told me, "I had what seemed like a mystical experience where in essence either my subconscious, or some outer information at least told me that I should be my essence, that I'm fine. And that the soul and essence is fine, it's whole and complete." The experience "gave me the belief that I needed to be my essence and my soul and that my essence and my soul were innately good." Throughout his life, Adrian explored psychology, Buddhism, and metaphysics to determine whether the experience had been "real" or simply "imagined." At the time of our recording, he still wasn't sure. Regardless, it was a touchstone that he revisited throughout his life and our oral history encounter.

Adrian sought to re-create these mystical experiences through dance. "I had come to appreciate those earlier spiritual experiences and insights," he wrote in a self-published book, "and I wanted to recreate these states of consciousness."[92] Adrian told me he left home in 1963, at seventeen, and enrolled in the San Francisco Ballet School, where modern choreographers were "freed from inhibiting rules and regulations."[93] Adrian gravitated to Glide's Intersection for the Arts, where dancers "attempted to eliminate the trained dancer's postures, positions, steps, and structuring"—the classical dance form—and instead found expression in "organic" everyday activity: running, skipping, hopping, and jumping.[94] He would put on a stack of records at full volume, turn off the lights, "strip off all clothes, and begin to move to the textural sound."[95] In these "ecstatic moments," he wrote, "one feels transported to what seems to be other realms."[96]

Adrian started dating a hustler he met in the Tenderloin, Joel Williams, and moved in with him at the El Rosa, a three-story hotel in the heart of the meat rack. "You had street people, you had some people who called them-selves hair fairies, and then there were also some drag queens," Adrian told me. A sociologist described the El Rosa in the late 1960s as a "queens ho-tel" where the newcomer has "a ready-made classroom and teacher. There was much for them to learn from the older queens" who were "constantly gathering in someone's room to dress a person's hair or to set a wig." In the process, "a large amount of information is exchanged among the girls," including "how to recognize the police, how to approach a prospect," and ultimately "how to survive."[97]

Adrian met El Rosa resident Billy Garrison, who, Adrian recalled, was in their early thirties, short with a slight build, and identified as a hair fairy, "which meant that the clothing he wore was heterosexual, you know, guy's clothes—jeans and a shirt—but then he had his hair ratted up and hair sprayed so it was stacked like a beehive almost." Garrison used an "eyebrow pencil, rouge, some lipstick, foundation, he did his nails—his nails were long and colored—and he wore some feminine jewelry." Before moving to San Francisco, Adrian told me, Billy passed as a heterosexual male and was a member of a Seattle street gang. According to Adrian, "Billy told me that the reason why he came to San Francisco is that it was noted to be gay tolerant, and he dressed the way he did . . . so men would recognize that he was available." According to Joel, Billy "looked like a very young pretty Elvis Presley with much too much makeup." Billy's lovers "were all young criminals."

Adrian and Billy Garrison talked about strategies for responding to the police abuse and discrimination in the Tenderloin. Adrian told me that Billy proposed a conflict resolution based on their background as a gang member. In response to conflict between Billy's gang and business owners, a minister reached out to both groups, held a town hall meeting, and encouraged dialogue between the warring factions. Gang members also helped elderly residents shop for groceries and repaired broken windows. "It mitigated the friction," Adrian said, "and people began to understand one another." Billy felt this model might work for street kids and hair fairies in the Tenderloin. Billy "wanted to try to apply the Seattle approach—bring the people together, see if they can resolve their differences, and can they support one another—and therefore you build a coalition."

Adrian told me that Billy "went to Glide Memorial Methodist Church." Phyllis Lyon agreed to sponsor a community meeting. Adrian and Billy advertised through "word of mouth" and posted fliers for a meeting designed to foster understanding between hair fairies, bikers, business owners, and police in the Tenderloin. At the first meeting, about forty people "from every demographic" met at the church. "You had street people, hippies, drag queens, I think there were some hustlers, elderly people, Russian, [and] Greeks." It was a "chaotic, semi-riotous scene," Adrian recalled. People who didn't like hair fairies shouted insults at Billy, who attempted to lead the meeting. Street kids complained about the church: "Why are we meeting at the church when the church burned us?" Mark Forrester attempted to impose his vision of organizing a broad base of the poor in the South of Market and the Tenderloin, "but the neighborhood kids did not like his model or political objectives," Adrian told me. "They wanted something specifically for the Tenderloin district and specifically for their own demographic—that's why they were meeting." Adrian felt that Vanguard formed organically out of a series of conflict resolution meetings.

Street Worker Programs and "The Tenderloin Ghetto"

While Adrian and Billy organized, reformers continued to reach out to Tenderloin youth. In February 1966, the Council on Religion and the Homosexual endorsed the establishment of central city as an antipoverty area and donated money to print a report by Forrester and Hansen, designed to win War on Poverty funds, titled "The Tenderloin Ghetto: The Young Reject in Our Society."[98] Distributed to politicians, social service providers, and churches, the report described a "very large group of youth and young adults" that "form a sub-culture that is generally ignored or condemned by middle-class oriented society." As a "depot for incoming persons" around the country, "the Tenderloin presents serious problems for both the new arrival and the subculture which exists there."[99] The report authors proposed several points of action: the use of "street workers" to "use 'on-the-spot' counseling," the involvement of local churches, tutoring centers, the development of a "Social Center-Coffee House," and the provision of housing, employment, education, and food.[100] In words likely designed to appeal to the dictum "maximum feasible participation," the authors also argued that the "young adults of the Tenderloin must . . . propos[e] solutions and [design] programs which meet their needs."[101]

One of the alternate titles for "The Tenderloin Ghetto" was "The White Ghetto," although it does not seem to have been extensively circulated.[102] Christina Hanhardt argues that the use of this alternate title demonstrates that the organizers understood race to be a primary framework for explaining urban poverty.[103] Reformers treated other nonconformities, such as sex work, promiscuity, drug use, and nonconventional gender expression, as blocks to the modes of integration and participation they most idealized. In this way, Hanhardt argues, the "white ghetto" is "both the place where white people might be consumed by the city's worst pathologies and a marker of the promise of assimilation through a certain kind of white (homosexual) identification."[104]

Toward this end, Forrester and Hansen began developing "street worker" programs, likely modeled on Youth for Service, to mobilize the Tenderloin's primarily white hustlers, hair fairies, and "undesirables." According to "The Tenderloin Ghetto," they aimed to train "street workers" to relate to kids on the meat rack: "Plush Doggie on Market Street, Chuckers, Compton's on the corner of Taylor and Turk, the Caboose, Pearl's, and the Lettermen Club."[105] According to an undated report written around April, street workers would act as "catalysts" to foster "indigenous leadership." Over time, "street workers may be able to encourage the potential leaders of the Tenderloin to assert themselves, and with some guidance to establish youth and young adult organizations in the area."[106] Youth could serve the elderly, staff senior centers, and otherwise "rehabilitate South of Market and the Tenderloin."[107] Forrester cofounded the Tenderloin Committee, an advocacy organization, which proposed in March 1966 the development of "experimental primary groups which will aid these young people in finding themselves." These "units," they wrote, "will have a structure comparable to an ordinary teenage 'gang.'" Units could be developed in "residence centers" and through "citizen-participation groups." Rejecting proposals that the Tenderloin be "cleaned up" or kids be "relocated," they planned to "use the existing . . . sense of community" to "aid in the very processes of individual self-discovery."[108]

In April 1966, the Tenderloin Committee formed the Tenderloin Citizens Committee, a "resident association" subgroup led by street kids, Tenderloin denizens, and "the finest medical, legal and professional talent in the City." The group's president was Shay, also known as "Miss Joyce Jenkins"; the vice president was "Tex," also known as Don Milendy; and the treasurer was the manager of the afterhours Lettermen Club.[109] Like many contemporary homophile organizations, the group interfaced with medical "experts" and the police in an effort to shift public opinion on homosexuality. A flier announced an April 24 meeting at the Lettermen Club with Elliot Blackstone, the San Francisco Police Department's liaison to the gay and lesbian community, on "the problems of the police in the Tenderloin" and "the relation between the police and the Tenderloin Community." A meeting on April 17 was scheduled with a doctor who would discuss "current scientific theories about homosexuality" and "then have an open discussion [about] what the kids in the Tenderloin think about this subject."[110] As such, reformers assisted in founding an organization led by the kids on the street months before Vanguard was established.

Meanwhile, Joel walked to Glide Methodist and talked with pastor Cecil Williams, an African American civil rights minister from the South, about the plight of street kids. He also stopped by the Society for Individual Rights (SIR) Center, just off the meat rack, which opened in April 1966 as the nation's first gay community center.[111] Joel said SIR was "very bourgeois, very middle class, and had no use for runaway kids. I got the idea, okay, they're doing gay liberation, and these kids aren't part of it." He picked up manila folders, filled them up with information from the American Civil Liberties Union (ACLU) and legal assistance, and handed them out on the street "so the kids knew—they didn't really have to put up with some of the crap they were putting up with." The kids started calling Joel "Rev," a reference to civil rights ministers. Joel told me Mark Forrester approached him after Joel started organizing. He said he "trained with Saul Alinsky and they needed to organize a group and they could get this federal funding." The Economic Opportunity Council wanted to "organize the people, in the neighborhood, in the street," Joel told me. "And here we are. I mean, there's nothing more visible than a whole bunch of teenage boys wearing eye makeup." Joel laughed. "And tight pants."

The Central City Target Area and "Vanguard Movement"

In May 1966, after a protracted battle, reformers won War on Poverty funds for the Central City Target Area of the San Francisco Economic Opportunity Council, a neighborhood antipoverty program covering San Francisco's Tenderloin and South of Market.[112] After half a century during which homosexuals were largely excluded from the civil sphere, the funds administered by this coalition signaled the beginning of a movement to establish the legitimacy of social relations that fell outside the conventionally gendered, white heterosexual nuclear family.[113] Don Lucas became director of the target area and hired Mark Forrester as a community organizer. The San Francisco Economic Opportunity Council approved an area budget of $124,500 for the next six months and set aside $100,000 for programs to be determined by an interim board.[114] Tenderloin street kids, including Joel Roberts, ran for elected seats on the interim board. "I made the strongest speech possible trying to communicate some of the desperation of the kids in the street," Joel wrote in June 1966. "My speech was full of the beautiful vulgarity of the streets, and when it was over . . . my voice was placed on the E.O.C. Interim Area Board."[115] Also elected to the interim board were Billy Garrison, Mark Forrester, and representatives of Goodwill, the Mattachine Society, and the Salvation Army.[116] The interim board characterized itself in an internal document as a "militant organization" whose programs would "strike at the redevelopment of people from one slum to another" and reject the idea "that only certain groups of poor people are rehabilitatable or deserving of help."[117]

There were profound class and cultural differences between street kids and the reformers who directed the Target Area. Reformers aimed to instill middle-class values in the "so-called 'Tenderloin sub-cultures,'" they wrote in a 1966 funding proposal, "which are growing in every major city in the country."[118] Above all, reformers sought to settle migratory youth. "Hundreds of these young people drift from city to city, supporting themselves by prostitution or other devices," Forrester wrote in 1967. "They should be given a stopping point to "help . . . get off the cycle."[119] Disentangling homosexual and gender-transgressive identities was crucial to the politics of respectability promoted by many homophile organizers. The Mattachine Society, in a proposal submitted to the Economic Opportunity Council in 1966, argued that street youth needed to "be freed from endless role assumption and theatricalism" by forming close relationships with "stable adult authority figures."[120] Reformers sought to impose a heterosexual/homosexual binary on a scene marked by butch/femme and trade regimes. For youth "without positively established sexual identity," read a 1966 proposal, their "heterosexual orientation may be reinforced through lay counseling and professional help." Reformers rejected the idea that homosexuality was a damaged identity, inextricably linked to vice and crime, and encouraged "confirmed and self-accepting homosexuals" to "accept their social responsibilities, including work at productive jobs . . . so that they will not be economically unproductive."[121] Homosexuality was increasingly cast by reformers as an affirmative and often white identity rather than a symptom of pathology.[122]

Joel explained that he felt a "tension between me living this life [on the street] and these [reformers], probably well-meaning, saying, 'We want to help you,' but in no way understanding us." Joel told me many reformers felt "their job was to send kids back home." Other reformers attempted to impose gender-normative behavior to integrate kids into the mainline economy. "I remember [adult] women who were part of the poverty program instantly wanting to help this young dyke to dress up and look like a woman. They thought that was the problem: that she didn't know how to act or look like a woman. . . . In no way did they understand what it meant to be a gay kid. None. All they wanted to do was at least make us act straight." Joel resigned from the interim board in protest.

Rising expectations and dashed hopes are familiar ingredients for insurrections. Joel wrote in June 1966 that a "Vanguard movement" began in May 1966 as a "rising tide of discontent set in against 'big brother' groups (e.g. Tenderloin Committee) which sought large federal poverty funds without organizing a base of people they were supposed to be helping," that is, the kids on the street. "Hopes had been raised by those seeking office and money, but in the weeks that passed not one visible sign of help arrived for the kids who had to pay hotel bills day by day."[123] He attributed growing frustration to food riots in the Tenderloin. "On Tuesday following the [board] election, those streets tingled with the sound of broken glass. A store owner who was notorious for his mistreatment of the street-kids had his place broken into and many on the street ate that night."[124]

Vanguard's Mutual Aid

Vanguard became a formal organization by June 1966, when, according to one account, "a group of the city's young 'Undesirables' met at Glide Church to formally proclaim the beginning of a grass-roots movement."[125] Billy Garrison became Vanguard's secretary, while Adrian Ravarour and Joel Roberts became key leaders.[126] Vanguard's president was Jean-Paul (also J. P.) Marat, a hustler and drug dealer who borrowed his street name from the radical French Revolution journalist who dubbed those in power "enemies of the people." Vanguard's first mission statement noted that it was made up of "youth in the Tenderloin attempting to get for its citizens a sense of dignity and responsibility to [*sic*] long denied. We find our civil liberties imperiled by a hostile social order in which all difference from the usual in behavior is attacked." Vanguard would "change these processes through the strength we develop for ourselves through our own efforts."[127] Among Vanguard's demands were a "Coffee House, Emergency Housing, Medical aid and a VD clinic, employment counseling, and Police cooperation."[128] The "coffee house" would be a store-front space, open twenty-four hours a day, where police would not harass the kids and where they could eat free food, talk with peers, and access services. They published screen-printed issues of *Vanguard Magazine* to broadcast their unique political vision.

Vanguard built on street kids' preexisting web of reciprocities to develop a politics of mutual aid. The kids who organized Vanguard, Joel told me, "instinctually knew if we're gonna make it at all, we're gonna have to all help each other. The choices are to die or to create some kind of family." If Vanguard members "turned a trick, you spent that money on your other friends, because when they turned a trick they did the same." Larry Mamiya, a Glide minister assigned to work with Vanguard in 1967, told me Vanguard "was a family. They took care of each other." If a member was in trouble with police, "the word was spread immediately among Vanguard members. If somebody needed housing, and if they had a place, they would share that. If there was a sugar daddy who's beating someone up, they tried to provide some protection."

Vanguard also provided resources to Tenderloin youth who were not active members. Organizers collected donations for a "T.L. Welfare Fund," which they "spent on providing kids on the street and people in need with the bare, cold necessities." They operated referral services for jobs and connected kids to welfare and disability benefits.[129] It listed in *Vanguard Magazine* the "clinics and missions," barber colleges for free haircuts, and locations for free meals. Vanguard organized weekly dances in Glide's basement to raise money to found its coffeehouse. "Most of these kids just wander in off the streets," the vice president told a reporter in 1966. "We try to feed them, give them a hot dog or something before they go."[130] It was "touching to see the kids together," a homophile organizer wrote of a dance. "Some you can't tell whether they are male or female—and I guess it doesn't make much difference—negroes and whites and chinese all mixed in together. . . . Some seem hardley [*sic*] in their adolescence, but I guess are in late teens—impossible to tell—identifications don't seem to mean much—they are just kids."[131]

Vanguard should be considered one of the many mutual aid programs active in the 1960s, including the Black Panther Party, whose survival programs included the Free Breakfast Program, a free ambulance program, and free medical clinics; and the Young Lords Party, which protested the lack of garbage pickups, provided free health care, and provided food and youth programs for Puerto Rican communities.[132] Dean Spade notes that people often come to social movements because they need resources or assistance, such as eviction defense, health care, or advocacy. Getting support through a mutual aid project that has a political analysis can help break stigma and isolation.[133]

Vanguard politicized the profound class and cultural differences separating street kids and homophile organizers at a time when black radicals came to view mainline groups like the National Association for the Advancement of Colored People (NAACP) as responding only to a middle-class constituency.[134] Vanguard positioned itself in opposition to the "99% of the homosexual organizations in the U.S. [that] are composed of and run by, the middle class, well established hidden homosexual." Vanguard was composed of "the other 1%," the "hustlers, who are bought and paid for by the same people who will not hire us to a legitimate job."[135] Vanguard is "an organization of 'kids on the street,'" wrote one organizer, "who feel there is no place for them within the organizational structure of the homophile organizations."[136] Organizers rejected the involvement of "professionals" and reformers. "We want people who are 'on the street,'" Joel Roberts said in July 1966, "not a bunch of nice type social workers. We believe that we can take care of a large portion of our problems without the interference of

> # VANGUARD
> # NEEDS YOUR SUPPORT
>
> This organization of, by, and for
> the "kids on the street"
> can use clothing,
> jobs,
> cash,
> a building,
> and many, many other items.
>
> *Our membership is limited to those who need help..*
>
> ## write: VANGUARD, % Glide Foundation, 330 Ellis, San Francisco

FIGURE 3.1.   Advertisement in Guy Strait's *Citizens News*, ca. August 1966.
Courtesy of GLBT Historical Society.

the Federal Government, head shrinkers or older people, most of whom do not at all understand the problems of the kids."[137]

While Vanguard presented itself as entirely youth-led, homophiles and Protestant ministers worked quietly behind the scenes to provide material support. Glide Methodist provided Vanguard an office, a telephone, and furniture.[138] Phyllis Lyon became a Vanguard sponsor, and the Reverend Raymond Broshears, a street minister I introduced in chapter 2, became the organization's "job counselor and advisor."[139] Larry Mamiya told me Glide ministers referred to Vanguard as an "organized street gang," suggesting that they considered it to be analogous to organizations like Youth for Service. Reformers shaped Vanguard's agenda and political rhetoric. Vanguard's mission statement, for example, appears to be a lightly edited version of the Society for Individual Rights' mission statement.[140] Vanguard's goal of opening a coffeehouse was likely shaped by reformers: Larry Mamiya told me that reformers working in "the poverty program" had as their "goal with Vanguard" the establishment of "a twenty-four-hour coffeehouse, in which we could plug in some adult help."

The fact that young adults considered Vanguard to be entirely youth-run demonstrates reformers' success in putting into action the War on Poverty's dictum of "maximum feasible participation." By forming an organization "to meet our OWN needs," as one of Vanguard's early broadsides stated, young people were at the same time putting into action War on Poverty goals.[141]

In a number of essays and interviews, Vanguard's president, Jean-Paul Marat, constructed a narrative remarkably consistent with reformers' goals of lifting the kids out of a "culture of poverty" through political organizing. Marat wrote in a 1966 issue of *Vanguard Magazine* that he grew up in a middle-class family "Victorian in their sex attitudes." He would hear "veiled references to 'fags' and 'queers': usually accompanied by the wish to kill all of them."[142] He "attempt[ed] to escape the harsh realities of being condemned by society for being 'different' by the use of drugs."[143] Traveling to Los Angeles, Marat pushed crystal and was arrested. He fled to San Francisco and began using crystal in the Tenderloin.[144] "Within a month my arms looked like pincushions," Marat wrote. "I started shooting 6–8 times a day. I went 8–10 days without sleep or food. I was a mess."[145]

Marat wrote that he kicked his drug habit after kids elected him president of Vanguard. "I realized that the objectives of Vanguard were much more important than my Crystal and the small amount of money I was making pushing." He decided to "come down" to contend with "problems that arose in the Organization and in the area."[146] The moral of his story is "that a 'hopeless junkie' can make it, that there is a way out which is not so difficult as to be impossible."[147] There was some truth to this story. By all accounts, Marat was a passionate organizer. "I want to help these kids," he told a reporter in 1966. "They're young—there are kids twelve and thirteen hustling on the street."[148] Others remember Marat for his ongoing love affair with speed. He was "Mr. Methamphetamine himself," Economic Opportunity Council organizer Calvin Colt recalled, "hollow eyed, twitchy, and very nervous and high strung." Mark Forrester exercised control over Marat's agenda. "[Marat] wanted to do this, that, and the next thing. And Mark was standing over there. 'No, we're not going to do that.'"[149] This account calls into question the notion that kids were fully in control of Vanguard's agenda or that political organizing dramatically transformed their lives.

FIGURES 3.2 – 3.5.   Images of Jean-Paul Marat and his artwork, ca. 1966. From the documentary film *Drugs in the Tenderloin*, directed by Robert Zagone, 1967. Screenshots by the author.

Fighting "Exploitation": Pickets, Riots, and Protests

At the center of Vanguard's political rhetoric was the argument that street kids should not be policed as criminals or undesirable blights but be viewed as young adults with value who were "exploited" by the police, meat rack business owners, redevelopers, and a broadly defined middle class. Jean-Paul Marat told a reporter in 1966 that kids formed Vanguard to end police harassment and "the exploitation of the kids in the Tenderloin by the middle-class people who run the businesses here."[150] Joel Roberts told me that he organized Vanguard "'cause I thought we were being exploited by . . . the police and society in general: our families that didn't want us," as well as "businessmen, police, [and] gays who weren't chicken queens, who had no use for us, who would walk down Market [Street] and just almost spit at us." Outside observers commented on this emerging theme. "In practically everything that has come out of Vanguard," Guy Strait told Vanguard organizers in late 1966, "there are overtones that you feel you have been exploited."[151]

Vanguard condemned as exploitative the meat rack business owners who excluded kids from places of consumption at a time when the rights of consumers took on great political significance.[152] For African American civil rights activists in the 1960s, historian Lizabeth Cohen notes, exclusion from sites of consumption was a "searing mark of unequal citizenship during a war fought to protect democracy."[153] The civil rights activist John Lewis, who organized with the Student Nonviolent Coordinating Committee, said the fact that African Americans "couldn't even get a hamburger and a Coke at a soda fountain" was an infuriating reminder of a lack of freedom "in what we believed was a free country."[154] Joel Roberts made a strikingly similar statement about the Tenderloin's cheap hot dog and hamburger stands: "The gay kids on the streets eating at these really sleazy joints, for nineteen cents you'd have a hamburger, but you weren't allowed to eat there, and the manager would yell at you, saying, 'Faggot, eat your hamburger outside.'" It "really got to me—my friends overdosing and not even being able to eat a goddamn hamburger in a sleaze joint."

Vanguard's racial makeup contributed to its analysis of exploitation. While historians often characterize Vanguard as representing the most hard-edged margins, it is critical to understand that it was composed of a relatively privileged subset of the street scene: young white men in their early twenties, many with some college education. Larry Mamiya recalled that "the vast majority were white. . . . There were a few Asians and blacks and Latinos, [but] not in great numbers." Trans activist Tamara Ching recalled that people of color did not feel welcome at Vanguard.[155] Felicia Elizondo, a trans woman of color who lived in the Tenderloin, told me the organization was "all white people." The organization also emerged at a time when growing numbers of white middle-class "runaways" set the stage for a dramatic shift in the public representation of street youth.[156] Widespread concern for a new group of white runaways began to spawn a more sympathetic image. The general public during the 1960s often saw white youth as socially needy "victims" in need of help rather than "criminals" to be incarcerated.[157] The general public would have been more likely to approach Vanguard's primarily white members as victims "exploited" by a variety of actors.

Vanguard organizers were also likely influenced by the rhetoric of the "low-income consumer," as developed through social science investigations like David Caplovitz's 1963 study *The Poor Pay More*, which exposed the consumer exploitation encountered by "ghetto" residents.[158] In a 1966 article titled "Exploitation," J. P. Marat denounced the Tenderloin's "slum landlord" who charged "fantastic rents for one room hovels," the "owner of the grocery store, whose scale is set to register just enough to make him a good profit," and land speculators who "buy these properties at a very low cost and sell them to redevelopment agencies at profits beyond imagination." Vanguard should "start fighting this exploitation."[159] A Vanguard broadside similarly protested the "endless profit adults are making off youth in the Central City," demanding "immediate corrections of the fact that most of the money made in the area is made by the exploitation of youth by so-called normal adults . . . off situations everyone calls degenerate, perverted, and sick." As such, Vanguard called into question the "morality" of a vice economy based on what it called "extreme degradation."[160]

Vanguard's first demonstration, likely in June or July 1966, appears to have been a picket in front of a Market Street theater designed to protest kids' exclusion from the meat rack's hot dog and hamburger stands. Joel Roberts told me that Vanguard organizers were inspired by the civil rights pickets they had "seen on TV with blacks." The kids designed the action, Joel said, to show "that we weren't even allowed to eat in the places we bought food in." Adrian recalled protesters holding signs that read "Hustlers Demand Rights" and "Drag Queens Demand Rights." Presenting themselves as excluded consumers appears to have been an effective strategy. "That actually hit a chord," Joel told me. "I remember very much the reporters being friendly. That's the first time I saw establishment people be friendly to us, really, unless they were coming down to buy us."

In July 1966, Vanguard held several pickets at Compton's Cafeteria after owners installed security and imposed a twenty-five-cent "service" charge, which Vanguard organizers felt was designed "to keep out those of us who have little or no money."[161] Ed Hansen wrote in July 1966 that there were "between 30 and 50" picketers "each night from 10 pm to midnight."[162] Vanguard distributed a mimeographed broadside at the picket that read, "We of the Tenderloin are constantly subjected to physical and verbal abuse by both the management and the Pinkerton Special Police Officers assigned here."[163] Compton's continued to deny kids service.[164] Jean-Paul Marat said he walked into the cafeteria and a cop said, "Get out, faggot. We don't want your kind in here."[165]

When the pickets failed to bring substantive change, street queens and hustlers rioted at Compton's Cafeteria in August 1966. The Reverend Raymond Broshears recalled in 1975 that the riot began "when police came into a cafeteria . . . to do their usual job of hassling the drag queens and hair fairies and hustlers." When the police "grabbed the arm of one of the transvestites, he [sic] threw his cup of coffee in the cop's face, and with that, cups, saucers, and trays began flying around the place and all directed at the police." The management "ordered the place closed, and with that, the Gays began breaking out every window in the place." The next day, "drag queens, hair fairies, conservative Gays, and hustlers joined in a picket of the cafeteria, which would not allow the drags back in."[166] The pickets and riot appear to have had limited impact. Vanguard's vice president reported in November 1966 that Compton's management promised "the kids would not be specifically harassed," but if they lingered too long over coffee they would be "pushing their luck."[167]

Perhaps Vanguard's most iconic action was its "Fall Clean Up" or "Sweep-In," a theatrical protest that took up and manipulated the symbolic terms of urban renewal and police sweeps that figured kids as "trash." A photograph printed in the October 1966 issue of *Vanguard Magazine* shows street kids and hair fairies, illuminated by streetlights, using oversize brooms to sweep Market Street. Young people wear signs that proclaim, "Market Street Needs a Cleanup. All trash is before the broom." According to Vanguard's press release, "Tonight a 'clean sweep' will be made on Market St; not by the POLICE, but by the street people who are often the object of police harassment."[168] Significantly, Vanguard swept the meat rack in front of the Plush Doggy, a business that had previously relied on the revenue hustlers generated but put into effect a "No Service" policy in 1964 and glassed in the front to keep hustlers out in 1965.[169] The action positioned youth as potential collaborators in the Tenderloin's revitalization. "We're considered trash by much of society," Marat said, "and we wanted to show the rest of society that we want to work and can work."[170] The action was almost certainly planned with Mark Forrester's assistance. Forrester's May 1966 "Workplan for Community Action" recommended "the use of local color" to "combine clever symbolic demonstrations with the threat of economic or political action."[171] He recommended "symbolic demonstrations in which people appear as they are, eg, transvestites picketing in 'drag.'"[172]

These collective actions empowered street kids to insist on the value of their lives and engage in more small-scale rebellions. For example, Adrian Ravarour told me that he and Vanguard organizer Dixie Russo walked into the Doggie Diner, a twenty-four-hour hotdog place in the meat rack, and asked for coffee. An Italian American from New York, Dixie identified as a queen or hair fairy, with "hair ratted up—wearing eyebrow pencil, foundation, lipstick, eyelashes, and I think fingernails."[173] An employee refused to serve Dixie until she took off her makeup. By this time, "we had done a number of demonstrations," Adrian said, "we had been having dances, we

FIGURES 3.6 – 3.11.   *This spread and previous page:* Vanguard "Sweep-In" on the Market Street meat rack in front of the Plush Doggy and Gallen-Kamp's shoe store, ca. September 1966. Photographer unknown. Courtesy of GLBT Historical Society.

were an organization, we felt empowered." According to Adrian, "Dixie said, 'Why? I'm a paying customer, here's my money, I want my coffee.'" The employee threatened to call the police, at which point Dixie picked up a sugar bowl and smashed it on the tile floor. "We were no longer intimidated," Adrian said.

Perhaps Vanguard's most lasting achievement was working with Tenderloin reformers to found Hospitality House, a social service "coffee house" that opened in January 1967 above the Lettermen Club.[174] The Economic Opportunity Council paid rent and salary for staff, who ran an information center and offered employment, food, health care, and information about drug use.[175] Vanguard offered free clothing and organized Friday and Saturday dances at Hospitality House in 1967.[176] Mark Forrester, identified by a newspaper in February 1967 as "the architect" of Hospitality House, said it would provide a chance for the more than four hundred youth in the Tenderloin, presently on a "'sabbatical' from responsibility and decision," to regain images of themselves as "functional."[177] Hospitality House director Kay Fullerton thought it was like a "settlement house," an institution in an inner-city area providing educational, recreational, and other social services. Charles Clay, a paid member of the Central City staff, said in 1968, "This place is a substitute for a family—and it's kind of like a common living room."[178] Hospitality House remains active to this day.

Keith St. Clare, Poetry, and *Vanguard Magazine*

A new cadre of young people began joining Vanguard in early 1967, including Keith St. Clare. I conducted an oral history with Keith at his house near San Francisco State University. He told me he grew up in a number of Texas towns in various stages of poverty, including living in a car "and sleeping on couches and all that kind of stuff." For two years, he lived in an orphanage "while the parents were fighting over who was going to get the children and the child support." Keith began studying for the priesthood at age twelve at a seminary across from the orphanage. At eighteen, he enlisted in the Vietnam War. In the course of his service, he read the *Realist*, a counterculture magazine featuring writings by the Beats and homophiles, and began identifying as a pacifist. Keith decamped to San Francisco in 1967 and, with kids he met at Compton's Cafeteria, lived in a gutted floor of a "skid row" hotel. Keith recalled being "hungry and essentially homeless," living one day at a time. Keith told me ministers at Glide Methodist found him a paid job at Intersection for the Arts, where he would read antiwar poetry "in an Air Force T-shirt, so it had some pith and marrow to it." He soon began organizing with Vanguard and editing its magazine.

Keith told me the Central City antipoverty program provided Vanguard a small office in the top floor of the Gayety (later the Gaiety) porn theater: "a little windowless office with a small plexiglass window and not enough room for chairs." The purpose of the office was to "establish peace" between warring factions in the Tenderloin, including bikers, gays, "butch women," and hair fairies. The space offered an alternative to the commercial coffeehouses by offering space for dancing, distributing publications, and celebrations. "We had a couple meals there," Keith said. "People would bring in turkeys and stuff like that. We would have food, and whatever we could get." Keith collated *Vanguard Magazine* at the Gayety using a Gestetner machine he paid for with the money he received when he left the military. He recalls posting signs at Tenderloin Laundromats asking for submissions. The "children of the night" submitted their art, literature, and poetry that "was comparable to," Keith said, "although certainly not as literary as Baudelaire or Genet, Sartre."

Keith also interviewed like a poet, responding to my questions with lyrical responses. As part of my sound check, I asked him what his favorite music was. "My favorite music is . . . silence." What is the date? "It's the twelfth—of Never." I asked for data: how many people, who made donations? Keith seemed less interested in facts than he was the rhythms and sounds of his poetic language—language that seemed designed to deliberately obfuscate. "If all of this seems confusing," Keith told me, "then you understand perfectly." All of this *did* seem confusing. I came in time to appreciate that Keith and other Vanguard informants were offering something more valuable than a staid chronological account of Vanguard's organizational history. By eluding, exceeding, and performatively tripping up my search for evidence, they were at the same time *performing* Vanguard's countercultural politics—a politics that often emphasized a "magical" sense of reality and sought truth in visions, dreams, and other nonrational states.[179] By playing with grammar, metaphor, and meaning, Keith's poetic narration "butt[s] against realism, which is a desire for completeness," and instead suggests a "world beyond," "all the more 'complete' because it cannot be completed."[180]

FIGURES 3.12–3.15. *Top and bottom left:* Cover art from *Vanguard Magazine* 1, no. 6 (ca. April 1967), and 1, no. 8 (ca. June 1967). *Top and bottom right:* Cover art and "Tenderloin Transexual" article from *Vanguard Magazine* 1, no. 9 (ca. July 1967). Courtesy of GLBT Historical Society.

Vanguard organizers enrolled in underground seminaries and were ordained as ministers in the queer street churches I analyze in the previous chapter. In early 1967, after meeting Raymond Broshears at a Vanguard meeting, Adrian Ravarour and his new boyfriend, nineteen-year-old Vanguard organizer Mark Miller, joined Broshears's seminary. According to Adrian, Broshears hoped to ordain gay couples as ministers, who would then go out into the country to form "gay churches," spreading the good word in evangelical fashion. "I thought it was a unique idea," Adrian told me, "and my mate Mark Miller wanted to go to the seminary." The two studied modules in the New and Old Testaments, the history of world religions, Eastern philosophy, Buddhism, and Sufi poetry. Broshears administered ministerial tests that touched on the New and Old Testaments as well as telekinesis, auras, astral projection, Buddhism, and the zodiac.[181] Adrian remembers reading "Madame Blavatsky's Theosophical writings" on metaphysics. "Ray was far out." Broshears ordained Mark and Adrian, bringing them into a brotherhood of activist-ministers.[182]

Adrian told me he walked the streets at night with Broshears and provided the kids referrals to social service organizations. Broshears "carried a wallet that was extremely thick with references. You need a place to stay, he'll look through his wallet, find a place, and get a home for a person for the night. You don't have any money, he'll reach into [his wallet]." If someone didn't have any food, "he would then look through his big notebook in his pocket and find different numbers." He "was the community switchboard before there was a community switchboard." Broshears's "life beatings made him . . . more generous of spirit and compassionate. . . . I saw him cry many times when he encountered people down on their luck and he heard their accounts. He was loud to get a point across . . . but he stood for the people."

Vanguard activist-ministers felt that that religion and movement culture could promote kinship or "brotherhood" among abandoned youth. In 1967 "Brother Mark Miller" wrote a paper for Broshears's seminary titled "Unity." He wrote, "We are not alone. Reach out, touch the hand of your brother and you touch the hand of God." The "key to brotherhood," he wrote, is "the total exclusion of all doubt, desire and ambition. To make a personal contact with another human being is to be sharing the blessings of God."[183] Miller expressed similar ideals in *Vanguard Magazine*. The "individuals in the Vanguard Movement," he wrote in 1967, should "guide each other as a brotherhood of friends." He asked that street kids, who have "the power of people," pledge to "work with one another."[184] Broshears similarly wrote in a 1967 issue of *Vanguard Magazine* that religion can provide feelings of "security" and "kinship with all people."[185]

Keith St. Clare told me he enrolled in Broshears's seminary soon after he arrived in San Francisco. In a December 1967 issue of Broshears's *Light of Understanding* newspaper, Raymond Broshears called St. Clare "the minister to the homosexual minority," someone who would "uplift others who are ashamed of themselves."[186] The Reverend Michael Itkin, a street minister I follow in chapter 2, ordained both Keith and Adrian as ministers. Keith told me that Itkin ordained him with a "formal laying hands on me and some sort of chalice and drinking this and that and he's dressed up and—something like that." Vanguard organizers became ministers in Itkin's Community of Jesus Our Brother, which Itkin noted is "a community of the concerned, ministers to the needs of their brethren even as they themselves are ministered to."[187]

Keith approached the theatricality of religious ritual as part of a larger repertoire of creative expression. He began operating the lights and costumes at a theater on Broadway, a neon-lined stretch of theaters in North Beach, and clothed himself and his other ministers in Franciscan robes discarded from one of their productions. Along with colorful scarves, Keith told me, they "became the trappings of our order." They led services, counseled people, and performed weddings. Organizations like the Universal Life Church, which offered nearly anyone ordination as a minister, democratized access to religious authority. Keith explained, "After all, we were surrounded by individuals [in mainline churches] who had titles and certificates and who had diplomas, and who had paper in frames on their walls. That's what gave them this magic. That they had these things. . . . These certificates and these ordination papers—they've become iconic devices. You need them." Keith and others could claim religious authority by "print[ing] brochures and certificates and banners and buttons and we can take pictures and we can dress up." According to Keith, "it was wonderment in itself."

Vanguard ministers drew on Christian scripture to find value in people deemed worthless. Larry Mamiya wrote in 1967 that the kids may be among the secular "prophets" who were "standing outside the confines of the institutional church," including groups like the freedom riders, the Student Nonviolent Coordinating Committee, and the Artists Liberation Front. "Per-

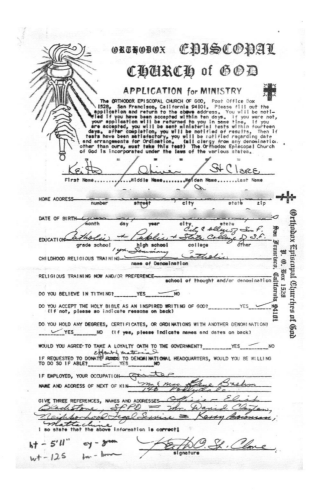

FIGURE 3.16.   Keith St. Clare's application for ministry with Raymond Broshears's Orthodox Episcopal Church of God, ca. 1967. Courtesy
of GLBT Historical Society.

haps I have seen the other prophets in the faces of some of the young people
who live and hustle in the Tenderloin," Mamiya wrote. "They are the ones
who have exhibited a kind of compassion which you and I are afraid to show.
They have allowed as many as eight or more homeless hustlers of Market
Street to sleep on their floors and to share their meals." Some "speak, even
in their personal loneliness, of a love that overcomes the barriers that have
placed them in society's garbage can."[188]

Vanguard organizers argued that kids were not undesirable blights on a downtown primed for redevelopment but young adults with worth, and potential collaborators in the district's revitalization. Their success was limited in this regard: the city began razing the meat rack in the summer of 1967, contributing to Vanguard's unraveling. The construction of Bay Area Rapid Transit, designed to funnel workers from the suburbs to downtown offices, tore up Market Street.[189] Guy Strait noted in 1967 that "the Gallencamp's shoe store (where all the less particular drag's bought their spikes), the news stand, the Plush Doggie, The Cavalier, are scheduled to be demolished." This was "the crux of the Meat Market and it will go away."[190] The city began demolishing a vast plot of the South of Market "skid row" and redeveloping it as the Yerba Buena Center.[191] As developers razed the central city, the Tenderloin absorbed many of the displaced and increasingly became a violent, low-income "landscape of despair."[192]

Sustained police sweeps, which accompanied redevelopment projects, appear to have contributed to a district that observers considered increasingly dangerous. "Market Street looks like a bombed out no man's land," a 1968 report from a minister read. "The 'enemy' [police] is everywhere, determined to 'clean up the Tenderloin.'" White gay youth in particular fled an increasingly violent Tenderloin for the countercultural Haight-Ashbury or relatively upscale Polk Street. Keith St. Clare told me that a fight broke out between bikers and hair fairies at the Gaiety Theater in 1967; he was soon on the street with printouts of "our next and least professional issue" of *Vanguard Magazine*. Keith told me he moved to the Haight-Ashbury and began publishing *Vanguard Magazine* in a building occupied by the Angels of Light and other counterculture luminaries.[193] Joel said that he left the Tenderloin and moved into a Students for a Democratic Society building in the Haight, occasionally returning to the Tenderloin. "Even though there's more opportunities . . . in the Haight-Ashbury," he told me, "I'm not giving up on those kids [in the Tenderloin]. But gradually what is happening in the Haight is much more interesting to me."

Conflicts over leadership also contributed to Vanguard's dissolution in the summer of 1967, about a year after it formed. Street youth "have an innate dislike for superstructure," according to a July 1967 issue of *Vanguard Magazine*. "Regretfully, organization brings about inequality. Inequality breeds distrust, discord; dissimulation. Eventually any leader will commit an error of judgment, misuse power, or fall victim to rumor; then the community will vanish." The magazine "has recorded the fluctuating passions, loyalties, and diversions of the T.L.'s children. Dynasties have risen and fallen with amazing ease. No single group has ever been able to serve all of their variances. No one has given unity."[194] Larry Mamiya attributed tension over leadership to the fact that many kids had been thrown out of homes and been stripped of status and authority. "Leadership positions were one of the few status positions that these kids had," he told me. "A lot of them come from unstable backgrounds, [and] that instability showed in the conflicts that they had. A lot of backbiting, spreading of rumors, that kind of thing." Two former members were far blunter in 1967: "Never will the youth of SF be anything but petty people and bitch fights."[195]

This conflict erupted into the present when two of my informants demanded that I recognize them as Vanguard's sole founder. When I told one narrator about a competing claim, he became enraged and cut off communication. Another informant sent me more than 150 emails from 2009 to 2014, most of them demanding that I name him founder. In the summer of 2013, a person claiming to be his lawyer called and told me it was "defamatory" to present him as "anything other than the adult founder of Vanguard." The conflict that erupted via our oral history encounters is ultimately about desire for authority. "It's really painful," one informant told me, "to not have social status." The emotional intensity of these encounters suggests that the traumatic dimensions of Vanguard's activism are not relegated to the past but can also be felt in the present.

While Vanguard was short-lived, street kids continued to organize mutual-aid programs in the Tenderloin. In the summer of 1967, for example, a group called the "Street Prophets" began serving a donation-only dinner at Glide Methodist and volunteering at Hospitality House. According to *Vanguard Magazine*, the Street Prophets were "creat[ing] a community feeling which is reminiscent of the best days of the Vanguard organization." Most of its members were "gay, impoverished and emotionally unstable" and were "dedicated to a multi-front improvement right on the local scene." Like Vanguard, the magazine predicted, the Street Prophets would dissolve in time. "However, that does not imply that it is not important. It is! It is the most important thing on the scene today."[196]

Historians claim Vanguard as one of the first gay liberation organizations in the United States because of its embrace of New Left ideology, its "militantly unapologetic tone," and its demands for "revolutionary change."[197]

But Vanguard is not a story about gay liberation or a gay rights movement that has seen incredible progress for (some) gays and lesbians. It is instead a story about economic and social inequality that has only grown more pronounced since the 1960s. Indeed, as I was conducting oral histories with Vanguard veterans, I was also out on the streets of the Tenderloin talking with kids whose lives shared uncanny similarities with the organizers of the 1960s. I developed a reenactment project in collaboration with marginally housed youth to examine links between past and present, an experimental project I present in the following "intervention."

Intervention   1.   Vanguard   Revisited

ON NOVEMBER 2, 2010, 54 percent of San Francisco voters approved a "sit/lie" ordinance that criminalized sitting and lying on city sidewalks between 7 a.m. and 11 p.m.[1] Sit/lie originated with complaints about street kids in the Haight-Ashbury district but quickly became a proxy for discussion about street youth in the city as a whole. Those promoting the law cast street kids as dangerous and criminal, their arrests necessary for public safety. An article in the *Wall Street Journal* called sit/lie an effort to "take back [the] streets" from "aggressive young vagrants."[2] After the ordinance passed, the gay Castro district became one site of police sweeps targeting street youth, many of them trans and of color, at the behest of white middle-class residents, most of whom were gay men. The Merchants of Upper Market and Castro supported the sit/lie ordinance, as did the Castro's gay representative on the Board of Supervisors.[3] While kids around the country fled to San Francisco because of its reputation as a safe haven, many found that their marked class, race, and gender identities positioned them as outsiders in a neighborhood they had imagined as their "gay mecca."

Homeless and marginally housed youth organized to tell a different story about their lives and worth. On May 14, 2011, roughly forty young people marched from the Tenderloin to the Castro. They pushed large brooms down the sidewalks, from the Pottery Barn to the iconic Castro Theater, holding signs that read "Housing = Safety" and chanting, "We won't be swept off the streets." This symbolic act of defiance, referencing the police sweeps that often targeted street kids, positioned them not as "trash" to be swept away but as people with worth and value. Some made a performance of it, turning a domestic task into a queer art form. "Work it, girl!" one young person shouted. "Work that broom!" The sweep was part of a day of actions designed to bring attention to budget cuts to social service organizations, demand housing and employment opportunities for homeless youth, and, most pointedly, put an end to sit/lie.[4]

As part of a historical reenactment project I launched in 2010, called "Vanguard Revisited," the sweep also consciously linked past and present, as it reenacted the 1966 Vanguard street sweep I analyze in the previous chapter. At a rally after the sweep, a nineteen-year-old trans activist named Mia Tu Mutch picked up a bullhorn and explained the significance of the reenactment. "In the sixties," she said, "Vanguard swept the streets to say, 'This is our community. You think it's disgusting, but this is our home. We value this, and we're actually going to clean up the filth that's on the ground, not the filth that are people, because people have value.'" Contemporary youth brought the sweep "back to life" to show they have "an investment" in the city. Kids "get harassed constantly by shopkeepers," Mia said, "and it's very evident that young queer people aren't welcomed in the Castro if you don't have money." Reenacting the action was "moving" but also highlighted persistent inequalities. "We're still protesting against laws that keep poor people down and keep queer people down in the one city in the US that's supposed to be our safe haven."

Vanguard Revisited

In this intervention, I show how Vanguard Revisited youth performed the Tenderloin's "countermemories": subversive histories that are not always discursively transmitted but are passed down and "publicly enacted by the bodies that bear its consequences."[5] Instead of simply transmitting historical evidence *to* contemporary youth, I developed a project that enlisted youth in documenting, interpreting, and performing the Tenderloin's history in relation to their own lives. Contemporary youth drew genealogical connections between themselves and youth in the 1960s, illuminating continuities and discontinuities in the lives of street kids over the previous fifty years.

FIGURE INTER1.1.   Vanguard "Sweep-In," ca. September 1966. From *Vanguard Magazine* 1, no. 2 (October 1966). Photographer unknown. Courtesy of GLBT Historical Society.

FIGURE INTER1.2.   Vanguard Revisited "Sweep-In," May 14, 2011. Photograph by
Matt Baume.

Through street theater, walking tours, and artistic productions, they revealed family rejection, economic deprivation, and anti-trans policing as structural continuities between the Tenderloin of the 1960s and the contemporary district. Just as importantly, they demonstrated that the shared set of morally inflected conventions around resource sharing, mutual protection, self-policing, and other survival strategies continued to animate the Tenderloin in the 2010s.

I launched the project at a time when San Francisco was increasingly organized to serve the social and economic interests of its white, wealthy residents in the growing technology sector. The city passed laws and policies designed to make it attractive to global capital, including tax breaks for corporations and tech companies, the privatization of public services, and policing strategies designed to drive perceived sources of disorder from gentrifying public spaces.[6] The gay rights movement's turn toward a politics of neoliberalism—privatized family rights, formal legal equality, state protections, and market visibility—further endangered those most vulnerable to regimes of homophobia. The rise of real estate, gay commodified businesses, and gentrified cities, Martin Manalansan argues, "are based on the very process of eradication and disappearance of the unsightly, the vagrant, the alien, the colored, and the queer."[7]

I conceived of Vanguard Revisited after locating in the GLBT Historical Society archive a dozen screen-printed copies of *Vanguard Magazine*, which young activists produced in 1966 and 1967. The beautifully constructed magazines called to me because of their blunt depictions of poverty, sex, and religion in the Tenderloin. What I found most surprising about *Vanguard Magazine* were the uncanny parallels between the Tenderloin of the mid-1960s and the Tenderloin of the early 2010s. Young adults in the 1960s flocked to San Francisco because of its reputation as a haven for outcasts. Attracted by the cheap housing, prostitution economy, and the anonymity of the central city, they pooled their money for food and housing and banded together for survival. As opposed to narratives that circulate widely today of dramatic improvements in the lives of queer people, and young people in particular, I found that disenfranchised people—especially trans women, immigrants, and people of color—continued to flock to the Tenderloin. Although there were critical differences between the kids of the 1960s and 2010s, the passage of "sit/lie" demonstrated that they continued to be deemed undesirable by the city, redevelopers, and many business owners, and were policed as such.

I began sharing these archival documents with the Reverend Megan Rohrer, a trans minister and activist in her early thirties who worked at a church off Polk Street. I felt that Megan, as executive director of WELCOME, a faith-based Tenderloin nonprofit providing social services to people experiencing homelessness, embodied the history of progressive, faith-based organizing I encountered in the archive. I began sharing archival documents with Megan, who found these documents compelling. Over dinner or on the street, we would imaginatively pair characters from the contemporary Tenderloin with uncannily similar characters from the Tenderloin's past. We saw similarities between the Reverend River Sims and the Reverend Raymond Broshears, for example, and between the antipoverty organizer Mark Forrester and a contemporary trans antipoverty activist who went by the name Beck. Megan and I discussed the possibility of creatively reconstituting Vanguard. I raised $20,000 from foundations and LGBTQ agencies. Megan and I started bringing together the actors and props we would need to creatively reenact Vanguard.

We ultimately structured the project as an imagined, cross-temporal conversation between two cohorts of Tenderloin youth: one that in 1966 founded Vanguard and another that in 2011 creatively "reconstituted" the organization by reenacting its street theater, artistic productions, and organizational structure. We hired Mia Tu Mutch, a firebrand trans activist who organized a weekly arts and activism program at the San Francisco LGBT Center, as our paid youth intern and developed partnerships with Larkin Street Youth, the city's largest homeless youth service provider; Faithful Fools, a faith-based drop-in center; Hospitality House, a twenty-four-hour service center; and RoadDawgz, a drop-in center located in the Hospitality House basement. We recruited youth through these organizations and held weekly meetings in their office and drop-in spaces. While queer scholars such as Myrl Beam show that the expansion of the nonprofit system—and its pernicious effect on queer politics—is an engine of homonormativity, we did not feel that collaboration with nonprofits was in contradiction with the spirit of the original Vanguard, which itself incorporated as a nonprofit organization in 1967.[8]

Megan, Mia, and I worked with a core group of young organizers—about eight to twelve people in all—though a much larger number participated in project events and direct actions. Most were people of color and trans women between the ages of sixteen and twenty-four. Many lived in emergency housing or SRO hotel rooms operated by nonprofit organizations. While I was initially surprised that several straight-identified youth showed up to meetings and participated in the project, I came in time to understand that the kids on the street didn't always define group identity based on shared sexual or gender identities but based on a shared sense of "disenfranchisement," as one young person characterized it at a project meeting.

Youth received stipends in exchange for their participation in street theater, self-defense trainings, intergenerational conversations, historical walking tours, and the creation of a historical "zine" that linked past and present. We asked youth to take leadership positions by facilitating meetings, defining project goals, and proposing project components. Mia's involvement likely assured many young people who may have been distrustful of Megan and me—both of us white, housed people in our early thirties. We held ongoing conversations about ways to increase youth power, including youth veto power on all project decisions, youth-led meetings, and gatherings at drop-in spaces rather than established nonprofit organizations.

FIGURE INTER1.3.   Vanguard Revisited project masthead combining photos of Vanguard Revisited participants and people working for the Central City Target Area, including Vanguard president J. P. Marat (*top center*). Courtesy of GLBT Historical Society.

Vanguard Revisited Magazine

Megan, Mia, and I began by presenting copies of *Vanguard Magazine* to roughly a dozen young people at Larkin Street Youth and talking with them about the possibility of creating a new magazine "in conversation" with the 1960s publications. One young man said it should be based on the same topics as the original magazine but about a "different era." Another said it should "enlighten youth, celebrate the *Vanguard Magazine*," and be "as blunt and honest as possible." Many participants felt excluded by the mainstreaming and whitening of gay politics. An increasingly neoliberal gay rights movement stressed marriage equality and service in the military instead of youth homelessness and economic justice.[9] The "mainstream gay movement," one young person said, was "leaving people out" and throwing marginalized people "under a rug." The magazine should be a voice for these people. Not all submissions needed to be written by queer or trans people, another person offered. They "should be written by disenfranchised youth," or those marginalized by race, class, or homelessness. The group eventually settled on themes to explore in a new magazine: faith and queer theology, loneliness and community, poverty and social stigma, drug use and sex work, sexuality and gender, and direct action.

A core group of young adults spent the next three months choosing articles, poems, and pieces of art from the original magazines and producing their own writings, art, or poetry "in conversation" with their chosen source documents. They also recruited contributors through their connections on the street, at social service organizations, through activist organizations like the Homeless Youth Alliance, and by talking with youth in areas where they were known to congregate. Because the original *Vanguard Magazine* included writings by queer urban ministers and antipoverty activists, we also asked contemporary adult organizers to submit writings and artwork. The group then collaboratively produced a new sixty-page publication, *Vanguard Revisited Magazine*, that combined material from the original magazine with submissions from contemporary Tenderloin denizens.

One of our core participants—a black, twenty-one-year-old gay man from Atlanta who went by the name Gotti—summarized the magazine goals in a letter addressed to the original 1960s Vanguard organizers. The letter begins:

My Darling VanGuard...

This is a Piece of Literature written in the mindset of rebellion...for oppression still reeks in the era I live.... before I lived in the T.L. I lived in a place where the rebel who speaks to you now... was confined with no way to express so much of what I feel and deal being... solely who I am.... Until I made a pilgrimage to San Francisco, and in the heart of the tenderloin I heard of "The Vanguard Boys"... I read your words and heard your voices in the depths of my soul, and now I wish to give you mine.... to [be] a part of what you started long ago. To see our hearts collide on paper. [10]

As such, the magazine manifested what scholar Carolyn Dinshaw calls a "queer desire for history," the longing to "collaps[e] time through affective contact between marginalized people now and then." [11]

The "collision of hearts on paper" revealed family rejection, economic deprivation, and social trauma as structural continuities between the Tenderloin of the 1960s and that of the contemporary district. For example, we paired the Reverend Raymond Broshears's 1967 essay titled "Loneliness in the Tenderloin" with the Reverend Megan Rohrer's response, an article titled "Tenderloin in the Loneliness." Broshears commented on the pervasive desire for "intimate relationships" in the Tenderloin and the difficulties he and other abandoned people had in creating them. Rohrer's 2010 article similarly argued that "the greatest poverty issue San Franciscans of all income levels face is loneliness." Living in the Tenderloin for seven years, "I've discovered that there are times when the Tenderloin makes the loneliness easier. It's a neighborhood that wears its loneliness, perversion, poverty, and sexuality on its sleeve. Sometimes the grime and the grit reminds me, that even in my deepest loneliness, I am still very well off. But I also see, in those who call me pastor, that the Tenderloin's above and underground economies are designed to feed off of the loneliness, destitution and desperation of the lonely souls who have been thrown away by families, society and in some cases their congregations."[12] We also reprinted a 1966 article from *Vanguard Magazine* that described an "economic system which youth can enter into very easily" in the Tenderloin, composed of prostitution, "drug abuse, and theft [which] may be considered by-products of a situation which begins by being without a family, without money, and without employability."[13]

The writings by contemporary queer youth reflected a sharp contrast between the lives of the authors and the newer public image of the "homonormative" subject. Gotti, in an article titled "Address to the People," acknowledged that LGBTQ issues were in the "public eye" but argued that people still considered street kids to be "a thing of darkness and of the night" or "fallen angels susceptible to perversion and drug addictions." Street kids

> are suffering dearly. If you don't have HIV, you have a serious drug addiction. . . . Could you deny that maybe we make it easy for the world to look at us as citizens of Sodom and Gomorra? Not wholeheartedly I can't. But in my ranting and raving . . . hope remains. Through all of the self-destructive beauty I have seen here in the Tenderloin I know goodness still remains among us. . . . people care to see us see our dreams and ambitions no matter how creative or outlandish, become real if we only need try. . . . We are shedding our blood wastefully and I will not stand for it . . . not when I have discovered people like the "vanguard boys," not after I left my life behind in another place far from San Francisco in search of a place to express all that lingers in my heart painfully, not after overcoming the fear and self-doubt! We are . . . angels who rise and achieve like any other.[14]

Contemporary youth identified with ongoing histories of mutual aid and activism. We paired a 1967 essay titled "People Power" with a contemporary article titled "People Power Continued." The 1967 essay by a Vanguard organizer read, "In an effort to establish identity, in order to give purpose to heretofore bitter lives, a small group of people have united in a single cause: to better themselves, to better their city, to better their nation, and, ultimately, all mankind. These individuals of the Vanguard Movement, idealists of the slums, have banded together to promote an environment of love and understanding between all peoples of the earth."[15] One young person responded with an essay titled "People Power Continued," noting that political activism was the main reason why youth produced *Vanguard Magazine* in the 1960s: "We are still fighting for equality, yet fifty years later we stand waiting for equality. San Francisco has broken a lot of those barriers. Yes, we can hold hands and kiss in public, but the mentality and the lack of education and open-mindedness has still failed us poorly. There are still people out there who want to postpone our equal rights. . . . This makes me wonder whether society knows anything about change, since the richest people in America usually make the rules and regulations."[16]

We paired Mark Forrester's 1966 essay "Central City: Profile of Despair," published in the first issue of *Vanguard Magazine*, and a response by Beck, a trans antipoverty organizer who became involved with the project, titled "Pt. 2 Profile of Desperation." Forrester wrote about the similarities he saw between the so-called skid row "derelicts" on Sixth Street and the hustler on the nearby meat rack. "In the youth and aged alike, you can read a terrible loneliness, a sense of futility, endless boredom, and the ennui of a waiting for the next happening. Somehow it is almost like a suspension of caring for self or others." But in the central city, "human beings are working out the riddles of personal existence, in ways that often shock yet still retain a flavor of committment [*sic*]." Forrester argued that the "real derelicts of this society" are the businessmen, white people who chant "white power" in the face of civil rights, those who wage war, and those who "pollute the air." They "hurt almost everyone else that they touch: the negro, the poor, the queers, the outcasts."[17] Beck responded to Forrester by writing about an expanding prison system, economic inequality, and the "poor young queens" who "fight tirelessly to get the scraps they need to survive from overworked non-profiteers, trekking from shelter to shelter, wondering where they would go from here." It's been fifty years since the first Vanguard flames, Beck wrote. "It's time to combine fires and to begin demanding humanity on the streets of San Francisco for the Outcasts, the Immigrant, the Black, the Queer, the Transgender, the Poor. Otherwise, the wait will slowly burn us from inside and from without."[18]

Gotti created the front and back cover art for *Vanguard Revisited Magazine*: a bleak collage in which a male figure holds his bleeding face while kneeling in front of a landscape littered with the bodies of dead men. A Christian fundamentalist holds a sign: "No Special Laws for Fags." Gotti talked with me about his illustration in an oral history interview. "When it comes to religion," he told me, "gay is just not depicted in a positive light." He pointed out the black background in the collage. "Gays are viewed in darkness." But Gotti found power in the story of Christ. "You can feel like you're being beaten, or being crucified, in other words, and that you've been forsaken by God." The "story of Jesus Christ is actually a perfect one." Christ went through "torture in order to assume the throne—or be crowned. And that, metaphorically speaking, resonated with me inside." Gotti told me about his experience of the project as a whole: "It was close to around the time that I was basically new here to San Francisco. I was really trying to pull my act together . . . and I knew then that any venue would help me. So I actually attached to this very quickly, because for one, I got to curse and I got to say whatever I felt without feeling like basically an outcast, so I just took that and ran with it."

The magazine project culminated with a release party, in February 2011, at St. Francis Lutheran Church, where we handed out about one thousand copies of the magazine to youth and veteran activists.

Project components following the release party included discussion groups, self-defense trainings, interactive historical tours of the Tenderloin, documentary screenings, and intergenerational conversations between young adults and veteran activists from the 1960s. At one gathering, for example, we screened Susan Stryker's documentary *Screaming Queens*, about the 1966 Compton's Cafeteria riots, with Felicia Elizondo, one of the film's narrators. In a discussion after the screening, one young person noted that a trans woman in the 1960s felt that "cops didn't treat us like we were human." She felt this continued to be true of the contemporary Tenderloin. "There have been many gay rights advances, but I think that's one of the things that hasn't changed: this very in-your-face further criminalization of poor people. Whether it's giving crazy crimes for people not being able to pay their bus fare, just all these little things that we have in place within San Francisco . . . that keep poor people poor." Another young adult agreed. "Our struggles are not just queer struggles," they said, "but poor struggles. Our roots are in the Tenderloin, not in the Castro, like we've been told."

FIGURE INTER1.4.   *Vanguard Revisited Magazine* cover, 2011.

Many Vanguard Revisited youth saw few substantive changes in the lives of Tenderloin street kids from the 1960s to the 2010s. "There's still your [SRO apartments]," one young person said at a project meeting, "there's still your heavy drug traffic, there's still your hustling." A young hustler felt that the kids founded Vanguard in the 1960s because of "very similar issues" he faced in the 2010s, including police abuse and familial rejection. "Power dynamics haven't changed, drug abuse hasn't changed," he said at a meeting. "My story isn't that much different than what [Vanguard youth] went through a long time ago." If contemporary youth felt disempowered by these similarities, they also found power in ongoing histories of mutual aid

FIGURE INTER1.5.   Vanguard Revisited participants at magazine release party, 2011.

FIGURE INTER1.6.   Vanguard Revisited walking tour flyer, 2011.

and kinship. Vanguard was about "struggle and sense of family," one young person said. "Everyone's been through so much hardship, and what it really gets down to is hardship, integrity, the ability to survive, and giving a shit about other people." Through Vanguard Revisited, "I was able to be part of that story, of that history in some way."

Mia Tu Mutch

Mia and I recorded an oral history after months of working together. I was struck by similarities between her story and those of the original 1960s Vanguard organizers. Mia told me she was assigned male at birth and was raised by "very conservative GOP Republican Southern Baptist parents, who, as I got older, didn't accept who I was." Her parents forced her to attend "de-gayification counseling" and "masculinity classes." She often left those sessions feeling suicidal. "In the notes that they gave you, that are very nasty, like very demeaning to women, the whole time I would pretend that I was writing notes and in all the blanks I would just fill in 'love.' Like 'love, love,

love.' Because to me, it was like, the only thing that would get me through this is knowing that later in life, people were going to love and accept me, and like fucking celebrate like who I am."

Mia drew strength from her religious background. "I grew up in a church that my parents had been going to for twenty years," she told me, "and I was always very active. I was on all of these leadership teams, I was in choir, and from a very young age I was very spiritual, I was very emotional, I was empathetic." Her parents thought she was going to be a missionary. "They always thought that I was going to do big things for other people, that I was gonna give my life to other people to, you know, to show my love for humanity, and to show my love for people, and to make the world a better place." Mia felt she was doing just that through her political organizing. "I came to queer organizing after escaping the degayification classes and the masculinity classes. And I always felt, you know, 'how did I survive,' [and] I wanted to go back for the people who are still in that."

After high school, Mia packed her things into "two little suitcases" and caught a plane to San Francisco. "I always wanted to move out, and in my mind, it was always San Francisco or Los Angeles, somewhere in California where there was sun and gay people. . . . When I moved to San Francisco, I felt like I was a new person. . . . People knew I was trans, but they didn't know my former name, they didn't know what city I was from, they didn't know all the trials that I'd been through." She renamed herself to start a new life. "I didn't want to forget all the bad things that happened to me. I wanted to take an active stance in reclaiming and using those things for good. And part of that was taking on the name Mia Tu Mutch, and reclaiming the fact that they said for the first eighteen years that I was 'too much,' and that was a horrible thing, and that I should be ashamed of being so over-the-top and being so flamboyant. And I took it back. And now people love that, and every time I introduce myself as Mia Tu Mutch, people say, 'Yes, yes you are. Of course you are.'"

Mia gravitated toward the Tenderloin, where she could afford to share an SRO studio with a friend. Finding a job was difficult during her transition. She was evicted from her apartment and slept in bathrooms and on friends' couches. But she found strength in the Tenderloin. The district "was supposed to be a place that I was supposed to clutch my purse tighter, a place that I was supposed to walk faster just to get through it." But it felt like a home. "I've experienced a lot of generosity and compassion from people that I'm taught to be scared of. . . . Seeing so many trans women on the corners," she said, "and just walking around during broad daylight, like I was like, oh, this is where I'm supposed to be. This is my community." The Tenderloin also helped her embrace a trans identity. "I got a lot of strength out of walking in the Tenderloin and at any given moment there would be three trans women walking across the street. Like I got a lot of strength out of, 'yes my life is hard, yes I don't know how I'm going to pay for rent this month.' But I see that trans girl over there and see her life is like that too, probably. And she's doing it, and I can do it too."

Mia felt that the kids in the Tenderloin continued to have each other's backs. "The street kids definitely have a sense of family and community," she said. "And trans women in the Tenderloin also have a strong sense of community." Trans sex workers have to "fight for money," she said. "All the sex workers go to the same four or five corners to fight for the same amount of money from the johns. I think that could divide us. But I think that ultimately, at the end of the day, the trans women are all going to see each other again, we're all going to be nice to each other, and if some john is trying to beat a girl up, you best believe a girl's going to come over there with her heels and defend her sister." Most of her friends are trans or queer, have engaged in sex work, are people of color and organizers. What brings them together, Mia felt, "is that we are different. . . . We all have been through stuff, [but] we all ultimately have each other's back when bad things go down."

She contrasted her experiences in the Tenderloin with the Castro, "where a lot of the gay youth sleep on the streets. I guess that they assume that they're going to get more compassion and more money from people walking by. Although my experience has been that the reaction is a lot more harsh from within the gay community, 'cause it's like 'you're making us look bad.' Like, 'you're poor, just go hide yourself, we don't want to see you here.'" She told me about an outside seating area, at the corner of Market and Castro.

Whenever youth try to access that space . . . they routinely get harassed by upper-middle-class gay men in the Castro, and also by the police who say you don't belong here. . . . And I think that was something that the Vanguard youth fought for in the sixties. One of the major things that they had on their list of demands was to have a coffeehouse, a meeting place where people could go and hang out any time, and a place where they could do organizing. And I think that we still, to some extent, lack that in San Francisco because anywhere that you want to meet you have to pay for the rental space or you have to pay for food and beverages to sit down.

As reflected in Mia's oral history, many young adults felt alienated not only from the heteronormative environments from which they escaped but also from the mainstream gay spaces and neighborhoods that some academics call "homonormative."[19] Many associated this politics with the Castro, which gained prominence as San Francisco's premiere gay neighborhood by the mid-1970s. As Christina Hanhardt notes, the Castro would not so much replace the Tenderloin as it would mark the fact that certain forms of homosexuality, especially those associated with whiteness, were no longer associated with urban "vice" and disorder. Many of the white and middle-class gay liberationists in the Castro would see the places and people of the Tenderloin as self-destructive, stuck in the past of new performances of pride.[20] By the 2010s, the Castro was populated primarily by white middle-class men and became the site of the targeting of street youth, many of whom were of color, in the name of public safety.

A bisexual woman at one meeting remarked on this dynamic at a project meeting: "It's the same people being targeted [through police sweeps in the 1960s and today], but in different ways. And sometimes it's our own [LGBTQ] community doing the targeting." The gay community "is fragmented in many ways," said a young man. "The primary one being forgetting about bad things that are going on in your community, be it HIV, drug addiction, or homelessness. They cut themselves off from it." Many young people felt left out of this mainstreaming of gay politics.

Megan, Mia, and I intended for Vanguard Revisited to inspire activism that would address these issues. We often opened meetings by presenting archival documents or oral history audio describing conflicts in the 1960s familiar to Tenderloin youth—police street sweeps, anti-vice campaigns, and the use of lewd-vagrancy and other laws to criminalize homosexual use of public space. Discussion about the policing in the 1960s often led to discussions of contemporary policing of public space, especially sit/lie, one of many anti-homeless laws throughout the United States designed to expel, punish, or otherwise discourage the presence of people deemed "undesirable" in public spaces.[21] Vanguard's successful efforts in the 1960s to foster community dialogue and police cooperation suggested alternatives to policing of public space in the 2010s.

Vanguard Revisited participants proposed a number of actions to respond to the criminalization of street youth in the Castro, including a performance in whiteface to highlight racial discrimination, setting up debate tables to increase understanding between queer youth and elders, and an action involving cardboard boxes to dramatize the need for improved housing. Ultimately, youth decided to organize a street sweep from the Tenderloin to the Castro, which would offer backtalk to historical narratives of gay progress that trace a monolithic community from the ghetto to respectable citizenship. The sweep reenactment dramatized the fact that the progress of a gay movement intent on state recognition and legal enfranchisement has been highly uneven, benefiting "housed" populations far more than those on the economic margins.

At a rally following the street sweep, a trans, marginally housed youth named Taylor picked up a loudspeaker to address the crowd. "Thousands of homeless queer youth sleep on the streets," she said. She noted that "cleaning the streets can make a city more appealing to tourists and potential new residents, but at what cost? Livelihood, safety, or even the sanity of a homeless youth?" And "even if we do find a place indoors . . . just because a building is abandoned yet infinitely safer than the not-so-great outdoors, we still get in trouble for it. All because we're trying to find a safe place to rest." She concluded, "Just because we're homeless doesn't make us any better or worse than those that are housed; just because we're queer doesn't make us any less deserving of anything than those who feel they aren't; just because we're youth doesn't mean we lack the experience or drive to get everything together."

Mia Tu Mutch spoke next. "Forty percent of homeless youth are LGBT, and there are fifty-seven hundred homeless youth in San Francisco," she said. "The top three needs in the queer community isn't marriage. It sure as hell isn't Don't Ask, Don't Tell. What we deserve as queer young people is supportive, family-style housing. That means that SROs aren't enough. Staying in a hotel where you don't even have a kitchen is not enough." The kids "don't need to be on the streets, we don't need emergency housing," she said. "We need safe housing."

By embodying a history stretching back half a century, Tenderloin youth prioritized economic and racial justice at a time when representations of queer life increasingly revolved around privatized family life and conspicuous consumption. They made visible the costs of the politics of neoliberalism as it manifested in LGBTQ politics and urban spatial practices, a politics that obscures the struggles of queer and trans people most vulnerable to regimes of state violence: the poor, the homeless, and the gender nonnormative among them. "Social negativity clings not only to these figures," Heather Love argues, "but also to those who lived before the common era of gay liberation—the abject multitude against whose experience we define our own liberation."[22] Given the new opportunities available to *some* LGBTQ people, the temptation to forget the humiliations of queer history and to ignore the ongoing suffering of those excluded by the rising tide of gay normalization is stronger than ever. In 2010, Vanguard Revisited youth demanded that we remember the Tenderloin's history of marginalization and resistance and care for those people who continued to survive in this zone of abandonment.

4.   The   Urban   Cowboy   and
the   Irish   Immigrant

FROM THE LATE 1960s through the 1970s, sustained police sweeps and redevelopment projects displaced the kids' scene from the Mid-Market meat rack to the Polk Street corridor, on the western fringe of the Tenderloin. From the 1970s through the 2000s, Polk Street's vice economies and material infrastructure—gay bars, nightclubs, SRO hotels, and cheap restaurants—called to young people across the country. "Every gay kid in the country knows about Polk Street," a gay activist told the *Los Angeles Times* in 1986. By gathering in protective street families, many migrants found a refuge and home, but life on Polk Street was precarious. "[They think] they're going to survive on their own," the activist said. "That's their fantasy. Some manage to survive. Some don't."[1]

In this chapter, I draw on oral histories and archival research to tell the stories of two white male migrants who attempted to survive on Polk Street in the 1980s and 1990s, stories that dramatize the promises and perils of the kids' performative economy.

I first tell the story of a thirteen-year-old boy, Coy Ellison, who escaped an abusive adoptive father in the late 1970s and hitchhiked west, lured to San Francisco by stories of peace and love. Joining the kids on Polk Street, he changed his name, affected an Irish accent, and began passing himself off as an "illegal Irish immigrant" on the run. The anonymity helped him dodge police who had previously returned him to an abusive home, and the "roaming gypsy" persona endeared him to bartenders who found him under-the-table employment in gay bars. Most importantly, the persona—which Coy developed over twenty years as a bartender and bouncer in the Tenderloin and on Polk Street—enabled him to confront and reinterpret the abuse from which he was running. Polk Street, he told me, was a great place to "find yourself."

I then tell the story of a nineteen-year-old, Corey Longseeker, who, in the early 1980s, escaped a fundamentalist family and charted a course to California. His blond hair and movie-star good looks made him an instant celebrity on Polk Street. With the "sponsorship" of wealthy men, he adorned himself with snakeskin boots and cruised the street in his own "mustang ford," reinventing himself as an "urban cowboy." In his heyday, Corey apparently made more money than many of Polk Street's aboveground businesses, but his decline was as swift and dramatic as his rise. By the time I met him in 2008, at age thirty-nine, Corey had been diagnosed with schizophrenia, compounded by years of methamphetamine use and AIDS-related complications—a triple diagnosis that was common on Polk Street. The street, many told me, was an easy place to "lose yourself."

Coy's and Corey's performances took on meaning via a performative economy that had long valued the paradox of masquerade. In this chapter, I situate their stories and performances in the broader economic and cultural history of Polk Street, from the 1960s to the 1990s, weaving in cultural history, social analysis, and psychological insight to conceptualize the rise and fall of a historically and geographically specific site in which the kids' scene took root. I analyze the emergence of a (primarily white) gay male economy in the 1960s and 1970s and show how the stock characters of the urban cowboy and the Irish immigrant, both of them reliant on tropes of white male masculinity, were the labor that brought my informants the recognition and support of Polk Street's primarily white bartenders, business owners, and johns. Finally, I show how two devastating epidemics—HIV/AIDS and methamphetamine—undermined the economic viability of Polk Street's vice economy and undercut the reciprocities, obligations, and moral norms that comprised the performative economy. An increasingly desperate population began competing for dwindling resources, leading to an environment many kids considered unsafe and exploitative.

Sweet Lips and Coy Ellison

In 2008 I set up an interview with the retired bartender, gossip columnist, and gay activist Richard Walters, better known in San Francisco as Sweet Lips for his acid wit. Sweet Lips was one of the bartenders who in 1962 formed the Tavern Guild, the nation's first gay business association, which formed to counter police harassment of gay bars, Alcoholic Beverage Control actions, and the chronic unemployment faced by gay bartenders.[2] I was excited to record Sweet Lips' oral history, but by the time I met him at his Polk Street apartment, he was in his mideighties and suffering from early-stage Alzheimer's. He had a difficult time remembering his past, much less recounting it. Sweet Lips' caregiver, a gay man in his forties named Coy Ellison, gently intervened and coached him through well-worn stories. "He's the oldest living writer for the *B.A.R.*," Coy said, referring to the city's gay newspaper, the *Bay Area Reporter*. "The first writer," Sweet Lips shot back. I asked Sweet Lips how they first met. "I don't know," he said. "We first met, where?" Coy suggested: "Were you working at the RendezVous?" Sweet Lips said, "I think so. And I wanted to give you a blowjob and you said, 'Get away from me.'" He laughed. Coy added, "When you said teeth optional, scared the daylights out of me."

In the process of helping Sweet Lips recount his personal history, Coy began telling his own. "I was basically a runaway all the time that would come to San Francisco," he told me. "Stop off at Denver, come to San Francisco. You could basically market yourself into a job in any situation on Polk Street, because it was a working-class neighborhood. If they knew you were willing to work, the bartenders would hook you up with a job and that's how I got to working with the bars. True, there were hustlers, there were both straight, gay, whatever, transgender, going up and down the street all trying to find themselves." Coy told me Sweet Lips was one of the bartenders who found him under-the-table work as a kid. "He was one of the people that would tell other customers, 'This guy could basically carry wood up for your fireplace for you.' He would set jobs for me." Now their roles were reversed as Coy cared for the aging Sweet Lips.

> It wasn't until later on in life that I became his caregiver. . . . I've been excited to hear all his stories from World War II up and the different areas in the city. It makes me very proud to have a sense of history. Coming from an area where your family is pretty much not your family bloodline

anymore, you develop this sense of family lineage and history by your community. I've seen community, the sense of gay community in this city, pretty much become a big joke. And [with] this field I'm in, home care, I see it forming again.

Coy began to recount the surprising way he crafted an identity on Polk Street. "The first time I came here," he said, "I came by a different name and just created a whole character and people accepted me.... It's like you're trying to get away from something to try to find yourself. And then when you find yourself, you are blessed to find out that you have friends in that area that understand that." A lot of people call Polk Street "the gutter," Coy said. "Well, you know, call it what you want—it's honest. You can look for your own lies and find your own truths there." I was captivated by Coy's storytelling. I wanted to know more about the character he developed and how it enabled him to "find" himself. Over the next few months, Coy and I recorded five oral histories in his Polk Street apartment. I also visited Coy at the Gangway, a gay tavern off Polk Street at which he bartended, and chatted with him, as customer-historian, over drinks. I present Coy's story here through a more-or-less-chronological narrative, placing his performance as "Irish immigrant" in the context of the migratory street scene and Polk Street's longer social and economic history.

"Child Protection" and Street Families

Coy told me he was born in 1966 in Gary, Indiana, on the southern tip of Lake Michigan to a Roman Catholic family. He was raised by his great-aunt and great-uncle, who he also called his adoptive father. He began running away at the age of nine. It was only in our last oral history recording that he told me he was running away because his great-uncle sexually abused him on a regular basis from an early age. Coy told me he identified as "a sexual-abuse victim," noting that his adoptive father forced him into sex. His father's power, and Coy's relative powerlessness, acted as a mechanism for coercing compliance and maintaining silence. This was a common story on Polk Street: many told me they ran away from sexually abusive homes.

Coy told me he first ran away to Denver around 1975, when he was nine, jumping trains and trucks and living with people in their vans. Police located him after a few months and sent him back to an abusive home. At age ten, Coy told me he ran away again, to Ft. Lauderdale, Florida. The police once again located him after a few months and sent him back home. The state's "child protection" system expanded significantly in the 1970s. Child-abuse reporting laws and the rising number of children in long-term foster care set off alarm bells in Congress, resulting in passage of the Adoption Assistance and Child Welfare Act of 1980.[3] The act required states to make "reasonable efforts" to avoid removing children from parents. The effort to preserve biological families, called "family preservation," historian John Myers shows, was "the dominant paradigm of child protection in the 1980s."[4] The irony is that the state's "child protection" system protected heterosexual, biological families—not children like Coy, who needed protection from their families of birth.

Coy found ways to subvert the state's family reunification policy when he ran away to San Francisco, around 1977, when he was eleven. In the Haight-Ashbury, Coy met a gay man named Moondrop and a lesbian named Leslie, who became his "hippie godparents." Coy learned to play the role of the "fake kid" as they posed as a heterosexual, nuclear family to obtain benefits from local charities and state agencies. "It was all a part of my job," Coy said, "playing the game with them, and that basically got me a place to stay." Playing the kid "got me clothes, it got me food, and that was pretty much all I needed." The three split rent in a rooming house for thirty dollars a week. Coy learned that he could evade the state and survive financially through manipulation of the truth.

Coy walked to the nearby Polk Street corridor, where he learned that gay businesses and bars served as de facto employment centers. Working-class bars and saloons had operated as employment agencies for itinerant workingmen at least since the late nineteenth century. These (heterosexual) taverns provided patrons with "free lunches" and sometimes doubled as employment agencies. Proprietors acted as bankers so that itinerant workers had safekeeping for their money.[5] Polk Street bars served a similar function for street kids. "There were so many odd jobs you'd be sitting there like it was a labor pool," Coy said. "Say there was someone needed their apartment cleaned, needed some stuff hauled up, couldn't haul the garbage out, needed their windows cleaned in a store, needed stock packed." Bartenders would connect street kids and business owners. "He'd say, 'This kid's not strung-out, this kid's actually trying to make it, why don't you give him a chance?'" Shop owners would pay Coy to sweep a sidewalk or clean windows. Because he was paid under the table, he could remain anonymous. "The reason I got attracted to the Polk was there were jobs. You could get paid for sweeping a sidewalk, cleaning windows, and stuff like that. The business owners actually took care of people who were willing to work. Next thing you know your foot's in the door in a job and you're finding your way off the street. There were a lot of people doing that."

It took Coy about a week to become a part of a street family made up of other runaways and "throwaways" on Polk Street, who banded together for safety and pooled money for food and housing in residential hotels. "I met other people who were homeless and basically if you took care of them, they took care of you. So there was a sense of community and a sense of family I never grew up with." Kids protected each other in an often dangerous environment. "The street family was basically a safety thing," Coy said, "because you had people with their dogs and stuff like that. You felt safer being in a group. It's warmer, like pigeons flocking together, and you pool your funds and your resources." Finally, he found that the kids were part of "a culture of nomads going from one city to another," often following changing weather patterns. Coy found on Polk Street the economic support and protection from his biological family the state was not providing.

Polk Street's Moral Economy

Coy began learning about Polk Street's history from bartenders and business owners who told fabulous stories about queer activism and belonging. Because Polk Street's history features so prominently in Coy's own self-fashioning, I offer historical background before moving forward with his personal story of transformation.

San Francisco's homosexual population exploded after World War II, as veterans like Sweet Lips migrated to the city in droves.[6] Polk Street, a commercial corridor populated by working-class heterosexuals and saturated with rooming-house hotels, bars, taverns, and bathhouses, became known as a gay district by the late 1950s and early 1960s, as the city's white population fled for newly constructed suburbs and the street's white, blue-collar, heterosexual population shrank.[7] Bar owners responded by "turning gay" to cash in on a growing homosexual market. "The owners [of Polk Street's Cloud Seven] confessed they weren't making any money," bartender Greta Grass recalled; in 1962 "they turned it into a queer bar . . . and when the owner opened it up as such he ended up doing four times the business without the headaches."[8] The heterosexual Rancho tavern became the gay Suzy-Q bar. In 1960 a gay bar called the Jumpin' Frog opened.[9] That same year, a gay couple opened the Town Squire, a "mod" clothing store. "Slowly people began to open more things that were gay oriented," a business owner named Randall Wallace told me. "It just began to multiply, and it was the place to be on the weekends and the weeknights." In 1964 *Life* magazine featured Polk Street in an article dubbing San Francisco the nation's "Gay Capital."[10]

It appears that at least some established merchants objected to Polk Street's transformation. In 1962 the Polk Street Merchants Association discussed the "problem of social variants in the Polk Street Area" and complained that "mothers, the PTA and others were always calling [the association] and objecting to some of the variants in the neighborhood." At an association meeting in 1962, homophile organizer Guy Strait told the members, "If they don't want the business of the social variant, all they need to do is to put a sign in their window to that effect and they will not then be at all bothered with it."[11] Profit appears to have trumped prejudice: by 1966 there were at least twenty-six gay bars and gay businesses on Polk Street, including restaurants, men's clothing stores, gay theaters, and transient hotels.[12] Businesses continued to "turn" gay through the 1960s. A cafeteria in the late 1960s "wasn't making it as a straight restaurant," according to the *Bay Gourmet*. "The ownership wanted to cash in on the large gay market" and reopened as the gay On the Q.T. In 1969 the French restaurant Alouette became the gay *P.S. Bar and Restaurant, a focal point for a growing scene.[13]

In the 1960s, homosexuals could gather legally in bars if they did not exhibit "immoral, indecent, disgusting or improper" behavior, but because these terms were ambiguously defined and up for interpretation, police regularly raided gay bars.[14] The largest vice raid in San Francisco history took place in 1961, when police arrested eighty-one men and fourteen women at the Tay-Bush Inn, an afterhours club in the Tenderloin that served beer and hamburgers to a mixed clientele. The police allowed the "respectable looking" and politically well-connected customers to leave but booked the largely queer, working-class, and dark-skinned remainder.[15] There was also widespread official corruption that came to light in the "gayola" scandal of 1961, in which San Francisco Police Department (SFPD) and California Alcoholic Beverage Control (ABC) officers were caught taking bribes from gay bar owners in exchange for not raiding their bars.[16] A researcher found in 1964 that gay bars in San Francisco "suppl[ied] goods and services as well as social interaction." A bar "may serve as a loan office, restaurant, message reception center, telephone exchange, and so forth."[17] As such, gay men crafted a collective consciousness in bars that was a necessary precursor for political organizations.[18]

Polk Street bars provided fertile ground for the establishment, in 1962, of the Tavern Guild of San Francisco, the nation's first gay business association. Phil Doganiero, a bartender at Polk Street's Suzy-Q bar, was elected the first president of the organization. Nan Alamilla Boyd has noted that the guild functioned in many ways similarly to a turn-of-the-century fraternal or ethnic organization: by pulling together collective resources, members were able to cushion the economic hardships of its members and protect each other from discrimination. The guild also "represents a marketplace activity that, in order to protect itself, evolves into a social movement." Bartenders founded the guild to bring business to alternating bars on slow days. But within its first year, the guild instituted policies that helped protect bartenders, bar owners, and patrons from police harassment and ABC actions. The guild established a phone networking system to track police and ABC movement, set up a loan fund for bartenders who became unemployed due to police raids, and fixed prices at reasonable rates.[19] As a result of the guild, its president said in 1966, "our businesses have a greater chance for survival, and the hazards of operation are minimized." At the same time, "the improved image takes the gay bar out of the class of a resort for social rejects" and establishes them as "social centers for our people, with a wholesome and safe atmosphere," and "a stronger front from a united 'Gay Community.'"[20]

The Tavern Guild spearheaded fundraising and service-oriented projects, the most prominent being the Imperial Court, founded in 1965 at an annual fundraiser for the Tavern Guild called the Beaux Arts Ball. Drag queen José Sarria, named "Queen" of the ball, responded by proclaiming himself "Empress of San Francisco" and founder of the Imperial Court. Part of the Tavern Guild's fundraising arm, the court elected a new empress each year who raised funds for housing, drug treatment, and mental health services. In 1969 Sarria organized a variety show benefit for a drug-abuse clinic serving homeless youth in the Tenderloin.[21] The same year, Sarria also led a costumed group down Polk Street, collecting money to provide a "holiday dinner" for Tenderloin youth.[22] Sweet Lips founded Operation Concern, a nonprofit devoted to gay mental health. Bar-based fundraisers were also organized, according to a 1969 article, out of a desire "to do something constructive as a group [and to] show the world that gay people can work in unison."[23]

It was not uncommon on Polk Street for young men to come into the gay world through the sexualized "sponsorship" of older men, through transactions that ran the gambit from "treating" to prostitution. Polk Street businesses appeared to have allowed commercialized sex if it was "respectable" and discreet. An informant told me that the Cloud Seven bar, which "turned" gay in 1962, had lip-shaped phones on numbered tables. "The johns were at the tables and the hustlers were all up on the bar," he said of the late 1960s. "The people at the table would call the bar and say, 'I'd like to talk to the third guy from the end,' and say, 'I'm over at table seven.'" The hustler would "go to table seven and they have a few quick words and out they go." At the restaurant On the Q.T., a 1971 article noted, "Brooks-suited businessmen sit next to tee-shirted youths, where friends can talk or friendships can be made." While a pianist entertained in a dining room decorated with "chandeliers disguised as hanging baskets of flowers," couples ate "Scalloped Chicken, Beef Burgandy," and "Frog Legs cooked in a wine sauce."[24] At the *P.S. Bar and Restaurant in the early 1970s, "there were older *older older* men with younger *younger younger* men," one informant told me. "There were all these good-looking men who were hugging and kissing and there was a little piano bar. And they were singing show tunes. . . . They didn't seem to mind calling each other girl 'n Mary 'n being very affectionate, and there wasn't a woman in the joint."

For white gay men in the late 1960s and early 1970s, San Francisco was a beacon of gay pride, and Polk Street was at its center. In 1970 organizers built the route of the city's first parade around Polk Street's gay bars and businesses.[25] The drag queen Cristal, owner of Polk Street's Left Bank art shop and Empress of the Imperial Court, was a main organizer of the first parade in June 1970, according to Randall Wallace. *The Advocate* reported that "twenty to 30 persons marched up Polk Street from Aquatic Park to Civic Center" that year.[26] Early the next year, Cristal took the court on a tour of the Tavern Guild member bars, including Totie's on Larkin and the Early Bird on Polk, as part of the Tavern Guild's "all out campaign to bolster and promote business in member bars."[27] Polk Street businesses were given prime real estate in the parade program. Listed in the centerfold were Empress Cristal's "Palace of Fine Arts," the Gramaphone record store, and several Polk Street gay bars, along with the directive: "When parading on Polk Street, Visit these Businesses." "There were a lot of businesses on Polk Street," John DeLeon, an organizer of the 1972 parade, recalled in an interview. "So therefore, it was worked out that the parade will take that part of the route."[28]

Polk Street's gay economic power contributed to growing political power, as throngs of gay men moved to the city in the 1970s. From 1970 to 1980, the number of establishments with on-sale beer and wine licenses more than doubled. By 1980 the Tavern Guild grew to claim at least 184 individuals and 86 businesses as members.[29] Tavern Guild member Rikki Streicher recalled that the guild achieved political success because "a buck is the bottom line at all times. And the bars had commanded an enormous amount of money in terms of the city. So when they began to invite politicians to their meetings, the politicians realized that here's an organized group and that, number one, they have money and, number two, they have votes."[30] Wayne Friday bartended at Polk Street's New Bell Saloon starting in 1975 and, in 1978, became the first bartender to be elected as president of the association. He used his position in the Tavern Guild to increase its influence and the overall political power of the San Francisco gay community. For gay men, "it was total freedom" in the 1970s, he told me. "Everything was out. The police had gotten over their inhibitions about gays. And they understood that the gays were becoming a political power in San Francisco."

If merchants on Polk Street cultivated a space of white male conviviality, the Tenderloin was composed of "the lowest income people," the trans activist and social worker Tamara Ching told me: "the immigrants, the elderly . . . That was an unwritten rule, that transgendered people, or people that lived 'that' kind of lifestyle, we would not step on their turf. Back then there wasn't a term *transgender* of course. We were known as either 'queens,' 'drag queens,' or 'the girls.'" The "little bit better—one or two steps higher—moved to the Polk Street area. Those people probably had jobs, they worked, they led normal lives. The gay kids there were different than the gay kids in the Tenderloin. In the Tenderloin, there were drunks, alcoholics, drug abusers. In the Polk Street, it could be 'fun' going to the bar, it could be 'exciting' walking down the street." People of color and trans people "stayed in the Tenderloin," Ching told me. "We never, never, never stepped on Polk Street in female attire, to prostitute, or even come down socially." People "that lived 'that' kind of lifestyle," she noted, "would not step on their turf." In the 1960s, Asians "did not frequent the Polk Area . . . because there was a lot of discrimination," she said. "In the bars, minorities were asked for three pieces of picture ID, were given bad service, were ignored."

Demographics began to change as redevelopment and street sweeps on Market Street uprooted the meat rack scene from the late 1960s through the early 1970s and displaced it to Polk Street. In 1969 the city launched a $34 million beautification project for Market Street. Supervisor William

Blake promised a "street of excellence, charm, and beauty which is going to attract . . . tourists from all over the country." Blake encouraged supervisors to adopt a policy of "no more pinball machines, arcades, nude movie houses or pornographic bookstores on Market Street."[31] A gay newspaper reported in 1971 that "the 'meatrack' was being 'swept' unmercifully" by the San Francisco Police Department's Tactical Squad.[32] A newspaper in 1972 noted that police were arresting hundreds of "young and poor on the streets of downtown" on "obstructing the sidewalk charges." Raymond Broshears told the paper that "the sweeps are being instigated by big business and property owning interests in the downtown area that are looking for the redevelopment of the Tenderloin area."[33] By 1974 Broshears reported that "male hustling is at an all-time low thanks to Lloyd Pluegher of the Downtown Association." Redevelopment plans "include greater police sweeps on that street." The "money is scarce, the police are hot, the thugs are making hits, merchants are short on cash, stock, and temper [and] drugs are on the increase in use."[34] The same year, an urban minister reported that "our city fathers are proud of the 'clean-up.' The police brag about a 'reduction in crime.' But if this is true, why is there so much fear? . . . Why are all the streets so barren?" The "shop-keeper and restaurant owner who complained about people loitering in their doorways had them arrested. And now they are gone. And the shops and restaurants are closed!"[35]

Redevelopment and sustained police sweeps forced the kids' scene to Polk Street by the mid-1970s. "More and more speedfreaks are abounding on [Polk] Street," a gay newspaper noted in 1974. "Cum to think of it, the street looks like the Tenderloin did back in 1966."[36] An informant named Michael Norton told me he stopped hustling the Tenderloin by the mid-1970s and started hustling Polk Street, which was a "place where you could party, where you could find decent restaurants that were gay, decent bars that were gay instead of skid row bars like in the Tenderloin. . . . You were around gay merchants, gay customers coming in and out. You didn't have to be ashamed of who you were." Rob Bennett, a native San Franciscan who began hustling Polk Street as a sixteen-year-old in the late 1970s, remembers an explosion of sexual energy through the end of the 1970s. "People seemed to have more money, so it seemed a little more carefree," he recalled. "A new batch of people started moving into the city, bringing money from I guess the Midwest, South, the East." Bennett began to hustle the streets shirtless and "have a normal stream of people doing their daily life, like old ladies grocery shopping . . . all walking past while I'm leaning against the wall, prostituting myself, half-dressed. It was a liberating feeling. I don't know what the feelings of the other people were that were walking by witnessing it, but for me it was a great feeling."

The gay male merchants on Polk Street viewed this influx with alarm. While intergenerational sex had long been a feature of the local economy, they perceived "trade" hustling as a threat to the local scene. In 1977 the Polk Street Merchants Association met with Mayor George Moscone to complain about the "teen-age prostitutes, drug addicts and shoplifters [who] are turning Polk Street into a nightmare." The president of the association said, "Old ladies with white gloves aren't shopping on Polk Street anymore." The owner of the Town Squire complained that "street youth, many of them gay hustlers," called women entering his store "the filthiest names you've ever heard."[37] The president of the Polk Street business association said in 1978 that Moscone responded with sustained police sweeps to remove people "believed to be displaced from the Market Street and Tenderloin areas where successful police efforts were making it difficult for these would-be lawbreakers."[38] The merchants association, Wayne Friday told me, "was always very powerful politically." If you want to run for supervisor, "you're naturally going to kiss ass to the merchants in the community, 'cause the merchants have the money." John Gallagher, a former beat cop on Polk Street, told me that in the 1970s, the merchants association "could call the mayor's office and get what they wanted. You wanted police around the clock on the beat, they'd do it."

Gay merchants won several police sweeps from 1977 to 1981.[39] The sweeps targeted hustlers, addicts, and street kids displaced from the Mid-Market area. Activists complained of indiscriminate checks by police and citations for jaywalking. A 1977 article noted that people "can get busted for 'standing,' 'sitting,' or even 'being' in private doorways or on your street!"[40] In 1978 the American Civil Liberties Union noted "numerous complaints . . . that the [loitering] ordinance has been extensively used by the police as a means to harass Gays on Polk Street."[41]

Coy appears to have been among the hundreds of kids arrested during the sweeps. He told me police arrested him around 1977, after he had been on Polk Street for about a month or two, and sent him to juvenile hall. Authorities eventually returned him to his abusive home in Indiana. Even though the sweeps were ordered by gay business owners, Coy remembered the street families, bartenders, and many business owners who cared for him on Polk Street. "It seemed like the only people who were willing to help me without asking for anything degrading," he said, "was on Polk."

In the late 1970s, as an eleven-year-old in Indiana, Coy began developing a persona for himself. He had learned from his hippie godparents, Moondrop and Leslie, that he could obtain benefits, find a place to stay, and evade a state apparatus by playing the role of the "fake kid." As a runaway in the South, Coy told me, he had met "tinkers," or "Irish gypsies": a small, itinerant Irish group in the United States who live primarily in the South and earn their living largely through construction jobs.[42] They were "roaming gypsies essentially," Coy told me, and "became a family for me." Coy was likely also inspired by widescale interest in Irish resistance in the United States. In the late 1970s and 1980s, organizations and individuals in the United States sent large sums of money to Ireland, much of which enhanced the Irish Republican Army's military campaign. Hundreds of existing and new Irish American associations protested British rule, a level of political engagement not seen in the United States since the campaign for Irish independence in the early twentieth century.[43]

Coy told me that he began experimenting with a persona he called "the illegal Irish immigrant." He tried it out for the first time at an Indiana mall. Coy approached strangers as the Irish immigrant and asked if he could "interview" them. "People fell for it and people were really opening up," he said. "The girls would get all giggly and the guys would get all tough and [I'd] say, 'Ah, so you're up for getting a pint of ale or something afterwards, eh? So you come from a good drinking family, do you?'" Coy realized he could manage others' perceptions of him. Through "interviews," he encouraged other people to "open up" to him.

Coy said he started using the persona on a regular basis when he began running away from home around thirteen. "The first time I tried it out I was a runaway," he told me, "trying to get away from abusive parents that were raising me, and I figured that the only way I could find a way for them not to find me was to create a totally different person. It was just a magical time because I was running from my past," he said. "I didn't want my parents to find me, so therefore the illegal immigrant hiding was my excuse for them not to find me, ever." Coy found that the persona enabled him to remain relatively anonymous when he ran away to various vice districts around the country. "That was my safety mechanism I had as a runaway," he told me. "If the area looked very scary, I would use the persona, so that if you needed to pull away you could." If he found under-the-table work at bars or businesses, "there were no records of you, so no one could find you, but you could set up camp and basically make a living."

Coy also began to understand the persona's performative benefits. Coy used the term *dissociation* to refer to the persona, likely narrating his story by borrowing from the rhetoric of the national child-abuse movement and psychological theories of "dissociative identity disorder" popular in the 1980s. Many psychologists at this time proposed repeated child abuse as a cause of "multiple personality disorder" or "dissociative identity disorder." According to this literature, multiple identities are caused by abuse that victims have forgotten.[44] In contrast to the theories based on forgotten abuse, Coy said he consciously created the Irish persona to manage and reinterpret a traumatic past. "Some people go crazy and get split personalities," he told me. "I didn't get a split personality. I developed one I knew wasn't real. It was the only way I could deal with the abuse and dissociate from my past. And try to create a better person with a better past."

The persona enabled Coy to reframe as romantic that which Erving Goffman calls "spoiled identity": an identity discredited by law, opinion, or social convention.[45] As a boy, Coy felt dominated by his adoptive father. "I was owned," Coy told me. "I was just running away, running away like a scared rabbit." The "scared rabbit" was inarticulate and small, vulnerable to what Coy called the "predators" that inevitably populated the vice districts to which he fled. The Irish immigrant persona was, in contrast, romantic, outgoing, and fearless. Instead of running from an abusive father, he created a past in which he was an illegal immigrant running from the law.

Coy told me he was scared and untrusting of people because of his history of abuse. The Irish persona allowed him to interact with people at a safe distance. As part of a growing child-abuse movement, people began to talk about a suffering that lay not only in the immediate assault, according to Ian Hacking, "but in an ongoing destruction of personality, a growing inability to trust anyone, to establish loving and confident relations with any human being."[46] Coy narrated his experience of social trauma similarly. "I didn't really have a connection except one friend," he told me. "He'd always play me [the song] 'Desperado' over and over again. And it wasn't 'til he was dead a year that I realized what he was saying. 'You gotta come down from your fences and open the gate. You gotta live life, you gotta feel it, you can't dissociate.'" By developing the Irish character, he told me, "I was feeling it from a safe distance, and I was slowly dipping into myself and finding myself."

Coy ran away to cities around the country in the 1980s, but he always remembered Polk Street. The kids on the street also talked about it as a prime destination. In Denver, hustlers told him about Polk Street. "The hustlers there in the bar would always talk about 'when it's winter in Denver, summer in San Francisco,'" Coy told me. "So there was this big migration back and forth and they'd always talk about the Polk." After graduating high school in 1984, at eighteen, Coy returned to Polk Street.

Polk Street had changed dramatically by the 1980s. By the late 1970s, the city's gay economic and political center had shifted from Polk Street to the affluent Castro district. In 1977 the Gay Freedom Day moved from Polk Street and began a route up Market Street from downtown to City Hall, and in 1982 added a celebration in Civic Center Plaza.[47] Starting in 1988, the parade route began in the Castro District, with the traditional end point in Civic Center Plaza.[48] Many of Polk Street's upscale gay merchants joined the exodus to the Castro. By the mid-1980s, a national recession, a spike in commercial rents, and a wave of shuttered businesses undermined the health of Polk Street's gay economy. A study in 1984 noted "the continual unraveling and chronic instability of Polk District businesses." Sixty-five percent of surveyed business owners reported knowing at least three cases where a merchant "had to close or move a business because of the high rents." Among the problems identified by merchants were the "streetwalkers, hustlers, drug dealers, panhandlers, and other 'unsavory elements' who are seen in the area" and the "high or rapidly rising commercial rents."[49] In the 1970s, a powerful business association could convince the city to order sustained street police sweeps. By the 1980s, the association was much less powerful, former beat cop John Gallagher told me. The city would "[just] look into it" when the association complained, Gallagher explained. "If you're not that powerful, it's the squeaky wheel that gets the grease." According to Polk Street business owner Steve Cornell, the city "responds to where the money is and the businesses are." The city no longer responded when hustlers congregated in front of empty storefronts. "With no merchants to tell them to leave, the empty storefronts attracted illicit behavior, such as drug dealing and hustling," Cornell recalled. "If you're a more establishment person, you get this uncomfortable feeling and you don't want to go down in the neighborhood."

Gay men and business owners on Polk Street developed a sexual economy—on the streets and in the hustler bars—that valued white male masculinity. Indeed, there were accounts of anti-Asian discrimination at gay bars in the early 1980s.[50] The N'Touch, a gay disco, for example, attempted to exclude Asians in 1981 by asking them for multiple forms of identification.[51] The Association of Lesbian and Gay Asians was founded in 1981 following several nights of protest at the N'Touch.[52] A country-and-western theme might code a bar as white: around 1983 the N'Touch became the Renegades, a Levi-western bar, and, according to one account, "Gay Asians ceased to attend it."[53] The Cinch, a western-themed gay bar, placed a wooden Indian in front of the bar. Coy himself remembered Polk Street as a "wild west" frontier: young people in western wear, "a bunch of city kids walking around with boots on, flared-out pants and fake spurs on the back of their boots . . . shoulder to shoulder people even in the daytime during the weekdays."

Polk Street became well known as the city's center for male prostitution. The *Baltimore Sun* described it in 1986 as part of the "continuing national tragedy of America's runaway and throwaway child population."[54] A 1981 government-funded study by a gay ethnographer noted that many gay kids on Polk Street saw hustling as an opportunity for self-discovery and upward mobility. Many hustlers "exhibited positive self-images, imagining themselves to be entrepreneurs, entertainers, and sexually desirable partners," and many clients were convinced that their relationships with hustlers were "mutually satisfactory."[55] Ron Huberman, a gay investigator with the District Attorney's office, made a similar point in 1984: "[Female prostitutes] become objects. Gay men don't see these boys as objects. They know the kids are here to come out. It's easier to have compassion for a young male prostitute whose hustling is a way to meet other gay men. You take care of your own."[56]

My informants remembered Polk Street as a carnivalesque space of masquerade and play. James Harris, a black gay man, told me he took a bus to San Francisco in 1978, at age twenty-one, and found himself drawn as if by magnetic force to Polk Street's packed bars, dance clubs, and sexually charged streets. "It was more than just a neighborhood really," Harris told me. "It was sort of like a carnival atmosphere." There was "a game people played there, because it was about the hustling. It was about people being more than what they really were sometimes. You know what I mean? People putting on this sort of charade, if you will, to make themselves more appealing to either another individual, or a young hustler, or just to satisfy their own shortcomings." Polk Street was a "ludic space," to use Roland Barthes's phrase, a space of play, what Barthes called a "privileged place where the other is and where we ourselves are other, as the place where we play the other."[57]

Coy told me he presented himself as the Irish immigrant when he arrived on Polk Street in the mid-1980s. The performance drew on tropes of white masculinity, offering Coy a white identity based not in domination but in subjugation. He built on the mythology surrounding the Irish Republican Army, which many considered a terrorist organization because of the tactics it used to oppose British rule. This may have appealed to Coy, who was still running from his father's domination, and it likely appealed to others on Polk Street who felt subjugated by a heterosexist world. Unlike his biological family of religious fundamentalists, his imagined family was pro–Irish Republican Army and "pro-freedom," he told me, "freedom fighters" who violently resisted the subjugation of foreign domination. "I had people believing that I had left a family that was involved in construction and building bombs," he told me. "Job security, you know." He developed an Irishness linked to a heritage of oppression and of opposition to British brutality against the Irish.[58]

The Irish immigrant masquerade endeared Coy to the street's primarily white male bartenders and business owners, who found him under-the-table work. "People were giving me jobs left and right because I was like the new thing," Coy told me. "And most of the bartenders knew I wasn't [Irish] but they're like 'The tourists are getting a kick out of this one, so let's have him sweeping outside the front,' and that went on for a while." As such, Coy's self-fashioning performance was the labor that brought him the recognition of Polk Street bartenders, who likely saw through his deception. A former bartender told me he remembered Coy as the "Irish immigrant." He wasn't convinced by Coy's performance, but, as in other transient or criminalized cultures, people on Polk Street did not delve too deeply into each other's past. Asking too many questions was the mark of a cop.[59]

Coy learned that bartenders were the eyes and ears of Polk Street. Bartenders knew the regulars, their patterns, and the complex relationships that tied together the local economy. The bartender at the Q.T., a gay man named John Hauser, facilitated hookups between street kids and clients. Coy told me Hauser "was basically the madam of Polk Street." He facilitated hookups between hustlers and johns and made money for the bar in the

FIGURE 4.1.   Leather-clad young man (named Linn or Lynn) in front of the Q.T.
hustler bar on Polk Street, 1980. Photograph by Blaine Dixon,
from his "Polk Gulch" series.

process. "A madam," Coy told me, "is someone who gets the hustlers to go
with the johns, the johns to go with the hustlers, and make sure it's safe in
between, that there's no problems in between. As a bartender, he facilitated
that and he was able to get tipped from both sides and make money from it
at the same time and provide a safety net for everybody." They remembered
the bartender fondly and referred to him with kinship terms. Coy told me
he "was like big mama to all the hustlers and the lost kids on the street."
He could "team you up with a date or a legitimate job or a place to stay." He
might team "the kids" up so they could pool their money and stay at an area
hotel. Many of the bartenders were former kids off the street.

If the street's moral economy provided opportunities for migrants to
avoid police and find support through under-the-table work, it also gave
cover to people looking to take advantage of young people lost and alone
in the city. "When you're lost," Coy told me, "there's a lot of predators out
there that jump out in front of you. I was lucky. I came from a predator, I ran
into a lot of predators, but I also ran into a lot of people." Many bar regulars

were spectators to these dramas. "When a new homeless kid would show up on the street," Coy said, "some of the cynical older people would make a bet to see how long it would be before the drugs would take them. And sure enough some of 'em would [succumb to drug abuse] and some of 'em would make it off the street and into a job."

Informants told me that hustler bars also served as de facto community centers where street youth could eat and socialize. Rob Bennett told me that most of the bartenders in the late 1970s were "very attractive boys from the street." Ron Huberman, a gay activist who worked in the District Attorney's office in 1981, recalled that many of the bartenders "had come off the streets themselves. Or knew people that had come off the streets. So they knew exactly what was going on." They were "the eyes and ears of Polk Street" and his "first source of information," providing him names of people who had committed crimes against customers or regulars. Bartenders provided economic opportunities for street kids, operated de facto community centers, and maintained safety. In an ideal situation, street kids, businesses, and clients developed shared moral rules and conventions to compel exchanges they felt were fair and just.

James Harris told me that hustlers, bartenders, and regular patrons would cooperate to ensure that financial transactions were handled smoothly, that regular patrons weren't ripped off, and that newcomers followed the unofficial rules on the street. "Hustlers used to do the circuit," James told me of the late 1970s and 1980s. "They used to go to L.A., and then they go to maybe Palm Springs, and then they come to San Francisco." Hustlers who were new on the street would "get violent," James said. "They would start talking trash to some of the . . . regular older bar patrons" or would rip them off. For example, one day a hustler who was new to the street ripped off a client who was a regular bar patron on Polk Street. James heard about this from Polk Street bartenders, who "understood what was going on" and "were very communicative with each other. Everybody was sort of interconnected." James and his friends approached the hustler and said, "Give him the money." The hustler said he didn't have it. "And I said, 'I tell you what, okay fine. When you get the money, you need to give it back to him.'" Later, "somebody had saw that he had scored with a john or something—seen him getting out of a car, y'know. And this is before the cell phone, so somebody just ran into the bar and said, 'So-and-so just got out a car with this guy.' We know he must have made some money, and so we ran down and

FIGURE 4.2.   Rob Bennett (*second from right*) and friends at a phone booth at Polk and Geary, ca. early 1980s. Courtesy of Rob Bennett. "These two payphones were notorious for tricks and drugs. I think right there, we're coming up from the Gay Pride, and we're on acid, and I think we're trying to buy some more. A friend of mine pulled by in the car and took our pictures as he was driving up the street."

said, 'Give it up.' Just like, 'Give it up or get your ass beat, one or the other. What do you want to do?'" He laughed. "So the guy gave us the money, and we went back and gave it to the guy. You know, 'cause he was a regular. We protected our own, we protected our community. 'Cause we didn't want anybody coming in and destroying it."

As Coy worked and performed at the bars, he continued to construct an even more elaborate history for his Irish immigrant persona, "studying up" in history books to add detail. "I told them I was from County Cork, and I had some family in Mayo and then some I didn't get along with in Donegal, up north." In the bars, Coy would sing "Some Say the Devil Is Dead," a "rebel song" about Irish nationalism. People "gobbled it up left and right." He drew heavily from Irish slang. "Oh no, I'd be sittin' on a high stool gettin' pissed if not. Haven' a bunch of crack—crack is just a slang for fun, you know. Getting pissed on the high stool is getting drunk and having a good time, being fully yourself, you know?" Coy also became part of a "gay family" on Polk Street. Coy and others on the street referred to the bartenders, clients, and street youth as a "family" consisting of "brothers," "sisters," and "moms." His "gay godparents" drove him around in their convertible and gave him dating advice. A beautician made sure he and other kids were clean. The kids called the beautician "mum," because "he acted like mom, he tried to insist, 'Oh, come put on some eyeliner, darling, come on, come on, you look good, we get you down to the Campus Theatre [a strip club], you'll make good money.'" Coy met Sweet Lips, who told his customers that Coy could carry wood up to the fireplace or wash their windows. A queen named Naomi, who owned an antique store, "would have you dust all his pottery and stuff like that and you'd make some cash that day. He would try to put the moves on you, but you could avoid it, it wasn't a thing that you had to do." During Christmas, a bartender would pay someone to paint the windows and mirrors of his bar. "It looked like something out of a Christmas novel and everyone would have food and drinks, it was free food. Everybody got fed and you had this sense of 'wow, I do have a family.'"

Coy's gay family enabled him to question what his family of birth taught him: if you were gay, "you're an anti-American, you're going to burn, you're going to catch a disease, you're defacing the country." His family of birth taught him that the only way to support your country is to get a job—maybe in a mill or the military—get married and have kids. On Polk Street, Coy learned a new set of values. "[I] was like 'Okay, what I was first taught doesn't always have to be right.'" Coy saw working gay couples with jobs, which suggested that he could have a domestic family—not only a "street family." The message he learned on Polk Street, he said, "was find out who the hell you are so we can know you . . . and if you're trying to be someone else at least believe in that person you are becoming." In other words, one should have confidence in one's own confidence game.

His new family taught him about the history of Polk Street and the folk tales people circulated in these areas. Indeed, in our oral histories, Coy referred to his "Irish immigrant" masquerade as the "Emperor Norton Syndrome," referring to a folk tale widely circulated in San Francisco. The story centers Joshua Norton, who traveled to San Francisco during the Gold Rush, made an unbelievable fortune, and, due to poor investment decisions, just as quickly lost it all. As the story is told, he appears to have lost his mind in the process. After disappearing from the city for several years, Norton returned in an officer's coat festooned with brass buttons and proclaimed himself "Norton I, Emperor of the United States and Protector of Mexico." In other cities, he would have been thrown in an asylum, but San Franciscans embraced him. Newspapers published his royal decrees. Merchants clothed him in royal regalia. Restaurants served him without charge. Norton was "emperor" until he died in 1880, when tens of thousands turned out for his funeral. San Franciscans, and queer San Franciscans in particular, have embraced this narrative of an outcast transformed into royalty. In the 1960s, Imperial Court founder José Sarria declared that he was Emperor Norton's long-lost widow, naming himself the "Widow Norton" and establishing a mythical lineage between two eras of San Franciscan bohemianism and extravagance.

The Emperor Norton story is an illustration of performativity: it is ultimately a story about how language and performance can construct or affect reality rather than merely describing it. The story Norton told about himself became a kind of "social truth" through its telling via a receptive audience. Like Norton, the success of Coy's Irish character required a receptive and appreciative audience. "I was glad that my friends didn't slam the door on me and shun me away, or else I probably would have ran and turned that part of myself off again." But Coy knew he couldn't "disassociate" forever.

The "Big Irish Thug Bouncer"

Coy came closer to confronting his past when, in the early 1990s, he became a bouncer at Polk Street bars and developed the persona of the "big Irish thug bouncer." This new performance built on stereotypes of the "illegal Mick" and Irish "paddy." As early as the 1830s, historian Dale Knobel shows, the stereotype of the Irish American "paddy"—the impoverished, drunken, unskilled Irishman—served as a foil for the sober, self-supporting Protestant farmer or craftsman.[60] Being the "illegal Mick," Coy told me, "grabbing one person who was irate from one bar and kindly getting them to another bar," went "perfectly into the persona of the pub-carrying Irish Mick. A bit of a paddy, you might say." Because work as a bouncer required him to use physical force to subdue others, he found himself uneasily occupying the subjectivity of his oppressor, a figure from whom, in his late twenties, he was still running. "Being a sexual-abuse victim and your abuser being your father—well, your adopted father—you all too often decide, 'Oh my God, I'm gay,' you worry that you're just like your father, another piece of the asshole that did this and that to you."

It may have been precisely because the qualities of the "big Irish thug bouncer" paralleled that of his childhood oppressor that Coy began to confront his past. The persona may have helped Coy realize the physical and emotional strength that childhood abuse had taken from him. The persona possessed the "best qualities that I had," Coy said, "and the safest qualities. They were strong, I was able to fight, no one was going to—hurt me." Coy fashioned the Irish persona to escape his father's control, but now he found himself figuratively face to face with the conditions of his domination.

Coy "bounced the bar" as part of a system various Polk Street bars had set up to defuse violence on the street. Coy worked jointly as a bouncer for four different bars. The managers had developed a system to rank the level of permissible intoxication and drug use in each bar. Bartenders would call him to one bar when a patron was too drunk or unruly and Coy would gently convince the patron to follow him to the next most permissive bar. In the course of one night, Coy might bounce the same person from one bar down the line to the next, ending at one bar that Coy called "the bottom of the line." For many, Coy said, seeing a uniformed person "triggers a lot of memories." The policy bars created helped "keep the cops out of the bars and cut down on the crime." This system was part of a longer tradition: Polk Street bars had long maintained their own policing strategies to defuse violence, increase personal freedom, and avoid unnecessary interaction with the authorities.

"I did find out that I was able to use my anger and subdue people," he said, "but afterwards I always felt bad about it, 'cause it always reminded me of my father." Risking repetition, Coy found he could use physical force not only to dominate, like his father, but also to protect. Coy remembers one "kid" who "was kind of strung up, enjoying his drug, whatever it was," and had alienated bar patrons to such an extent that Coy "had to protect him from the rest of the bar, because they were going to beat him up." He brought the young man outside, sat him down, and helped him sober up. In this instance, the "big Irish thug bouncer" protected a young person with whom Coy may have identified. He was able to overcome a fear of identifying with the role of abuser (associated with his violent father) by taking on a persona that closely resembled him.

Coy also increasingly perceived himself as an adult caring for young people migrating to Polk Street. When Coy was young, a bartender at Reflections always had a free cup of coffee for him "and [would] pay me about ten bucks to sweep behind the bar and stuff like that." When Coy began working as swamper—an assistant worker who performs odd jobs—he would "sit and do the same thing with other homeless kids that were coming in." The relationship was mutually beneficial. When it was raining, Coy would invite youth to sit inside and buy them a cup of coffee. Late at night, if Coy ever had a problem outside the bar, "I knew I had the street kids, the street kids would have my back if I had a problem walking home." This, too, could mark Coy's successful incorporation, as an adult, into Polk Street's performative economy. Being an adult did not mean dictating young people's behavior, since authoritarianism is precisely what people came to Polk Street to escape. It did mean providing opportunities should young people want to take advantage of them.

Love, Coming Out, Forgiveness

Coy narrated a crucial turning point in his story. One night in the late 1990s, when he was in his thirties, he was watching the Super Bowl at the Rendez-Vous bar. Coy the Irishman was drinking a lot those days. That night he had twelve kamikazes and a few shots. He started watching "this little Latino. . . . I walked up to him and said, 'Hi, my name's Coy,' and he said, 'Hi, my name's Sal, are we going to fuck or what?' And I sort of stood back," Coy told me, "and after a couple of cocktails we kissed on the way home, and I spent the night with him." They started dating. Coy always presented himself as the Irishman. "I didn't want a relationship when I met Sal," he told me, "but I fell in love." After a year, Coy moved in with Sal. This was the first time, Coy told me, that he really had a "home" instead of merely "a place to sleep." He told me he was untrusting and scared, but every day with Sal "I was getting closer and a bit of me was coming out." Two years passed, and Coy slowly began revealing more of his past. "And eventually it all had to flood out," Coy said, "which meant I had to remember everything that happened to me in the past. And relive it and share it, which I did *not* want to do." He finally "came out" to Sal. Sal thought the relationship was based on a "lie"—Coy's invented past—and wanted to break up. He eventually understood and forgave Coy.

Coy ultimately took the risk of being known by another. As he narrated his story, Coy was able to transition from "scared rabbit" to "survivor." The "Irish thug" and "scared rabbit" had been separate identities. Now, as Coy revealed the "scared rabbit" to Sal, he began recognizing them as aspects of an integrated consciousness. "The past was a lie, the accent was a lie," Coy said, "[but] the person was real." Sal and Coy also went on a joint journey to "forgive" Coy's stepfather. Coy had long tried to "sever the connection" with his father through the "Irish thug" persona, but he now decided he could only do so through "forgiveness." His father told Sal, "Now it's your turn to take care of him," Coy said, "and it was kind of his way of saying I accept you." Coy found a "nice part" of his father, he told me, a "closet-case World War II veteran" not unlike many men on Polk Street. Sal "met some of my family and understood. When you're driving on the road and you see cloth-wrapped crosses, you kind of understand, okay, there's a good reason you're not here."

Coy ended his story as a conventional account of coming out and settled, domestic life. In 2008 he told me that he and Sal had been united in a domestic partnership. "And now here I am," he concluded his story, "Coy the homosexual, in a domestic partner relationship for ten years." This new, almost ritual language of reconciliation seems to be at odds with the narrative strategies of masking and masquerade Coy used earlier in his life. But there were hints that Coy continued to revel in the creative and performative storytelling that had long characterized the performative economy. Coy said his friends know the "truth" about his past, but some of them—he called them his "drinking buddies"—refused to accept it. They "want to keep the illusion alive in their heads," Coy said. For those who prefer masquerade to "truth," the persona remained a kind of "drinking game."

FIGURE 4.3.　　　　Coy Ellison at the Cinch, 2008. Photograph by Gabriela Hasbun.

Corey Longseeker: The Urban Cowboy

Polk Street may have been the stage on which Coy's emancipation occurred, but there were as many exploitative dynamics operating within this world as threatening it from without. The street that enabled migrants to performatively reframe the abuse from which they were running appears to have drained the life and vitality of others. Countless people—hotel managers, social workers, bartenders, and business association members—told me about one man who "lost himself" on Polk Street. His name was Corey Longseeker, and his story had become the stuff of myth: the most beautiful sex worker on Polk Street—a gentle artist and poet who, people told me, "could have been a model"—who had become one of the street's most destitute and lonely. By the time I met Corey in 2008, when he was thirty-nine, he was among the many homeless on the street. I would see him sitting on the sidewalk, rocking back and forth, long hair covering his face, or shuffling slowly down an alleyway. He sometimes stooped over and made cupping motions with his arms. People told me he was picking up imaginary children. I tried to talk with Corey, but he was not able to tell a story about his life in a way that I found legible. I instead pieced together an account of his life through the stories others told about him, as well as letters that Corey wrote in the 1990s. I found that Corey's story dramatized the rise and fall of the kids' performative economy as it manifested on Polk Street.

One of the first people I interviewed about Corey was Dan Diez, a gay man in his sixties with thinning gray hair. We met at an upscale coffeehouse on Polk Street where Dan and many of his retiree friends gathered to talk, watching people walk past from their sidewalk tables. Dan had been a city government employee living in the East Bay before retiring and moving to the city. When I met him, he was cochair of a new neighborhood association. Along with other association members, he believed that homeless people like Corey were driving down property values and scaring away potential residents for new condominiums. But for more than a decade after meeting Corey in 1990, I learned, Dan considered himself part of Corey's surrogate family.

Dan told me he first saw Corey in 1990 while looking out the window of the Q.T. hustler bar. The kids on Polk Street were "just like the flower children who came to San Francisco in 1968," Dan explained. "And it was lively, a lot of the kids on the street were hustling." But Corey stood out from the crowd. He "wasn't what I expected someone like a hustler to look like," Dan said. "He just didn't fit it. Because alotta times hustlers, if they do drugs, you can tell . . . or some kids may be really hard on their luck." Corey "didn't look like any of that. . . . I cannot tell you, this kid had movie star written all over him. He was six foot three, and he was probably about 190 or 210 pounds. He had very nice long blond hair, very attractive eyes. He was extremely clean and very attractive, and he just looked like somebody who walked out one of these suburban towns. Which in essence is really what it was about with him because he was new at that time when I first saw him here."

Dan told me he befriended Corey. He occasionally slipped Corey twenty-dollar bills when he saw him on the street. He would also drive Corey to Burger King, where Corey would always order the same meal: "double whopper with cheese, onion rings, and a big chocolate milkshake." They would sit in his car in the Burger King parking lot, listening to seventies rock music, while Corey drew illustrations and wrote poetry. Dan told me their relationship wasn't sexual. "I did not pick up [hustlers] at that time," he assured me. "Corey was the only person I was really interested [in] 'cause he was something different. He was a person with a creative bent, which I really admired. He

FIGURE 4.4.   Polaroid image of Dan Diez and Corey Longseeker (and Marilyn),
                   December 18, 1993. Courtesy of Dan Diez.

was someone I liked being around. It was just really a nice relationship." The
two became closer over the years. Dan would bring Corey to the movies, he
told me, or take him to a spa to wash and take his clothes to a Laundromat.

By the early 1990s, Corey and other hustlers were Polk Street's primary
economic engines. Just as heterosexual bars on Polk Street "turned" gay in
the 1960s, Polk Street gay bars in the late 1980s and 1990s increasingly
"turned" hustler. Businesses—bars, sex clubs, and restaurants—increasingly
relied on the revenue sex workers generated, including those that made up
the street's business association. Steve Cornell, the owner of a Polk Street
hardware store, told me that many business owners in the 1980s didn't like
the kids hanging out on the street. "But if there are male prostitutes out there

and there are businesses that thrive on that, they're part of the business association too." Because businesses increasingly relied on a sex work economy, "maybe things aren't going to get done." According to a 1984 news report, "40 to 50 hard-core juvenile prostitutes are on that street at any one time."[61] On a typical night, a 1985 newspaper story read, "teen-age boys can be seen loitering in doorways, offering their bodies for hire."[62] The same year, a Polk District Merchants Association member complained that male hustlers were "doing better business than we are."[63] While her statement may have been hyperbolic, it pointed to the relative economic power of sex workers.

With his movie-star good looks, Corey became an economic powerhouse. Dan gave me a series of letters that Corey wrote Dan in the mid- and late 1990s. In a letter dated 1995, Corey referred to Dan as one of his "sponcers." Dan was one of many men, also called "uncles," who provided Corey with cash, meals, and often drugs. One man bought him a car. Corey wrote that his sponsors "made me into a liveing legand at the age of twenty two years old by letting me have enough money" and named as his "boss" a bartender at the Q.T. known for facilitating hookups between johns and hustlers.[64] James Harris told me he called Corey "Thor" because of his long, flowing blond hair and his height—about six two. "He coulda been a model," James told me. "No question about it. And you know, he was the envy of a lot of people."

Corey embraced the (white) masculine freedom of the urban frontier by fashioning himself as a modern "Old West" cowboy, a performance that likely appealed to his primarily white sponsors and clients. "I used to have my apartment," Corey wrote in a letter dated 1996, "and a 'mustang ford' and I wore a black leather trench with a marshal's badge on the trench coat." He pinned a marshal's badge to his shirt. "All right, so I got that badge from a leather cowboy boot, belts, and hat store up by the Castro," he wrote, "but it added to my snake skin boots and trench coat nicely." As I show in previous chapters, the cowboy has long been romanticized in popular culture, first by dime-store fiction and then by Hollywood, including John Schlesinger's 1969 film *Midnight Cowboy*. Corey also went by the name "Tiger," which appears to have long been a common street name among hustlers. In his 1963 novel *City of Night*, John Rechy refers to a hustler named Tiger, a name "as obviously emphatically masculine as the queens' are emphatically obviously feminine."[65]

Corey also began to tell Dan about his past. Dan learned that Corey was born David Royal Lundy Jr. in 1970 and grew up in a devoutly religious family in a small Minnesota town. (According to public records, David Royal Lundy Jr. was born in March 1970.)[66] Corey told Dan that his mother and father worked in factories and hunted and fished in the countryside. "He used to be a wrestler in school," Dan said. "He told me about that. He was very active with his family in hunting and fishing—so he's a very active outdoor type of person." Dan learned that Corey left Minnesota for San Francisco when he was around eighteen, before graduating high school, around 1988. "Something happened in that family," Dan said. "Either he did something really wrong, and they could not put up with him, or they did something wrong, and he could not put with up with them, or both—I don't know."

Corey shared clues about his past in a series of three letters he wrote to Dan in 1996 from jail, where he was incarcerated on drug-related charges. The kids at school, he wrote in one letter, "were always cruel" to the "kind-hearted kids that were soft like a marsh mellow inside." Corey also described three "recurring nightmares" from his childhood in a series of letters, which I have since archived at the GLBT Historical Society. The nightmares were "true life stories," he wrote, and "part of my past survived existence." His accounts are "intended to be an explanation of an actual experience I had once," he wrote, "just so long as the reader is intelligent enough . . . to comprehend" them.

"DAVID ROYAL LUNDY JUNIOR"

C-TANK CELL #1

850 BRYANT STREET

SAN FRANCISCO CA

Dear "Dan Diez," Hello it's me "Tiger," and I'm writing you finally. I've written to "Rust" [another "sponsor"] also, and he keeps sending me post cards. . . .

I had recurring nightmares and one of them was of a form of a cesspool, or a swamp like a play pen, a square brick room, and in that room, a large bunch of kids close to my age, we were all a bunch of little gay boys. We were all the same age, and we were all much more loveable that any of the smart ass kids that I knew at school. . . .

It was me and a group of kids my age we were in a pool similar to a swamp water-filled empty basement, and it was filled with little pokey stickers, and the water was slightly salty so every time a sticker would poke one of us on our feet the ankle deep salt water would torture our feet and make us cry, but we were the more loveable kids out of every one else. Would quickly arrive to comfort and help pull stingers out of the others feet while we cuddled to stay warm in the cold salted water.

We were all nude from heads to toes and all of us were scared. We were scared of the cruel Demon, or wicked witch. And the wicked witch used to make us do naughty naughty favors for her and each other. We all cared for each other, and we each had our own boyfriend, or special partner, who we chose to be with, and that one special partner meant enough to us that we were willing to do anything that wicked creature who owned the play pool was making us do.

All the while we were very special loveable, talented, and caring, our very own parents used to laugh and giggle, and be cruel to us. And no matter how gifted each child was, our parents watched us and made harsh comments, and truly not funny jokes, and they forced us by broken pride, trust, and rejection to survive in Satan's swamp. Only because we were black sheep, either overly talented, and before our time, or because we loved too strong to let go of one another, and watch them grow sick, and Die, because of a few late bloomers, and spiritually altered bodies, and minds.

Boys who were boys proud to be boys, who loved other boys who were boys, and loved them as boys, shoved back into a playpen. Lucifer's swamp, by the end of a rude pokey stick used by Satan himself in the ribs, or the belly as we would fall back into the stickers and salt water. That was like a basement for lovers, or couples, who were not allowed to live a normal life one on one with their partners, among lost immediate family, and unforgiving, misunderstanding, or nonaccepting religious traditional old fashioned folks.

And the harder we would cry for fear or try to help, the crueler the tough love from the parents not intelligent or mature enough to accept the warmth of their own flesh and blood. . . .

I suppose we're at our thirty year generation lapse of the generations cycle, and where some parents are not willing to understand the flower children of the nineties. . . . [We are] on the edge of the biggest wave. A wave of Spirit that hasn't been here since 1969, and like the hippies once did, so will we rise above once again. . . .

In this "true life" story, Corey appears to present Polk Street as "Satan's swamp": the metaphoric hell to which his fundamentalist family had relegated him. Street kids, rejected by their own "flesh and blood" and "nonaccepting religious . . . folks," cared for one another. They withstood the pain of being on Polk Street, pulling stingers out of the others' feet and "cuddl[ing] to stay warm." The moral authority of Corey's account of this nightmare derives in part from the figure of the innocent (abused/abandoned) child and his desire for community and social bonds, which he developed with other kids on the street by calling on the history of the "flower children." In this dreamscape, Corey also appears to combine two periods of his life—his childhood in Minnesota and early years on Polk Street—as if to suggest continuities in the social trauma he experienced during these two periods. His letter suggests that he was not only attempting to manage the affective and economic impacts of homophobic violence and physical abuse that he experienced at home. He was also attempting to manage those forms of social trauma as they were restaged in "Satan's swamp."

Twin Epidemics: AIDS and Methamphetamine

In the late 1980s, two devastating epidemics—HIV/AIDS and methamphetamine—undercut the social formations my informants called "street family," leading to an environment that many kids considered unsafe and exploitative. Coy spent the bulk of his time on Polk Street starting in 1984. He was able to forms bonds and friendships with a street family and expansive "gay family," find work at gay businesses and bars, and eventually climb the local employment ladders to become a swamper, bouncer, and bartender. Corey arrived on the street around 1989. The delicate tissue of social norms and reciprocities motivated reciprocity as an exchange pattern and served to inhibit the emergence of exploitative relations that would undermine the meat rack economy.[67] While Corey arrived on Polk Street just a few years after Coy Ellison, he encountered a vastly different neighborhood with far fewer economic and social opportunities. In the early 1980s, according to a field note by ethnographer Toby Marotta, Polk Street had been "a bustling, entertainment district, filled with homosexuals and heterosexuals out for every form of sexy pursuit." By 1987 "the bars are half empty, the shops and restaurants and outdoor eateries seem barely attended," and in its place was "a larger, more pathos filled, more starkly highlighted prostitution scene, bigger than that it's even been in S.F. from what I can guess."[68]

San Francisco was an early center of the HIV/AIDS epidemic and for many years had the highest per capita rate of AIDS cases in the United States. The first AIDS cases, reported in 1981, were primarily among the affluent, white gay men in the upper-income Castro. A second epicenter emerged in the low-income Tenderloin by 1984, particularly among injection drug users and men who have sex with men.[69] From 1988 through 1992, the epidemic progressed rapidly among men who have sex with men in the Tenderloin. The low-income Tenderloin, rather than Castro, emerged as a primary epicenter for AIDS at this time. In the Tenderloin, HIV/AIDS cases were predominantly among men who have sex with men, including male hustlers, but also included large numbers of injection drug users, heterosexuals, and trans women.[70] By the late 1980s, HIV/AIDS was wreaking havoc on Polk Street. "AIDS just decimated the beauty parlors," Randall Wallace told me, "and boys from the Town Squire. At the *P.S., the waiters used to wear satin basketball shorts, and they got really, really cute kids, and they began to go." James Harris recalled, "The feeling back then was that there was no cure for this disease. Some people just woke up one day and had lesions on them and stuff like this, and so it was a scary time, as we started watching these younger people start to disappear." With the advent of AIDS, James said, "the character of the street changed, the philosophy of the street started changing. You started to see this turmoil start to take place, in what was pretty much a calm place. . . . We started to see more young kids on the street, strung out from dope. Myself included. You started to see this—desperation. Looked like there was no hope left."

While street kids had used methamphetamine for decades, it became an epidemic among sex workers with the onset of AIDS. The drug made it easier to "perform," Lala Yantes told me. Speed produced feelings of euphoria, a sense of invulnerability, focus, and a desire for sex. The drug "numbs your mind," Lala said. "You don't think about what you're doing, you're just a mindless individual performing a task, just like any other factory worker." Speed is "the drug of choice on Polk Street," an article from 1986 read, "and much of the underground society is built around how and where to buy it."[71] Methamphetamine undermined the obligations and reciprocities that had defined the street scene. The ethnographer Toby Marotta wrote that by the mid-1980s "the whole southern end of Polk Gulch was being transformed because of methamphetamine use." While the drug "produced long mind-escapes," it also "completely undercut the personal relationships and social obligations essential to functioning community."[72] The boys who had been "partying and having a good time," Rob Bennett told me, with "just the flick of a switch you would see them totally strung out, sitting on the street, no shoes, talking to themselves, picking themselves raw."

Clients' fear of AIDS decimated the hustling economy and drove down hustling rates. "All you're going to get now is these cheap street trash dates," one sex worker reported in 1987. "These rich guys . . . won't spend money anymore because they're scared."[73] A hustler told an ethnographer in 1989, "It used to be that people up and down the street would have money all the time [in the early 1980s], but now you go out there and nobody has money."[74] A twenty-six-year-old white transgender woman said in 1987 that "there used to be a time when I could make $3000 a week. And you're lucky if you can get half now."[75] Another trans sex worker on Polk Street told a researcher in 1988 that "a good 60% of clients I have had do not . . . come around. . . . The money is not there now cause they're scared of AIDS and I don't blame them."[76] Rob Bennett told me that, in the early 1980s, "sixty dollars was good money for a trick." By the late 1980s, "they were only offering twenty dollars." An increasingly desperate population began competing for dwindling resources. Kevin "Kiko" Lobo told me that "for those of us that depended on the street to survive, the money was harder and harder and harder to make. And that's what [began] the downward spiral." Those who were able left the street and advertised in newspapers. Only the most desperate street kids remained.

The HIV/AIDS and methamphetamine crises eroded the reciprocities and moral codes that had animated the performative economy in the 1970s and early 1980s. This contributed to a relationship between sex workers and clients that many of the kids considered exploitative. Rob Bennett told me the street "attracted a different kind of john, where it was mostly guys looking to give drugs to the boys to make them freaky and have sex." James Harris agreed. "The johns became different. They became the predator. They preyed on these young boys, and they knew that they could probably get them not for much money, all they had to do is get a bag of speed." As a result, "you saw this sort of deterioration of respect for these kids, you saw a more increased use of speed with these kids, and you saw a more desperate type of youth." Addiction also led to increased homelessness. In a 1992 field note, ethnographer Toby Marotta wrote about a "network of men, straight and bisexual as well as gay, who were in the down-and-out homeless crowd" and lived on General Assistance (GA) and Supplemental Security Income (SSI)— "what one respondent called 'the welfare circuit.'" Many had been "middle class and well educated men" who "thanks to their years of methamphetamine use and their current heavy usage . . . were homeless."[77] These crises decimated the mutual obligations, reciprocities, and local vice economy on Polk Street, which had once offered opportunities to youth.

Corey was among the kids whose mental and physical health was decimated by speed. His artwork "became wilder and wilder," Dan recalled.

Corey's blond hair turned brown. Spa staff began to refuse Corey service when Dan took him in. Dan told me he worried that by continuing to give Corey money, which he used to buy speed, he was "keeping him where he was at" instead of helping him. "I eventually always gave in because I always wanted to see him have something better," he told me. Corey became increasingly paranoid. He started losing his teeth. He would wander into the street to pick up his imaginary children or talk with imaginary people. "One he'd call Tommy, his little Tommy," Dan said. "And people would see him bend over to pick up his little Tommy off the sidewalk. He went into a lot of gibberish or psychobabble," Dan recalled. "He started to look almost Charles Manson–like." Anthony Cabello, who managed an SRO hotel on Polk Street, remembers Corey as "innocent" when he first arrived, with a "kind of farm boy quality to him," but noted that his decline was rapid. Anthony saw the same thing happen to a lot of kids in the 1990s especially. "I don't think there's brochures that they print up saying, 'Come to Polk Street: you'll find your dreams.' 'Cause I think sometimes when you come to Polk Street you find your nightmares. There's alotta drugs out there and alotta people who are willing to take advantage of somebody who isn't ready for 'em," Anthony told me. "That's what I see a lot of." Corey, he explained, is "one of the fortunate ones that's basically still around and breathing. Other people haven't been that lucky."

Speed, heroin, and HIV/AIDS also decimated the forms of mutual aid that had animated Polk Street's bar economy. Gay bar patronage decreased citywide in the 1980s and 1990s as the result of AIDS-related deaths and the rise of the internet as a social networking tool. Many bar owners, who purchased property at the height of the gay economy in the 1970s, retired and sold their bars. The Tavern Guild disbanded around 1995.[78] In the early 1990s, a heroin dealer threatened Coy Ellison while he was working at a Polk Street bar, and the bartender—a client of the dealer—refused to call the police. "I realized that Polk Street really has changed and it really broke my heart," he said. "The bartenders would all have each other's backs, the bar owners used to work with each other. They stopped doing that." A bartender interviewed in 1992 said he had left the employ of a Polk Street bar where the majority of the patrons and staff were using speed because it "got so rough and the manager didn't care. He didn't keep the place free of violence." He went to work at another bar where management "told me to do everything with a soft touch. . . . He turns his back on [drug use]. He's

FIGURE 4.5.   Corey Longseeker, 1999. Courtesy of Dan Diez.

making his money from the bar customers. Unless it's blatant, they want the customers to come back."[79] Polk Street bars had historically provided work for street kids, as bartenders, bouncers, and swampers. These opportunities began drying up for young migrants.

James Harris felt that Corey's decline resulted in large part from the breakdown of Polk Street's economy. James told me he left the street in the mid-1990s; when he returned in 2001, he barely recognized Corey.

> I looked at him again, and I—I started crying. I just lost it. I just could not believe what I was seeing. What was once a strapping, good-looking young man had been reduced to this homeless, toothless guy. And I just, it just freaked me out. It freaked me out so bad, and it took me a little while to get over it. It really did. But see it—that's what happened to a lot of the hustlers. As that mentality changed, they became the prey of these delusional men, because there were these guys who that's all they did, they just abused hustlers, y'know. The whole mentality of what a hustler and a john was changed. . . . And this [is] what it became, y'know, a drug-induced boy who would go home with this guy, and this guy would just abuse him sexually, throw him back out on the street.

If Corey came to Polk Street in 1980, James told me, "he would have a job as bartender maybe, working somewhere, maybe living in the Castro," he said. "No question about it."

"DAVID ROYAL LUNDY JUNIOR"
JAIL # 6TH FLOOR
C-TANK CELL #1
850 BRYANT STREET
SAN FRANCISCO CA

Dear "Dan Diez,"

Hello how are you, I thought I would write you another letter, and this time I thought I would tell you about another night mare that I lived in my past!

I suppose you don't enjoy to here about the night mares. But that is part of my past survived existence so I hope you're still patient, because this night mare was a recurring night mare also and I used to have this night mare about the men wearing neatly tailored uniforms and they all had badges.

Every time I had the dream I was still only approximately four, or five years old, but in the nightmares I was a full grown man, and I had already grown hair on my legs, and I was weak, I could no longer run, walk, or fight, and these two soldiers would carry my nude dying body over the gravel and the dust was filling my nose and my ears and my mouth as these two men carried me by my hands and my feet over the gravel.

At the end of the nightmare I would awaken . . . crying from the experience of the two men wearing uniforms swinging me just like a baby cradle then releasing me through the air where my nearly lifeless body [fell] onto a pile of dead naked men in a large pit, or hole that had been dug in the gravel . . .

After that was a third dream of the set of three dreams that were childhood nightmares of mine. But I'll wait til my next letter to explain about the third and after that these stories are true life stories, but they are from my past and after the third one they get happier for a while. If you could I would appreciate it if you would hold on to these for me. I'll write to you again soon until then please tell "Michael, Hey Now," "Robert," and "Mr. Ricky Ricardo" and yourself that I love . . . and like you a hell of a lot.

Polk Street remained the city's primary zone for male (and increasingly transgender) street prostitution in the mid-1990s. A newspaper article in 1995 called it the city's "best-stocked boulevard of sex for sale. Young, home-less, and far from their dismal pasts, boys come from all over the country to Polk Street, one of the last frontiers of male prostitution in America."[80] Hustlers were highly aware that they remained Polk Street's main attrac-tions. "Let's be real," one hustler said in 1991. "Who do you think brings in the revenue here?"[81] David McCleve, part of a street family of hustlers who occupied an abandoned Polk Street building in 1994, wrote that the Q.T. relied on the revenue they generated. "He [the Q.T. manager] will let any young hustler go in and sell his body," he wrote. "That's the only reason he still has his business standing. He lets all of the young hustlers bring in all the business for him."[82] By 1997 the Q.T. manager was president of the business association—a dramatic sign that sex work remained the street's main economic engine.[83]

In the late 1990s, a new bloc of business owners became a powerful po-litical force. New business owners remade many of the remaining hustler bars into upscale heterosexual or mixed drinking establishments serving new residents attracted by low rents during the dot-com era. A new busi-ness association, Lower Polk Neighbors, became a powerful political force. The association hired private security, steam-cleaned the alleyways, planted trees, and successfully pressured city officials to increase the number of po-lice patrols in the area and drive out the drug dealers, homeless, and hustlers who had long claimed space on the street. Corey and other hustlers, once the street's primary economic engine, were now bad for business.

In the late 1990s, Corey was arrested on a string of drug-related charges and returned to Polk Street. Corey wrote about the cops who "illegally ha-rassed him" on the street. "If they've driven passed me twice in a half of an hour, then they've stopped gotten out of their cars, and patted me down, as well, as run my name, and place me in cuffs, twice in a half of an hour without reason simply because they saw me walking in the neighborhood where I live." This on "a public sidewalk built for young San Franciscans." In 1997 Corey was arrested, sent to a state hospital, and diagnosed with HIV. Corey told his mom, he wrote Dan, "and she may be a little upset, be-cause I told her I was diagnosed with HIV+." But Corey's letters remained surprisingly childlike. In a letter to Dan, he said he'd like to go to Disney

Land and was "looking forward to going to the international house of pancakes." In 2001, writing from the Mercy Mountain Mission Bible Training Center, he said that he wanted to raise kids and buy a guitar. "And I'll be ready to rise above my obsticals. . . . I'll be home freshly bible studied, and freshly cleaned." But he needed money, he told Dan. "I was going to ask if you could send some more money."

With the collapse of the mutual obligations that animated street families, the responsibilities for Corey's care increasingly fell to new nonprofit workers. In 1996 a nonprofit called the Welcome Ministry was founded out of Polk Street's Old First Presbyterian Church. I talked with the Reverend Megan Rohrer, its twenty-eight-year-old director, who estimated that "98 percent" of the Polk Street homeless she served had been part of the sex-work economy. When Megan first met Corey in 2001, he had "the decision-making skills of probably a fourth grader, unable to keep his room up, unable to keep keys, unable to manage money." As Corey began losing his memory, he did remember that he lived in front of the Old First Presbyterian Church, and he often slept in front of the church. Megan recalled that Corey would have "loud, yelling conversations" on the sidewalk outside the church.

> Most people call it schizophrenia, believing that he was talking to people who didn't exist, but as I started listening to the conversations that Corey was having, I realized that he was having an argument with his mom. He was having the conversation of the day he came out to her, and his mom was always trying to tell him why he couldn't be gay and why it was a bad thing. And he was always trying to have the conversation that that was who he was, and it was how he loved. And he just kept having the conversation over and over and over, trying to have a different result, which never happened.

If others perceived Corey's screams as illegible outbursts, Megan heard them as a haunting scene of familial rejection. "People thought it was mental illness or drugs," she told me, "and it was just having a broken heart—out loud in a visible place where everyone could see it."

Megan began taking over the responsibilities that Dan and other "uncles" once fulfilled. A category of queer kinship on Polk Street, uncles provided food, clothing, and other resources to sex workers who had aged into the general homeless population. An uncle "would take care of them," Megan said, "because for years and years and years they had used their services." They "usually have more information than the Social Service people who

Megan Rohrer at Old First Presbyterian, 2008. Photograph by Gabriela Hasbun.

are trying to take care of them. . . . You can't tell if this person's taking advantage of [the unhoused person], which they probably are, or if it's a completely mutual relationship—it's just so impossible to know." Dan once kept Corey's Social Security card, money, and other personal items safe for him. He told me that he handed those items to Megan and her nonprofit organization. Megan went to doctor's appointments with Corey and visited him in jail. She would "babysit" his imaginary children when he went out to look for housing. Megan had been raised in the Midwest with a relatively supportive family and community. Polk Street "feels like the space that I'm supposed to be where the midwestern queer kid meets the other midwestern queer kids who didn't have it so well—and can try to be family for them," she said. "It kinda feels like a going full circle for me." Corey, rejected by a fundamentalist family, may have found solace in Megan, a minister who didn't ask him to change to be part of her church.

Corey ultimately received services and medication because of complaints from new business owners and residents. "The neighbors were getting really angry and wanted to get rid of the homeless from the area," Megan told me. Corey was one of the loudest and most disruptive at the time. In 2005 police arrested Corey on drug charges and he was declared mentally unfit to stand trial because of his schizophrenia. The court sent him to Napa State Hospital, a mental facility where he was required to take medications. "Finally, Corey was getting the mental health services he needed," Megan explained. Corey was at Napa for nearly a year on medications. "Corey make some really good strides there," Dan recalled. "He was also at his artistic high points. He built balsawood airplanes that he gave to children." When Corey was declared competent to stand trial and sent back to San Francisco, "he was like a completely different person," Megan said. "He was able to tell these long stories and advocate for himself, and could talk about—it was kind of like he woke up and he was like a normal, beautiful person. He was really clear about what he wanted and where he wanted to go." But the hospital didn't give him a single one of his medications, Megan noted. By the time Megan got his mental records from the hospital, two months later, "he had slowly gone back into his deep funk of schizophrenia and was at a point where he wasn't willing to go back on the medications again. It was like watching Corey emerge in this beautiful way and then to disappear in two because he had just been dumped." Corey never went back on medication, and his condition never improved. Evicted from city housing, he eventually moved back to the sidewalk in front of Megan's church.

Al Casciato, head of San Francisco Police Department's Northern Station, told me that Corey's story was common. "The problem we have is that we do not have a front end to the criminal justice system in the health arena. What happens is that we wait until they get in trouble in order to put them in jail to get them off the street and then try to get them into services," he told me. "We should be trying to get them into services first, but we do not have the capacity to accept everybody into services." Even after police convince a person to use services, "they fall back into their pattern of either drug abuse, or if they have a mental health issue, their depression starts to spin out again." In 1990 San Francisco mayor Art Agnos cited as the causes of homelessness in San Francisco "the critical shortage of low-cost housing, along with mental illness, drug and alcohol abuse, unemployment and family breakups."[84] The deinstitutionalization of state mental hospitals and rollback of the welfare state contributed to an increase in the number of mentally ill people being incarcerated across the country in the 1990s. Responsibility for mentally ill homeless individuals was displaced to a criminal justice system that was not designed to appropriately care for people's mental health needs.[85] Many, like Corey, ended up without services or housing.

Dan and Megan interpreted Corey's dramatic decline differently: while Dan focused on individual responsibility, Megan pointed to a failure of the social safety net. Dan had "hardened" about homelessness and had stopped talking with Corey, he told me. "I was an enabler for him, which I didn't like doing but I was always hoping that what I was doing was helping him," he said. "But maybe not. Corey made choices, and maybe they weren't good choices. And you can't blame that on the city." Megan blames Corey's decline in part on a failed social safety net. "There's a barrier to getting mental health services that seems like it's set up so that people will fail," she told me. "The hospital does not even have the capacity to help those that police deem a threat to themselves or others."

Dan and Megan both felt that Corey's decline resulted in part from social and economic changes on Polk Street and the demise of the moral economy that once thrived on the commercial corridor. "When there were gay bars here," Dan said, "there were affluent men, and that's not here anymore," he explained. "The bars are gone, those people who went to those bars don't come anymore, and Corey's just a remnant. He's just existing. He's surviving. He's just something that's eventually going to disappear from the scene." Megan felt that many of the homeless along Polk Street were "the litter of a changing economy." When someone gets "too drugged up, or too mentally ill to continue being a sex worker," she said, "they're just kind of stuck in this nowhere place."

"DAVID ROYAL LUNDY JUNIOR"
JAIL # 6TH FLOOR
C-TANK CELL #1
850 BRYANT STREET
SAN FRANCISCO CA

Dear "Dan Diez,"

I still have the last of the three Nightmares to tell you about. And I know that must not be your favorite part of these letters that I've written to you, but after you hear this one you will understand or comprehend much better why I WROTE ABOUT THE FIRST TWO. They are all truly nightmares that I experienced, while I was from three til approximately six years old . . .

I used to dream about floating in a space of nothingness. Nothing, no gravity, no breath, no friends, no houses, and no parents, no nothing except a soft low tone of a low humming noise that slowly and painfully sounded. And continuously I was floating, my head hurt from a swelling feeling like if there was absolutely no atmosphere it was like if I was all by myself totally there was no other existence accept for me and my bed. And that's all: just me and my bed, and I held on to my bed with all of my strength.

Me, my pajama bottoms and my shorts and my bed and there was no other existence, just me, my pajamas, my bed, and I was crying, because I was afraid of the nothing, and as I floated through space I was in pain, a pain that tortured me, a pain that wouldn't go away. I was dead. And I was crying for someone close to me, someone who loved me to catch me as I fell from the sky. . . .

See now I am trying to step out of a nightmare and back into a Dream . . . if someone is man enough to take some attitude adjustment rather than leaving people parts in dumpsters as far as I'm concerned . . . God bless them.[86] *See they'll keep the bloode off the streets and kickstart the new flower child era, and we'll bring so many happy campers back to "San Francisco" that we'll have the richest city in the world again just like it was five years ago rather than a ghost town like we have today!*

"A Traveler of Time and Space"

I had originally been wary of conducting an oral history with Corey, as I was unsure if he could reasonably give his consent, but Megan encouraged me to visit and talk with him. One day in 2008, I ran into Corey and asked him if he'd like to record an interview. His eyes lit up. He opened a Bible he was carrying to the title page, where the address of his SRO apartment was scrawled in pen. I told him I would come visit. Megan told me to bring crayons and paper when I visited. "As 'out of it' that Corey is and as mentally ill as he seems to be," she said, "if you give him a box of crayons, or a guitar, he will tell you the most lucid stories you've ever heard. He'll talk about his family that lives in a garage in Minnesota. He'll tell you stories about driving around in the fancy cars that he had."

A few days later, I brought paper and crayons to Corey's SRO building. His one-room apartment was an improvement over the streets, but it was

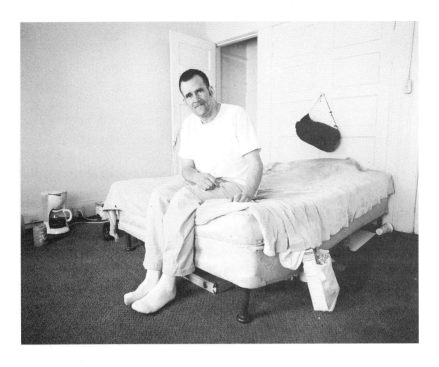

FIGURE 4.7.　　　　Corey Longseeker, 2008. Photograph by Gabriela Hasbun.

unclear whether Corey was capable of living on his own. A sink fastened to the wall was clogged with brackish water. The carpet was filthy with cigarette butts. I suppressed a scream when a mouse ran over my foot. Cartoons played on the television.

I set up my recording equipment and sat with Corey on his bed, the only piece of furniture in the room. Corey started drawing. I asked him what he was sketching. "A cute little pudgy dragon," he told me. I asked him why he came to San Francisco. "I came to San Francisco," he said, "because I wanted to be an artist." He spoke softly and slowly. "When I first got here, there were a lot more people. We used to play guitars and drink beers or smoke a joint and just hang out and stay out of trouble." He had a "fancy mustang" and apartment, he said. But "that was an awful long time ago."

He paused as he labored at his little dragon drawing. "There used to be a lot more people on Polk Street, it used to be a lot more fun. There used to be a lot more people, we used to play guitar and sing and dance and smoke and just have a good old time and now there's not so many people on Polk Street anymore. It makes me feel strange. Sometimes it hurts my feelings, sometimes it feels strange." A tenant knocked on the door as we were recording and stuck his head in. "I brought you a couple smokes," he said, "one for you and one for your friend." Corey thanked him and took a cigarette. I told his friend I didn't smoke. He retreated into the hallway. I asked Corey why it felt strange. "Because there's not very many people that I know out there anymore," he said. "Because I've been trying to protect my little self and my little brother and I'm about five hundred homicides behind and I don't know how to bump and grind to pick up the little morsels and the pieces of the people I liked and loved the way I used to know how to. . . . So I just keep on."

I asked Corey how long he had been in the hotel. "I've lived in this hotel now for a little more than three months, but I've seen myself as a traveler of time and space and I've seen my little brother as a traveler of time and space and I've been trying to get that cleared up and cleaned up." He paused. "Otherwise I don't know what else to say." I asked him, what does it mean to be a traveler of time and space? "I don't know how to explain that part," he said. "I'm not exactly sure how to explain that." He told me he wasn't sure where his "little brother" was. "I've been having a hard time seeing them in myself, and I've been having a hard time organizing it, because that's where they've been trapped as a traveler of time and space. And I don't know how to explain that part."

I wasn't sure what else to ask. I was also overcome by sadness while talking with him. I told him I would see him on the street and began packing up. Corey's caseworker arrived as I was leaving. "Well, I came to see what kind of condition your room is in," she told him. "What do you think?" Corey told her it was okay, that he was planning to take a nap. "Do you think we can clean up our room before we take a nap? Because this is the only time I'm going to be able to see you this week." Corey said, "All right." He addressed his imaginary child as I left, extending his arm and cupping his hand as though he was holding a child's hand. "Come in here, nincompooper," he said.

Weeks later, as I was reading through Corey's letters, I found that "little brother" referred to his former boyfriend, a hustler known on Polk Street as "Hey Now," who died years before of a drug overdose. I also learned that the phrase "traveler of time and space" likely referred to the Led Zeppelin song "Zashmir"—Megan told me that Corey was a huge Zeppelin fan. The song features the lyrics "Oh let the sun beat down upon my face, stars to fill my dream / I am a traveler of both time and space, to be where I have been" and continues "Here is the path that led me to that place / Yellow desert stream / My Shangri-La beneath the summer moon." If Corey was searching for meaning and an identity—a "Shangri-La," or the "flower child era" he references in his letters to Dan—he instead ended up lost and often alone.

Corey died in his hotel room in August 2013, five years after I visited him. Megan and I contacted the city's gay newspaper, which printed Corey's obituary, noting that his death "serves as the latest mark in the passing of the Polk neighborhood." A reporter reached out to his mother, Wendy Lundy. During a phone interview, she wept as she recalled the "very soft-spoken and kind-hearted, very, very well-behaved" artistic child she still called "Davey." The reporter asked his mother if she'd had trouble accepting her son's homosexuality. "I guess you could say that," she said. She added: "He lost himself in San Francisco."[87]

5.   Polk Street's Moral Economies

IN JUNE 2008, demonstrators from Gay Shame gathered at a site that had become emblematic of gentrification on Polk Street: a condominium building and ground-floor Congregational church being constructed on the razed remains of a former hustler bar called the RendezVous. On first glance, the demonstrators may have been taken for an out-of-season Halloween party. Ghostly painted faces and costumes drew honks from passing cars and double takes from pedestrians. Many protesters wielded saxophones, loudspeakers, and bullhorns. But the costumes served a more spiritual purpose. "This is a séance," an organizer announced through a bullhorn, "to summon the ghosts of Polk Street's past!"

They focused their rancor on a new neighborhood association, Lower Polk Neighbors (LPN), which was holding a meeting inside the Congregational church. A small group of business owners was visible behind the floor-to-ceiling glass walls. An organizer took up a bullhorn. "We are protesting the Lower Polk Neighbors," he shouted, "who are bent on erasing anything that does not fit into a white picket fence!" The demonstrators roared their approval. "They shut down the RendezVous and other poor queer watering holes to try to change the demographics and makeup of this entire neighborhood! It used to be mixed, multicultural, fucking working class, queer—

and we're not gonna take it." He was at full volume, the bullhorn distorting: "We're not gonna take it! The drug addicts are not going to take it! The working-class queers are not going to take it! We oppose cultural erasure!" Two people held a banner to the glass: "Don't Erase Our Past."

Demonstrators responded by calling on the district's ghosts and asking them to haunt those who would obliterate their memory. "What do people feel like doing now?" the organizer asked the crowd. "Do you want to channel the spirits?" People shouted their approval. "It's time to summon the spirits!" A saxophone rose above a track of discordant electronica. The organizer yelled again: "Channel the spirits!" The demonstrators shouted even louder. Trumpets blared. The saxophone became wild and the electronic music grew louder. Car alarms began going off. I covered my ears. The buttoned-up businesspeople meeting inside the church looked out onto the sidewalk, startled and confused.

In the late 2000s, Polk Street was in transition, and in crisis, as monied, primarily white, heterosexual residents claimed space in the area. The most vulnerable and fugitive members of the street family, such as homeless and transgendered people of color, were fighting a losing battle against the neoliberal, homonormative neighborhood boosters who wanted them gone, "sweeping the streets clean" of trash. Management of a transgender club called Divas alleged that Alcohol and Beverage Control (ABC) tried to revoke their liquor license at the behest of merchants. New merchants attempted to rename the district "Polk Village," a point of contention that became symbolic of a battle over the area's very identity. The Gay Shame séance was one of many dramatic conflicts and daily tensions that took place as people from vastly different backgrounds fought for their right to the city.

Overview and Methods

In this chapter, I draw on ethnographic and archival research to examine the transformation of Polk Street in the late 2000s from a working-class queer commercial corridor to a gentrified entertainment destination serving the new economy's tech elite. I take the reader on a walk up and down Polk Street—in and out of the district's alleyways, taverns, posh new clubs, and SRO hotels—and introduce them to some of the people I met. I talked with patrons and staff at the transgender Divas nightclub, populated primarily by immigrants from Asia and Latin America; patrons and street kids at Kimo's, Polk Street's last hustler bar; the owners of the RendezVous; and the new

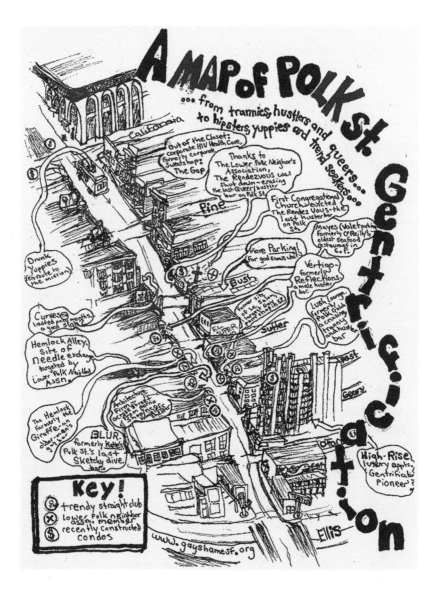

FIGURE 5.1.   "A Map of Polk St. Gentrification," Gay Shame, ca. 2007.

business association leaders seeking to transform the street's economy and culture. In the process, I outline the competing moral and economic norms at play in the transformation of Polk Street. While conflicts were of course triggered by the razing and closing of spaces in which queer working-class and homeless people lived, socialized, and worked, these grievances were grounded in a set of shared moral values, social norms, obligations, performance practices, and conceptions of justice—a shared performative economy. It was outrage to these moral assumptions, just as much as the demise of the local economy, that generated such strong feelings of exclusion and anger.

I show in chapter 4 that the HIV/AIDS and methamphetamine crises undermined the performative economy in the 1980s and 1990s. The death knell, I show in this chapter, was urban neoliberalism: a set of practices and laws designed to make urban spaces attractive to global capital and the creative classes that comprise the high-tech new economy, including the reinvestment of capital in central cities, often through governmental tax breaks for large corporations; public-private partnerships; and new waves of policing strategies and campaigns that drive perceived sources of disorder from gentrifying public spaces.[1] The economic and social transformations associated with urban neoliberalism radically undermined the preexisting social patterns—the reciprocities, obligations, and moral codes kids developed for limiting competition and controlling pricing—that constituted the performative economy, leading to a more competitive marketplace in which kids and those who made up the larger vice economy no longer "had each other's backs." These structural changes permitted clients, the police, and businesses to increasingly violate the moral economy, leading to an environment the kids considered exploitative.

While the story I tell in this chapter is specific to a few square blocks in San Francisco, these local conflicts highlight pressing issues—gentrification, economic inequality, and the policing of public space—that have transformed central cities across the country. Gentrification is so damaging because it restricts the availability and viability of new and inventive forms of kinship, politics, and alternative social projects. Gentrification, as Sarah Schulman defines it, is "the removal of the dynamic mix that defines urbanity—the familiar interaction of different kinds of people creating ideas together." The privatization of public space restricts the viability of new cultures and politics, contributing to what Schulman calls the "gentrification of the mind."[2] What is at stake in the transformation of districts like Polk Street is our ability to remember the politics of mutual aid that once defined the migratory scene and to imagine new ways of being and becoming.

A Sexual Marketplace: 1980s–2000s

Polk Street demographics changed dramatically over the 1980s from a primarily white gay male space to one populated by racialized minorities and transgender women. By the early 1980s, Tamara Ching told me, "you started to see a sprinkling of Asian, Latino, and Black gay men." The N'Touch was populated by young Asian men and older white men who might as often be objects of desire as dismissed as fetishistic "rice queens." Polk Street became the center of the city's transgender street prostitution scene when the owner of a gay bar, the Motherlode, "turned" it transgender around 1989, attracting the clientele of the Black Rose, a trans club in the Tenderloin that was, according to one article, "having a tough time avoiding prostitution and drugs."[3] The owner of the Motherlode "originally wanted to open it up as a gay bar for Asian boys," an informant told me, but "he was making more money off the transgenders than he would be the gay boys." The Motherlode "turned into a huge meat rack. The girls were hanging out the window, they were stopping traffic. Many times there were accidents, just from people taking a double take as to what was going on." In 1998 the Motherlode moved across the street and was renamed Divas. The three-story club was populated primarily by trans women of color, many of them immigrants from Asia or Latin America.[4] My informants thus described Polk Street in the 1990s as a sexual marketplace in which clients—primarily white men—could fulfill sexual and often racialized fantasies.

The 1997–2001 dot.com boom triggered an affordability and rental crisis across San Francisco. Many neighborhoods had already undergone gentrification and displacement, but the sudden influx of tens of thousands of Silicon Valley tech workers caused rents and no-fault evictions to skyrocket. Artists and young people were among the first wave of Polk Street gentrification. According to a 1997 article, "young people, especially artists," flocked to Polk Street because of its relatively low rents and abundant housing. Many characterized Polk Street as "hip" and appealing because of the hustling scene. Drag queen Juanita MORE! said in 1997 that "all the hustling and drugs and the trannies who are here—I like them here, and I think they are part of what makes the neighborhood cool and hip and what it is." Polk Street "is fun," according to an artist who moved to Polk Street

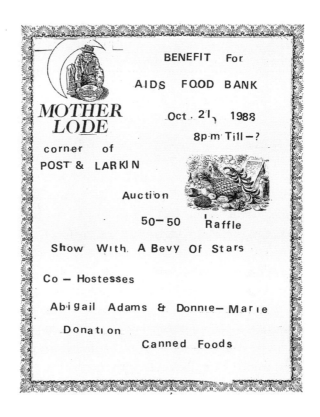

BENEFIT For

AIDS FOOD BANK

MOTHER
LODE

Oct . 21, 1988

8p·m Till – ?

corner of
POST & LARKIN

Auction

50– 50 Raffle

Show With A Bevy Of Stars

Co – Hostesses

Abigail Adams & Donnie– Marie

Donation

Canned Foods

FIGURE 5.2.   Motherlode flier, 1988. Courtesy of GLBT Historical Society.

because of the cheap rents and organized a club night at a local bar. "You party with the old men and the street hustlers. Everyone knows each other at the bars." Meanwhile, the manager of the Q.T. hustler bar began beefing up the police presence. "My attitude was, I'd lose my business unless I did something," he said in 1997. "We had the highest crime rate in the city. We're talking heavy-duty crimes: rape, murder, you name it. We demanded police protection. As a result, today we have bike and foot patrols. They prevent crimes just by their presence." As a result, violent crime was down and "the neighborhood is showing signs of a renaissance. Empty storefronts are less common, new businesses have moved in, and old businesses are being refurbished." A newspaper article in 1997 declared that "virtually everyone shares the same sentiment: Polk Street is on its way back."[5]

New business owners lured by Polk Street's relatively low rents and central location also framed Polk Street as an unsafe space plagued by "undesirables" and began to police them out of the district. Many began buying up hustler bars and reopening them as upscale heterosexual or "mixed" bars. In 2000 a merchant bought out two queer bars, which he called magnets for "bottom-feeder gay men," and turned them into upscale bars serving an upscale clientele. "With a vigilante spirit," an article read, "he drove the transgender prostitutes out of the Lush Lounge" and "chased drug dealers off the sidewalk." This formula "not only has worked to attract young bar-hoppers (most straight, some gay) but also is inspiring a new social scene."[6] In 2005 the *San Francisco Bay Times* noted "a trend" on Polk Street as gay bars "change hands, redecorate . . . then put in a bid for a new clientele; often straight"—"in other words, hustler-free zones."[7] Management at Divas alleged that ABC tried to revoke their liquor license at the behest of merchants. In 2005 ABC conducted several undercover operations, made arrests for prostitution, and suspended the club's liquor license on the basis that the bartenders had failed to prevent sex work.[8] An article in a gay newspaper in 2005 denounced what the journalist called the "de-gaying" of Polk Street.[9] And smaller, daily tensions arose as people from vastly different backgrounds—merchants, service providers, police, sex workers, and street youth—came in contact with one another.

Lower Polk Neighbors, founded in the early 2000s, worked jointly with the City of San Francisco to remake Polk Street. District Attorney Kamala Harris responded to LPN pressure by ramping up the street's police presence and installing high-tech surveillance equipment. Supervisor Aaron Peskin convinced the Mayor's Office of Economic and Workforce Development to include Lower Polk in its Neighborhood Marketplace Initiative, a program designed to "revitalize" business districts. In 2005, LPN secured a $90,000 grant from the Department of Public Works to "clean up" the streets and alleyways and won $1 million from a city program to install new lights and plant trees like those in front of the architecture studio. In 2006 the association created the Lower Polk Community Court, overseen by the District Attorney's office, whereby a jury of local residents sentences those who commit "quality-of-life offenses" to a fine or community service. Lower Polk Neighbors also sought to drive out needle exchanges, liquor stores, drug dealers, and, above all, the homeless and sex workers, and the bars that welcomed them. Their efforts exemplify "urban neoliberalism," where public-private partnerships and Business Improvement Districts are designed to attract private investment while policing strategies drive perceived sources of "disorder" from public spaces.

The neighborhood association was made up of business owners and residents who formed bonds across differences of sexual identity through their shared interest in property values and what scholar George Lipsitz calls an "investment in whiteness."[10] Some association members also made a distinction between what they called "good" and "bad" gays: the (primarily white) homosexuals who contributed to the street's gentrification, on the one hand, and the homosexuals (including street kids, the homeless, and racialized populations) who were a potential threat to capital, on the other. In these imaginaries, Christina Hanhardt and other queer scholars show, wealthy gay consumers are good investors, and poor queer people, people of color, street kids, and sex workers are detrimental to "quality of life."[11] Neighborhood association representatives claimed they were simply working to promote "safety" and cleanliness. "I had no idea," LPN cofounder Carolyn Abst told the *Wall Street Journal* in 2006, "that cleanliness, beauty, and safety could get people so riled up." Anti-gentrification activists, the author of the *Journal* article claimed, "aren't fighting the usual gentrification battle over displacing low-income families. Instead, they are fighting for the neighborhood's gritty ambience."[12]

Center of the Conflict

The center of the conflict, when I arrived in 2007, was a glass-walled architecture studio at the base of Polk Street. The studio, Case+Abst Architects, had been the workplace and home of husband-and-wife Carolyn Abst and Ron Case since 1999. The two cofounded Lower Polk Neighbors. Heavy black gates protected the studio's floor-to-ceiling glass walls. Two palm trees, freshly planted in front of the studio, were conspicuous on a street largely devoid of greenery. Across the street was a porn shop featuring a wall-to-ceiling Technicolor image of a mustached, shirtless man promising "Hot Bareback Action!" Next door was a large homeless shelter.

I visited Ron Case at the studio in 2008. A slim man in his fifties, wearing a crisp dress shirt and khakis, Case was welcoming, almost ingratiating. He seemed eager to present himself as something other than a "gentrifier" or "homophobic," two words that were bad for business in liberal San Francisco. When he and his wife first arrived on the street, Case told me, many of the businesses were vacant and crime was rampant. But they weren't discouraged. The studio was a great price and located near City Hall, the ballet, and Union Square. "I gotta take a gamble," he told me. "I gotta take

FIGURE 5.3.   Ron Case, 2008. Photograph by Gabriela Hasbun.

a chance." One of the first people they met was Steve Black, who "came over and welcomed us to the area and started telling us some of the problems," Case said. "And he's investing in the neighborhood and trying to clean [it] up, least his area." Case appealed to the safety of children and families to justify gentrification and displacement. He founded the neighborhood association in 2006 after seeing "two little kids," he said, "step over this guy who's passed out on the sidewalk to get on the school bus." Case appeared to care only about the "little kids" on their way to school. Case presented the person on the street as merely an obstacle to be removed, not a human in need of help.

The RendezVous was among the "problem" businesses that Lower Polk Neighbors succeeded in ejecting from the neighborhood. Case told me he never entered the bar but was troubled by the "shady element" congregating outside. "It wasn't a place you even wanted to walk by. People were yelling and screaming and it was just—it was just total chaos in a way." I asked him what exactly was "shady" about the men. "When we see prostitutes," he explained, "they have the really skimpy outfits on, you look at them and say,

'That's not really what you go to work in, that's not really what you stand around in.' It was the same way with the kids. The shirts were off. The poor kids looked like they were being prostituted." Case also expressed distaste for displays of queer sexuality. "You would have the guys hangin' out with no shirts on—just a lot of people hangin' out. More than just smoking. And that became, for the whole neighborhood, everybody started to recognize that as a potential problem." The association blamed bar owners for the hustlers who gathered at the bar.

The association asked the bar to pay for private security and demanded that it exclude street kids from the sidewalks in front of the building. According to 2005 LPN meeting minutes, Case asked the bar owners to look into "finding ways to improve its clientele."[13] The RendezVous owners objected. "When the association talks about these 'undesirable elements,'" RendezVous bar co-owner Paul Xaviar was quoted as saying in a 2005 article in the *Bay Area Reporter*, "in actuality, some of those people are probably our patrons standing outside having their cigarette. . . . There's this idea of the gay culture conflicting with their moral ideas."[14] Case told me the owners "didn't feel like they were doing anything wrong. I'm not saying they were promoting [prostitution]. They just allowed it to happen. . . . We were more shocked than anything that they thought this was acceptable." The association told the city's Planning Department that the owners weren't "good neighbors," Case said. The Planning Department responded by denying the RendezVous's request to remain open. "There used to be young kids all up and down Polk Street," Case told me. After they closed the RendezVous and razed it to the ground, "that was the last time that we actually saw kids hanging out. That was the last vestige of kids on the street that we saw."

A few weeks later, I walked up Polk Street to the former site of the RendezVous, where the First Congregational Church and several high-end condominiums were being constructed. Pastor Wilfried Glabach and steering committee member Ken Tipton took me on a tour of the two-story church. It was, as Wilfried put it, "very modern": exposed brick walls, floor-to-ceiling windows, and a second-floor worship space with an open glass ceiling. Thirty-two condominium units were under construction next to the church. An advertisement on the building boasted apartments with custom cabinets and granite counters priced at $630,000 each. Wilfried and Ken told me that they moved to Polk Street after it became clear that a shrinking congregation could no longer cover the rent on their downtown building. Polk Street was one of the only affordable areas left in the city during the dot-com boom. They were unprepared for the neighborhood's negative reception. "A lot of people were really scared," Wilfried said, "or upset when they heard a church was coming to Polk Street. And they felt that we were a very fundamentalist church, and that we just moved there because we hate gay people, and we wanted to transform this neighborhood." Ken agreed. "There were things in the [gay newspaper] *Bay Area Reporter*, and people saying negative things about the church on the street that were reported back. And it was like, how can it be so negative when we're so positive?"

Ken and Wilfried, both white gay men, were bewildered by charges of homophobia, lobbied by the gay press, protesters, and residents on the street. "I mean it's ridiculous," Ken told me. "We have a gay group, we have a track record of being the most liberal Christian denomination supporting gays." He told me their national church body voted to affirm marriage equality. "I mean"—Ken laughed, incredulously—"our denomination—*our denomination*—let me repeat that, has had films in the gay film festival, produced by *our denomination*." Wilfried said, "People should really see who we are and what we are doing and that we are really not judgmental at all." This said, Ken himself made distinctions and judgments about different queer ways of being in our interview. "We're not *necessarily* against any segment of the gay community," he told me. "We do feel that maybe the young hustlers are needing more help than they're getting from that way of life, and that finishing education and having secure living arrangements are probably what they need." The RendezVous "was an underage hustler club," he said. "So yes, that no longer is an option on this corner. So we're aware of that. It's just that we have gotten more compliments for that than negatives."

Deco Lounge: "History You Can Talk with Today"

When they were ejected from the neighborhood, the owners of the RendezVous—David Kapp and James Beales—opened a new bar, Deco Lounge, further into the Tenderloin. David and James cooked a free lunch every Thursday in their apartment above the bar for their regular patrons. I stopped by on a Thursday afternoon in 2008. When I arrived, 1950s-era big band jazz played over the speakers. Many Polk Street "old-timers" were there, some in their eighties, many making the trek from their SRO apartments. I found that many were part of the post–World War II migration of gay veterans to San Francisco in the 1940s and 1950s. Patrons were celebrating the birth-

FIGURE 5.4.   David Kapp and James Beales, 2008. Photograph by Gabriela
                    Hasbun.

day of an elderly man named Dennis. "We're having S.O.S.," one person told
me. "Collard beans, peas—because that's what we ate in the army." (S.O.S.
is World War II troop slang for chipped beef on toast.) A man in his early
forties introduced himself as Kiko and explained he was the bar's "resident
DJ and security." Kiko told me he arrived on the street as a hustler before
working as a bouncer at the RendezVous. Wearing a baggy football jersey,
Kiko greeted the patrons by name, hugging and joking with them.

    In an oral history after the meal, David and James told me they'd been
living together as a couple and working in Polk Street bars for more than
twenty years. The Deco Lounge, James said, "reminds me of the old days of
Polk Street, because all the old fogies hang out here." David agreed. "The
last remaining," David called his clientele. David told me he moved to San
Francisco from Pennsylvania in 1982. James grew up in a family of auto factory workers in Toronto before coming to San Francisco in 1986, at nineteen, to "come out" in the gay mecca. When he first arrived in the city, James
was leery of Polk Street, "having heard typical stories that you'd hear about

it being a hustler area, drugs, and old men going after boys. But it really wasn't like that at all once I got down there." James found what he called a "typical neighborhood—very diverse, racially. There were a lot of bars on the street there, a lot of older people there. . . . People with nine-to-five jobs who work in the office, who otherwise don't fit in other places, always fit in on Polk Street. Always."

David and James became part of the reciprocal obligations of street kids and bartenders on the street. "The bartenders on Polk Street, I discovered, knew each other and looked out for each other," James said. "There were the runaways on the street, the young kids, they sort of looked out for each other too. There's a lot of friendships. People went to all the bars. All the bars were their home." The two joined the Tavern Guild and went on picnics and trips with the group. James learned about Polk Street's history from his aging patrons.

> It's an old neighborhood. And being a bartender on Polk Street, people told me stories about how they were young. These people were fired from their jobs, they were in the military, they had to be careful, they had to be closeted from their families. They lost their families and had come to San Francisco to reconnect and make new families. They worked as bartenders, they worked with the Tavern Guild, which formed to fight police discrimination. . . . I have a lot of respect for these men and women who went through such hard times to give me a better life and freedoms. These people are alive today and I respect what they did.

James was tapping into a living history, he told me, a "history you can talk with today."

David and James explained that they began to approach street kids as engaged in a way of life that may have operated in ways that were at odds with conventional morality but that they accepted as valid. "The kids on the street, the hustlers," James told me, "when you're working there every day, you get to know them. And once you got to know a person you didn't really judge them for being what they were." They found that the kids were part of an extended family on Polk Street. "It was more like a family," David told me. "I'd see customers taking care of these kids." David and James began to accept divergences from the norm among many people on the street. There were "a lot of crazy characters," James said. A man named Chip "was a bald man who shot his wife and spent time in jail." He had a "gimp arm" and "would make lewd comments about it. He's one of these people when

I came down to Polk Street, I thought, 'Who is this? I don't want to know him.' But having to deal with him every day, you relax your attitudes. He soon became a fun guy and we used to joke around all the time. . . . We all accepted each other, and I thought that was a great feeling."

James and David bought a bar, which they called the RendezVous, and felt they were keeping Polk Street's traditions alive through various functions and charities. They hired bartenders who lived in the neighborhood. Drag queens in the Imperial Court held their functions at the bar. The Rendez-Vous helped organize "Bar Wars," in which groups of patrons walked from bar to bar, raising money for AIDS-related charities. In 1985 Bar Wars benefited the Godfather Service Fund, a standing committee of the San Francisco Tavern Guild Foundation, which provided services directly to patients of the AIDS ward at San Francisco General.[15] James and David played in a bar-based baseball team called the Hustlers, some of the members hustlers themselves, which also raised funds for area charities. James continued to talk with older patrons, who sometimes brought James photos and other ephemera from the 1960s and 1970s. "They would bring me photos of what they looked like then, before the AIDS crisis." James slowly amassed an archive in his apartment and used these materials to curate historical wall exhibits at the RendezVous. David occasionally hired kids to wash the windows for twenty dollars or invited them in for a free meal or drink. James said the kids "were allowed in the bar as long as they were discreet" and "conducted themselves like gentlemen. Whatever arrangements they made in secret or by themselves were up to them."

James and David were outraged that the neighborhood association strong-armed them off Polk Street. However, their anger and indignation resulted not just from the closure of their business but from the outrage to the shared moral assumptions and reciprocities that made up the street scene. "I was just upset," James said, "that when we tried to hold the Club RendezVous as one last bastion of the gay history and culture on Polk Street that we were stamped out like that at the end. To be sent out like that was wrong, it was like salt in the wound." David was angry about the "authoritarian" style with which the neighborhood association pushed them off the street. He felt "betrayed" by the merchants. "Bunch of Gestapos, that's what I felt like, I thought I was in Germany"—David laughed—"being prosecuted." Both David and James acknowledged that the economics of owning a gay bar on Polk Street were "just not feasible." David said he'd seen the bar rents double in some cases, and the clientele dropped after the AIDS crisis. "Business nowadays couldn't support that many bars on the street," James said. "I think that the demise of the Polk Street gay scene was a natural progression."

I returned to Deco Lounge a few weeks later and interviewed Kevin "Kiko" Lobo on the top floor of the bar. "I've been around the Polk Gulch area since about 1982 when I was about—let's see, '82—I was about eighteen years old," he said. He told me he was born in the primarily Latinx Mission district of San Francisco. His dad was a cop, his mom a housewife. Kiko "chose to be the black sheep of the family." He was part of a street gang in the Mission before hustling Polk Street.

Like others, Kiko remembered Polk Street as a sexual marketplace. "Each bar was unique in its own fashion," Kiko told me, "because each had its own crowd. The N'Touch: Asians, if you wanted Asian street boys you could go there. The White Swallow: mostly older crowd. The Cinch: country western. Reflections: street guys, hardcore. And the Q.T. was pretty boys. And then there was the corners. Austin Alley, Hemlock Alley. Pretty much all of Polk Street from about O'Farrell Street all the way up to Washington Street you could pretty much get what you wanted. It was a smorgasbord." Kiki also explained, "There were a lot of kids on the streets so [Polk Street] was full. The action was constant. It was never dull, ever, that I can remember." Kids would also migrate. They would do "the L.A. tour, as we like to call it. We would migrate to Los Angeles and hustle down there."

In the 1980s, Kiko would hustle Polk Street and pool money with other kids to rent a hotel room and buy food and liquor. "There'd be four or five of us in hotels staying up in the hotels," he told me. "We all needed each other. Everything was family. We all looked out for each other. If you didn't make any money that day, it didn't mean you were going to sleep on the street. Your brother or your sister . . . made sure that you had a roof over your head or a place to sleep." Kiko said he developed a sense of self-worth by watching out for the most vulnerable. He may have looked like a "thug," he related, "but I looked out for my bro. . . . We milled together to be safe, to have something to cling with because all of us were lost souls." Kiko also came to terms with his own sexuality through sex work. "I was kinda homophobic," he explained, but his clients included high-ranking politicians, police officers, and people in the District Attorney's office. These were "people of power and meaning and substantiation here in San Francisco," Kiko said. If they could be gay, he thought, "then I can be comfortable and not afraid." Kiko counted them as his friends.

Kiko told me about a Polk Street bartender at the Q.T. who in the 1980s facilitated transactions between hustlers and clients. When Kiko was too young to hustle in the bars, "I was always on the corner or walkin' around out in front." One day a bartender "just invited me in and he told me don't worry about—just sit and do your thing." The bartender "was probably my best friend, my best influence. I guess that he introduced me to pretty much everybody I know." The bars depended on revenue generated by sex workers. The bartender invited him in, Kiko told me, "because he knew I could bring in people. People would come and sit down with me at the bar and spend money and drink." In return, the bartender introduced Kiko to clients. "Nobody lost," he said, "because the bar made money, I got a few drinks, and I met clients." Kiko remembered him fondly. "He was kind of like my other dad and my brother. He was a very caring and dear man to me." Kiko worked his way up Polk Street's employment ladder in the mid-1980s, first as a bouncer. "Who better to be able to deal with the street kids, my family, [than] me."

The kids banded together to protect each other, but violence was endemic on the street. Kiko told me about his friend Tommy Wenger, whom people found chopped up in a dumpster on Polk Street. Tommy "was very well known in the community," Kiko said. "He was a hustler. He was gay. He was young. He was a very pretty, blond, blue-eyed boy from—I think he was from the Midwest. He was one of my close friends on this street." Kiko remembers people being murdered on the street because they were hustlers.

> Tommy was the worst. It was very sickening to walk by a roped-off alley and know that the bags you see them pullin' out of this fucking thing is your friend. . . . We became a lot more tightknit as street hustlers. If you were hustlin' the corner, you stood there in a group. Two, three. Somebody always got the license plate number of the car—or the description of the car—or remembered what the person looked like. You had a backup. You weren't doing this shit by yourself. We always made sure that after that that nobody, nobody was by themselves. Nobody deserved to die like that, especially kids. We were not throwaways. We were not nobodies. We're not garbage. I have no love for people that want to abuse those that are weaker than them.

Kiko told me he still saw the "remnants" of his street family hanging out on Polk Street. Many of them had been jailed, or developed severe mental illnesses, or became part of the homeless population. "Some are incarcer-ated, due to what the street turned them into," Kiko told me. "Some of my friends are just really fucked-up on dope and pushing shopping carts around or talking to themselves. . . . For me, it was a better change. My family was my family and that's what my concern was. I spent more time worrying about other people on Polk Street and dealing with other people on Polk Street than I cared to worry about myself." He said he was trying to keep his family alive at Deco.

> I think what we remember [at Deco] is that we were together as a family, as a unit, as a community. It's just the best way I can describe it. . . . I'm here because these people are my family. I would probably be pushing a shopping cart if it wasn't for this place and my friends and my family that have been with me through the thicks and the thins and the ups and the downs of my life. I miss it a lot. We are a part of which is becoming a fast nonexisting thing now. We're losing our community.

Alexis Miranda and Divas

Developers were also targeting Divas, a three-story transgender club just across the street from the Case+Abst architecture studio. Lower Polk Neigh-bors complained about street prostitution outside the club, and ABC re-sponded by targeting the business. The first time I walked into Divas, in 2007, manager Alexis Miranda was showing off the club's new zebra-print carpet to customers and making sure they knew that it matched her zebra-print bodysuit. "No jacking off at the bar," she joked. "We just got new carpet." A few men sat at the bar. Others played video poker. The Motherlode's iconic neon sign was hanging behind the first-floor bar, a reminder of the club's history. When I told Alexis I was researching the history of Polk Street, she sidestepped my requests for an oral history and instead lectured me about transphobic media representations of the club. Over the next few months, I came back every other day, as customer-historian. I would sit at the bar buy-ing drinks, watching Alexis patiently answer questions posed by visitors—or stare down an unwelcome customer until they slinked out of the bar—all while filling drinks for the girls.

I chatted with Alexis one day as she stood outside the club. She pointed to a bar across the street. Until 2000, it was a cruisy transgender and hus-tler bar called the Polk Gulch Saloon. Now it was the upscale Lush Lounge,

FIGURE 5.5.   Alexis Miranda, 2008. Photograph by Gabriela Hasbun.

where white twenty-something heterosexuals sipped apple-pie martinis. Alexis said that the owner ejected her when she went to welcome him to the neighborhood; she responded by reporting him to the Human Rights Commission. Alexis recalled, "We've all been thrown out of there." A twenty-eight-year-old trans woman with curly brown hair said she was also thrown out. "We don't accept your kind here," a bartender allegedly told her. "If you're a tranny," she said, "you're a whore or a freak." Alexis explained: "The people coming in here with money want to take out the life that has always been Polk Street. And create their own ambience. They want to gentrify the neighborhood."

Alexis finally agreed to an oral history after I organized several mediated dialogues between warring factions on Polk Street, which I describe in the "intervention" following this chapter. One night, after her shift at Divas, she brought me to her rent-controlled apartment in the Mission—filled with wigs, feathers, and trophies—which she shared with drag queens. (Alexis told me she identified as a "female impersonator.") While Alexis took off her makeup and wig, I chatted with her housemate Big D about the Tenderloin in the 1960s, when it was teeming with sailors, hustlers, and hair fairies. The hair fairies, she told me, were "nelly little boys who wore makeup and fluffed their hair up" and who "paraded through" the street. When police ramped up their harassment of people in the Tenderloin in the 1970s, she told me, "sensible people moved on" and Polk Street became the center of "the scene." Alexis returned to the living room in a nightgown and slippers. We sat on her couch and I began to record.

Alexis began her story with a keen sense of the ways in which familial abandonment is the "common ground" for queer kinship on Polk Street. "Most people that come to San Francisco, particularly with Polk Street, don't have a bond with their family," Alexis explained. "Which is why they come here to create their own. And you create your role models, and they later become your parents, or your family, I would say. That's the common ground there: that you're ostracized in your own family so you come to San Francisco to be yourself, and that's exactly how my story came to be."

Alexis's conception of "family" and queerness is shaped by her Cuban American background. Scholars have established that "familism," a concept that emphasizes loyalty, solidarity, and interdependence with family, is important for many Latino groups. Familism refers to familial honor, the belief that the individual is responsible for preserving the family name, and subjugation of self for family, the belief that an individual must respect family rules.[16] Alexis told me she grew up in Miami and was raised by parents who emigrated from Cuba. "I wanted to get as far away from Florida as I could," she said, "so I did not embarrass or tarnish the family name. I wanted to live my life without having to run into anyone I knew to judge me." She clarified: "Not that I consider myself an embarrassment. But in the straight world, or in the Latino world, Cubans specifically, my lifestyle might not exactly be welcome. So this way I can live the way I want."

Alexis began performing drag at a young age. "In Florida, I came into the drag community when I came into the drag gay bar," she said. "I saw a lot of the drag shows and I was mesmerized by that, and I thought, Oh, I can do that." Alexis heard San Francisco was "the gay capital, that a lot of things were happening, that I could be myself." At nineteen, in 1986, she decided to move to the city. "I hopped the bus, and seven days later I was in San Francisco." The Greyhound bus station was in the Tenderloin, "so I walk a couple a blocks and the first hotel I saw that had rooms available, I took it." She hung out at a transgender nightclub in the Tenderloin called the Black Rose, "and I just sat there and watched everything and how it happened. And a couple weeks later, they had asked me to enter a lip sync contest and that's how I started entertaining." She hung out at Esta Noche, a queer Latinx bar in the Mission district. After a few months on General Assistance, Alexis got a job at Denny's, "and then moved on to Sizzler, and on Polk Street, while I was working in the daytime, I went out at night and was carousing the shows. So I was doing the shows for twenty dollars a week and I was lovin' it."

Alexis met a Cuban American drag queen, Lola, at the Latinx drag bar Esta Noche. Lola became her "drag mother." (In talking about Lola, Alexis alternated between "he" and "she" pronouns.) Lola "was Cuban like I was, so we had a lot of things in common," Alexis told me. "I respected him." Lola taught Alexis how to make dresses and entertain at clubs. "He taught me how to embellish dresses and put rhinestones on them, and I made jewelry at that time because I couldn't afford jewelry, so I made all of it with him." Lola helped Alexis understand the differences between exploitation and mutual reciprocity in the central city. "I had to tell the difference between my friends and family and acquaintances," Alexis said. "Lola was just telling me, 'You have a lot of growing up to do. People are not all honest and people are not all giving and they're not always gonna do what's right for you.'" She learned the difference between her "family and acquaintants," she said. "Your friends and your family will be there for you—and not necessarily blood, just family as in gay people, or trannies even. And then there's people who want to take advantage of you and get whatever they can out of you. You learn that through time." Being on Polk Street—what Alexis called the "core of the party"—opened up a variety of possibilities and challenges, which Lola helped her navigate. "The bathhouses were here, nightclubs, bars, drugs," Alexis said. "And from that spans a lot of different things: disease, drug addiction, homelessness, everything. On the up side, you have people willing to work together, and not judge you if you do do drugs, or if you do do drag, or if you're black or Asian, they deal with you."

Alexis became involved with the Imperial Court, a fundraising organization founded in 1965. The first time Alexis saw an empress, "I just saw this big, beautiful girl walking down the street in beaded dresses and furs, and everyone said, 'Oh, that's the empress.' And it was a big deal back then. You would walk into a bar and people would applaud and give you respect and all of that stuff. And I wanted a piece of that." In 1998 Alexis was elected the thirty-third Empress of the Imperial Court. "I was the first Latina elected empress in San Francisco and that means a lot to me because my heritage means a lot to me," she said. Alexis called it the Imperial Family—a vast kinship network that cared for the most marginal. "If somebody is homeless," she explained, "we do fundraisers for organizations that would supply a home for them. If you have AIDS, it covers the AIDS Emergency Fund. If you're hungry, Project Open Hand is there. 'Cause you never know when you're going to fall and you're going to need those services." The Imperial Court "taught me how to be giving, selfless. . . . You learn to work as a team, 'cause at the end of the day, you're still part of a family."

In the process of becoming Lola's drag daughter, Alexis became part of a longer family lineage on Polk Street. Lola's mother was Big D, the queen I talked with before interviewing Alexis. "If Lola was still alive, I would still be her daughter. Like my so-called grandmother, who is Big D, who was Lola's mother, is still alive, so I call her my grandmother. 'Cause she taught Lola, Lola taught me." In time, Alexis herself became a mother to many of the kids on Polk Street. Most of her girls had been thrown out of families of origin, and many were undocumented immigrants from Asia or Latin America. Alexis took on her first daughter, a young Puerto Rican named Jason, in the late 1990s. (In talking about Jason and other daughters, Alexis alternated between "he" and "she" pronouns.) "His name was Jason and he was on drugs," she told me. "At that time, she wanted to be a tranny, and her boyfriend was beating her up and she was on the streets and she was high. She needed somewhere to go, and she came to my house. And we went through a lot of traumas and stuff." Alexis mentored Jason and helped them survive. "If I wasn't there, he would have died long ago, because somebody was there to pick him up when he fell—*every* time he fell. And I would be there again. A lot of other people consider him an outcast. Well, you know, people can be judgmental: 'That person's on drugs and high, we don't want to deal with them.' They're broken basically. And nobody wants anything broken." Alexis made it clear that "judgment" was not a valid part of her family. "Some of the girls I call my daughters are prostitutes," Alexis said, "but I don't lead their lives for them. I just try to be there for them when they need me. And they help me in the same way. . . . 'Cause one of the best things I did moving to San Francisco is living my life the way I wanted to, which means I make a living in a dress, and a lot of people like it that way, and so do I."

Alexis taught one of her daughters "how to be self-supportive to where she's no longer prostituting at all," she said, "and now she sews clothes for a living." Alexis bought her daughter her first sewing machine, "and she worked it off for me and made me some dresses." Alexis also trained her daughters to make money as drag queens and bartenders. "I've nurtured and helped a lot of people do performances and do shows," she explained. She became a mother to one transgender girl who was thrown out of her family and wanted to avoid the streets. Alexis taught her to bartend. She was off drugs and working at Divas. "I have another daughter that came to me years later, Kipper, she's Hawaiian, beautiful tall girl. And I met her and she was very naive. And now she's one of the top bartenders at the bar. . . . In my two and a half years of knowing him, he's gone from being an androgenous club kid to being a full tranny, working, going to school, entertaining . . . and I'm a positive role model." At the time we recorded the interview, a dozen girls called Alexis "mom."

Alexis ultimately created a sense of self-worth on Polk Street as a mother, empress, fundraiser, and female impersonator. Polk Street "will make or break you," she told me. "I've seen a lot die on Polk Street, chased down by a car and hit, get into fights and just bash their head and die right there." For people struggling with addiction, "it can be the worst place. But if you know all of those things and you overcome it, that creates a strength and a power for you—and it did exactly that for me." Polk Street "made me a stronger person, because it made me feel that I was worth something, and I was able to do something to help, in my life and in my community. . . . Where when I was a kid, I was told I wasn't going to amount to anything. I was an abused child, and when you're young they push that into you—and you come here and there's open arms, without judgment." She was part of an alternative moral economy against which the worth of her life and others could be measured.

If gentrifiers painted Divas as a space of crime and violence, Alexis presented it as a vital space for queer and trans kinship. "If Divas was closed, transgender girls would have nowhere to go. So that's my stake on Polk Street and Divas, is to make sure that there's a place for the girls to go to. And the people who admire them and respect them." She acknowledged that the networks of care that once defined the street were disappearing. There was a time "where we did a lot of fundraising, where there was a lot of community service up and down the streets." It's not so "community oriented" anymore, she said, "it's like every man for himself, but the people who've been on Polk Street a long time, way before any of that gentrification come in, we still communicate with each other and keep each other sane." Polk Street "is unique," Alexis told me. "It's family oriented—whether you like each other or not, it's family oriented. 'Cause I know the hooker on the street, I know the drug dealer on the street, I know the bar owner. Everybody knows everybody. So to lose that, it would be a shame."

O'Reilly's Holy Grail

One day I walked up Polk Street, past Case+Abst and Divas, to conduct an oral history with Myles O'Reilly, the owner of an opulent new restaurant called O'Reilly's Holy Grail. When I arrived, a pianist was playing soft jazz on a black grand piano. Waiters wore starched pastel button-down shirts. Wearing a tailored black suit, Myles greeted me and took me on a spirited tour, pointing out the imported stained-glass windows, hickory pecan floors from South America, and a 250-year-old Spanish chandelier. But he sounded defeated when he bemoaned his "multimillion-dollar jewel in the middle of the desert." The restaurant was only a couple of blocks from City Hall, "but tourism doesn't come this way." He took out his cell phone to show me photos. "This is defecation on the sidewalk," he said, pointing to a smudgy image. "This is condoms on the sidewalk. There are one thousand condos being built here. Something has to be done to restrict the number of street people."

We sat down in the back room and Myles told me he immigrated to San Francisco in 1989, during a national recession in Ireland. "I came out seeking my Holy Grail," he said. In 2004 he spent $6 million to purchase and renovate a shuttered building on Polk Street across the street from the RendezVous. "They talked about Lower Polk, about it being very tough and very rough and a lot of gay people here," he told me. "And it didn't really make any difference to me if there was Zulu warriors living on Polk Street. I really wanted to be over here." The area, he explained, "was in a big state of disarray." A "destination area for male prostitutes wasn't encouraging for someone like myself from a business point of view." But the price was right. "I couldn't really afford to go anywhere else [in the city], really. I didn't have funds to buy a building that was going to be twice as expensive."

Myles transformed a low-rent residential hotel above the space into fourteen European-style hotel suites, and opened his restaurant in 2005. He wanted to revive the "glory years" of Polk Street. These were the years before what he called the "undesirables" moved in, and before the city became "so liberal." He encountered resistance from the local community. "I know people spat in my face when I started off here, first which were gay people," he said. "But there's a difference in gay people, there's a difference in straight people . . . there's good gay people, there's good straight people . . . and there's bad people too, there's bad white people, they call them white trash and there are a lot of them out there." The difference between desirable and undesirable populations, in other words, was not necessarily a matter of sexual orientation but class status and gender nonnormativity.

Myles credits his financial investment in the area with the beginning of a larger transformation on the street. The neighborhood association "decided to crank up the involvement of the merchants," creating a fund to hire private security and steam-clean the alleyways, a favorite site for hustling and drug dealing. Lower Polk Neighbors often used the coded language of "cleanliness" to dehumanize street kids and justify their displacement. Myles made these connections explicit. He was cleaning the alleyways, he said, because it was "a playground for undesirables." He enforced a dress code at O'Reilly's Holy Grail because he had to "make some kind of a stance" on the street. "People who are not desirable will not come," he said, "because they will not be welcome." Coy Ellison, whom I follow in the previous chapter, told me that one night he arrived with a friend in drag who was served a beer with a fly in it. When they complained, the waiter told them she'd get another "but you'll probably get another [fly] in it." If you don't like the place, she said, "you don't have to come back." Coy said he'd "never been politely told so well to get the fuck out of here, you faggots." Those deemed undesirable clearly included the working-class and gender nonnormative people.

With the goal of transforming the area, Myles also teamed up with a new business association, Polk Corridor Business Association, to rebrand Polk Street as "Polk Village." The association, which was circulating a petition to legally change the name, sponsored the installation of fifty colorful banners on the street that read, "Welcome to Polk Village: Working Together to Build a Cleaner, Safer, More Beautiful Community." What they were working to build, of course, was not beauty or cleanliness but capital. The business association couldn't "raise a dime on the [name] 'Tenderloin,'" Myles told me. The name "Polk Village," inspired by a redeveloped Greenwich Village, would "attract a lot of people," Myles said. At the same time, "we're going to get more police even if we have to go out there and hire them ourselves," Myles explained. "Foot patrols, the presence of the SFPD uniform, and anybody with any backbone in them will always respect a uniform."

Kimo's and Michael Norton

I heard a different story at Kimo's, a gay bar just down the street from the Holy Grail. Kimo's opened in 1977 as a gay Hawaiian bar, but by the time I arrived, it was serving two vastly different groups: downstairs, an aging gay male population and hustlers; upstairs, a young hipster crowd that came for indie band concerts. When I visited one afternoon in 2009, a young man sporting a shaved head and hoodie was hanging out in front, holding a skateboard with flames stenciled on the bottom. An older, paunchy man walked to the door, chatted with the young man, and brought him into the bar. The young man looked suspiciously at a fresh-faced young blonde woman wearing Ugg Boots, who breezed in with two friends, laughing, and headed up the stairs.

A sign in front read, "No Loitering in Front of These Premises." A bartender, John David, told me that Alcohol Beverage Control mandated the warning, the result of pressure from the neighborhood association. "Kimo's is the new whipping boy," he said. "RendezVous is out, and now it's our fault that people are on the streets." He told me the "Polk Village" proposal was meant "to make everything with the twinkle lights, to get rid of the characters, to get rid of the character of the street [and] make this part a yuppie land. Does this look like a village to you? Paint it anywhere you want and it's still a city." An elderly man in an American flag cap, green cowboy boots, and a mustache waxed at the ends told me he'd been coming to the bar for fifty years. "This was the original Castro," he said, "this is where the gay community first began, this was the street where the first gay pride was held, gay parade, and slowly but surely things are changing. And I guess that's just a fact of life."

A bartender at Kimo's named Charlie, who told me he'd been on Polk for twenty-seven years, introduced me to the phrase *Polk Street trash*. The phrase, Charlie explained, referred to people who had "experienced it all" on Polk Street—"the hustlers, and the drug addicts, and the homeless people . . . and the ones in close association with them, the ones that picked up the hustlers and the ones that hung out late at night and went to the bookstores that used to be there." Charlie told me that being a bartender involved more than just pouring drinks: "You have to put up with a lot of drunks, a lot of personalities, a lot of fights." It also required him to be an entertainer: I watched him perform the same kind of cultivated vulgarity as a bartender that he performed in an oral history I recorded with him. In Polk Street's dirty bookstores and sex arcades, he told me, there was "the smell of flesh, the smell of dick." He laughed as he showed me a photo book of his tricks from his years working as a bartender, a kind of sexual inventory— "a little book of all the penises, all the dicks, all the vergas, all the chorizos, all the chili peppers of Polk Street." He pointed to one photo. "This is Markie, a pretty little boy skateboarder," he said. He pointed to another. "I can't remember who that was, bending over for me. That was right before I plowed him in the office." He turned the page. "I don't remember who that is. That's a pretty dick, though. He was such a pretty little kid. I asked him, 'You want a line of cocaine? That's gonna cost you, little boy.' So we went to the office and I gave him a blowjob and a good line of coke." He was performing the role as the dirty old man, but I felt like I could trust him, that he cared about me and others. Indeed, one day, after I talked with a john at Kimo's who gave me his number and agreed to an interview, Charlie warned me against this particular man, who he felt was untrustworthy. "You know what he's going to expect."

One day I talked with Michael Norton, a tall man in his midfifties with shaggy brown hair, standing on the sidewalk outside Kimo's. Handsome and trim, with deep wrinkles marking his face, he told me he'd been hanging out in front of the bar for two hours. "Nothing's going on. Normally I don't like to come out here, but I'm in between jobs now." He'd heard that Kimo's was going to be sold and new owners were planning to hire security guards. "Going to chase all the hustlers out." Michael said he originally came to Polk Street, in the 1970s, for mutual support and guidance. "It wasn't just money for me," he explained. "This was a good place to come and get advice, comfort, support. There are people that need people, and they're going to take that all away. San Francisco is going down the tubes. All the heterosexual people are moving in. They like the police-state mentality."

I started seeing Michael around the street after that. I often saw him hanging out at a Polk Street convenience store. The store owner later told me that he acted as unofficial security in exchange for the use of a phone or food. I ran into Michael at an internet café that allowed street people to linger over coffee. He spent time in the café typing on an aging laptop, compiling what he told me were screeds against fascism. I also ran into Michael at Old First Church, off Polk Street, where he regularly volunteered for a nonprofit organization serving the homeless and marginally housed.

I conducted an interview with Michael at Old First Church in 2008. He told me he started hustling in San Francisco at age seventeen, in 1969, after fleeing the "redneck, racist town" of Martinsville, Indiana, when he was in tenth grade. "By the time I got here in '69," he told me, "the party was crashing down fast. It was not the peace-loving, incense-and-peppermint leprechauns and munchkins. It was kids sleeping in doorways with needles in their arms, starving—and in those days there was no programs to speak of that would help kids. You were on your own." In his early twenties, Michael lived in the meat rack and shared a hotel room with someone who was murdered soon after they moved in. "Got three bullets in his head. That was the same week when two of my other friends were killed. One was pushed out of a hotel eight stories up. Another one was tied to a bed and the whole house was set on fire. That's when I realized this gay world is not a big party. I'd always known you had to survive but I now knew survival was the only thing that counted."

Michael and other hustlers shared resources and housing to survive in the Tenderloin. "If one had a place to live, then three or four or five others would be living there. Each one would pitch in. But none of us went hungry. Nobody stayed homeless more than a few days. . . . In the days of oppression, gay people stood together to a lot larger degree than they do nowadays. They had to. It was kind of like a ghetto mentality. We had to watch out for each other. 'Cause you never knew when it was gonna be your turn next," he explained, "to go hungry, to be arrested for being gay." In the 1970s, Michael said, hustling

> was an occupation. Just like any real waitress is determined to be guided by professional work standards when she's waiting tables, hustlers had a code. You were as professional as you can be. Once you had been at it for a while, you learn to overcome the disdain you had for the johns, customers, whatever you wanna call them, tricks. You became neutral emotionally when you were with them. You didn't love them, but you didn't hate them. But through it all, you were a professional. You maintained your honesty, you maintained your integrity, you always knew that you were more than a piece of flesh, a lump of flesh. You were a person who had a mind, you had a soul whether or not these tricks wanted you to show you were intelligent or not.

Like other narrators, Michael described Polk Street in the 1980s as a sexual marketplace, each bar and dirty bookstore catering to specific desires. "The Q.T. was more for the older guys who were, say, like, bald and fat, but they had money." The Giraffe "was more like the cocktail scene. The hustling went on but it was not throw-it-in-your-face type. It was let's talk about politics, let's talk about philosophy, let's talk about existentialist dialectics as opposed to historical idealism—that whole type of thing." At the RendezVous, "people would grind their dicks against each other's asses or just be trashy-mouthed. Didn't mean that's the way they really were but that was the image while you were in the bar." And "if you were the trick who wanted to be trashed out as much as possible—so you didn't have to live by your boring upper-middle-class lifestyle of being totally respectable in front of everything and everybody—you went to the dirty bookstores. The Ben Hurs, the Locker Rooms. Frenchy's. You got down on that floor on your knees with everybody's pee and sperm all over the floor, glory holes right in front of your face, and you did the nasty." He laughed. "It was good money by the end of the day. You end up staying in these little booths that are like three-by-three or three-by-four. You sit there for hours trapped like you're in a jail cell, putting up with all these weird slimed-out people, 'cause some people love to get trashed out and there was as trashy as you could get in a bookstore."

One particular story Michael told me was about a man he met in one of the dirty bookstores who countered stereotypes of hustlers: "that we are garbage, that there's nothing redeeming about us, that we're lazy or we're parasites." His story dramatizes the mutual obligations people created on the street. Around 1990, when Michael was about thirty-eight or thirty-nine, he met "this mostly het blind guy. He could still see but he was heading towards total blindness. He wasn't much to look at—the most boring personality I had met in years." He started coming in three to four times a week to see Michael. "Some other hustler who had known him said, 'You better hook on to that guy—he's worth a fortune,' and I thought, 'Sure, he's easygoing.' But I also found out that he was just naturally a real nice sincere guy. He didn't believe in manipulating people, didn't believe in using them. He was like the old school of gay people, say like the World War II generation or what came after them. . . . To make a long story short, I guess, we just became the best of friends."

Michael moved in with the man. For the next eighteen years, Michael was the man's caretaker and lover in exchange for housing and financial support. "I scrubbed this man's toilets, I scrubbed his living rooms. I answered his phone calls. I did his shopping. I lugged his luggage around when nobody else would." In contrast, "his nice 'respectable' friends just wanted to be with him so he could treat them to nice dinners at the restaurants, but they were not going to help him in ways he needed the help." Michael said he fell in love with the man. He was like "the old school of gay people," a product of the "days of oppression," who "supported each other and treated each other nice." He was "somebody who's honest, moralistic, and will believe in you no matter what." Michael told me the man died a few years before our interview. "I found love," he told me, "and it's all because of a dirty bookstore on Polk Street."

Deeth, Yoyo, and the Kids on the Street

The few hustlers and kids who remained on Polk Street told me that gentrification had radically undermined the fraternal accumulation of obligations, mutualities, and reciprocities by which they could "watch each other's back." One day I ran into Deeth, a thirty-year-old cisgender woman, who was folding her clothes at a Laundromat. She had previously told me she lived in a nearby squat with her pet rat and hustler boyfriend. "I got lucky," she told me at the Laundromat, "and ran into these Christians that help me out every once in a while. They gave me money to do my laundry." Deeth agreed to record a short interview. After she finished her laundry, we sat at the corner of Austin Alley and Polk Street, just a block away from Kimo's, and began recording.

Deeth told me she was born in Los Angeles, off Hollywood Boulevard, and hitchhiked to Polk Street when she was sixteen, around 1998. "I was down there [in Los Angeles] selling a lot of speed and getting really high on speed, so I got kinda bored with that." She hitchhiked to San Francisco, "and the first place that my friends brought me was Polk Street. . . . I got stuck up here for just a couple months when I was sixteen because I fell in love with this little thirteen-year-old. He was so cool. I was into punk rock before I got up here, but he got me more into it, like into the Misfits and shit. And it was just so cool, man." The kids slept in Fern Alley, she said. "The kids were able to hang out and not get messed with by the cops. . . . We watched out for each other and it was just one big family back then." Deeth remembers the street being relatively safe for the kids because older people watched out for them. "The older cats that had been there forever were really overprotective of us when we were younger," Deeth said. "No one fucked with the kids, because if you fucked with the kids you were going to get fucked with." Deeth also had a steady income selling drugs. "Every time I came up here," she said, "I had some kinds of means of support. I don't sell drugs

FIGURE 5.6.   Deeth (*right*) and boyfriend Ian, 2008. Photograph by Gabriela Hasbun.

anymore, but I was still selling drugs and using drugs, and I didn't really have to worry about too much."

Deeth told me that gentrification had created a more competitive, unsafe, and exploitative environment. "There's a lot of rich people coming up here, a lot of condominiums going up. It's changing, the way the neighborhood wants it to change. They want to get all the street people out, but they want to get them out of the Tenderloin too." The businesses were increasingly hostile. "The only hip place is that coffee shop over there. . . . You can go in there and plug in your laptop and they are not going to be prejudiced or fascist against you. As long as you're buying something. They didn't used to be like that on Polk Street. You didn't have to be buying something." Deeth felt that the street was less safe than it had been when people were watching each other's backs. "It's a place where [people] can get away with ripping off kids. I've woken up before and since I'm such a tomboy, they think that I'm a boy. I sleep in a cardboard box and some guy was trying to get his hand in my pants, saying he was trying to get my dick. I woke up and I'm like 'Who the fuck are you? Get away from me, man.' Then you go tell the cops, the cops are like 'Well, you're sleeping on the street.'"

Other kids also told me that redevelopment upended the hustling rate structures and related social rules, leading to a more competitive environment. A forty-five-year-old hustler who had been hustling Polk Street eighteen years told me, "The clientele is dropping drastically. The kinds of bars that are popping up are not . . . the kinds of bars you wanna hustle out of. They're more like yuppie, straight, whatever." The rates for sex workers have "dropped," he said, "plus now a lot of people are on the internet." A thirty-six-year-old hustler, who started hustling Polk Street at twenty-five, also told me about changes over the previous decade. "Back then we used to stick together, look out for one another," he told me. "If one of us was dope sick one would help the other out. . . . If there was a john on the street that was rough . . . we would tell each other." A lack of cooperation among street kids led to decreased safety and a more exploitative environment. "We don't stick up for one another like we used to. And the johns notice that," he said. "Before, we got more respect." Now we're "looked down upon. The johns don't treat us as well as they used to, that's for sure. . . . We don't care what happens to the other, or most of them don't, you know what I mean?"

In 2008 a public defender gave me a phone number of a former street kid named Shane Gibson, who went by the name Yoyo and lived at the New Pacific Hotel, an SRO that served the formerly homeless, one of many similar hotels lining Polk Street. I called Yoyo, told him about my project, and he agreed to an interview. I was a little wary of the crowd milling around the hotel when I arrived. At least one person offered to sell me crystal. I walked up the stairs to the main desk, showed my ID to the attendant, turned left, and found Yoyo's door wide open. Yoyo was inside chatting with a friend and moving about the space. He saw me and immediately put me at ease, greeting me warmly, with a thick southern accent, and cracking a few jokes. Yoyo was a wiry figure, six foot, wearing wire-rim glasses and a beanie over a crew cut. Queer Nation stickers covered his mini fridge. He sat on the mattress, next to a collection of stuffed animals, and rolled a cigarette. I sat on a green upholstered chair by the door and started recording.

Yoyo began his story, like many others on Polk Street began theirs, with an account of childhood abuse. "I was born and raised in the backwoods of Georgia in a little town in Marietta," he said. "My childhood as a young child was basic—you know, cartoons, Tonka trucks. I was three when my

FIGURE 5.7.   Yoyo, 2008. Photograph by Gabriela Hasbun.

father held me down the first time and a friend of his injected me with just enough heroin to where it would be much easier for him to pass me around amongst themselves and his friends. This went on for numerous years." I was shocked the first time I heard stories on Polk Street about sexual abuse, but by the time I talked with Yoyo, it was a common origin story on Polk Street. Yoyo continued: "I knew what it was like to feel so dirty that I don't care how many times you washed your body, you couldn't get clean, or to feel like 'Oh my God, what did I do to initiate this?'"

Yoyo narrated a turning point in which he stood up to his father's abuse and ran away. "At fourteen I finally one day had enough," he said. "I was out back doin' my chores, rakin' leaves. My father came out, knocked me to the ground, started cussing at me, called me a crude, rude, retarded unaccept- able piece of shit one too many times. So I grabbed the rake, which had a metal head on it—I grabbed it, I swung it around and stuck it through the bottom half of his leg and stood up and announced to him, I said, 'You son of a bitch, I'm leaving. And you better pray I never come back, because if I do, you're going to hell and I'll be right behind you.'" That day "I decided to stop being a victim. And I left." Yoyo traveled the country working odd jobs. In the winter months, he "lumped" semitrucks, loading and unloading furniture. During the summer, he worked the "carnival circuit" as a ride jock for Reed Entertainment. This is where he picked up his nickname. "My ride was the Yoyo," he explained, "which is a swing that's on the chain that swings out. And the rule of the carnival was if you can take it apart and put it back together without killing yourself or anybody else, then it's your ride." The name Yoyo stuck. "If you watch me, you'll see it fits. I have mood swings that would put PMS and menopause *to shame*. I guess that makes me just a moody girl."

Yoyo told me he hitchhiked to San Francisco at seventeen, in 1983, in part because he heard about the city's gay Castro district. "I knew I had sugar in my tanks," he said. "All my life I've known that my bread was buttered on a very special side, so that's what levitated me was basically being closer to my type of people." He wanted to find himself. "I was numb still. I was still searching for myself, still trying to put all the things that happened to rest in my mind. And that's basically why I came here, to find me. . . . I wanted to be able to live to be myself and not be scared of what—of failings I had, and what my desires were and preferences were." In San Francisco, Yoyo found the soup kitchens and the day labor pools where he could find work on construction sites. People also told him he could make fast cash on Polk Street. "You know, I actually enjoyed sex," Yoyo told me. "I mean, for me that was my way of venting, even though I had been exposed to different types for so long." He often exchanged sex for drugs rather than cash. He said he wasn't doing it primarily to get paid. "I was basically into it for the gay sex." He would look for the "tweak and freak dates," he said, "where there's no money involved but they give you a real good hit of speed and then it was on for three, four days."

Yoyo met other young people on Polk Street who were fleeing their families and their pasts. He became part of the web of reciprocities and obligations that made up the street scene. "When I first came to Polk Street," Yoyo said, "Scooby, Dagger, Crystal, [and I] were four teenagers out there." Together they formed what he called a street family. "Let me explain what I mean by family," Yoyo said. "You don't have to be blood to be related to somebody. Back when I was first here, we watched each other's back. Like somebody needed to get well, we helped out with that. A couple would go to a needle exchange or get carryout back for us from different places to eat. Make sure our blankets and gear was watched. . . . We were a big family. We'd share expenses, camping and watching out for each other." Street families provided mutual aid and protection in a dangerous area while also offering vital emotional support. "We came here broken, scared, confused, and it was here that we found a family that gave a damn," Yoyo told me. "You know emotionally we stopped growing when things started happening" in abusive families of origin. "So you know, one of us might have made it to a little more mental stability. Someone would have already gone through what we were going through so they helped guide us through that. And so vice versa: where one lacked the wisdom of one certain thing, one of us said, 'Hey, let's try this.' So it was like with all of us in the same group, it was like we all had one working brain. Basically, we were a whole person."

Yoyo also met his husband, Fred. "He started out as a trick, believe it or not, but I fell in love with him." To many outside observers, and even those who were part of the scene, Fred might appear to be an exploitative person. He would "get guys off Polk Street and take 'em home, get 'em on speed and have his way with them," Yoyo said. This dynamic might seem to reiterate Yoyo's experience of childhood abuse, but Yoyo suggests that this relationship enabled him to also reframe and reinterpret those experiences. "If someone like me goin' through all the shit I went through as a kid could find something to love about him . . . He was a boy chaser, he was a scamp, but he was *mine*." Polk Street was "where I found myself, my true self, to where I was able to put a lot of things to bed. To be able to forgive my father, knowing now that what he did was a very vicious cycle. I've learned how to love myself and be myself—once I was able to identify with my sexual identity, as it were."

Anthony and the Palo Alto Hotel

About a block up the street from Kimo's was the three-story Palo Alto Hotel, one of the many SRO hotels off Polk Street. One day I met the manager, Anthony Cabello, an infectiously bubbly man in his early fifties, who lived on the bottom floor with his lover in an apartment packed with paintings and statues of the Virgin of Guadalupe. Anthony chatted me up, told me about the "extra" roles he's played in recent movies, and told me he was excited about documenting Polk Street's history. A few days later, Anthony gave me a tour of the hotel and the small, single-person rooms he rents out primarily on a short-term basis. "Polk Street is populated with places like this," he said, opening a door to an empty room. "They're not always as kept up as they should be, which kind of sucks, 'cause it's not fair to the tenants when you let things disintegrate." In his thirteen years as hotel manager, "a lot of people have come and gone, and those people have been straight and gay and young and hustlers and drag queens and a lot of them turn to an SRO as a means to survive. My goal has always been to give them an opportunity to do this and to feel comfortable and to feel safe." Anthony greeted two women walking by in the hallway. "Hey, honey, how's it going?" To me, in a stage whisper, he said, "Working girls are using that room for now. I'm giving them two weeks." Anthony continued the tour. "I'm happy to have the opportunity to give people a chance," he said, "'cause a lot of things have transpired in the last twenty years where people don't always have the opportunity to call a space home. I like to try to give people a break, because Polk Street has always been kind of a jumping-off point for people, and a starting point. It was a jumping-off place for me. A lot of my roots come back to Polk Street."

We walked back to his apartment and sat down for an oral history. Anthony told me he grew up in a working-class Mexican American family in Fresno. "I came from an abusive household," he said. "My father was an alcoholic, my mother, unfortunately, got sick at a very early age. She had three children, and when my father used to threaten her or beat her up or try to bring other men home to sleep with her, she would take the three of us off to the movies. We got to escape that way. So one of my goals was always to make her happy, and surprise her and appear on the silver screen." Anthony attended Catholic schools throughout his childhood. "Catholicism basically kept me going and gave me inroads to reach my main goal, which was to live in San Francisco," he said.

Anthony said he started having sex in the late sixties when he was twelve. Among his sexual partners were several Catholic priests. "I don't feel like I was molested," Anthony assured me. "I had a great time, it was really hot." One priest brought him to San Francisco. "There were a couple of residences—places that the Catholic Church owned—that were private. I was, I guess, the traditional altar boy sleeping with the hot priest." The priest brought him to San Francisco "under the guise of going to seminars 'n religious little things," Anthony said, "and there were rewards for being such a good altar boy." Anthony looks back at the relationship as a positive experience. "It was okay to be with this older man," he said. "We could walk down the street—he wouldn't necessarily hold my hand, but it was nice to be seen with a handsome man. There were a lot of other men on the block, as we walked up and down and got in 'n out of the car, they kinda turned to

FIGURE 5.8.   Anthony Cabello, 2008. Photograph by Gabriela Hasbun.

him and winked. It was kind of a badge that he wore, that he was with this little cute thing. I thought it was great. I was treated like a little prince, in that I was made to feel special on Polk Street."

Anthony said he met many of the kids on Polk Street. "Back then it seemed to be more of a brotherhood," he told me. "The hustlers kind of watched out for each other." He mentioned "one real special black queen" named Leland, who took Anthony under his wing. Leland told him, "Yeah, I just want you to be careful, 'cause you got this cute little tiny butt, and you just seem like you're a sweetheart, and you just gotta watch your shit." The queen took Anthony to a coffeehouse and said, "Well if you're here hustling, you gotta be careful about that. If you're thinking about making this your home, look out for this, look out for that." Anthony learned "that the best knowledge you can get is from shit you see on the street, and the best way you can take care of yourself is to watch how other people aren't taking care of themselves." The queen told Anthony: "When I first came to the city, somebody sat my ass down. And I'm sittin' yours down." In the early 1970s, as a student at a nearby college, he formed lifelong relationships with men on the street who treated him to posh hotels, plays, and dinners. "I did not mind the monetary help, but that wasn't my primary concern," Anthony said. "I was getting exposed to things that normally I wouldn't have the ability to do." He characterized the street's economic exchange not as prostitution but as "a proud sponsorship."

Anthony felt that the Polk Street social economy had changed dramatically since the 1970s. "Back in like the sixties and the seventies, it was like a big party atmosphere. I, fortunately, was taken under several people's wings. But now people don't have the time and the energy, it seems. Or the cash flow, 'cause economically times have really changed." Many people died during the AIDS epidemic, or they left the street because businesses changed hands. "It was pure economics after that." The "gay dollar" is simply not as strong. "My contemporaries, the ones that are left that didn't die from—during the epidemic—those people have really tightened their grips, and they're not as open as they used to be. They're a little afraid of getting bruised 'n hurt 'n ripped off, and I can't blame them."

Anthony felt he was able to carry on the tradition of Polk Street at the hotel.

> Polk Street to me has always been someone—or something—that accepts. . . . And I think through this hotel I've been able to give people opportunities that they normally wouldn't get at other hotels. Opportunities to be themselves and opportunities to rent, and be accepted, as long as they don't screw up. I kinda feel like I am offering, through my open-door policy, I'm giving people a chance. . . . I kinda do feel like I'm carrying on the tradition of Polk Street, in that way of trying to be accepting to everybody. . . . And it's also good for me because I kind of feel that . . . people like the clergymen and Leland and all those wonderful people they gave to me and I wanna give back. This is all I have to give, at this point.

Whose Families? And Safe for Whom?

Most of my informants told me they traveled to San Francisco because of its reputation as a safe haven. In contrast to their often abusive families of birth, they privileged mutual aid and care. New business owners and neighborhood associations instead stressed the need for "safety" and order, ejecting the people and institutions that were once synonymous with Polk Street's wide-open character. Whether we refer to Polk Street's transformation as revanchism, urban neoliberalism, or gentrification, it is a story of social trauma that has long been inflicted on the kids: the most vulnerable members of a street family fought a losing battle against the neighborhood boosters who wanted to "sweep the streets clean." In 2008 I developed a public humanities and storytelling project to intervene in this conflict, which I outline in the following "intervention."

Intervention 2.   Polk   Street   Stories

IN THIS INTERVENTION, I reflect on my experience directing "Polk Street: Lives in Transition," a public history project that challenged gentrifiers' claims to be promoting "safety" and "family" on Polk Street by positing alternative understandings of both concepts—alternatives drawn from oral histories I recorded with trans women, street kids, and working-class people on the corridor. Oral history enabled me to document a local past rich in nonbiological family structures, which I interpreted through public "listening parties," professionally mediated neighborhood dialogues, a traveling multimedia exhibit, and radio documentaries. These programs enabled me to intervene in debates about homelessness, queer politics, and public safety in the highly polarized setting of gentrifying San Francisco. If gentrifiers claimed they wanted to make Polk Street "safe" for families and children, the oral histories I recorded and publicized raised the questions: Safe for whom? And whose families?

I build on Edward Said's argument, in *Culture and Imperialism*, that imperialism was a battle over land, but when it came to who had the right to the land and who could define its character, these issues were "reflected, contested, and even for a time decided in narrative."[1] Said argued that the "power to narrate," or to block counternarratives from emerging, was central to processes of colonization. Narrative is likewise central to processes of gentrification. Gentrifiers use narrative to justify displacement and claim a right to the city. In the early 2000s, developers, neighborhood association leaders, public officials, and the media had the power to narrate Polk Street as an "unsafe" space plagued by "undesirables" and police them out of the district. Neighborhood associations framed their law-and-order approach as an effort to promote "safety" and "cleanliness." They justified their actions by appealing to the safety of families and children. As such, the power to narrate is central to the displacement of working-class people.

Storytelling is also a method by which subjugated people can assert their own identity and the existence of a collective history. My informants told powerful stories of mutual aid and survival. My goal in broadcasting their stories was not to stop gentrification: the economic forces animating urban neoliberalism are simply too powerful. However, the project did provide platforms for people to assert their identities and insist on the existence of a collective history; fostered dialogue and compromise among groups competing for urban space; and forced developers, neighborhood associations, and public officials to acknowledge the histories of those they were displacing. Each of these outcomes was a precondition for future mobilization. Documenting the existence of marginalized lives is a key goal of queer oral historians.[2] But we can accomplish more than simply documenting marginalized histories. We can also amplify counternarratives to intervene in political debates.

Mediated Dialogues

I spent months before recording oral histories attempting to cultivate trust with the bartenders, street kids, and working-class queer and transgender people on Polk Street. Linda Shopes notes that oral history often requires the cultivation of trust, especially when one is working with marginalized individuals with less social power than the investigator, and who have therefore good reason to be wary of their intentions. Often, such wariness leads to a sort of "test," or an implicit request for proof of commitment to being on the narrator's side.[3] My positionality as a young, white, queer college graduate situated me as a bridge between the two social groups at war with one another: working-class queer and transgender people, many of them people of color; and middle-class business owners, most of them white and heterosexual. My positionality also marked me as an outsider in both camps. I spent months attempting to cultivate trust by volunteering with social service providers and attending neighborhood association meetings. I found that many remained distrustful of my intentions. The warring groups demanded to know "whose side" I was on.

I ultimately decided to demonstrate my commitment not by explicitly "taking a side" but by engaging in a long-term process of dialogue between warring factions. I partnered with Community Boards, a conflict resolution organization, and invited a wide range of stakeholders from Polk Street to a mediated dialogue. The goal of the gathering, I wrote in an invitation, was to "strengthen relationships [and] to discuss solutions to conflicts arising from issues such as prostitution, crime, and housing." While it required some persistence to get key stakeholders to come to the meeting, most people I talked with seemed to recognize the importance and value of dialogue. In September 2008, roughly a dozen stakeholders met at a Polk Street storefront for a mediated dialogue. These included representatives from Divas, the First Congregational Church, a nonprofit serving the homeless, the neighborhood association, a representative from the Mayor's Office of Economic and Workforce Development, and the director of the San Francisco AIDS Foundation.

We began the session with introductions, personal histories, and hopes for the dialogue. Warring groups had literally been shouting at each other across the street. They were now encouraged to be quiet and patiently listen to each other's personal histories. The dialogue provided a venue for people on both sides of the conflict to tell their stories, listen to others' stories, and better understand various points of view about the street. "I've been here twenty-two years now," Divas manager Alexis Miranda told the group. She came to the dialogue "to see if we can include ourselves in being a solution, rather than the problem." The Reverend Megan Rohrer, whom I introduce in intervention 1 and chapter 4, said her organization had been on the street for seven years. She hoped she could "listen more" at the mediated session and "come together where our values are similar." Ron Case introduced himself as head of the neighborhood association, which he founded six years prior "with goals of making the neighborhood safer and try to beautify the neighborhood." He hoped to find common ground through dialogue. "I think there's more similarities we all realize."

Adela Vázquez, a Cuban American transgender activist and performer, highlighted the importance of safety for transgender women. "I belong to many communities," she told us, "but right now I'm just representing the transgender community." Hailing from Cuba during a time of political uprising, Vázquez told us she sought asylum and migrated in the Mariel boatlifts in 1980. She moved to the Tenderloin district in the early 1980s and organized with the HIV-prevention organization Proyecto ContraSIDA por Vida. "A lot of young people come to the area 'cause of the hotels and prostitution," she told us. "They're rowdy, they're loud, but they're part of this neighborhood." She told the group that increased policing did not make trans women safe. It often meant increased harassment. Trans sex workers, many of them immigrants from Mexico, the Philippines, and Thailand, she said, were "increasingly being pushed into the alleyways, into unsafe spaces."

Participants then discussed points of contention with the help of the mediators. Business owners new to the street felt that "problem" businesses were attracting drug dealing and prostitution. Participants debated the significance of businesses operating on a street corner: a liquor store, Divas, and a medical marijuana dispensary. Long-term residents and employees offered a different perspective. "Polk Street," Alexis Miranda said, "has always been a place where people come to do things that they normally wouldn't do in their own lives. . . . We have a place for transgenders where they can go and clean up and look respectable. We have a place where people can go and change needles. We have a place where people can go and buy pot. And it all centers within five blocks." She felt that policing simply moved people from one street corner to the next. If a street corner was policed, drug dealers "would go down two blocks to Cedar Street to you, and all we're doing is schlepping the problem off to the next doorstep. . . . All we did is shrink the problem off to the next person, so we don't have a resolution. We have to find a way to work with the city as a group to say, we're trying to do our part. Help us to do our part. But the police isn't always our solution. As a matter of fact, sometimes they view us as the problem. Because of their prejudice."

The mediators asked who was listening and who wanted to reflect back. Ron Case raised his hand. "I agree with that," he said. "We all have to work together. The issues will always be there. If we move them around, move them next door, we're pushing it over at someone else." He responded to Alexis: "If we could get rid of [the liquor store] on the corner, we'd probably all be much happier. But as a community—" Alexis cut him off. "But you're saying 'getting rid of.' And I'm sorry for interrupting. In the eighties, there used to be bathhouses up and down Polk Street. Just 'cause you got rid of the bathhouses doesn't mean that you got rid of addiction or AIDS. You just got rid of the bathhouses. And the medical marijuana place [that opened next to

Divas] . . . are there for people who need them." Case responded, "But J+D sells liquor." Alexis said, "Well, there's liquor on one side, Divas in the middle, and marijuana on the other side. You have all three, right at your feet."

Adela Vázquez responded:

> I've been working with the community for fifteen years, and I worked with needle exchange in the early nineties. I would encourage everyone here to volunteer with the needle exchange for a day. You learn a lot. What I'm listening to from everyone is that there is no communication between the communities within the Polk, and that's important to happen, otherwise I don't think we are going to solve anything. . . . Sometimes you can find a lot of interesting stuff just listening to what people have to say. The liquor store, the corner stores in San Francisco, people go there for nutrition and survival. You think that it is just liquor? They buy their food there. . . . In my work, couple of workshops for them to buy the nutrients from the corner store, and I have spent hours in corner store—what is there to make a meal out of? There is corn, there is black beans. That's how they live. And believe me I have told the people in the streets where they can get free meals, free beds, free needles, but they choose to live there, and be in the street. That's what they do. And if we want to have a prosperous neighborhood, we have to accept those things.

A neighborhood association representative pointed to a hypodermic needle exchange operating in an alleyway off the street. They argued that used needles were a threat to public safety and demanded that the exchange be moved. A representative from the San Francisco AIDS Foundation, which legally distributed the syringes, explained that they chose the alleyway because it had historically been a place where homeless people gathered. "My perception is that some people think the needle exchange encourages people to come to the neighborhood," he told the group, "when in reality, as studies have shown, it's absolutely the opposite. The people who inject have chosen that alley, that area, those blocks, as their home." He presented evidence that needle exchange, far from being a threat to public safety, dramatically stemmed the spread of HIV and hepatitis C.[4] Fifteen years earlier, he said, people sharing needles caused 12 to 15 percent of all new HIV infections. In part because of the needle exchange, new needle-related HIV infections were at the time of the conversation less than 1 percent of new infections. "The needle exchange actually does make people safer," he said. "Getting rid of it does not make people safer." As such, Keith asked that the association rethink its delimited definitions of "safety."

The dialogue raised a central question: whose safety is being prioritized when people talk about "safety" on Polk Street? Gentrification and policing didn't eliminate violence and crime; it simply pushed drug dealers, sex workers, and needle exchanges to other neighborhoods in the city. The "safety" that gentrification created benefited those who could afford to stay and face the rising rents. The dialogue generated a few concrete results. The neighborhood association committed to holding regular social service presentations at its meetings and to the formation of a committee to organize a community-wide event dedicated to dialogue. Megan made headway on plans for public restrooms that had been stalled for years due to poor neighborhood relations. "Now we have some people interested in helping us find a storefront space for a bathroom and shower," Megan told me. Megan told me that the same businesspeople who used to blame the ministry for bringing homeless to the district began supporting the group's community garden project, which aimed to grow food for the homeless. Merchants began planning a seventy-five-foot mural project that would celebrate Polk Street's queer history. As such, I found that mediated dialogues can be a powerful way to "give back" to the communities in which we are working and researching. I also found that the mediated dialogues enabled me to develop trust and record stories that were originally closed to me. People who were initially suspicious of my intentions found they had something at stake in the oral history project: namely, addressing neighborhood tensions and, in the case of people like Alexis Miranda, potentially saving their businesses from closure. People began seeking me out to record their stories.

Audio Portraits

I recorded oral histories with bartenders, social service providers, and neighborhood association members who introduced me to others, who in turn introduced me to others—a process that oral historians call the "snowball method." I used a digital recorder with an eye toward producing radio documentaries and conducted as many as four interviews with the same narrator. Each oral history generated a more complex account of their lives and the social worlds of which they were a part.

I chose several stories and edited them into three- to five-minute "audio portraits." My goal was to produce compelling, detail-rich narratives that dramatized my informants' understanding of "safety" and "family." I sought to avoid what oral historian Alexander Freund calls the "storytelling phenomenon," or the confessional mode of storytelling and enabling industry that motivates people to produce and buy depoliticized stories of individual triumph over adversity.[5] This kind of storytelling, Freund argues, "collapses individual memory—filtered through social discourses of individualism, survival, and therapy—and history." As a result, when we listen to many podcasts and radio programs, we are often hearing only one story, what Freund calls the "neoliberal story of individual triumph and, implicitly, the success of the free market and the failure of the state."[6] I edited my audio portraits to highlight the politics my informants foregrounded: a politics of mutual aid and reciprocity, of queer redefinitions of safety and family. I also highlighted the culturally specific meanings people ascribed to different spaces and businesses on Polk Street.

For example, I recorded three separate oral histories with Alexis Miranda. Each oral history enabled me to better understand her sense of subjectivity, her history in the area, and her understanding of the stakes of gentrification. I then edited a three-minute audio portrait from the interview sessions. The transcript of the audio portrait is included here. Ellipses indicate an omission or edit of audio material rather than a pause.

> Most people that come to San Francisco, particularly with Polk Street, don't have a bond with their family. Which is why they come here to create their own. . . . And you create your role models . . . and they later become your parents, or your family, I would say. . . .
>
> That's the common ground there that you're ostracized in your own family so you come to San Francisco to be yourself, that's exactly how my story came to be. But once you're here, you have to find a way to be productive, fit in and be accepted. . . .
>
> In Florida, I came into the drag community when I came into the drag gay bar. . . . I saw a lot of the drag shows and I was mesmerized by that, and I thought, Oh, I can do that. . . . But in the straight world, or in the Latino world, Cubans specifically, my lifestyle might not exactly be welcome. . . .
>
> I heard it was the gay capital . . . and I hopped the bus, and seven days later I was in San Francisco. . . . I got a job at Denny's and then moved on to Sizzler, and on Polk Street, while I was working in the daytime, I went out at night, and was carousing the shows and everything. . . .

And I met this person called Lola . . . Lola was my drag mother in the city. When I first came to the city, I was asking my friend Lola at the time and Big D, why do people do the things they do. 'Cause I was young and I say, why is that one beating up on that one or why is that one selling drugs or why is that one lying to her and telling her she's pretty when she's god ugly, why can't she tell her and help her? . . .

Lola was just telling me, you have a lot of growing up to do. . . . I had to tell the difference between my friends and/or family and acquaintances, 'cause there's a huge difference, your friends and your family will be there for you . . . and then there's people who want to take advantage of you and get whatever they can out of you. You learn that through time, like anything else. . . .

And I respected him . . . and he mentoring me into MCing . . . and then he taught me how to—at that time I didn't know how to sew—he taught me how to embellish dresses and put rhinestones on them, and I made jewelry at that time because I couldn't afford jewelry, so I made all of it with him . . . and he got me into MCing, and how to deal with people, and how to deal with audiences. . . .

So I was doing the shows for twenty dollars a week and I was lovin' it. . . .

If Lola was still alive, I would still be her daughter. Like my so-called grandmother, who is Big D, who was Lola's mother, is still alive, so I call her my grandmother. 'Cause she taught Lola, Lola taught me. . . .

In the trans community, some of them call me mom. I have twelve girls that I mentor.

The first daughter I took on . . . was ten years ago, his name was Jason, . . . and he was on drugs, . . . at that time she wanted to be a tranny, and her boyfriend was beating her up and she was on the streets and she was high . . . and she needed somewhere to go, and she came to my house. . . .

And we went through a lot of traumas and stuff . . . and if I wasn't there, he would have died long ago, because somebody was there to pick him up when he fell, every time he fell. And I would be there again. A lot of other people consider him an outcast. Well, you know, people can be judgmental. That person's on drugs and high, we don't want to deal with them. They're broken basically. And nobody wants anything broken. . . .

Polk Street will make or break you. I've seen a lot die on Polk Street, chased down by a car and hit, get into fights and just bash their head and die right there. It can be the best place for you or the worst place. . . . If you have an addiction problem, it can be the worst place for you. . . .

It made me a stronger person, because it made me feel that I was worth something, and I was able to do something to help, in my life and in my community. Where when I was a kid, I was told I wasn't going to amount to anything. I was an abused child, and when you're young, they push that into you, and you come here and there's open arms without judgment. . . .

Some of the girls I call my daughters are prostitutes, but I don't lead their lives for them. I just try to be there for them when they need me. . . . And they help me in the same way. . . .

'Cause . . . one of the best things I did moving to SF is living my life the way I wanted to, which means I make a living in a dress, and a lot of people like it that way, and so do I.

I've been the manager of Divas now for six years. . . . If Divas was closed, transgender girls would have nowhere to go. So that's my stake on Polk Street, to have a place where the girls go to, and the people who love and admire them. . . .

I just wish that people would open their minds to some of the diversity that's on Polk Street and not try to change it. Clean it up possibly, but don't try to change it. Because that's what makes Polk Street what it is. It's unique. It's family oriented—whether you like each other or not, it's family oriented. 'Cause I know the hooker on the street, I know the drug dealer on the street, I know the bar owner. . . . Everybody knows everybody. . . . So to lose that, it would be a shame.

I shared these stories about mutual aid and reciprocity at neighborhood association meetings. I found that members were responsive to different perspectives in a way that they had not previously been. Ron Case pointed to Alexis's audio portrait as a turning point in neighborhood relations, especially what he called her "concern for having a place where transgender women could go and feel safe. . . . This understanding of a safe place for people of all types was something that we all could relate to, and this understanding helped in easing neighborhood tensions." If new residents and business owners understood Divas as an "unsafe" space for drug dealing and prostitution, or a danger to families and children, Alexis's story encouraged them to consider it as a "safe" space for transgender families. Her narrative is compelling not because it is a simple story of triumph but because it is a more complicated, even ambiguous story about making do in difficult circumstances.

Listening Parties

I built on these generative experiences at neighborhood association meetings by organizing a "listening party" on Polk Street. More than seventy people gathered to listen to the audio portraits I had crafted. I found that city officials would attend events where their constituents are gathered. Among the attendees were City Supervisor David Chiu and representatives from the Mayor's Office of Economic and Workforce Development. I also presented a historical narrative based on archival research. I highlighted, for example, the role of gay bars as vital community institutions. Historical context helped new residents understand the intensely emotional reactions to the closure of gay bars. I told the audience that many new residents and business owners approached the homeless as sources of crime, and then I played a short clip from bartender Coy Ellison to present his perspective on the ways street kids might help stop crime on Polk Street.

> I knew most of the homeless kids that were out on the street, that were old enough to sit in the bar. I would buy them a cup of coffee and they would sit by me inside the bar. A lot of the kids, and they weren't causing any problems. But late at night, if I ever had a problem and I was cleaning the sidewalk and it was two in the morning or four in the morning, and a pimp would be chasing his hookers up onto Polk Street and chasing with a gun, I knew I had the street kids, the street kids would have my back if I had a problem walking home. . . . We had homeless people on the street on Polk that *stopped* crime. When I was a bouncer, if you treated the kids decent, you didn't have muggings on the block. Someone was watching your back late at night.

Chris Schulman, a representative from the Mayor's Office of Economic and Workforce Development, told me after the storytelling event that there was "a definite breakthrough in relationships as an understanding was formed between persons who normally do not work together." He told me he learned of the strong sense of "family" on Polk Street. "Businesses looked out for newcomers, runaway youth had some options, there was mentoring, there was self-policing; it was safer in a lot of ways." Schulman said he wanted to "take that spirit and rebuild." The programs encouraged developers, neighborhood association leaders, and public officials to consider different points of view about the street, but it is unclear if those who wielded power acted differently because their thinking changed. In retrospect, I would have built on this public history project by building alliances with housing rights advocates to directly influence policy. A powerful model for this type of work is the Anti-Eviction Mapping Project, a data-visualization, critical cartography, and multimedia storytelling collective documenting dispossession and resistance in gentrifying landscapes. Working with community partners and housing movements, volunteers study and visualize entanglements of racial capitalism and political economy while providing tools for resistance via digital maps, narrative multimedia work, murals, reports, and community events.

Multimedia Exhibit

I also showcased Polk Street's history through a traveling multimedia exhibit. "Polk Street: Lives in Transition" opened in January 2009 at the GLBT Historical Society, located in the South of Market, and then moved to a backroom gallery at the worker-owned, feminist sex shop Good Vibrations, on Polk Street, during the latter half of the year. The exhibition consisted of sixteen audio portraits, available on iPods and headphones, paired with sixteen framed photographs of the narrators by the professional portrait photographer Gabriela Hasbun. Guest-book comments suggest that the pairing worked well. "The idea of having the recordings and the photos together was especially nice," one wrote. "It really did feel like you were having a conversation with them."

I invited narrators to lend personal objects that represented their personal histories. I then paired those loaned objects with related archival materials from the GLBT Historical Society. For example, Alexis Miranda loaned me her Imperial Court coronation crown, from 1999, which I paired with a "royal edict" by Imperial Court founder Empress José Norton I, from 1965. The pairing showcased the living history of the Imperial Court and the role of Latinx drag queens in leadership positions. I also paired "Polk Gulch" (ca. 1970) and "Polk Village" (2006) banners to highlight the different ways people have attempted to define the street's character over time. The San Francisco AIDS Foundation loaned an antique baby buggy, which activists used in the late 1980s to clandestinely distribute needles when state law prohibited the practice. The buggy, which I placed at the center of the ex-

boys and some very pretty girls have become very
the gentrificational change of the neighborhood.
... here [at Deco Lounge]

FIGURE INTER2.1.   Kiko at "Polk Street: Lives in Transition" exhibit, January 15,
                     2009. Photograph by the author.

hibit, was emblematic of the early effort to stem the spread of HIV among IV
drug users. James Beales loaned a collage of photographs he saved from Q.T.
bar. As such, the exhibit was collectively curated by people on Polk Street.
I arranged and juxtaposed materials in a way that would encourage people
to interpret the past in a way that might illuminate contemporary conflicts.

The exhibit was accessible to people who lived on the street because of
its location at Good Vibrations and appears to have spoken to those who
made up the scene. "Polk Str. has been a place where I had to survive the
last six years and this exhibition captures it all," read one guest-book com-
ment. "It brings tears in my eyes to see the invisible struggle be visible and
that this allows to share the strength we bring in this harsh environment."
People saw their lives reflected in the exhibit. "Experiencing this exhibit is
experiencing a large part of my life, espec. being low income, disabled, and
a female-to-male trans guy." Perhaps the highlight of the project, for me,
was at the exhibit opening party when Alexis Miranda, always imperious
and critical—as a former empress should be—listened to her audio portrait,
walked over to me, and said, simply, "You did a good job." The exhibit helped
outsiders understand a street-based world that was often vilified. "These
stories give perspective and histories and a personal touch to the streets I've

FIGURE INTER2.2.   Ron Case and Alexis Miranda at exhibit opening, January 15, 2009. Photograph by the author.

always thought of as seedy," one person wrote. Many people found them emotionally charged. "I [got] emotional listening to the stories and have not spent so much time in a gallery before," one visitor wrote. Another wrote, "I was moved and am now emotionally exhausted, but in a good way."

While many visitors appreciated the effort to "make visible" the lives of marginalized people, at least one felt that the focus on storytelling foreclosed a more structural analysis. "This was awful!" they wrote. "No discussion of social justice issues, people forced out of long term rent controlled homes, bars forced out by the gentrification. . . . This community was destroyed in a class war, the rich won." Additional historical and political analysis may have added depth to the exhibit. But for those who listened closely, the personal stories I presented did dramatize social justice issues, the stakes of displacement, and the importance of local bars and businesses as centers for queer kinship and resistance. For example, I presented an audio portrait of Cecilia Chung, then chair of the San Francisco Human Rights Commission, which highlighted the importance of transgender clubs as spaces for personal transformation and collective politics. Reprinted here is her audio portrait.

I think for my parents it was okay for them to deal them with the fact that I was gay, but they didn't know how to relate to me anymore when I came out as a woman. And because of that experience, I was kicked out of my family apartment, and I was becoming homeless instantly. . . .

It was in the Polk that I found a place to stay. . . .

Being a Chinese immigrant who's queer identified, it was hard enough for me to find a place that I would feel comfortable, not to mention a place that I belonged . . . and when I came to Polk St. I just feel like those feelings were lifted from me, and I felt like I've never been as free as I was at that time. . . .

I started going to the transgender bar called the Motherlode. . . .

It was one of the seediest bars in the city. You know that there was a lot of wheeling and dealing in and outside of the bar. . . . And I felt that I found paradise. . . .

There was a little stage at the corner of the club . . . where the girls would just go up and parade themselves, dancing as if they were angelfish in a fishbowl. And trying to attract attentions. And that's our sexuality, that's how we felt like we were sexual beings, and that's when we felt like we were important, because everyone was looking at us. . . .

That's where I was able to see my true self through other people's eyes. . . .

And being part of that community, that club called the Motherlode, was not the best place on this planet, but that's where I found the validation I needed, to know I found myself. I was able to see my true self through other people's eyes. That's a gift—regardless of how many things attached to that gift, it's a gift. You know, it came with a lot of negative consequences, but it was equally fulfilling to find answers that I'd been looking for all my life, in that little bar. . . .

I learned to hustle like everyone else, I learned to depend on nobody but myself. . . .

And I was doing a lot of hotel hopping, and so for three years that's how I survived, that really hard time in my life. . . .

And I survived it. And getting self-medicated seemed to be a necessity at that time, in order to live through that. . . .

There is definitely that element of extreme freedom and extreme despair, and definitely violence. And that's definitely how to define Polk Street. It's a big paradox. And at the same time, people find validation, people find their connection to their own sexuality to their own self-discovery, and to a community that's forgotten by most people outside. . . .

I was sexually assaulted multiple times, which also involved a police officer from San Mateo County who was driving around picking up girls and threatening to arrest them if they don't give him sexual favors. And . . . I was kidnapped by two guys and I got stabbed. And that was the darkest time in my life. . . .

I still remember testifying for both cases in court as if I was being tried. They kept questioning about my sexuality, my gender identity, and what I was doing in that neighborhood, as if I deserved that kind of consequences. Being raped or being stabbed. And there was definitely no antidiscrimination law at that time to protect the transgender community. And . . . no anti-stigma effort around extending support to the sex worker in the neighborhood. . . .

When you come out of that bottomless pit, if you manage to find your way out of that bottomless pit, I think you would realize there's a lot to fight for. And that's what happened. For me, I felt that I have a lot to fight for. . . .

And after that, I started to realize I want to find ways to help this community. I started working as a substance abuse counselor, and an HIV counselor, and . . . I got appointed to the Human Rights Commission in September 2004. . . .

And that's what gives me hope on a daily basis. To know that I am actively helping. Not judging. Not point my fingers, but actually roll up my sleeves to do something to help make people's lives better. To just offer them more choices.

For Cecilia, "safety" included the need for protection from biased police and courts, changes in the law, antidiscrimination laws to protect the transgender community, and anti-stigma efforts around responses to sex work. She promoted the concept of harm reduction, a set of public health strategies aimed at reducing negative consequences associated with drug use. Her story highlights the importance of transgender clubs as spaces for personal transformation. Cecilia told me she appreciated the larger Polk Stories project because she felt that Polk Street merchants needed to "practice more empathy." She felt it was important to note that as a result of the project, some of the merchants acknowledged "the deep-rooted history of the Tenderloin." Through mediated discussions, she told me, "both mer-

FIGURE INTER2.3.   Cecilia Chung, 2008. Photograph by Gabriela Hasbun.

chants and [service] providers were willing to set aside differences to look at ways that all would feel supported." She felt that the project had a "profound effect on so many audiences" because it contained "timeless stories" about human resiliency.

Radio Documentary and Theatrical Performance

I reached a larger audience by producing two radio documentaries. Radio has the capacity to convey the aural nature of oral history but also, Siobhan McHugh notes, "the ability to reach a potentially much wider audience than the rather self-selecting field of, for example, readers of books or visitors to museums."[7] You don't need to be literate to listen to oral histories and you don't need abundant leisure time, since listening to the radio can be a secondary activity. Oral historian Daniel Kerr, for example, found that a sizable number of homeless people in Cleveland carried portable radios and listened to the programs he developed. Broadening an audience through radio not only reached an educated public; it also reached working-class residents and the homeless.[8]

In October 2009 I released "Polk Gulch: The Story of Corey Longseeker" for KALW, a local San Francisco radio station. The twenty-five-minute piece told the history of Polk Street through the story of Corey Longseeker, whom I follow in chapter 4. In 2010 I worked with National Public Radio (NPR) producer Jay Allison to create a one-hour documentary, titled "Polk Street Stories," for his public radio website Transom.org that was distributed nationally via NPR. Allison invited me to travel to Woods Hole, Massachusetts, where he walked me through the process of crafting a longform documentary. We decided to run my audio portraits, unedited, in a sequence and to frame the audio portraits with a first-person narrative of my own, highlighting my own personal connection to Polk Street and my motivation for documenting the street's history. We also decided that I would provide the bare minimum of framing copy. This approach enabled us to avoid the usual spoon-fed public radio mode—that is, where the narrator tells the audience what they need to pay attention to—and instead encourage audiences to resolve ambiguities and make their own connections between narratives, therefore participating in the interpretation of the stories.

The stories moved people across space and time in unexpected ways. In 2012, for example, a nineteen-year-old undergraduate at Georgetown University heard the program on NPR while driving with his mother. He asked if I would be willing to let him adapt "Polk Street Stories" for the stage. I gave my consent after checking in with several oral history informants. The play was produced in March 2013 by two student drama societies. The group partnered with Honoring Individual Power and Strength (HIPS), which specializes in outreach to sex workers and drug users in Washington, DC. At each production, one actor each night stepped forward, during curtain call, and made an announcement that they would be raising money for the organization. They used Polk Street stories to engage with the politics of the local community, which was undergoing parallel issues of gentrification and marginalization.

What are the lasting impacts of "Polk Street: Lives in Transition"? The project did not, of course, stem the tide of gentrification that has transformed Polk Street and the city as a whole. It did provide platforms where people had the power to narrate their identity and the existence of their own history. The project demonstrated that the kinship networks my informants call "street family" were critical forms of survival and are overlooked frameworks for understanding the formation of queer public cultures. "Polk Street: Lives in Transition" raises larger questions as public historians respond to the erasure of queer spaces. Gregory Samantha Rosenthal argues that community history projects can "make cities queer again" by renaming and reclaiming urban space, thereby resisting a gentrification that threatens to erase the queer past.[9] The project also laid the groundwork for the many historical memory projects that would follow in the Tenderloin, as I show in this book's conclusion.

C o n c l u s i o n

Memory is a process that depends crucially on forgetting.

—Joseph Roach, *Cities of the Dead*

IN THE SUMMER OF 2013, Coy Ellison organized a grassroots "Tenderloin History Awards" at the Gangway, a nautical-themed gay tavern off Polk Street at which he bartended. Coy was concerned that people were forgetting the Tenderloin's history as the district gentrified, businesses closed, and the kids on the street were policed away. In the months leading up to the event, Coy asked people to nominate awardees who represented the best of the district. I nominated the Reverend Megan Rohrer, my primary collaborator on the Vanguard Revisited project. On the day of the awards, I walked up Larkin Street through "Little Saigon," which houses Southeast Asian and Vietnamese businesses, to the Gangway, located on the ground floor of an SRO hotel housing the formerly homeless. Jutting above the Gangway entrance was a massive re-creation of a ship bow. Posted at the bar entrance were photographs of pickpockets and a sign warning: "PLEASE WATCH OUT FOR THIEFS."

Inside was a dark, windowless tavern designed to resemble the interior of a ship. Circular mirrors on imitation wood suggested marine windows. Walking into the Gangway always felt to me like walking back in time. Its maritime theme, as I romanticized it, called to mind the homoerotic icon of the merchant marine, San Francisco's history as a port city during World War II, and the many gay veterans who created a social world in the Tenderloin. The ship itself has long been the "greatest reserve of the imagination," according to Michel Foucault, a symbol without which "dreams dry up, espionage takes the place of adventure, and the police take the place of pirates."[1]

Coy was standing behind the bar, pouring drinks and chatting with the regulars, a dozen older gay men and a few trans women huddled around the bar. I sat on a stool next to Megan, who was wearing a clerical collar and joking with one of the regulars. Coy poured me a stiff drink and began handing out awards.

The first award went to Latiya Pryor, a black trans woman also known as Miss Classy. "One can't start to begin to talk about Miss Classy without acknowledging her long record," Coy began. "And no, we're not talking about the one down at the police station, though I have heard it's impressive too." Coy paused for laughter. "Miss Classy has overcome many things and used that life experience to mentor others in the Tenderloin." She was a hospice worker and led night classes to teach "the working girls" their rights, Coy said. "No easy task when you live from day to day, and somehow find the time to save the world." Coy handed her a framed plaque. He gave a second plaque to Three Finger Susie, who once managed a Tenderloin trans bar called the Black Rose. Susie, sitting at the bar with her chihuahua Peanut, graciously accepted the award. Coy gave another prize to Megan Rohrer for providing resources to marginally housed people on Polk Street. Coy honored those people, in other words, who animated the webs of reciprocity, mutual support, and mentorship that comprised the Tenderloin's performative economy.

Coy began regaling me—as customer-historian—with an account of the Gangway's history. He told me the space opened in 1910, survived prohibition, and began catering to a gay clientele by the 1960s. He took me into the bar's cellar and told me there were once a series of secret underground tunnels that connected it to other gay bars. Patrons could escape the police by hiding in tunnels or moving from bar to bar. He took me upstairs and turned over a barstool to reveal the names of former employees scrawled on the underside: *Debi Sue / Suzie, started Jan 21 1972 | Billy Smith, man-*

FIGURE C.1.   José Sarria funeral notice, the Gangway, 2014. Photograph by the author.

ager, hired 1969 | Page, retired 1975. He brought me to the front of the bar, which was covered with newspaper articles commemorating Polk Street's history: an article titled "Gay Political Power Growing" emblazoned with a photo of Sweet Lips, an announcement for the 1972 pride parade, and an announcement of the death and funeral of the Imperial Court founder José Sarria. He pointed to the walls around the bar, which were lined with marble and silver plaques from empresses and emperors of the Imperial Court. Each plaque acknowledged the Gangway for its financial support of their charitable causes. "The Elegant Black & White Court of Salt & Pepper," read a plaque from the 1980s, "Thanks you for all Your Support This Past Year."

Back behind the bar, Coy told me and Megan an even more extraordinary story about the Gangway's history. The Tavern Guild held its first and last meetings at the Gangway, Coy said. "Two of the original members are still here," he said, pointing to a small ship suspended above the bar. "They were cremated. Their urns are in the ship." I was spellbound by this visceral connection to queer history and felt an overwhelming desire to see the urns. Megan and I excitedly hatched a plan. Aided by Coy's stiff drinks, and with

Megan's encouragement, I climbed up onto the bar to see into the ship. Patrons looked up from their drinks and hollered, egging me on. But when I peered into the hull, I found that there was nothing there—it was just me, making a self-mortifying spectacle of myself.

The point of a story in the Tenderloin, I should have understood by that time, is not always to describe an objective reality but to call forth and create a social world of fantasy and belonging. Coy's story transformed the seemingly abject, profane Gangway into a mausoleum—a sacred space of memory—and drew me affectively into Polk Street's performative economy. If his story led me into making a spectacle of myself, it also inducted me into the kinship networks chartered by real or imagined homophile founders. To be "taken in" by a story in the Tenderloin can mean more than to be tricked and exploited; it can also mean to be tested, inducted, and incorporated into a family, a social world, and the informal economies and memories that sustain it. The two possibilities are never far removed from one another in any given transaction, just as the historical testimonies told in the Tenderloin are never entirely divorced from mythological memory.

Historical Memory and Urban Neoliberalism

Coy wanted people to remember the Tenderloin's history, but in the early 2020s, a person walking down Polk Street would be hard pressed to recognize the traces of its queer past. The New Pacific Hotel, where I interviewed Yoyo, was converted into an upscale boutique hotel called EPIK in 2015.[2] The Gangway closed in 2018 and was transformed into a Laundromat. Skyrocketing rents forced Divas to close a year later.[3] "Most of our community has left the city," Divas manager Alexis Miranda told me in 2019. "Gentrification has ruined San Francisco and a very diverse community is gone." Meanwhile, the Tenderloin Mid-Market area has become ground zero for battles over the future of San Francisco. In April 2011, with a push from Mayor Ed Lee, the Board of Supervisors passed a city ordinance that gave tech companies a 1.5 percent city payroll tax cut in return for operating in the Mid-Market area. Twitter moved its corporate headquarters to the Mid-Market corridor in 2012 and other tech industries followed.[4] The payroll tax exclusion zone vastly increased the property value of the area, and the influx of highly paid tech workers dramatically increased rents and evictions of longtime tenants. While redevelopment efforts were blunted by the COVID-19 pandemic, in 2021 Mayor London Breed announced an

$8 million "Mid-Market Vibrancy and Safety Plan," which will saturate the Mid-Market Tenderloin with police officers and redevelop the area.[5] The city and business interests have policed, priced out, and swept away much of what remains of the performative economy.

At precisely the same time, the city and business interests have begun acknowledging and memorializing the history of the people they are displacing. Through private-public partnerships, they have founded Tenderloin museums, created historical districts, commissioned queer history murals, renamed gentrified streets after transgender icons, and created transgender cultural districts. Why this sudden interest in a queer and trans history? It is not an altruistic desire to remember what has been lost. At a time when historic preservation and "cultural heritage" projects are common components of urban redevelopment projects across the United States, the City of San Francisco and business interests are appropriating the history of the kids on the street beyond recognition for the economic and political aims of the new economy. We are witnessing what theorist Barbara Kirshenblatt-Gimblett calls the "deconstruction of cultural forms under the pretext of preservation." Paradoxically, she argues, "remembering is a prelude to forgetting."[6]

In this conclusion, I examine efforts in the late 2010s and early 2020s to remember (and forget) queer and trans histories on Polk Street and the Mid-Market corridor—two sites where the kids' performative economy took root. I first show how the city and business interests are using historic preservation—historical murals, museums, street renamings, and historic districts—in a way that distorts, rather than preserves, the queer history I chart throughout this book. In Pierre Nora's terms, the Tenderloin's environment of memory—embodied memory that takes refuge "in gestures and habits, in skills passed down by unspoken traditions"—is being replaced by places of history, via institutions such as museums, archives, and journals. Powerful actors are generating historical narratives about the Tenderloin for their own political and economic aims.[7] I then document initiatives that seek to commemorate the Tenderloin's history in a way that might contribute to queer world making and counter urban neoliberalism, including the Compton's Transgender Cultural District, founded by queer activists and black trans women in 2017 as the world's first legally recognized transgender cultural district. Organizers hope to build on historical memory to enrich the lives of trans residents via what they call a "reverse gentrification model."[8]

In 2010 the Mayor's Office of Economic and Workforce Development and Lower Polk Neighbors (LPN)—the neighborhood association that aggressively policed street people and queer businesses out of the corridor—joined forces to commission two murals depicting Polk Street's queer history. Lower Polk Neighbors chose to locate the murals in Hemlock and Fern alleys, a site they had long sought to police of its hustling, drug use, and the legally operated needle exchange. The murals, according to the call for artists, were intended to "establish a positive street identity, deter graffiti," and "contribute to the economic vitality [and] revitalization of the merchant district."[9] The neighborhood association hired two artists and asked them to "design a mural depicting the influence of Polk Street's Beat poet community on the LGBT movement."[10]

In January 2011, the two artists unveiled their mock-ups at an LPN meeting. The association members were outraged by the murals, which they felt depicted San Francisco's rebellious neighborhood as riotous. One mock-up depicted thousands of people marching on City Hall, including Harvey Milk, José Sarria, and protesters clashing with police. Another depicted a street hustler, among other subjects. "It looked like there were riots going on," LPN president Ron Case commented to a local newspaper reporter. The executive director of the Community Leadership Alliance, a neighborhood services group, told a reporter that the mock-ups didn't "fit into the spirit of what Polk Street is trying to do," referencing redevelopment and policing efforts. "Folks are concerned it might incite anger from people on the street."[11] One of the muralists told me he was shocked by the association's response. "If you research the history of Polk Street," he explained, "you will see that this illustration is somewhat mild compared to what was *really* going on on that street."

The explanation for neighborhood association outrage is clear: business interests were attempting to transform Polk Street's historically "seedy" image and redevelop the alleyways. The association felt that a mural depicting sex workers and riots wouldn't help calm the area. Instead, the association wanted a whitewashed history that would demonstrate its embrace of "diversity" while also furthering its redevelopment agenda. Polk Street's history is "fraught with conflict," a newspaper reported in 2011. "Incidents of police harassment and brutality are well-documented," but many "don't want to acknowledge that history."[12] A few months after the mock-ups were revealed, the Community Leadership Alliance held a meeting to revisit the mural project. What did they want the mural to depict? "Something beautiful," Ron Case said, "like flowers."[13] The association ultimately decided to change the mural theme from queer history to the more generic topic of "transportation."

In 2016 Lower Polk Neighbors again attempted to commemorate Polk Street's queer history by commissioning an architecture firm to "preserve and improve the Alleyways" by creating "medallions."[14] The firm developed a proposal to create medallions, embedded in the sidewalk, that would mark significant sites of queer history. A firm representative told me in 2017 that the medallion project would highlight Polk Street's queer history and "imbue the streets with the sense of this history and place." The architecture firm was also "interested in establishing an LGBTQ Polk Street district, to pay homage to the LGBTQ movement's history in this neighborhood."[15] Significantly, the firm's proposal focused on the period before 1971, when Polk Street was a primarily white, middle-class gay district—medallions would commemorate the first pride parades, early gay bars and gay-owned businesses, the Tavern Guild, and similar organizations. The proposal did not mention street kids, sex work, or transgender people.[16] Meanwhile, LPN continued to call on police to sweep away people who claimed space in the alleyways. In late 2019, police "cleared out" a homeless encampment of more than two dozen people living on Willow Street.[17]

Queer activists also organized commemorative marches in the 2010s and 2020s to work through the shared feelings of loss and anger in an increasingly unlivable city. In March 2018, Damon Scott and Trushna Parekh document, a group of queer leaders, community activists, drag queens, and neighborhood residents—including Coy Ellison (now Coy Meza)—gathered on the sidewalk in front of the Gangway, which had closed several months earlier. They then embarked on a two-hour procession to "Remember and Reclaim" twenty shuttered gay bars and businesses along the Polk Street corridor. Complete with a brass band, drag queens dressed in mourning, and black banners, participants stopped at the sites of former gay bars and other establishments, where they laid wreaths, offered eulogies, and remembered the significance of these places. By attending to the felt conditions of urban development, Scott and Parekh argue, the shared sentiments they performed opened up "relief from, if not alternatives to, the ongoing displacements and dispossessions of the neoliberal city."[18] The march offered participants a momentary respite from the feelings of loss, alienation, and precarity of an increasingly unlivable city.[19]

In June 2021, I attended a "People's March and Rally," which consciously drew on historical memory by taking the route of the first march in 1970, down Polk Street to City Hall. Led by an all-black-and-brown committee of queer and trans community leaders, artists, and performers, the march called for racial and economic justice. People held banners promising to "make racism wrong again."

Remembering (and Forgetting) the Tenderloin

Meanwhile, the city worked to redevelop the downtown Mid-Market area, helping turn San Francisco, an article in the *New York Times* reported in 2014, "into Silicon Valley's newest, and perhaps most dynamic, extension."[20] Historic preservation has been one component of the city's broader redevelopment agenda. In 2014, for example, Mayor Ed Lee helped kick off the opening of the Tenderloin Museum, which is housed in the Cadillac Hotel, an SRO residential hotel near the old meat rack district. Lee explained that neighborhood improvements start with the arts. "Let's bring a light to this whole area," Lee said. A museum will provide a "way to look at the Tenderloin in a very different light." He mentioned the payroll tax exemption, which will "incite positive investment in our community." He promised the crowd, "You'll see startling recoveries."[21]

If tourism stages the world as a museum of itself, Kirshenblatt-Gimblett argues, museums "play a vital role in creating the sense of 'hereness' necessary to convert a location into a destination."[22] Randy Shaw, the executive director of the Tenderloin Housing Clinic, a nonprofit organization, spearheaded a campaign to launch the museum. The museum built on an earlier effort in 2009 to designate the Tenderloin as a national historic district, a designation that makes it eligible for state and federal tax credits.[23] Both aim to redevelop the area. As Shaw said in 2011, "the whole goal is to be able to show people this is a historic district and it's a place they should walk around, eat in the restaurants and it's a good place to hang out in."[24] A slate of museum activities is designed to attract tourists. "By attracting tourists to the Tenderloin during the day," Shaw noted in 2014, "the museum will also expose them to dining spots, bars, and theater that they can return to at night."[25]

The Tenderloin Museum tells a story about the "rise and fall" of the Tenderloin, focusing on the period before the 1960s when it was an upscale apartment district and promising to bring us back to those imagined glory days. "If you look at the old photos," Randy Shaw told a reporter in 2014, "people used to come to the Tenderloin dressed in suits." It was known, he said, as "the Paris of the West." A volunteer told the reporter he focused on the year 1917. "At that time, it was an upscale apartment district," he said. "There were uptown residential hotels and a rich nightlife with dance and dining clubs." [26] The museum walls showed off black-and-white photos and news clippings about the Tenderloin's journey, according to a business newspaper, "from a thriving entertainment district to one that guidebooks caution tourists to avoid." [27] The Tenderloin Housing Clinic also touched up fading vintage advertisements on buildings in the district. A $41,000 city grant helped "bring those old advertisements back to life," according to a 2011 article. "If you look beyond the grittiness of San Francisco's Tenderloin," it reads, "you'll find ample evidence of its glory days." [28] The museum and murals are meant to "revitalize" the Tenderloin by bringing us back to the imagined glory days before impoverished queer people claimed the district as their own.

The city also memorialized trans and queer history by literally mapping it onto the city streets. In 2014 I joined a crowd at Turk and Ellis as members of the Board of Supervisors and gay activists renamed the 100 block of Turk Street "Vicki Mar Lane" after Vicki Marlane, a trans woman and drag performer who became an icon at the Tenderloin's Aunt Charlie's Lounge. A member of the Harvey Milk LGBT Democratic Club welcomed the crowd to what they called the "birthplace of the LGBT community, and . . . to the rebirth of our history." Marlane "helped ignite an era of trans activism that is most widely associated with the August 1966 riots at Gene Compton's Cafeteria." Board of Supervisors representative David Campos said that "we cannot be a GLBT community without protecting the rights of trans people" but also reminded the crowd of the trans women "who are being pushed out of San Francisco, who cannot afford to live in this city." Two years later, Supervisor Jane Kim launched a successful bid to rename the 100 block of Taylor Street "Gene Compton's Cafeteria Way." But as trans activist Aria Sa'id explained it in 2020, "the [trans] community didn't want it to be [renamed] Gene Compton. They wanted it to be Compton's Cafeteria Riot, but the city did not want to have the word 'riot' in a street sign." [29]

The driving force behind cultural district development is the belief that the arts and "heritage" are a primary tool for urban revitalization that can promote economic growth. Protected by legislation and supported through tourism, heritage becomes an instrument of urban redevelopment.[30] If cultural districts often have the aim of gentrifying public space, queer and trans activists have also attempted to create a transgender cultural district as a form of "reverse-gentrification." In the mid-2010s, activists, many of them black trans women, used a historic preservation document to question whether a development project should be allowed to demolish buildings along the Mid-Market. The controversy birthed the Compton's Transgender Cultural District, now the Transgender District, the world's first legally recognized transgender cultural district. In collaboration with the city, organizers seek to memorialize trans history while developing economic power for contemporary trans people of color. "If the world won't help us survive," District executive director Aria Sa'id said in 2020, "we can create our very own economy."[31]

This story begins in the early 2010s, when a team of historians and historic preservationists developed a "context statement" for LGBTQ history, which was approved by the Board of Supervisors in 2015.[32] The sites documented in the report stood a chance of being protected from demolition under state historic preservation laws, according to the report's authors, which provide communities "an opportunity to use their collective voice to oppose projects that would destroy the historic fabric of San Francisco's LGBTQ enclaves."[33]

In 2016 queer and trans activists cited these laws to question whether a real estate development company should be allowed to construct a luxury hotel on Market Street. The project would demolish or endanger several buildings listed in the context statement, including the former sites of businesses that sustained the Tenderloin's hustling scene: the Old Crow, a bar that operated from the 1930s until 1980; the Flagg Brothers shoe store; the Silver Rail; the Pirates Den; the Club Turkish Baths; the Pleasure Palace; Turk Street Follies; the Dalt Hotel; and the Chuckkers. Activists also argued that the development would endanger the former site of Compton's Cafeteria. "The important political and cultural history of the transgender, and broader lesbian, gay, and bisexual movement at and around the 950 block of Market Street," activists wrote the Planning Commission in 2016, "may be permanently erased if the current development plans are allowed to proceed."[34] One of the organizers, drag queen and trans activist Honey Mahogany, recalled the activists' mindset. "We realized that if we didn't do something," she said in 2019, "the Tenderloin was quickly going to become gentrified and our history was going to be completely erased."[35]

This group of activists soon entered into negotiations with the developer. Brian Basinger, executive director of Q Foundation, a nonprofit in the neighborhood that focuses on preventing homelessness for people living with HIV/AIDS, filed a declaration in opposition to the developer's assessment that, as Sa'id recalled, "there was no historical value to that neighborhood, that the neighborhood was just filled with substance users and poor people, and that there's no actual historical value within the block."[36] Basinger partnered with St. James Infirmary, an occupational health and safety clinic for sex workers and their families, and Sa'id, then the program director for St. James, began working to memorialize the Tenderloin's transgender history. "We started our effort internally [at St. James] and as a sort of newly bound unofficial coalition [in summer] 2016," Sa'id recalled. "We were working with historians and lawyers, fighting the developer."[37] Honey Mahogany recalled the argument this coalition presented to developers. "If you are going to . . . create a development that is going to not only displace people who actually live in this neighborhood but also erase the history of that neighborhood," she said in 2019, "then you need to provide some sort of mitigation to help us combat that displacement."[38]

As part of a compromise with the activists and their allies on the Board of Supervisors, in January 2017 the developer was allowed to proceed with construction but agreed to pay $300,000 into a fund, administered by the Mayor's Office of Economic and Workforce Development, that would be used to establish a transgender cultural district.[39] The same month, the Board of Supervisors passed legislation that created the first legally recognized transgender district in the world. Additionally, in November 2018, the city passed a measure that would appropriate about $3 million for cultural districts around the city, including $215,000 for the Compton's Transgender Cultural District.

Three black trans women led the process to develop the Cultural District: Aria Sa'id, Honey Mahogany, and Janetta Johnson, the executive director of Transgender, Gender Variant, and Intersex Justice Project (TGIJP). Johnson and Sa'id drew on their own histories as marginally housed trans women to imagine the district as a hub of economic opportunities and a place to honor the community's history. Johnson arrived in the Tenderloin in the late 1990s. "A lot of people who came to San Francisco came here broken and looking for a better quality of living," she said in 2019. "The Tenderloin was a passage that a lot of trans people went through upon coming [here], wherever they were coming from." Sa'id said in 2019 that she came to San Francisco "with $60 in my purse," took the Greyhound bus, "and was dropped off at the Caltrain station." The Tenderloin "is probably the only area of the city where trans women are socially accepted, and it's the only place that we can actually afford to live."[40] There is "an intense stigma in living in the Tenderloin, both as a trans person and as a poor person." She imagined a cultural district that would create "pride . . . in loving and living in the neighborhood."

As trans activists build the infrastructure for a cultural district, they are also building a "reimagined world," their website reads, "in which transgender people are socially, culturally, and economically empowered and genocide against us is eradicated."[41]

Sa'id hopes to contest gentrification by developing the Transgender District. "Oftentimes when we think of urban planning and we start doing things like expanding sidewalks and putting in trees," she said, "it's because white people are moving in. It's not designed for the people that currently live there." She instead wants to create "urban beautification projects . . . that support the people that actually live here and not doing it as a way to . . . displace the people that live here with hopes of new crops of residents coming in, but rather saying, you know, 'you deserve to live in a nice neighborhood just like anyone else, and you've lived here' and we're just beautifying it for the folks that already are here." Organizers hope to serve trans people of color by offering opportunities to obtain job training; gain affordable housing opportunities; and cultivate transgender business ownership, including a transgender people-of-color-owned cannabis club. The goal is to provide workforce development for trans people with the aim of keeping residents and small businesses from being priced out. If successful, the district could be a model for drawing on historical memory to develop political power and keep gentrification in check.

The commemoration of the Compton's Cafeteria riots sparked new forms of memory making. On June 18, 2020, hundreds of protesters gathered for a Black Lives Matter march from downtown San Francisco to Turk and Taylor, the site of the 1966 riot. As rallies demanding racial justice and the defunding of police departments swept the country, protesters trained their eyes on a private prison, disguised as an apartment building, that occupied this historic site of resistance. Susan Stryker wrote a few days before the protest, "Why not liberate the historic site of trans resistance from its occupation by a private for-profit prison, and turn it into something that truly serves these many unmet needs? . . . Why not demand that the City of San Francisco divert money from its police and jails to support a community-led effort to support Black Trans Lives . . . by turning a private jail into low-income housing, as part of a broader demand for the abolition of all prisons, public or private?"[42] At the rally, Ms. Billy Cooper, a black trans woman in her sixties, told protesters she was a thirty-five-year resident of the Tenderloin. "I remember back in the late seventies, and we didn't have any hope that we would even be alive now." Levi Maxwell, a black trans woman, said, "The Tenderloin is the place where the city has put the most marginalized people." After the rally, the crowd marched through the Transgender Cultural District to demand that the private prison be shut down.

Kids on the Street

What will be remembered about the kids on the street who traveled from tenderloin to tenderloin, connecting zones of abandonment through migratory circuits? I have shown in this book that cities constructed tenderloin districts as zones of abandonment, spaces where the degradation and immorality associated with the urban poor, sexual dissidents, and racialized populations could be contained and cordoned off from white, respectable families and homes. The social trauma many experienced lay in the ongoing experience of a specific kind of scene: at each point, people who stood in for the moral order—police, medical authorities, redevelopers, business owners—made them feel that they were worthless and unwanted, unworthy of care and deserving of abandonment.

Abandoned youth responded by creating a distinctive counterpublic complete with rituals for renaming new members, conventions for collective housing, self-policing mechanisms, and networks for pooling resources to increase the chances of mutual survival. They developed a flexible set of reciprocities, obligations, and moral norms that they instantiated, embodied, and transmitted via religious rituals, kinship terms, and other performances. Many banded together to develop an alternative set of values against which the worth of their lives could be measured.

Centering the experiences of street kids—those who live at the intersections of economic precarity, racialized surveillance, and sexual respectability politics—brings to the fore a politics of reciprocity and mutual aid, values that stand in stark contrast to the individualism prevalent today in the United States. If I came to Polk Street looking for a queer history I could claim as my own, this is what I found: a queer public that "watched each other's backs." This history is even more vital today, as the historical erasure that takes place through gentrification risks foreclosing other possible ways of being in, and relating to, the world.

ABBREVIATIONS

BAR	*Bay Area Reporter*
GLBTHS	Gay, Lesbian, Bisexual, Transgender Historical Society
GLBT-OH	GLBTHS Oral History Collection
LARC	Labor Archives and Research Center
NACP	National Archives at College Park
NYPL	New York Public Library
ONE	ONE National Gay and Lesbian Archives
Painter Collection	Thomas N. Painter Collection, Kinsey Institute
SCRC	Special Collections Research Center
SFHC	San Francisco History Center
SFLC	San Francisco Labor Council Records
SFNM	San Francisco Night Ministry Records
UMAH	United Methodist Archives and History Center

Introduction

1   Bobby White, "San Francisco's Red-Light Denizens Fight to Stay Seedy," *Wall Street Journal*, October 24, 2006.
2   Throughout the book, I refer to narrators using the names that they themselves used when they interacted with me. These may have been "given" birth names, street names, or pseudonyms. In some cases, I use multiple names to refer to the same person.
3   S. Hartman, *Lose Your Mother*, 15.
4   Heap, *Slumming*, 19.
5   D. Taylor, *Archive and the Repertoire*, 89.
6   Rechy, *City of Night*, 88.
7   Larry Littlejohn et al., "Drugs in the Tenderloin: A Publication of the Central City Target Area Board," January 1967, box 14, folder 13, Lucas (Donald Stewart) Papers, GLBTHS.
8   On assemblages, see Bennett, *Vibrant Matter*.
9   Conquergood, *Cultural Struggles*, 35.
10 For this formulation, see J. Scott, *Moral Economy*, 6.
11 Povinelli, *Empire of Love*, 128.
12 Schechner, *Future of Ritual*, 1.
13 Conquergood, *Cultural Struggles*, 127–69.

14   On the term *kids* in the 1920s and 1930s, see D. Johnson, "Kids of Fairytown," 98.

15   Guy Strait, "Young Rejects Form Organization," *Cruise News & World Report* 2, no. 7 (July 1966). See also Guy Strait, "The Tenderloin Report Rejected," *Cruise News & World Report* 2, no. 5 (May 1966). Guy Strait published several "bar rags" from 1961 to 1967, including *L.C.E. News*, *The News*, *Citizens News*, *Bar Rag*, and *Cruise News & World Report*.

16   Laurence Tate, "Exiles of Sin, Incorporated," *Berkeley Barb*, November 11, 1966.

17   DePastino, *Citizen Hobo*, 72–75.

18   Boag, *Same-Sex Affairs*, 17; Canaday, *Straight State*.

19   Anderson, *On Hobos and Homelessness*.

20   Kunzel, *Criminal Intimacy*, 66–67; Chauncey, *Gay New York*, 89; Canaday, *Straight State*, 99.

21   Thomas Painter, "Male Homosexuals Vol 2: The Prostitute," ca. 1941, p. 135, series II, D. 1, vol. 10, Painter Collection (hereafter Painter, "Prostitute").

22   Painter, "Prostitute," 71.

23   Rechy, *City of Night*, 32.

24   Guy Strait, "The Lavender Lexicon, Dictionary of Gay Words and Phrases," Strait and Associates, June 1, 1964, GLBTHS.

25   Moran, *Teaching Sex*, 20.

26   Canaday, *Straight State*, 99.

27   Rechy, *City of Night*, 132.

28   Untitled document ca. 1930s, p. 8, box 128, folder 7, Ernest Watson Burgess Papers, 1886–1966, SCRC.

29   Baker, "Introduction," 8–9.

30   Nestle, "Flamboyance and Fortitude," 18; Newton, "'Drag Queens,'" 132.

31   Kennedy and Davis, *Boots of Leather*, 379.

32   Reay, *New York Hustlers*, 16.

33   Kunzel, *Criminal Intimacy*, 109.

34   Kunzel, *Criminal Intimacy*, 237.

35   C. Cohen, "Punks, Bulldaggers, and Welfare Queens," 444.

36   DePastino, *Citizen Hobo*, xvii.

37   Holmes, "End of Queer Urban History?," 161.

38   C. Cohen, "Punks, Bulldaggers, and Welfare Queens," 480.

39   J. Scott, *Moral Economy*, 168.

40   On reciprocity, see Malinowski, *Crime and Custom in Savage Society*; Mauss, *Gift*; Belshaw, *Traditional Exchange and Modern Markets*.

41   For this formulation, I am indebted to Newton, *Mother Camp*.

42   Stack, *All Our Kin*, 29.

43   Stack, *All Our Kin*, 25.

44   Berlant and Warner, "Sex in Public," 558.

45   J. Scott, *Moral Economy*, 240.

46   Spade, *Mutual Aid*, 11.

47 Spade, *Mutual Aid*, 1.

48 Lisa Duggan defines "homonormativity" as a politics that does not contest heteronormative assumptions and instead embraces "a privatized, depoliticized gay culture anchored in domesticity and consumption." See Duggan, *Twilight of Equality*, 50. Sara Warner defines "homoliberalism" as the "quest for acceptance, legitimacy, and formal equality through a program animated by individual economic interests, a privatized sexual politics, and a constricted notion of national-public life." See Warner, *Acts of Gaiety*, 2.

49 Cvetkovich, *Archive of Feelings*, 11.

50 On queer studies of affect, see Sedgwick, *Touching Feeling*; Love, *Feeling Backward*; Halperin, *What Do Gay Men Want?*; Cvetkovich, *Archive of Feelings*; Darieck Scott, *Extravagant Abjection*; La Fountain-Stokes, "Gay Shame, Latina- and Latino-Style"; Halberstam, "Shame and White Gay Masculinity."

51 Sedgwick, *Touching Feeling*, 63–65.

52 Halperin and Traub, *Gay Shame*, 10.

53 Love, *Feeling Backward*, 2.

54 Paul Welch, "Homosexuality in America," *Life*, June 26, 1964, 68.

55 Canaday, *Straight State*, 99.

56 Hanhardt, *Safe Space*, 49.

57 Love, *Feeling Backward*, 28.

58 Love, *Feeling Backward*, 29.

59 Chris Roebuck makes a similar observation in his study of Polk Street. See Roebuck, "'Workin' It.'"

60 Littlejohn et al., "Drugs in the Tenderloin."

61 Gould, *Moving Politics*, 41.

62 J. Scott, *Moral Economy*, 3; Stack, *All Our Kin*, 25.

63 Sandberg, "Moral Economy and Normative Ethics," 177.

64 E. P. Thompson, "Moral Economy of the English Crowd"; J. Scott, *Moral Economy*.

65 E. P. Thompson, "Moral Economy of the English Crowd," 79.

66 E. P. Thompson, *Customs in Common*, 271.

67 J. Scott, *Moral Economy*, 3.

68 Wilson, *Intimate Economies of Bangkok*.

69 Stout, "When a Yuma Meets Mama," 668.

70 Shah, *Contagious Divides*, 77–104.

71 Sides, "Excavating the Postwar Sex District," 359; Symanski, *Immoral Landscape*, 134; Shumsky and Springer, "San Francisco's Zone of Prostitution."

72 Boyd, *Wide-Open Town*, 15.

73 Arondekar et al., "Queering Archives," 222.

74 W. Benjamin, "Theses on the Philosophy of History," 263.

75 D. Taylor, *Archive and the Repertoire*, 89. On performance historiography, see Roach, *Cities of the Dead*; Jackson, *Lines of Activity*; Bernstein, *Racial Innocence*.

76 D. Taylor, *Archive and the Repertoire*, 20.

77 D. Taylor, *Archive and the Repertoire*, xvii.

78 Conquergood, *Cultural Struggles*, 40.

79 Roach, *Cities of the Dead*, xii.

80 Rechy, *City of Night*, 32.

81 Rechy, *City of Night*, 360.

82 Roach, *Cities of the Dead*, 36.

83 Roach, *Cities of the Dead*, 28.

84 Roach, *Cities of the Dead*, 89–90.

85 Roach, "Mardi Gras Indians and Others," 462.

86 Garland, "What Is a 'History of the Present'?"

87 The bartender James Beales collected materials from his aging patrons and stored them in his Polk Street apartment. He donated these materials to me, and I, in turn, donated them to the GLBT Historical Society. Similarly, Dan Diez gave me a series of letters that Corey Longseeker wrote him in the 1990s. Beales's and Diez's materials are now archived as part of the Polk Street Project Collection. Additionally, I traveled to Tucson, Arizona, and accessioned the Toby Marotta collection of Prospero Project records, which is now stored at the GLBT Historical Society.

88 Groth, *Living Downtown*, 133–37.

89 Roach, *Cities of the Dead*, xi.

90 On social history methods, see Abrams, *Oral History Theory*, 153; P. Thompson, *Voice of the Past*, 8.

91 "The Hu$tler," *Two: The Homosexual Viewpoint in Canada*, 1964, 24.

92 Thomas Painter, "Homosexuality: An Introduction," 1941, p. 29, series II, D. 1, vol. 8, Painter Collection.

93 Scholars trace the term *performative* to J. L. Austin's 1962 "How to Do Things with Words." Austin attacked the philosophical view that utterances chiefly serve to state facts and thus can be deemed true or false according to the truth or falsity of the facts they state. He introduced the "performative" as a category of utterance that has no truth value since it does not describe the world but acts on it—it is a way of "doing things with words." See Austin, "How to Do Things with Words"; Butler, "Performative Acts and Gender Constitution"; Sedgwick, *Touching Feeling*, 5.

94 Kennedy, "Telling Tales," 61.

95 E. P. Johnson, *Sweet Tea*, 8.

96 E. P. Johnson, *Sweet Tea*, 9.

97 Cvetkovich, *Archive of Feelings*, 7.

98 Cvetkovich, *Archive of Feelings*, 167.

99 Chanfrault-Duchet, "Narrative Structures," 81–82.

100 Boyd, "Who Is the Subject?," 188.

101 Love, *Feeling Backward*, 28.

102 Howard, *Men Like That*, 13.

103 I borrow the phrase *social trauma* from Judith Butler, who defines it as an "extended experience" that takes the form "of an ongoing subjugation, the restaging of injury through signs that occlude and reenact the scene." See Butler, *Excitable Speech*, 36. I borrow the phrase *moral drama* from Kathryn Dudley. See Dudley, *Debt and Dispossession*, 139.

104 Sedgwick, "Queer Performativity," 13.

105 On the development of transgender as an identity category, see Stryker, "(De)Subjugated Knowledges"; Valentine, *Imagining Transgender*.

106 Somerville, "Queer."

1. A Performance Genealogy of US Tenderloins

1 On migration and queer publics, see Tompkins, "Intersections of Race, Gender, and Sexuality"; Povinelli and Chauncey, "Thinking Sex Transnationally."

2 S. Hartman, *Wayward Lives*, xiv.

3 Halberstam, *Female Masculinity*, 13.

4 Fraser, "Rethinking the Public Sphere," 61.

5 Heap, *Slumming*, 20.

6 Keire, *For Business and Pleasure*, 3.

7 Keire, *For Business and Pleasure*, 9.

8 On the construction of tenderloin districts, see Heap, *Slumming*; Keire, *For Business and Pleasure*; Sears, *Arresting Dress*; Capó, *Welcome to Fairyland*; LaFleur, *Natural History of Sexuality in Early America*; Wild, "Red Light Kaleidoscope."

9 See Povinelli, *Economies of Abandonment*; Keire, *For Business and Pleasure*, 7.

10 Keire, *For Business and Pleasure*, 11.

11 W. Taylor, *In Pursuit of Gotham*, 95.

12 Gilfoyle, "Policing of Sexuality," 297.

13 Newspaper articles from the late nineteenth century note that areas with vice economies offered "prime cuts" for madams and graft opportunities for politicians and police officers. See Gilfoyle, *City of Eros*.

14 Keire, *For Business and Pleasure*, 3; Rosen, *Lost Sisterhood*, xii.

15 Keire, *For Business and Pleasure*, 138.

16 Symanski, *Immoral Landscape*, 129.

17 Califia, "City of Desire."

18 On the construction of whiteness, see Roediger and Barrett, "In Between Peoples"; Roediger, *Working toward Whiteness*.

19 Painter, "Prostitute," 121.

20 See Roediger, *Working toward Whiteness*; Holmes, "End of Queer Urban History?"

21 Holmes, "End of Queer Urban History?"

22 "Dear Cornelia," letter from Thomas Painter, January 18, 1966, p. 1, Painter Collection.

23 Letter from Thomas Painter to Alfred Kinsey, August 23, 1966, p. 3, Painter Collection.

24 Chauncey, *Gay New York*, 34.

25 Benjamin and Masters, *Prostitution and Morality*, 316.

26 "Nightmare, U.S.A.," *Salute: The Picture Magazine for Men* 3, no. 2 (March 1948): 4.

27 Gilfoyle, *City of Eros*, 202; Painter, "Prostitute," 22.

28 Painter, "Prostitute," 22.

29 "Alexander Stahl, Age: 19 Years," n.d., p. 41, box 98, folder 5, Ernest Watson Burgess Papers, 1886–1966, SCRC.

30 Thomas Lanigan-Schmidt, "Mother Stonewall and the Golden Rats," 1989, handwritten text to accompany the exhibition *Mother Stonewall and the Golden Rats* at the Gay and Lesbian Community Center in New York City.

31 Don Lucas, "Interview with Steve," August 21, 1964, box 6, folder 31, Lucas (Donald Stewart) Papers, GLBTHS.

32 James P. Driscoll, "Transsexuals," *Transaction* 8, nos. 5–6 (March/April 1971): 28–37.

33 Tom Ramsay, untitled and undated document, box 15, folder 4, Lucas (Donald Stewart) Papers, GLBTHS.

34 "A Summary of the Data on Homosexual Behavior and the Law in New York City 1951," p. 2, Alice Fields Collection, Kinsey Institute.

35 George L. Kirkham and Edward Sagarin, "Transsexuals in a Formal Organizational Setting," *Journal of Sex Research* 5, no. 2 (1969): 99.

36 On vagrancy laws, see DePastino, *Citizen Hobo*, 7; Shah, "Between 'Oriental Depravity' and 'Natural Degenerates,'" 713; Kunzel, *Criminal Intimacy*, 151; Capó, *Welcome to Fairyland*, 42; Boyd, *Wide-Open Town*, 216.

37 Sonenschein, *Some Homosexual Men*, 203.

38 Estes, *Stilettos and Steel*, 71.

39 On the construction of adolescence, see Shah, "Between 'Oriental Depravity' and 'Natural Degenerates,'" 708; Kett, *Rites of Passage*, 243; Moran, *Teaching Sex*, 136.

40 Moran, *Teaching Sex*.

41 Shah, "Between 'Oriental Depravity' and 'Natural Degenerates,'" 708; Gibson, *Street Kids*, 31.

42 A. Platt, *Child Savers*, xvii.

43 Guy Strait, "The Young Homosexual, He's Got Problems," *Cruise News & World Report* 3, no. 2 (January 1967).

44 Lipschutz, "Runaways in History," 328.

45 Gibson, *Street Kids*, 51; Bush, *Who Gets a Childhood?*; Gilbert, *Cycle of Outrage*.

46 Kaye, "Male Prostitution in the Twentieth Century," 39.

47 Kaye, "Male Prostitution in the Twentieth Century," 20.

48 Libertoff, "Runaway Child in America."

49 Kett, *Rites of Passage*.

50 Painter, "Prostitute," 134.

51 Mr. Mark Forrester and Mr. Calvin Colt, "Joint Proposal: Central City Citizens Council and the Tenderloin Committee in Cooperation with the Job Corps and Glide Memorial Methodist Church: A Community Facility Service-Training Program for the Central City Area of San Francisco," August 1966, p. 2, box 14, SFLC, LARC.

52 Kamel, "Downtown Street Hustlers," 49.

53 DePastino, *Citizen Hobo*, 9.

54 Paulson, *Evening at the Garden of Allah*, 26.

55 Syrett, "Busman's Holiday in the Not-So-Lonely Crowd."

56 Painter, "Prostitute," 72.

57 Drew and Drake, *Boys for Sale*, 145.

58 Atack, "Transportation in American Economic History," 23.

59 Painter, "Prostitute," 29.

60 Painter, "Prostitute," 50.

61 "Dear Cornelia," letter from Thomas Painter, January 18, 1966, p. 1.

62 Guy Strait, "Annual Migration Underway," *Citizens News* 4, no. 14 [ca. Summer 1965?]: 24.

63 Painter noted in 1941 that hustlers' "wandering" was dictated by Mardi Gras, fairs, and conventions. See Painter, "Prostitute," 134.

64 T. Williams, *One Arm and Other Stories*, 10–11.

65 Rechy, *City of Night*, 343.

66 "Dear Cornelia," letter from Thomas Painter, January 18, 1966, p. 1.

67 Symanski, *Immoral Landscape*; James, "Mobility as an Adaptive Strategy," 353.

68 Guy Strait, "Prostitution," *L.C.E. News*, April 1963.

69 Painter, "Prostitute," 135.

70 Henry, *Sex Variants*, 450.

71 Kamel, "Downtown Street Hustlers," 51.

72 For the historiography of queer migration, see D'Emilio, "Capitalism and Gay Identity"; Weston, "Get Thee to a Big City," 41; Howard, *Men Like That*.

73 Shah, *Stranger Intimacy*, 15.

74 On queer temporalities, see Halberstam, *In a Queer Time and Place*.

75 Freeman, *Time Binds*, 3.

76 Paulson, *Evening at the Garden of Allah*, 24.

77 Woodlawn and Copeland, *Low Life in High Heels*, 54.

78 Groth, *Living Downtown*, 119.

79 Newton, "'Drag Queens,'" 116.

80 H. Benjamin and Masters, *Prostitution and Morality*, 333.

81 Sylvia Rivera, interviewed by Martin Duberman, October 12, 1990, audiotape 02888, Martin B. Duberman Papers, NYPL.

82 Duberman, *Stonewall*, 67.

83 Toto le Grand [pseudonym for Lou Rand Hogan], "The Golden Age of Queens," *Bay Area Reporter*, September 4, 1974, 6.

84   Kamel, "Downtown Street Hustlers," 130.

85   H. Lawrence Ross, "'Hustler' in Chicago," *Journal of Student Research*, no. 1 (Fall 1959): 7.

86   McNamara, *Times Square Hustler*, 39.

87   Ross, "'Hustler' in Chicago," 7.

88   Carter, *Stonewall*, 59–60.

89   Donald Stuart, "Report by the Night Minister," July–September 1968, SFNM.

90   Nels Anderson, "The Juvenile and the Tramp," *Journal of the American Institute of Criminal Law and Criminology* 14, no. 2 (August 1923): 290–312.

91   Document in folder marked "Male Homosexuality," ca. late 1970s, p. 3, Marotta Papers.

92   Wild, "Red Light Kaleidoscope," 729.

93   Donovan Bess, "In the Tenderloin Underground: Stories of 'Boys for Sale,'" *San Francisco Chronicle*, March 2, 1966.

94   Martin F. Stow, untitled document, ca. early 1970s, Marotta Papers.

95   Ross, "'Hustler' in Chicago," 5.

96   Interview excerpt from Zagone, *Drugs in the Tenderloin*.

97   Ross, "'Hustler' in Chicago," 8.

98   Newton, "'Drag Queens,'" 120.

99   Newton, "'Drag Queens,'" 43.

100 Larry Littlejohn et al., "Drugs in the Tenderloin: A Publication of the Central City Target Area Board," January 1967, p. 10, box 14, folder 13, Lucas (Donald Stewart) Papers, GLBTHS.

101 Painter, "Prostitute," 137.

102 Ross, "'Hustler' in Chicago," 8.

103 Drew and Drake, *Boys for Sale*, 171.

104 Hammer, *O My Land, My Friends*, 362.

105 Henry, *Sex Variants*, 383.

106 "Consultation on the Church and Homosexuality," meeting minutes, February 1966, p. 31, Lucas (Donald Stewart) Papers, GLBTHS.

107 Chauncey, *Gay New York*, 34.

108 Chauncey, *Gay New York*, 56.

109 Chauncey, *Gay New York*, xxii.

110 Document with no title, n.d., ca. late 1930s, p. 4, box 128, folder 7, Ernest Watson Burgess Papers, 1886–1966, SCRC.

111 Driscoll, "Transsexuals," 34.

112 Roach, *Cities of the Dead*, 29.

113 Halperin, *What Do Gay Men Want?*, 95.

114 Hauser, *Homosexual Society*, 74.

115 Susman, *Culture as History*, 280.

116 "Case J," n.d., ca. late 1930s, box 128, folder 7, Ernest Watson Burgess Papers, 1886–1966, SCRC.

117 Anonymous letter to John V. Moore, January 12, 1965, Moore, John V. Collection, Pacific School of Religion Archives.

118 Werther, *Female-Impersonators*, 70–71.

119 Werther and Herring, *Autobiography of an Androgyne*, 65, 68.

120 Werther, *Female-Impersonators*, 171.

121 Werther, *Female-Impersonators*, 205.

122 Werther, *Female-Impersonators*, 6.

123 Chauncey, "Policed," 320.

124 Young, *San Francisco*, 547.

125 Boyd, *Wide-Open Town*, 44; Sides, "Excavating the Postwar Sex District," 359.

126 Le Grand [Hogan], "Golden Age of Queens," 8.

127 Le Grand [Hogan], "Golden Age of Queens," 8.

128 Sweet, "Political and Social Action in Homophile Organizations," 79.

129 Driscoll, "Transsexuals," 34.

130 Gould, *Moving Politics*, 41.

131 Document with no title, n.d., ca. late 1930s, p. 8, box 128, folder 7, Ernest Watson Burgess Papers, 1886–1966, SCRC.

132 Genet, *Thief's Journal*, 65.

133 Untitled document starting with "In Mr. K's case history we," ca. late 1930s, box 128, folder 7, Ernest Watson Burgess Papers, 1886–1966, SCRC.

134 George Henry and Alfred Gross, "Social Factors in the Case Histories of One Hundred Underprivileged Homosexuals," *Mental Hygiene* 22 (1938): 605.

135 Guy Strait, "Radio," *L.C.E News*, December 6, 1962, 5.

136 "Miss Destiny," *ONE Magazine*, September 1964, 7.

137 "Miss Destiny," *ONE Magazine*, September 1964, 9.

138 Ralph "Mezzeppa" Dulberg, letter to the editor, "Dear Senator," *The News* 2, no. 18 (June 10, 1963): 7.

139 Thomas Painter, "Autobiography," unpublished essay, 1944, p. 142, box 2, series II, D. 2, vol. 1, Painter Collection.

140 Painter, "Prostitute," 25.

141 Painter, "Prostitute," 87.

142 Letter from Thomas Painter to Alfred Kinsey, August 1944, p. 1, box 2, series II, D. 2, vol. 1, Painter Collection.

143 Painter, "Prostitute," 113.

144 Painter, "Autobiography," 155.

145 Jones and Wills, *American West*, 94.

146 Pérez, *Taste for Brown Bodies*, 23.

147 Pérez, *Taste for Brown Bodies*, 16.

148 Document with no title, n.d., ca. late 1930s, p. 4, box 128, folder 7, Ernest Watson Burgess Papers, 1886–1966, SCRC.

149 "Regarding the love affair of Jim and Rodney. Told me by Rodney," n.d., box 98, folder 3, Ernest Watson Burgess Papers, 1886–1966, SCRC.

150 Keith St. Clare, "Lavender in Uniform," *Vanguard Magazine* 1, no. 6 (ca. April 1967).

151 Kamel, "Downtown Street Hustlers," 102.

152 Goffman, *Presentation of Self in Everyday Life*, 28.

153 Rechy, *City of Night*, 291.

154 Rechy, *City of Night*, 291.

155 Sesto Chiarello, "Orpheus . . . In-bound," *Vector Magazine*, May 1968, 5.

156 "Case of Mr. H," n.d., p. 6, box 98, folder 2, Homosexuality interviews, Ernest Watson Burgess Papers, 1886–1966, SCRC.

157 No author, "Dear Senator," *The News* 2, no. 18 (June 10, 1963): 7.

158 Painter, "Homosexuality: An Introduction," 87.

159 Painter, "Prostitute," 88.

160 Painter, "Homosexuality: An Introduction," 37.

161 Ross, "'Hustler' in Chicago," 3.

162 Chauncey, "Policed," 324.

163 Chauncey, "Policed," 323.

164 Painter, "Prostitute," 2.

165 Oral history conducted by Marc Stein with Bill Brinsfield, October 27, 1993, OutHistory.com, accessed July 22, 2021, https://outhistory.org/exhibits/show /deweys-sit-in/oral-histories.

166 Rechy, *City of Night*, 180.

167 Rechy, *City of Night*, 32.

168 Keire, *For Business and Pleasure*, 35.

169 Keire, *For Business and Pleasure*, 10.

170 Driscoll, "Transsexuals," 28.

171 "RendezVous for the City's Outcasts," *San Francisco Chronicle*, May 9, 1969.

172 Rechy, *City of Night*, 237.

173 Letter from Thomas Painter to Alfred Kinsey, March 10, 1966, Painter Collection.

174 D. Johnson, *Buying Gay*, 25.

175 Floyd, "Closing the (Heterosexual) Frontier," 111.

176 D. Johnson, *Buying Gay*, 160.

177 Guy Strait, "How to Deal on the San Francisco Meat Market," *Citizens News* 5, no. 8 (August 1966): 7.

178 Guy Strait, "Homosexual Prostitution," *Cruise News and World Report* 2, no. 2 (December 1965). (Strait claims that this segment of his newspaper is a transcript of Norm Woodruff, "The Market Street Proposition," a radio program on KFRC.)

179 Strait, "How to Deal on the San Francisco Meat Market."

180 Ross, "'Hustler' in Chicago," 7.

181 McNamara, *Times Square Hustler*, 62.

182 Guy Strait, "In Defense of Prostitution," *Cruise News & World Report* 2, no. 10 (October 1966): 3.

183 Letter from Thomas Painter to Alfred Kinsey, April 2, 1947, Painter Collection.

184 Kenneth Ginsburg, "The 'Meat Rack': A Study of the Male Homosexual Prostitute," *American Journal of Psychotherapy* 21 (1967): 174.

185 McNamara, *Times Square Hustler*, 63.

186 William Marlin Butts, "Boy Prostitutes of the Metropolis," *Journal of Clinical Psychopathology* 8 (1946–47): 675.

187 Henry and Gross, "Social Factors in the Case Histories of One Hundred Underprivileged Homosexuals," 606; see also Ross, "'Hustler' in Chicago," 5.

188 Gouldner, "Norm of Reciprocity."

189 Toby Marotta, field note, March 31, 1991, Marotta Papers.

190 DePastino, *Citizen Hobo*, 233.

191 Heise, *Urban Underworlds*, 172.

192 Letter from Thomas Painter to Alfred Kinsey, March 10, 1966, p. 1, Painter Collection.

193 Quoted in Faderman and Timmons, *Gay L.A.*, 1.

194 Faderman and Timmons, *Gay L.A.*, 2.

195 Stein, *City of Sisterly and Brotherly Loves*, 245.

196 Stein, *City of Sisterly and Brotherly Loves*, 246.

197 Joel Roberts, "Street Youths Organize," *SDS Regional Newsletter* 1, no. 11 (June 29, 1966): 2–3.

198 Stein, *City of Sisterly and Brotherly Loves*; Stryker and Silverman, *Screaming Queens*.

199 On urban neoliberalism, see Smith, *The New Urban Frontier*; Hackworth, "The Place, Time, and Process of Neoliberal Urbanism"; Beckett and Herbert, *Banished*; Mitchell, "The Annihilation of Space by Law."

200 Dave Poster and Elaine Goldman, "Gay Youth Gone Wild: Something Has Got to Change," *The Villager* 75, no. 18 (September 21–27, 2005).

201 Weiss, "Queer Politics in Neoliberal Times," 112.

202 McNamara, *Times Square Hustler*, 125.

2. Street Churches

1 For this formulation, see Nietzsche, *On the Genealogy of Morals*, 17.

2 J. Scott, *Moral Economy*, 240.

3 Povinelli, *Empire of Love*, 122.

4 On the Old Catholics, see "Old Catholics," in *The Columbia Electronic Encyclopedia* (New York: Columbia University Press, 2021), accessed May 16, 2022, ebsco.com. See also Byrne, *Other Catholics*; Pruter, *Old Catholic Sourcebook*; Anson, *Bishops At Large*.

5 W. Platt, "African Orthodox Church."

6 Byrne, *Other Catholics*, 12.

7 On Hyde's ministry, see Anson, *Bishops At Large*, 265; letter from Bishop George A. Hyde to Reverend Raymond Broshears, February 12, 1977, box 4, George Hyde file, Broshears (Raymond) Papers, GLBTHS; George Hyde, interview with J. Gordon Melton, July 6, 2005, LGBT Religious Archives Network, accessed May 16, 2022, https://lgbtqreligiousarchives.org/media/oral-history/george-augustine-hyde/GHyde.pdf.

8 Talley, "Queer Miracle in Georgia," 17.

9 Helen Pappas, "Happy Birthday Jesus!," *SAGA* (December 1976): 8, International Gay Information Center collection, NYPL.

10 Letter from Rev. George Hyde, December 29, 1964, box 2, folder 10, Hyde, Rev. George C. General Correspondence, Old Catholic Church records, NYPL.

11 "His Dream: A Derelicts' Haven," *Hudson Dispatch*, June 6, 1963, box 2, folder 8, Old Catholic Church records, NYPL.

12 St. Kasmer's Oratory Newsletter, May 1966, box 2, folder 7, Gerard, Rev. Bro. Lawrence, General Correspondence, 1965–73, Old Catholic Church records, NYPL.

13 Letter from Rev. Fr. Lawrence Gerard, likely an alias of Brother Marion Gerard Greeley, c. 1966, box 2, folder 7, Gerard, Rev. Bro. Lawrence General Correspondence, 1965–73, Old Catholic Church records, NYPL.

14 Enroth, *Gay Church*, 100.

15 Editorial response to a letter to the editor, *Vector* 6, no. 11 (November 1970): 9.

16 Michael Mitchell, "Profile: Father Feldhausen," *G.P.U. [Gay People's Union] News*, March 1972, 12.

17 James Stephens, "Two Women Plan to Be Married; File Suit; Make It a Federal Case," *Jet* 41, no. 6 (November 4, 1971): 24.

18 Church of the Beloved Disciple Sunday Bulletin, July 19, 1971, p. 1, Roy Birchard Collection, Flora Lamson Hewlett Library, Berkeley, quoted in White, "Proclaiming Liberation."

19 "Beloved Disciple: What Does It Do?," n.d., Printed Ephemera folder, Old Catholic Church records, NYPL.

20 On George Hyde and Clement, see J. Gordon Melton, "Eucharistic Catholic Church (Canadian Branch)," accessed September 15, 2004, http://netminis tries.org/see/churches/ch04614; Ward, *Independent Bishops*; Hyde, *Genesis of the Orthodox Catholic Church of America*.

21 Frederick Brittain, "Book Review: Bishops At Large," *Theology* 67, no. 532 (1964): 67.

22 Lester Kinsolving, "The Paper Priests," *San Francisco Examiner*, October 11, 1971, 33.

23 Letter from Michael Itkin to "Members of the Holy Synod of the North American Old Roman Catholic Church," July 20, 1962, Old Catholic Church records, NYPL.

24 See advertisements in *Grecian Guild Pictorial* 2, no. 1 (January 1957): 27; no. 26 (September 1960): 45; and no. 29 (March 1961): 44. The advertisement in each issue reads: "The Very Reverend Geoffrey P. T. Paget King, J.D.C., of the Old Catholic Roman Catholic Church, the Chapel of Saint Thomas of Canterbury . . . celebrates Mass every month at 8:00 A.M. on the last day of the month for the intentions of the Grecian Guild and all its members."

25 Lloyd, *For Money or Love*, 14.

26 "United States Government Memorandum, 4/15/69," to Mr. Gale, "Subject: Raymond Broshears Information Concerning," Broshears (Raymond) Papers, GLBTHS.

27　Hanhardt, *Safe Space*, 93.

28　"Reverend Ray," ca. 1973, Broshears (Raymond) Papers, GLBTHS.

29　Interview of Raymond Broshears conducted by Steve Jaffe, James Alcock, and Louis Ivon, "Broshears #4," August 8, 1968, p. 6, John F. Kennedy Assassination Records Collection, Papers of Jim Garrison, Broshears, Reverend Raymond files, National Archives at College Park, MD (hereafter Broshears files, NACP).

30　Superior Court of the State of California, City and County of San Francisco, Lawrence Gerrard, Plaintiff, v. Raymond Broshears, et al., Defendants, no. 763864, p. 3, Broshears (Raymond) Papers, GLBTHS.

31　United States Federal Census, 1940, National Archives and Records Administration, Washington, DC.

32　According to his headstone, he was a private in the US Army in Korea during the Korean War. The San Francisco National Cemetery lists the name Charles Raymond Broshears, born August 11, 1936, died January 10, 1982. "Raymond Charles Broshears," Find a Grave, accessed July 22, 2021, https://www.findagrave.com/memorial/3521814/raymond-charles-broshears.

33　Control files, Broshears (Raymond) Papers, GLBTHS.

34　Superior Court of the State of California, City and County of San Francisco, Lawrence Gerrard, Plaintiff, v. Raymond Broshears, et al., Defendants, no. 763864, Broshears (Raymond) Papers, GLBTHS.

35　Memorandum of SA Irving R. Dean, to director, FBI, from SAC, San Francisco, April 7, 1969, Broshears (Raymond) Papers, GLBTHS.

36　George Mendenhall, "Heaven Can't Wait! Broshears Gets Final Call," *Bay Area Reporter*, January 14, 1982, 1.

37　Wacker, *Heaven Below*, 7.

38　Hood, *The Psychology of Religious Fundamentalism*, 84.

39　Hood, *The Psychology of Religious Fundamentalism*, 112.

40　Stanford Lawsuit file, "The Orthodox Episcopal Church of God," pamphlet, box 3, Broshears (Raymond) Papers, GLBTHS.

41　"Deaths—Raymond Broshears," *San Francisco Chronicle*, January 11, 1982, B9.

42　"Inmate Ill-Treated at Medical Facility, 'Gay' Minister Charges," *Vacaville Reporter*, no. 26 (April 3, 1972).

43　"Illinoisan Sentenced on Morals Conviction," *St. Louis Post-Dispatch*, November 15, 1964, 14.

44　"C.O.R.E. Aid Jailed on Morals Charge," *Chicago Tribune*, November 15, 1964, 41.

45　Raymond Broshears, "Thoughts and Opinions," *Bay Area Reporter* 6, no. 1 (January 1976): 7, Broshears (Raymond) Papers, GLBTHS.

46　Memorandum to Jim Garrison, District Attorney, from Stephen Jaffe, Investigator, re: Rev. Raymond Broshears, August 8, 1968, p. 1, Broshears files, NACP.

47　Interview of Raymond Broshears, conducted by Steve Jaffe, James Alcock, and Louis Ivon, "Broshears #4," August 8, 1968, p. 1, Broshears files, NACP.

48　Memorandum to Jim Garrison from Stephen Jaffe, August 8, 1968, p. 6, Broshears files, NACP.

49 Memorandum to Jim Garrison from Stephen Jaffe, August 8, 1968, p. 4; interview of Raymond Broshears, conducted by Steve Jaffe, James Alcock, and Louis Ivon, "Broshears #4," p. 2, Broshears files, NACP.

50 Broshears, "Thoughts and Opinions," 7.

51 Donovan Bess, "The Cops vs. City's Sin Jungle," *San Francisco Chronicle*, February 25, 1966, 1, 24.

52 Raymond Broshears, unknown title, *Light of Understanding* 2, no. 6 (May 1968), Broshears (Raymond) Papers, GLBTHS.

53 Broshears, "Thoughts and Opinions," 7.

54 Alan Stanford Lawsuit file, ca. 1979, box 3, Broshears (Raymond) Papers, GLBTHS.

55 Unknown title, Raymond Broshears, *Light of Understanding* 2, no. 6 (May 1968), Broshears (Raymond) Papers, GLBTHS.

56 Raymond Broshears, "The Minister to the Homosexual Minority," *Vanguard Magazine* 1, no. 5 (ca. March 1967).

57 "Interview with Rev. Broshears," *Vanguard Magazine* 1, no. 9 (ca. August 1967): 5.

58 See Broshears's scrapbook, box 4, "Orthodox Episcopal Church of God" file, Broshears (Raymond) Papers, GLBTHS.

59 Letter from Raymond Broshears to Internal Revenue Service, April 7, 1970, "Orthodox Episcopal Church of God" file, carton 4, Broshears (Raymond) Papers, GLBTHS.

60 Raymond Broshears, *Light of Understanding*, July 1969, Broshears (Raymond) Papers, GLBTHS.

61 "Reverend Ray," ca. 1973, Broshears (Raymond) Papers, GLBTHS.

62 "Ministerial Test," n.d., box A, Broshears (Raymond) Papers, GLBTHS.

63 "Fellowship," August 1, 1974, box 4, "Orthodox Episcopal Church of God" file, Broshears (Raymond) Papers, GLBTHS.

64 Raymond Broshears, *Light of Understanding* 2, no. 5 (April 1968), Broshears (Raymond) Papers, GLBTHS.

65 Raymond Broshears, *Light of Understanding* 2, no. 5 (April 1968), Broshears (Raymond) Papers, GLBTHS.

66 Raymond Broshears, "History of the Orthodox Episcopal Churches of God, Inc. in America!," box 4, "Orthodox Episcopal Church of God" file, Broshears (Raymond) Papers, GLBTHS.

67 Handwritten letter dated "October," no year, folder 17/1, Lucas (Donald Stewart) Papers, GLBTHS.

68 Letter from Bob Graham to Raymond Broshears, n.d., Bob Graham file, Broshears (Raymond) Papers, GLBTHS.

69 Letter from Bob Graham to Raymond Broshears, January 13, 1981, Bob Graham file, Broshears (Raymond) Papers, GLBTHS.

70 Eric Markowitz, "The Most Dangerous Gay Man in America Fought Violence with Violence," *Newsweek*, January 25, 2018.

71 Raymond Broshears, "San Francisco GAA," *Gay Scene* 2, no. 4 (1971): 17.

72 Untitled article in *The Advocate*, December 22, 1971, Broshears (Raymond) Papers, GLBTHS.

73 "Gays Liberate Mason St.," *Berkeley Barb*, October 15–21, 1971, 10.

74 Sandy Green, "Queens Liberation Alliance," *Gay Pride Quarterly* 3 (Winter 1973): 10.

75 Raymond Broshears, "History of the Helping Hands Community Center," *San Francisco Crusader*, no. 11 (July 1974): 4. Broshears ran numerous newspapers, including the *Crusader*, *Gay Crusader*, *San Francisco Crusader*, *Gay Pride Crusader*, and *Gay Focus*, titles he appears to have used interchangeably. Most of the articles in these papers appear to have been written by Broshears.

76 Broshears, "History of the Helping Hands Community Center," 2.

77 Raymond Broshears, "Transsexuals—Transvestites & Drag Queens," *Crusader*, no. 17 (May 1975): 5.

78 Raymond Broshears, "Gay Liberation Is Dead . . . Long Live Gay Revolution!," *Gay Pride Quarterly*, Spring 1973, 7.

79 Raymond Broshears, advertisement, *San Francisco Crusader*, no. 11 (July 1974): 1.

80 Hanhardt, *Safe Space*, 93.

81 "SIR Sics Pigs on Rev. Ray," *Berkeley Barb*, September 17–23, 1971, 4.

82 "The Sexes: The Lavender Panthers," *The Advocate*, January 5, 1972, Broshears (Raymond) Papers, GLBTHS.

83 "Lavender Panthers Disbanded," *Berkeley Barb*, May 24–30, 1974.

84 "The Sexes: The Lavender Panthers," *Time*, October 8, 1973.

85 "Gay Vigilantes to Fight Back," *San Francisco Examiner*, July 7, 1973.

86 "Gay Guerillas Hit Beaux Arts Ball," *Berkeley Barb*, October 29–November 4, 1971, 11.

87 Unknown publication, unknown title, July 11, 1973, Broshears (Raymond) Papers, GLBTHS.

88 GAA [Gay Activists Alliance] "Zap Letter," n.d., Broshears (Raymond) Papers, GLBTHS.

89 Enroth, *Gay Church*, 97.

90 Raymond Broshears, "Thoughts and Opinions," *Bay Area Reporter* 6, no. 1 (January 1976): 8.

91 Control files, Broshears (Raymond) Papers, GLBTHS.

92 Walter P. Morgan, "Quandry," *Forum*, September 27, 1972.

93 "Community of Jesus Our Brother, Affiliated with the Brotherhood of the Love of Christ," in folder labeled "Itkin, Mikhail, Bishop III," unprocessed box, ONE.

94 Michael Itkin, "Act of the Consecration of Life," p. 3, box 107, Correspondence, Living Theatre Records, Beinecke Rare Book and Manuscript Library (hereafter Living Theatre Records, Beinecke).

95 Keller, "Walt Whitman Camping," 114.

96 J. Lewis, *Peculiar Prophets*, 127. See also Ian Young, "Mikhail Itkin: Tales of a Bishopric," *Gay and Lesbian Review Worldwide* 17, no. 6 (November/December 2010): 26–27. On the People's Institute, see Pehl, "'Apostles of Fascism,'" 456.

97 Letter from Michael Itkin to "Friends," May 21, 1958, box 107, Correspondence, Itkin, Michael, Living Theatre Records, Beinecke.

98 Letter from Francis Itkin to Mrs. Salisbury, April 5, 1971, Correspondence, Itkin, Michael, Living Theatre Records, Beinecke.

99 Young, "Mikhail Itkin," 26–27.

100 Letter from Primitive Catholic Church, Itkin, to Members of the Holy Synod of the North American Old Roman Catholic Church and the Primatial See of Caer-Glow, England, July 20, 1962, Old Catholic Church records, NYPL.

101 Untitled letter from George Hyde, ca. 1961, p. 2, box 2, folder 10, Hyde, Rev. George C. General Correspondence, Old Catholic Church records, NYPL.

102 Letter from Chancellor's Office, United Old Catholic Bishops, World Union, to Msg. AC Whitehead, Long Island, NYC, February 17, 1961, Old Catholic Church records, NYPL.

103 Undated and unsigned letter, likely written by Lawrence Gerard, ca. 1966, box 2, folder 7, Gerard, Rev. Bro. Lawrence, General Correspondence, 1965–73, Old Catholic Church records, NYPL.

104 Letter from Byzantine Primitive Catholic Church to Msg. AC Whitehead, Long Island, NYC, February 17, 1961, Old Catholic Church records, NYPL.

105 Letter from the Most Reverend Michael Augustine S.A. Itkin (Bishop Primus, Free Catholic Communion, NYC 52, NY) to Rev. Francis MacNamara, O.S.J., November 20, 1961, General Correspondence, 1960–62, Old Catholic Church records, NYPL.

106 Document titled "Community of Jesus Our Brother, Affiliated with The Brotherhood of the Love of Christ," ca. 1970s, p. 2, folder labeled "Itkin, Mikhail, Bishop III," in unprocessed box, Itkin (Mikhail) Papers, ONE.

107 Michael Itkin, "Community of Jesus Our Brother," pamphlet, ca. 1969, folder labeled "Itkin, Mikhail, Bishop III," in unprocessed box, Itkin (Mikhail) Papers, ONE.

108 Letter from Michael Itkin to "Sisters, Brothers, Comrades, Friends and Lovers," March 16, 1974, Living Theatre Records, Beinecke.

109 Itkin, "Community of Jesus Our Brother," 3.

110 Michael Itkin, letter to the New York Committee for the General Strike for Peace, January, 26, 1962, Living Theatre Records, Beinecke.

111 "Unionists Back Negro Protests on Segregation," *Gaffney (SC) Ledger*, April 14, 1960, 14.

112 "22 Pacifists Start 150-Mile 'Peace Walk,'" *Meriden (CT) Record*, August 8, 1960, 14.

113 "Two Clerics Guilty in a Sit-Down," *Daily News* (New York), May 22, 1962, 397.

114 Martin, *Theater Is in the Streets*, 4.

115 Martin, *Theater Is in the Streets*, 4.

116 Sullivan, *Radical Bishop and Gay Consciousness*, 52.

117 Michael Itkin, "Act of the Consecration of Life," 14, box 107, Correspondence, Itkin, Michael, Living Theatre Records, Beinecke.

118 Itkin, "Act of the Consecration of Life," 14.

119 Michael Itkin, Brotherhood of the Way, the People's Church of Human Divinity, "Bond of Fellowship," March 27, 1959, pp. 1–2, "Itkin, Mikhael, Bishop III" folder, Itkin (Mikhail) Papers, ONE.

120 Letter from Michael Itkin to Constantine Whitehead, Catholic Episcopal Church, May 1, 1961, General Correspondence, 1960–62, Old Catholic Church records, NYPL.

121 Michael Itkin, "Faith and Practice Being the Confessional Statement of the Brotherhood of the Love of Christ and Evangelical Communion," Brotherhood of the Love of Christ and Evangelical Communion, Old Catholic Church records, NYPL.

122 Jon Jacobson, "The Man Don't Dig Church," *Berkeley Barb*, January 24, 1969.

123 Young, "Mikhail Itkin," 26–27.

124 "Two GLF House Residents Are Ordained as Priests by an Evangelical Catholic Sect," *Washington Blade*, July 18, 1972.

125 "Exiles from Roman Catholicism Form Their Own Congregation at the GLF House," *Washington Blade*, September 1971.

126 Letter from Mikhail Itkin to Mr. Roy Birchard, December 11, 1972, Birchard Collection, quoted in White, "Proclaiming Liberation," 115.

127 Letter from Rev. Thomas A. Fairbanks, Arlington, VA, cc. Ray Broshears, Itkin, to Rev. Yves Junod, Switzerland, May 5, 1971, Broshears (Raymond) Papers, GLBTHS.

128 Enroth, *Gay Church*, 103–4.

129 "Christ and the Homosexual," Christmas 1969 sermon at the Community of Jesus Our Brother, San Francisco, box 2, Gay Clergy file, Broshears (Raymond) Papers, GLBTHS.

130 Folder labeled "Itkin, Mikhail, Bishop III," p. 3, in unprocessed box, Itkin (Mihkail) Papers, ONE.

131 "Christ and the Homosexual," Christmas 1969 sermon.

132 On the West Hotel, see "West Hotel," *Up from the Deep*, accessed May 3, 2014, http://upfromthedeep.com/2010/11/05/west-hotel/.

133 For Itkin's title, see Lester Kinsolving, "The Paper Priests," *San Francisco Examiner*, October 11, 1971.

134 Description of consecration, Itkin file, Broshears (Raymond) Papers, GLBTHS.

135 Raymond Broshears, "Paper Priests . . . Battle for Their 'Recognition' Is Underway by the Many Many Many Paper Priests and or . . . Bishops!," *San Francisco Crusader*, January 22, 1981, 6.

136 Young, "Mikhail Itkin."

137 Thumma and Gray, *Gay Religion*, 116.

138 Rivera, "Queens in Exile," 77.

139 Rivera, "Queens in Exile," 67.

140 Rivera, "Queens in Exile," 68.

141 J. M. Murphy, "Santería," in *Encyclopedia Britannica*, July 18, 2008, https://www.britannica.com/topic/Santeria.

142 Barnet, "Religious System of Santería," 81. On Sylvia Rivera's devotion to Santería, see Ellison and Hoffman, "The Afterward."

143 Rivera, "Queens in Exile," 77.

144 Sylvia Rivera, interviewed by Martin Duberman, October 12, 1990, audiotape 02888, Martin B. Duberman Papers, NYPL.

145 Duberman, *Stonewall*, 67.

146 Duberman, *Stonewall*, 83; Sylvia Rivera interviewed by Martin Duberman, October 12, 1990, NYPL.

147 Kasino, *Pay It No Mind*.

148 Rivera, "Queens in Exile," 70.

149 Sylvia Rivera interviewed by Martin Duberman, October 12, 1990. See also Duberman, *Stonewall*, 67.

150 Walsh, *Latino Pentecostal Identity*.

151 Villafañe, *Liberating Spirit*.

152 S. Cohen, *Gay Liberation Youth Movement in New York*, 102.

153 Sylvia Rivera, "Sylvia Rivera's Talk at LGMNY, June 2001, Lesbian and Gay Community Services Center, New York City," *CENTRO: Journal of the Center for Puerto Rican Studies* 19, no. 1 (Spring 2007): 116–23.

154 David Isay with Michael Scherker, "Remembering Stonewall," premiered July 1, 1989, on weekend edition of *All Things Considered*.

155 Rivera, "Sylvia Rivera's Talk at LGMNY," 120.

156 On STAR, see "Street Transvestite Action Revolutionaries," ca. 1971, box 19, Street Transvestite Action Revolutionaries file, International Gay Information Center collection, NYPL; S. Cohen, *Gay Liberation Youth Movement in New York*, 95; Negrón-Muntaner, *Boricua Pop*, 92.

157 Leslie Feinberg, "Leslie Feinberg Interviews Sylvia Rivera," *Workers World*, July 2, 1998.

158 Sylvia Rivera, interviewed by Martin Duberman, October 12, 1990.

159 S. Cohen, *Gay Liberation Youth Movement in New York*, 134.

160 Duberman, *Stonewall*, 254.

161 Lynette Holloway, "Young, Restless and Homeless on the Piers; Greenwich Village Reaches Out to Youths with Plan for Shelter and Services," *New York Times*, July 18, 1998.

162 David Isay, "I Never Thought I Was Going to Be a Part of Gay History," *New York Times Magazine*, June 27, 1999, 66.

163 "The Query Newsletter," Metropolitan Community Church of New York, September 2002.

164 Laqueur, "Deep Time of the Dead," 817.

165 Durkheim, *Elementary Forms of Religious Life*; Douglas, *Purity and Danger*, 159. Giorgio Agamben coins the phrase "theory of the ambivalence of the sacred" in *Homo Sacer*.

3. Urban Reformers and Vanguard's Mutual Aid

Epigraph: Unknown author, "impression of the Tenderloin written by a 22 year old while he was high on Methedrine," in Larry Littlejohn et al., "Drugs in the Tenderloin: A Publication of the Central City Target Area Board," January 1967, p. 26, box 14, folder 13, Lucas (Donald Stewart) Papers, GLBTHS. (It is very likely that the author of this "impression" was Jean-Paul Marat, Vanguard's president, who was twenty-two in 1967 and credited as one of the "researchers" for the "Drugs in the Tenderloin" publication.)

1   Joel Roberts, "Street Youths Organize," *SDS Regional Newsletter* 1, no. 11 (June 29, 1966): 2–3.
2   Spade, *Mutual Aid*, 11.
3   Roberts, "Street Youths Organize," 2–3.
4   Sedgwick, "Queer Performativity," 4.
5   Agee, *Streets of San Francisco*, 163.
6   Hirsch and Spitzer, "Witness in the Archive," 155.
7   Hirsch and Spitzer, "Witness in the Archive," 158.
8   On activism in the Tenderloin, see D'Emilio, *Sexual Politics, Sexual Communities*, 193–95; Meeker, "Behind the Mask of Respectability"; Members of the Gay and Lesbian Historical Society of Northern California, "MTF Transgender Activism in the Tenderloin and Beyond"; Stryker and Silverman, *Screaming Queens*.
9   Littauer, "Sexual Minorities at the Apex of Heteronormativity."
10 Kunzel, *Criminal Intimacy*, 90.
11 Baker, "Introduction," 8.
12 Valentine, *Imagining Transgender*, 53.
13 "In My Father's House Are Many Mansions: Prospectus of the Walt Whitman Guidance Center (For Men of All Faiths and All Races) Presented as a Public Service by ONE, Incorporated," box 90, folder 1, ONE Incorporated records, Social Service Division Records, ONE.
14 "In My Father's House Are Many Mansions."
15 Letter from Jim Kepner to One Inc., February 27, 1955, p. 1, box 41, Coll 2011-001, ONE Incorporated records, Correspondence, series 3, 1955, ONE.
16 Quoted in Lyn Pederson, "Meeting God on Hoover Street," *In Touch*, March/April 1976, First Church of One Brotherhood Collection, 1956–76, ONE.
17 Jim Kepner, "Angels of the News: God Met on Hoover Street," *The Advocate*, August 15, 1971.
18 Paul Welch, "Homosexuality in America," *Life*, June 26, 1964, 68.
19 C. Hartman, *Yerba Buena*, 96.
20 Don Lucas interview conducted by John D'Emilio, November 23, 1976, International Gay Information Center collection audiovisual materials, Interviews Conducted by John D'Emilio, NYPL. See also "Calling Shots," *Mattachine Review*, January 1959, 27–28. For more on the social service function of the Mattachine Society, see Meeker, *Contacts Desired*.
21 Don Lucas, n.d., likely 1965, p. 7, box 7, folder 8, Miscellaneous Writings and Subject Files, Lucas (Donald Stewart) Papers, GLBTHS.
22 Untitled report, 1962, p. 26, box 90, folder 1, Coll 2011-001, ONE Incorporated records, Social Service Division and Satellite Offices Records, Administration, Social Services, 1954–63, ONE.

23 Will Oursler, "Revolution in the Ministry," *Parade*, August 29, 1965.

24 White, *Reforming Sodom*, 83.

25 Crysdale, *Churches Where the Action Is!*, 9.

26 "Toward Understanding Older Youth-Young Adults: What Is the Church's Ministry to Persons in Transition from Youth to Adulthood?," 1962, p. 15, "Reference Materials" series, file titled "Older Youth and Young Adult," Records of the General Council on Ministries, 1934–90, UMAH (hereafter Older Youth and Young Adult file).

27 "Combined Report of Two Young Adult Consultations: What Is the Church's Ministry to Persons in Transition from Youth to Adulthood?," 1962, p. 14, Older Youth and Young Adult file, UMAH.

28 Metropolitan Young Adult Ministry booklet, 1966, p. 14, Administrative records of the General Board of Discipleship, 1890–2005, "Discipleship Resources" series, folder titled "Metropolitan Young Adult Ministry / booklet, 1966," UMAH.

29 Consultation on the Church, Society, and the Homosexual, London, August 1966, box 19, folder 20, Lucas (Donald Stewart) Papers, GLBTHS.

30 Ted McIlvenna, "'Freewheeling' Mission to Young Adults," *World Outlook*, June 1965.

31 J. W. Bell, "The Older Youth / Young Adult Project, A Report of Progress, September 10, 1964," Older Youth and Young Adult file, UMAH.

32 Robert M. Mennel, "Attitudes and Policies toward Juvenile Delinquency in the United States: A Historiographical Review," *Crime and Justice* 4 (1983): 214.

33 Mennel, "Attitudes and Policies toward Juvenile Delinquency in the United States," 214. See also Heap, "City as a Sexual Laboratory"; D. Johnson, "Kids of Fairytown."

34 Schlossman et al., *Delinquency Prevention in South Chicago*, 14.

35 Schlossman et al., *Delinquency Prevention in South Chicago*, 15.

36 Agee, *Streets of San Francisco*, 159.

37 "Youth for Service," 1950s film, available on YouTube, July 20, 2019, https://www.youtube.com/watch?v=PRRehjUZ9Gg&ab_channel=PeriscopeFilm.

38 Agee, *Streets of San Francisco*, 162.

39 Lawrence Lipton, "The Wasp," *Los Angeles Free Press*, February 19, 1965, 2.

40 Homophile representatives included members of the Mattachine Society, the Tavern Guild, the League for Civil Education, the Daughters of Bilitis, and Louise Lawrence, a trans activist known for her advocacy work with medical and psychiatric professionals. "Report to Governing Board and S.F. Chapter Re: New S.F. Community Project Now in Planning Stage," January 28, 1964, Barbara Gittings and Kay Tobin Lahusen gay history papers and photographs, NYPL.

41 Letter from Del Martin to Barbara Gittings, February 29, 1964, Governing Board Minutes, box 54, folder 15, Barbara Gittings and Kay Tobin Lahusen gay history papers and photographs, NYPL.

42 For a list of consultation participants compiled by Mark Bowman, coordinator of the LGBT Religious Archives Network, see the online exhibit "The Council on Religion and the Homosexual," accessed May 12, 2022, http://www .lgbtran.org/exhibits/crh/Image.aspx?AID=13. Participants included the Lutheran Church, Washington, DC; Glide Urban Center; Orville Luster; Kilmer Myers from the Chicago Urban Training Center; Methodist Board of Social Concerns; the Tavern Guild; the Mattachine Society; the Daughters of Bilitis; and the League for Civil Education.

43 The Committee on Religion and the Homophile, Outline Report of Meeting, June 1–October 31, 1965, box 9, folder 13, Lucas (Donald Stewart) Papers, GLBTHS.

44 Boyd, *Wide-Open Town*, 232.

45 "How It Started," n.d., p. 34, box 17, folder 14, Lyon (Phyllis) and Del Martin Papers, GLBTHS.

46 CRH By Laws and Founding Summary, "brief background on the founding," ca. late 1964, Lucas (Donald Stewart) Papers, box 19, folder 18, GLBTHS.

47 D'Emilio, *Sexual Politics*, 176.

48 For more on the Chuckkers and the spelling of the club's name, see Guy Strait's photograph of a sign posted in front of the Chuckkers in February 1966, which reads, "The Chuckkers—Famous for its Unusual Entertainment—Now Presents Police Harassment!" Guy Strait, untitled article, *Citizens News* 5, no. 4 (February 1966).

49 Guy Strait, "Police Week," *L.C.E. News*, May 1964.

50 Ed Hansen described the scene at the Letterman Club in a letter to his parents, January 24, 1966, Hansen (Ed) Papers, GLBTHS.

51 Guy Strait, "Homosexual Prostitution," *Cruise News & World Report* 2, no. 2 (December 1965). (Strait claims that this segment of his newspaper is a transcript of Norm Woodruff, "The Market Street Proposition," a radio program on KFRC.)

52 Members of the Gay and Lesbian Historical Society of Northern California, "MTF Transgender Activism in the Tenderloin and Beyond," 354.

53 Document authored by Mayor Shelley labeled "rough draft," July 29, 1964, Market Street vertical file, Market Street Design Task Force, SFHC.

54 Market Street Development Project, "What to Do about Market Street: A Prospectus for a Market Street Development Project, an Affiliate of SPUR: The San Francisco Planning and Urban Renewal Organization," 1962, 23.

55 Raymond Broshears, "Thoughts and Opinions," *BAR* 6, no. 1 (January 1976): 6.

56 "90,000 San Francisco Perverts—Startling Police Report," *San Francisco News*, March 18, 1965, Marinissen (Jan) Collection, GLBTHS.

57 Guy Strait, "Let Them Be Crucified and You Will Be Next," *Citizens News* 4, no. 10 (ca. March 1965): 8.

58 Night Minister report, December 1964 to March 1965, SFNM.

59 C. Williams and Mirikitani, *Beyond the Possible*, 78.

60 *San Francisco Chronicle*, January 5, 1965.

61 *San Francisco Chronicle*, May 9, 1960; *San Francisco Chronicle*, April 2, 1963.

62 "Bar Blasts Juveniles' Treatment," *San Francisco Examiner*, January 9, 1963.

63 Charles Lewis interviewed by Paul Gabriel, February 8, 1997, GLBT-OH, GLBTHS.

64 Mark Forrester, "A Funding Proposal for a Half-Way House-Residential Facility for Youth in the Tenderloin," ca. July 1966, p. 8, box 14, SFLC, LARC.

65 Rowland's plan, a homophile organizer wrote in July 1964, was "far in advance of our capacities at that time" but "might well be incorporated into plans for the future today." See letter from Dorr Legg to Reed Erickson, July 7, 1964, Reed Erickson correspondence with Dorr Legg, 1964–86, Reed L. Erickson papers, ONE. On the Tenderloin-based halfway house, see Rev. Edward Hansen, Mark Forrester, and Rev. Fred Bird, "The Tenderloin Ghetto: The Young Reject in Our Society," 1966, p. 29, box 15, folder 7, Lucas (Don Stewart) Papers, GLBTHS.

66 Mark Forrester, Cecil Williams, and Ted McIlvenna, "A Halfway House," ca. 1964, Lucas (Donald Stewart) Papers, GLBTHS.

67 Bauman, *Race and the War on Poverty*, 18.

68 O. Lewis, *La Vida*, xlvi.

69 Matusow, *Unraveling of America*, 13.

70 Schryer, "'Culture of Violence and Foodsmells,'" 153.

71 Meeker, "Queerly Disadvantaged," 23.

72 Clayson, "Barrios and the Ghettos Have Organized!"

73 See Meeker, "Queerly Disadvantaged."

74 Mark Forrester, ca. late 1965, untitled report on Inner-City Methodist Churches of San Francisco letterhead, box 9, folder 13, Lucas (Don Stewart) Papers, GLBTHS.

75 [Ted McIlvenna,] "Action/Research Project (Inner City) 1962–1965 Design 7 San Francisco Team History of Change," p. 7, Older Youth and Young Adult file, UMAH.

76 [McIlvenna,] "Action/Research Project (Inner City) 1962–1965 Design 7 San Francisco Team History of Change," 5.

77 See, e.g., Jesse Hamlin, "Life Met Art Here / Part One: 1965–75," SF Gate, June 13, 2005, https://www.sfgate.com/entertainment/article/LIFE-MET-ART-HERE-Part-one-1965-75-Forty-years-2628356.php.

78 Will Oursler, "Revolution in the Ministry," *Parade*, August 29, 1965.

79 Oral history interview conducted by John D'Emilio with Mark Forrester, International Gay Information Center collection audiovisual materials, Interviews Conducted by John D'Emilio, November 23, 1976, NYPL; Consultation records, box 20, folder 4, Personnel, Lucas (Don Stewart) Papers, GLBTHS.

80 Boyd, *Wide-Open Town*, 227–29.

81 Oral history interview conducted by John D'Emilio with Mark Forrester, International Gay Information Center collection audiovisual materials, Interviews Conducted by John D'Emilio, November 23, 1976, NYPL.

82 Susan Stryker, oral history interview with Ed Hansen, GLBT-OH, GLBTHS.

83 Rev. Ed Hansen, "The Tenderloin Project," *Vector Magazine*, February 1966.

84 See letter from Ed Hansen to dad, mom, brother, sister-in-law, January 24, 1966, Hansen (Ed) Papers, GLBTHS; transcript of "The Church and Homosexuality: Consultation with the Board of Directors, Northern California Conference, and the Conference Church and Community Commission," February 26, 1966, box 9, folder 17, Lucas (Don Stewart) Papers, GLBTHS; and Guy Strait, "The Tenderloin Report Rejected," *Cruise News & World Report* 2, no. 5 (May 1966).

85 Consultation transcript, February 1966, box 9, folder 17, Consultation on the Church and Homosexuality folder, Lucas (Don Stewart) Papers, GLBTHS.

86 For more on the South Side Hotel, see Guy Strait, *Citizens News* 5, no. 2 (December 1965).

87 Oral history with Edward Hansen by Martin Meeker, Regional Oral History Office, University of California, Bancroft Library, Berkeley, 2009.

88 Guy Strait, *Citizens News* 5, no. 2 (December 1965).

89 Oral history with Edward Hansen by Martin Meeker, Regional Oral History Office, University of California, Bancroft Library, Berkeley, 2009.

90 Untitled essay by Moore, n.d., p. 15, Moore, John V. Collection, Pacific School of Religion Archives.

91 Oral history with Edward Hansen by Martin Meeker, Regional Oral History Office, University of California, Bancroft Library, Berkeley, 2009.

92 Ravarour, *Keys to Spiritual Being*, xiv.

93 Ravarour, "Energy Flow Dance."

94 Ravarour, "Energy Flow Dance," 19.

95 Ravarour, "Energy Flow Dance," 19.

96 Ravarour, "Energy Flow Dance," 2.

97 James P. Driscoll, "Transsexuals," *Transaction* 8, nos. 5–6 (March/April 1971): 32.

98 Hansen, Forrester, and Bird, "Tenderloin Ghetto," 24.

99 Hansen, Forrester, and Bird, "Tenderloin Ghetto," 2.

100 Hansen, Forrester, and Bird, "Tenderloin Ghetto," 13.

101 Hansen, Forrester, and Bird, "Tenderloin Ghetto," 17.

102 Edward Hansen, Fred Bird, Mark Forrester, and Victor de Marais, "The White Ghetto: Youth and Young Adults in the Tenderloin Area of Downtown San Francisco," n.d. (ca. February 1966), p. 17, box 15, folder 5, Lucas (Don Stewart) Papers, GLBTHS.

103 Hanhardt, *Safe Space*, 48.

104 Hanhardt, *Safe Space*, 57.

105 Hansen, Forrester, and Bird, "Tenderloin Ghetto," 23.

106 Untitled report by Forrester and Hansen, ca. April 1966, p. 13, box 15, folder 26, Lucas (Don Stewart) Papers, GLBTHS.

107 Hansen, Forrester, and Bird, "Tenderloin Ghetto," 27.

108 The Tenderloin Committee, "Proposal for Confronting the Tenderloin Problem," n.d., p. 7, Subseries D: Other Anti-Poverty Organizations and Programs, March 9–April 1966, box 15, folder 1, Lucas (Don Stewart) Papers, GLBTHS.

109 Forrester and Hansen, "A Funding Proposal for the Tenderloin Project," ca. April 1966, p. iii, box 15, folder 26, Lucas (Don Stewart) Papers, GLBTHS.

110 Flier advertising future Tenderloin Citizens Committee meetings with the heading "Attention—Tenderloin Meeting," ca. April 1966, box 15, folder 1, Lucas (Don Stewart) Papers, GLBTHS.

111 "Community Center Opens," *Vector Magazine* 2, no. 6 (May 1966): 1.

112 Kramer, *Participation of the Poor*, 60.

113 See Canaday, *Straight State*; D. Johnson, *The Lavender Scare*.

114 Kramer, *Participation of the Poor*, 54.

115 Roberts, "Street Youths Organize," 2–3.

116 Anti-Poverty Programs Central City Target Area Correspondence and Memoranda, January 30, 1968–August 20, 1969, n.d., box 13, folder 15, Lucas (Don Stewart) Papers, GLBTHS.

117 Economic Opportunity Council, untitled document, n.d., p. 3, box 14, SFLC, LARC.

118 Forrester, "A Funding Proposal for a Half-Way House-Residential Facility for Youth in the Tenderloin," 1.

119 Mark Forrester, "A Funding Proposal for a Tenderloin Community Center / Clinic Facility," ca. 1967, box 4, folder 13, Tavern Guild of San Francisco Records, GLBTHS.

120 Tenderloin Committee, "Proposal for Confronting the Tenderloin Problem: A Proposal Submitted to the Economic Opportunities Council," 1966, p. 3, box 15, folder 1, Lucas (Don Stewart) Papers, GLBTHS.

121 Tenderloin Committee, "Proposal for Confronting the Tenderloin Problem," 7.

122 Hanhardt, *Safe Space*, 55.

123 Roberts, "Street Youths Organize," 2–3.

124 Roberts, "Street Youths Organize," 2–3.

125 Roberts, "Street Youths Organize," 2–3.

126 Membership cards, ca. late 1966, name J. P. Marat as president and Billy Garrison as secretary. See Personal Papers, Membership Cards Date: 1950–1971, box 17, folder 9, Lucas (Donald Stewart) Papers, GLBTHS.

127 "Statement of Purpose for VANGUARD," *Vanguard Magazine* 1, no. 1 [ca. September 1966]: cover.

128 Laurence Tate, "Exiles of Sin, Incorporated," *Berkeley Barb*, November 11, 1966.

129 *Vanguard Magazine* 1, no. 4 (ca. February 1967): 9.

130 Laurence Tate, "Exiles of Sin, Incorporated," *Berkeley Barb*, November 18, 1966.

131 Letter from Foster Gunnison to Richard Inman, September 19, 1966, p. 1, Barbara Gittings and Kay Tobin Lahusen gay history papers and photographs, 1855–2009, NYPL.

132 Spade, *Mutual Aid*, 11; Nelson, *Body and Soul*.

133 Spade, *Mutual Aid*.

134 L. Cohen, *Consumers' Republic*.

135 "Vanguard Statement," box 20, Lyon (Phyllis) and Del Martin Papers, GLBTHS.

136 J. P. Marat, "The Views of Vanguard," *Cruise News & World Report*, October 1966, 10.

137 Guy Strait, "Young Rejects Form Organization," *Cruise News & World Report* 2, no. 7 (July 1966).

138 "Shedding a Straight Jacket" oral history interview with Lewis Durham by Paul Gabriel, July 18, 1998, GLBT-OH, GLBTHS.

139 "Interview with Rev. Broshears," *Vanguard Magazine* 1, no. 9 (ca. August 1967): 5.

140 Vanguard duplicated the phrases "get for its citizens a sense of dignity" in a "hostile social order" in which they are "forced to accept an unwarranted guilt." For the Society for Individual Rights' mission statement, see letter from Beardemphl and Forrester, n.d., ca. 1964, p. 1, box 11, folder 3, Lucas (Don Stewart) Papers, GLBTHS. For Vanguard's mission statement, see note 127 above.

141 Tate, "Exiles of Sin, Incorporated," November 11, 1966.

142 Anonymous [Jean-Paul Marat], "Why Drugs in the Tenderloin," *The Needle, V—The Magazine of the Tenderloin*, November 1966, GLBTHS.

143 Anonymous [Marat], "Why Drugs in the Tenderloin."

144 Tate, "Exiles of Sin, Incorporated," November 11, 1966.

145 [Jean-Paul Marat], "From an Addict Who Has Made It," in Littlejohn et al., "Drugs in the Tenderloin," 18.

146 [Marat], "From an Addict Who Has Made It," 17.

147 [Marat], "From an Addict Who Has Made It," 19.

148 Tate, "Exiles of Sin, Incorporated," November 11, 1966.

149 Oral History with Calvin Colt by Martin Meeker, 2009, p. 37, Regional Oral History Office, University of California, Bancroft Library, Berkeley, CA.

150 Tate, "Exiles of Sin, Incorporated," November 11, 1966.

151 Guy Strait, "Advice Is Cheap and Usually Worth It," *Cruise News & World Report* 3, no. 1 (December 1966).

152 L. Cohen, *Consumers' Republic*, 188.

153 L. Cohen, *Consumers' Republic*, 189.

154 L. Cohen, *Consumers' Republic*, 189.

155 Stryker and Silverman, *Screaming Queens*.

156 On the racialization of street kids, see Gibson, *Street Kids*, 51; Bush, *Who Gets a Childhood?*; Gilbert, *Cycle of Outrage*.

157 See Kaye, "Male Prostitution in the Twentieth Century"; Gibson, *Street Kids*.

158 L. Cohen, *Consumers' Republic*, 355.

159 J. P. Marat, "Exploitation," *Vanguard Magazine* 1, no. 1 [ca. September 1966]: 3.

160 Vanguard, "We Protest," Vanguard, 1966–67, box 11, folder 17, Lucas (Don Stewart) Papers, GLBTHS.

161 Guy Strait, "Young Homos Picket Compton's Restaurant," *Cruise News & World Report* 2, no. 8 (August 1966): cover.

162 Letter from Ed Hansen to parents, July 25, 1966, Hansen (Ed) Papers, GLBTHS.

163 Letter from Ed Hansen to parents, July 25, 1966.

164 Strait, "Young Homos Picket Compton's Restaurant."

165 Tate, "Exiles of Sin, Incorporated," November 11, 1966.

166 Raymond Broshears et al., "History of Christopher Street West–SF," *Gay Pride*, June 25, 1975, 8.

167 Tate, "Exiles of Sin, Incorporated," November 18, 1966.

168 "From the Press Release," *Vanguard Magazine* 1, no. 2 (ca. October 1966): 4.

169 Night Minister report, December 1964 to March 1965, SFNM. See also Guy Strait, "Roving Report," *Citizens News* 3, no. 7 (June 8, 1964): 11.

170 Quoted in "From the Press Release," *Vanguard Magazine* 1, no. 2 (ca. October 1966): 4.

171 Mark Forrester, "A Workplan for Community Action Based on the Alinsky Approach to Community Mobilization," Central City Citizens Council, May 24, 1966, p. 9, box 14, folder 4, Anti-Poverty Programs, Lucas (Don Stewart) Papers, GLBTHS.

172 Mark Forrester, "Leadership Training Manual: An Outline for Study," September 1966, p. 20, SFLC, LARC.

173 Joel Roberts told me Dixie was "one of the queens, and they did facial makeup, usually not lipstick, but lots of eye makeup and foundation makeup and their hair impeccably teased."

174 Esther Wanning, "The History of Hospitality House," January 10, 1990, Hospitality House records, Hospitality House, San Francisco, CA. According to *Vanguard Magazine* 1, no. 6 (ca. April 1967), "as much as we'd like to take credit for the new, free Tenderloin coffee house," the founders were "Glide, The Tenderloin Committee, the Letterman Club, and the [EOC] Governing Board."

175 Wanning, "The History of Hospitality House."

176 "Points of Interest," *Vanguard Magazine* 1, no. 6 (ca. April 1967).

177 "Health Center: New Plan for Tenderloin," *SF Progress*, February 1–2, 1967.

178 Rob Haeseler, "A Street for the Pariah but No Carnival of Crime," *San Francisco Chronicle*, May 11, 1968, 5.

179 On the importance of nonrational states to the counterculture, see Roszak, *Making of a Counter Culture*; Steven Watson, *Birth of the Beat Generation*, 6.

180 Taussig, *I Swear I Saw This*, 13.

181 "Ministerial Test," box A, Broshears (Raymond) Papers, GLBTHS.

182 Broshears wrote in 1977 that Adrian Ravarour studied with him for seven months in 1967. He "excelled in the area of metaphysics, and in the concepts of eastern mysticism" and was "worthy of acceptance into the Brotherhood of Light." Letter from Reverend Raymond Broshears to Antioch College West, Monterey, CA, October 7, 1977, Broshears (Raymond) Papers, GLBTHS.

183 Mark Miller, "Unity," n.d., Broshears (Raymond) papers, GLBTHS.

184 "People Power," *Vanguard Magazine* 1, no. 4 (ca. February 1967): 3.

185 Raymond Broshears, "Loneliness in the Tenderloin," *Vanguard Magazine* 1, no. 4 (ca. February 1967): 7.

186 Raymond Broshears, "The Minister to the Homosexual Minority," *Light of Understanding* 1, no. 5 (December 1967).

187 Document in folder labeled "Itkin, Mikhail, Bishop III" in unprocessed box, ONE.

188 Larry Mamiya, untitled, n.d., "Religion—General folder," box 19, folder 5, Lyon (Phyllis) and Del Martin Papers, GLBTHS.

189 C. Hartman, *City for Sale*, 9.

190 Guy Strait, *Citizens News*, March 1967; Night Ministry report, July–September 1968, SFNM.

191 C. Hartman, *City for Sale*, 66.

192 Dear and Wolch, *Landscapes of Despair*.

193 *Vanguard Magazine* articles highlighted "Wisdom of the East" and "Sex within the Creative Order" along with articles on antiwar activism, abortion reform, and bisexuality. See "Krishnamurti on Sex and Love," *Vanguard Magazine* 1, no. 8 (ca. July 1967).

194 "Street Prophets Prediction," *Vanguard Magazine* 1, no. 8 (ca. July 1967): 12.

195 Doug Patrick and Carolyn V. Fronty Smith, "To the Membership of Vanguard the Youth Organization, Inc.," *Vanguard Magazine* 1, no. 7 (ca. April 1967): 32.

196 "Street Prophets Prediction," 12.

197 See S. Cohen, *Gay Liberation Youth Movement in New York*, 18; Carter, *Stonewall*, 108; Armstrong, *Forging Gay Identities*, 63.

Intervention 1. Vanguard Revisited

1 City and County of San Francisco Department of Elections, "Results Summary November 2, 2010—Consolidated General Election," accessed July 15, 2011, http://www.sfelections.org/results/20101102/.

2 Heather Mac Donald, "San Franciscans Try to Take Back Their Streets," *Wall Street Journal*, October 2, 2010.

3 "Scott Wiener, District 8, Castro—San Francisco Supervisor Candidate Profile," *San Francisco Chronicle*, accessed July 15, 2011, https://web.archive.org/web/20110122071715/http://www.sfgate.com/district8-scott-wiener/.

4 "Civil Sidewalks Ordinance," San Francisco Police Department, accessed July 15, 2011, https://tinyurl.com/287pcj6m: "On November 2, 2010, the voters of the City and County of San Francisco passed Proposition L, 'Sitting or Lying on Sidewalks.' Proposition L added Section 168, 'Promotion of Civil Sidewalks,' to the San Francisco Police Code. Section 168 prohibits individuals, with certain exceptions, from sitting or lying on the City's public sidewalks between the hours of 7 AM and 11 PM."

5 Roach, *Cities of the Dead*, 26.

6   On urban neoliberalism, see Hackworth, *Neoliberal City*; Don Mitchell, "The Annihilation of Space by Law: The Roots and Implications of Anti-homeless Laws in the United States," *Antipode* 29, no. 3 (1997): 303–35.

7   Manalansan, "Race, Violence, and Neoliberal Spatial Politics in the Global City," 152.

8   On Vanguard's nonprofit status, see Laurence Tate, "Exiles of Sin, Incorporated," *Berkeley Barb*, November 11, 1966; and "President's Page," *Vanguard Magazine* 1, no. 4 (ca. February 1967): 1. See also Beam, *Gay, Inc.*, 7.

9   In 2007 the National Gay and Lesbian Task Force estimated that between 800 and 1,600 of the approximately 4,000 homeless youth in San Francisco are LGBTQ, a calculation based on research that demonstrates that 20 to 40 percent of all homeless youth identify as LGBTQ. See Nicholas Ray, "Lesbian, Gay, Bisexual, and Transgender Youth: An Epidemic of Homelessness," National Gay and Lesbian Task Force Policy Institute and National Coalition for the Homeless, January 30, 2007.

10 Gotti, "My Darling VanGuard . . . ," *Vanguard Revisited Magazine*, February 2011, 1, ellipses in original.

11 Carolyn Dinshaw et al., "Theorizing Queer Temporalities: A Roundtable Discussion," *GLQ: A Journal of Lesbian and Gay Studies* 13, nos. 2–3 (2007): 178.

12 Megan Rohrer, "Tenderloin in the Loneliness," *Vanguard Revisited Magazine*, February 2011, 8.

13 "Summary of the Tenderloin Problem," *Vanguard Revisited Magazine*, February 2011, 7, reprinted from *Vanguard Magazine* 1, no. 9 (ca. August 1967).

14 Gotti, "Address to the People," *Vanguard Revisited Magazine*, February 2011, 17, ellipses in original.

15 "People Power," *Vanguard Revisited Magazine*, February 2011, 23, reprinted from *Vanguard Magazine* 1, no. 4 (ca. February 1967): 3.

16 Juan A. Cerna-Aviles, "People Power Continued," *Vanguard Revisited Magazine*, February 2011, 24.

17 Mark Forrester, "Central City: Profile of Despair," *Vanguard Revisited Magazine*, February 2011, 41, reprinted from *Vanguard Magazine* 1, no. 1 (ca. September 1966): 8.

18 Beck, "Pt. 2 Profile of Desperation," *Vanguard Revisited Magazine*, February 2011, 42.

19 Duggan, *Twilight of Equality*.

20 Hanhardt, *Safe Space*, 78.

21 Marina Fisher, Nathaniel Miller, Lindsay Walter, and Jeffrey Selbin, "California's New Vagrancy Laws: The Growing Enactment and Enforcement of Anti-homeless Laws in the Golden State," February 12, 2015, https://papers.ssrn.com/sol3/papers.cfm?abstract_id=2558944.

22 Love, *Feeling Backward*, 10.

1   Steve Brewer, "Hard Life for 'Throwaways' in Polk Gulch: Hundreds of Homeless Youths Hustle in Gay Bars, Sidewalks of S.F.'s Polk St.," *Los Angeles Times*, July 27, 1986, 3.

2   Boyd, *Wide-Open Town*, 223.

3   Myers, "Short History of Child Protection in America," 455.

4   Myers, "Short History of Child Protection in America," 459.

5   Averbach, "San Francisco's South of Market District," 204–5.

6   See Boyd, *Wide-Open Town*; Bérubé, *Coming Out under Fire*. Allan Bérubé argues that the war constituted a "national coming out." Gathered in military camps, homosexual service people often came to terms with their sexual desires and began to name and talk about who they were.

7   C. Hartman, *City for Sale*, 8.

8   Mary Richards, "Once Upon a Time in San Francisco," *BAR*, April 4, 1996, 34.

9   Guy Strait, "Roving Report," *L.C.E. News*, April 1, 1963.

10   Paul Welch, "Homosexuality in America," *Life*, June 26, 1964, 68.

11   Guy Strait, "Polk Street," *L.C.E. News* 2, no. 3 (November 12, 1962): 9.

12   The San Francisco LGBTQ Sites Database, compiled by Eric Garber and Willie Walker, available for use in the GLBTHS reading room, GLBTHS.

13   Article in the *Bay Gourmet*, date unknown, L. James Beales personal collection, now part of the Polk Street Project Collection, GLBTHS. See also Michael Flanagan, "*P.S. They Loved You," *BAR*, November 23, 2015.

14   Boyd, *Wide-Open Town*, 207.

15   Stryker and Buskirk, *Gay by the Bay*, 43.

16   Stryker and Buskirk, *Gay by the Bay*, 43.

17   Achilles, "Development of the Homosexual Bar as an Institution," 230.

18   For the political role of homosexual bars, see Chauncey, *Gay New York*; Bérubé, *Coming Out under Fire*; Kennedy and Davis, *Boots of Leather, Slippers of Gold*; Stein, *City of Sisterly and Brotherly Loves*.

19   Boyd, *Wide-Open Town*, 223.

20   Bill Plath, "The Tavern Guild: A Record of Accomplishment, Address to the Tavern Guild of San Francisco," April 5, 1966, Tavern Guild of San Francisco Records, GLBTHS.

21   "Press Conference," n.d., box 13, Sarria (José) Papers, GLBTHS.

22   Tequila Mockingbird, "The Bar Tour," *Vector Magazine*, July 1969.

23   Tequila Mockingbird, "The Bar Tour," *Vector Magazine*, August 1969.

24   Article in the *Bay Gourmet*, date unknown, L. James Beales personal collection, now part of the Polk Street Project Collection, GLBTHS.

25   "Shedding a Straight Jacket," oral history project with Bill Beardemphel and John DeLeon by Paul Gabriel, July 1997, GLBT-OH, GLBTHS.

26   "SF March, Gay-In Held," *The Advocate*, July 22–August 4, 1970, 2.

27   "An Evening Out," *BAR*, April 1, 1971.

28   Interview with John DeLeon, GLBT-OH, GLBTHS.

29   San Francisco Alcohol Fact Book, November 1983, p. 23, Tavern Guild of San
      Francisco Records, GLBTHS.

30   Boyd, *Wide-Open Town*, 226.

31   Unknown article in *San Francisco Chronicle*, November 14, 1969, 4.

32   "City within the City," *Gayzette*, no. 48 (ca. 1971), box B, Broshears (Ray-
      mond) Papers, GLBTHS.

33   "SF Pigs Sweeps Rapped," *Berkeley Barb*, April 7–13, 1972, 4.

34   Raymond Broshears, "Tenderloin Times Tuff," *Gay Crusader*, April–May
      1974, p. 12, Broshears (Raymond) Papers, GLBTHS.

35   San Francisco Night Ministry report, second quarter, 1974, SFNM.

36   Mavis Mockingbird, "Mavis Mockingbird Blitzes the Bars," *Gay Crusader*,
      February–March 1974, p. 6, Broshears (Raymond) Papers, GLBTHS.

37   "Polk Street a Jungle, Merchants Gripe," *San Francisco Examiner*, September
      30, 1977, 4.

38   "Police Honored by Polk Area Merchants," *BAR*, January 19, 1978.

39   "S.F. Police Wrap Up Narcotics Sweep," *San Francisco Chronicle*, January 9,
      1980, 2. See also C. Hartman, *City for Sale*, 377.

40   "Repeal Anita Bryant's New Vagrancy Law in S.F.," *Polk Street News*, no. 2
      (September 1977).

41   "Polk Harassment? ACLU Protests New Loitering Law," *BAR*, March 2, 1978, 6.

42   Andereck, "Irish Travelers."

43   Sanders, *Inside the IRA*, 96.

44   Hacking, *Rewriting the Soul*, 3.

45   Goffman, *Stigma*.

46   Hacking, *Rewriting the Soul*, 63.

47   "History of Pride 1977," SF Pride, accessed June 12, 2014, http://www.sfpride
      .org/heritage/1977.html.

48   "History of Pride 1988," SF Pride, accessed June 12, 2014, http://www.sfpride
      .org/heritage/1988.html.

49   Public Research Institute of San Francisco University, "A Neighborhood Com-
      mercial District in Transition: A Pilot Survey," April 1984, p. 9. According to
      this survey of eighty-seven businesses that were part of the Polk District Mer-
      chants Association, the neighborhood saw an 18 percent turnover rate and a 42
      percent average rent increase from 1981 to 1984.

50   Edward Sebesta, "An Account of the Campaign against Anti-Asian Discrimina-
      tion in San Francisco Bars, 1980–1981," author's personal collection, courtesy
      of Randy Kikukawa.

51   "One's Own Kind," letter to the editor, *San Francisco Sentinel*, December 12,
      1980, author's personal collection, courtesy of Randy Kikukawa.

52   Felix Racelis, "Bill Matsumoto: Finding Community, Fighting Discrimination,"
      The Advocate, March 17, 1983, p. 24; Alice Reports, the Monthly Publication
      of the Alice B. Toklas Memorial Democratic Club, February 1981; Mark Dyer,
      "Discriminatory Practices at the N'Touch," all in author's personal collection,

courtesy of Randy Kikukawa. See also Brochure for ALGA and ALGA Newsletter, January 1986, ALGA file, Groups Ephemera Collection, GLBTHS.

53 Sebesta, "Account of the Campaign against Anti-Asian Discrimination," 8.

54 Michael Satchell, "Kids for Sale: The Exploitation of Runaway and Throwaway Children," *Baltimore Sun*, July 20, 1986, 408.

55 Toby Marotta, "A Study of Juvenile Prostitution: Executive Summary," US Department of Health and Human Services, October 1981, Toby Marotta collection of Prospero Project records, GLBTHS.

56 "Polk Street Hustle: The Gay Life That Isn't," *San Francisco Examiner*, August 14, 1984, A1.

57 Barthes, "Semiology and the Urban," 96.

58 Smyth, "Irish American Organizations," 38.

59 Hoboes protected their comparative freedom by withholding personal information and did not inquire into others' pasts; asking for a name was the mark of a cop or a spy. See DePastino, *Citizen Hobo*, 79.

60 Knobel, *Paddy and the Republic*, xx.

61 "Polk Street Hustle: The Gay Life That Isn't," *San Francisco Examiner*, August 14, 1984, A1.

62 "Polk Merchants Take Hard Line on Drugs, Hustling," *San Francisco Examiner*, June 13, 1985, B1.

63 "Hustling the Hustlers off the Street," *United Press International*, June 13, 1985.

64 Letter from Corey Longseeker to Dan Diez, 1995, courtesy of Dan Diez. All subsequent quotes from Corey's letters are from a series of letters he wrote to Dan in the mid- and late 1990s. Spellings are reproduced as they appear in the originals.

65 Rechy, *City of Night*, 127.

66 See Ancestry.com, US Public Records Index, 1950–1993, vol. 2. According to Corey's mother, he left the Midwest when he was about eighteen, around 1988. See Seth Hemmelgarn, "Former Polk Sex Worker Mourned," *BAR*, September 5, 2013, 11.

67 Gouldner, "Norm of Reciprocity."

68 "Field notes #1 Toby," October 30, 1987, Toby Marotta collection of Prospero Project records, GLBTHS.

69 Willi McFarland, ed., "Atlas of HIV/AIDS in San Francisco: 1981–2000," HIV/AIDS Statistics and Epidemiology Section, AIDS Office San Francisco Department of Public Health, November 15, 2002, 44, https://www.sfdph.org/dph/files/reports/RptsHIVAIDS/HIVAIDSAtlas19812000.pdf.

70 McFarland, "Atlas of HIV/AIDS in San Francisco," 46.

71 Brewer, "Hard Life for 'Throwaways' in Polk Gulch," 3.

72 Toby Marotta, Prospero Project interviews, n.d., Toby Marotta collection of Prospero Project records, GLBTHS.

73 Toby Marotta, Prospero Project interviews, n.d., Toby Marotta collection of Prospero Project records, GLBTHS.

74 Toby Marotta, Prospero Project interviews, December 1989, Toby Marotta collection of Prospero Project records, GLBTHS.

75 Toby Marotta, Prospero Project interviews, n.d., Toby Marotta collection of Prospero Project records, GLBTHS.

76 Toby Marotta, Prospero Project interviews, June 10, 1988, Toby Marotta collection of Prospero Project records, GLBTHS.

77 Toby Marotta, "Summary Statement, Field Notes, 3/6/92," Toby Marotta collection of Prospero Project records, GLBTHS.

78 Guide to the Tavern Guild of San Francisco Records, 1961–93, GLBTHS, processed by Martin Meeker and Heather Arnold, 2003.

79 Toby Marotta, Prospero Project interviews, January 22, 1992, Toby Marotta collection of Prospero Project records, GLBTHS.

80 Andrew Meier, "Innocence Lost," publication unknown, January 8, 1995, "Polk Street" vertical file, SFHC.

81 Toby Marotta, field note, March 31, 1991, Toby Marotta collection of Prospero Project records, GLBTHS.

82 "Writings from Red Balloon House," by the tenants of 1211 Polk Street during the Homes Not Jails occupation, June 14 through July 11, 1993, Polk Street Project Collection, GLBTHS.

83 Mark Mardon, "Polk Street Unplugged," publication unknown, August 30, 1997, L. James Beales personal collection, now part of the Polk Street Project Collection, GLBTHS.

84 Art Agnos, "Perspective on the Homeless: Off the Streets, into the Safety Net," *San Francisco Examiner*, July 23, 1990.

85 John R. Belcher, "Are Jails Replacing the Mental Health System for the Homeless Mentally Ill?," *Community Mental Health Journal* 24, no. 3 (Fall 1988): 185–95.

86 Corey may have been referring to the high-profile murder and dismemberment of Tommy Wenger, which took place on Polk Street around the time Corey wrote this letter. See chapter 6 for more about this incident.

87 Hemmelgarn, "Former Polk Sex Worker Mourned," 11.

5. Polk Street's Moral Economies

1 On urban neoliberalism, see Hackworth, *Neoliberal City*; Beckett and Herbert, *Banished*; Mitchell, "Annihilation of Space by Law."

2 Schulman, *Gentrification of the Mind*, 27.

3 Jeff Stark, "Moving Is a Drag: The Mayor Stonewalls the Motherlode Bar's Plans to Relocate on Post Street," *SF Weekly*, April 19, 1995.

4 Christine Beatty, "Motherlode Finally Victorious," *Spectator Magazine*, December 25, 1998.

5 Mark Mardon, "Polk Street Unplugged," publication unknown, August 30, 1997, Polk Street Project Collection, GLBTHS.

6 Lisa Lambert, "The Resurrection of Polk Street," *Oakland Tribune*, May 22, 2005.

7   Don Baird, "The Closing of a Bar . . . and the Rebirth of English Punk Rock," *San Francisco Bay Times*, January 6, 2005.

8   Human Rights Watch, "Sex Workers at Risk: Condoms as Evidence of Prostitution in Four US Cities," July 19, 2012, 64, http://www.hrw.org/reports/2012/07/19/sex-workers-risk-0. See also Alcoholic Beverage Control Appeals Board of the State of California, Berkey v. ABC, AB-8331, June 20, 2005, https://abcab.ca.gov/wp-content/uploads/sites/27/2020/03/8331.pdf.

9   Zak Szymanski, "Concerns about Efforts to 'De-gay' Polk Street," *BAR*, February 17, 2005.

10 Lipsitz shows that home ownership, education politics, inheritance patterns, and federal policy have made "being white" a valuable commodity in economic and cultural terms. Lipsitz, "Possessive Investment in Whiteness," 371.

11 Hanhardt, *Safe Space*.

12 Bobby White, "In San Francisco, Red-Light Denizens Fight to Stay Seedy," *Wall Street Journal*, October 24, 2006, A1.

13 Lower Polk Neighbors General Meeting Notes, Cathedral Hill Hotel, January 10, 2005, accessed June 4, 2018, https://lowerpolk.org/meetings/.

14 Szymanski, "Concerns about Efforts to 'De-gay' Polk Street," 2.

15 Wayne Friday, "The Rock Hudson Debate," *BAR*, August 8, 1985, 9.

16 On the concept of "familism," see Steidel and Contreras, "New Familism Scale for Use with Latino Populations"; Acosta, "'How Could You Do This to Me?'"

Intervention 2. Polk Street Stories

1   Said, *Culture and Imperialism*, xii–xiii.

2   On "queer oral history," see Murphy, Pierce, and Ruiz, "What Makes Queer Oral History Different"; Boyd and Roque Ramírez, *Bodies of Evidence*; Cvetkovich, *Archive of Feelings*.

3   Shopes, "Commentary."

4   "History of Health: Needle Exchange in San Francisco," San Francisco AIDS Foundation, accessed October 7, 2018, http://www.sfaf.org/client-services/syringe-access/history-of-needle-exchange.html.

5   Freund, "Under Storytelling's Spell?," 96.

6   Freund, "Under Storytelling's Spell?," 131.

7   McHugh, "Affective Power of Sound," 187.

8   Kerr, "'We Know What the Problem Is,'" 36.

9   Rosenthal, "Make Roanoke Queer Again," 38.

Conclusion

1   Foucault, "Of Other Spaces," 27.

2   "Game Changer: Polk Street 'SRO' Going Upscale," Socketsite, February 10, 2015, http://www.socketsite.com/archives/2015/02/renovated-polk-street-sro-aiming-go-upscale.html.

3   Amy Graff, "Fabled Transgender Bar Divas Closing Its Doors after Throwing One Last Party," *San Francisco Chronicle*, March 22, 2019.

4   Adam Hudson, "The Bleaching of San Francisco: Extreme Gentrification and Suburbanized Poverty in the Bay Area," *Truthout*, April 27, 2014, http://www.truth-out.org/news/item/23305-the-bleaching-of-san-francisco-extreme-gentrification-and-suburbanized-poverty-in-the-bay.

5   Megan Cassidy, "S.F. to Put $8 Million into Mid-Market," *San Francisco Chronicle*, May 19, 2021, B1.

6   Kirshenblatt-Gimblett, *Destination Culture*, 159.

7   Nora, "Between Memory and History," 13.

8   "About the District," Transgender District, accessed May 12, 2020, https://www.transgenderdistrictsf.com/about.

9   "Polk Street Alleys Mural Project Call for Artists," March 7, 2011, https://web.archive.org/web/20110501023659/http://artsandmedia.net/2011/03/polk-street-alleys-mural-project-call-for-artists.html.

10 Matt Baume, "Polk Neighbors Derail LGBT History Mural," *BAR*, February 16, 2011.

11 Erin Sherbert, "Polk Street Mural Depicts Neighborhood as Seedy, Enrages Neighbors," *SF Weekly*, January 19, 2011.

12 Matt Baume, "Tenderloin Activists Reject Gay History Mural," *NBC Bay Area*, February 22, 2011.

13 Sherbert, "Polk Street Mural Depicts Neighborhood as Seedy."

14 Lower Polk Alleyways Vision Plan, July 25, 2016, https://issuu.com/lowerpolk neighbors/docs/15.07-15_lpadocument_-_for_web.

15 Email from Erica Waltemade to the author, July 3, 2017.

16 "LQBTQ History in Middle and Lower Polk Neighborhood," document titled "17.09-05 LGBTQ Slideshow," author's personal collection.

17 Laura Waxman, "Homeless Swept from Polk Street Alley despite Lack of Shelter Beds," *San Francisco Examiner*, December 4, 2019.

18 Damon Scott and Parekh, "Three Recent Scenes in the Affective Life of Gentrification," 302.

19 Damon Scott and Parekh, "Three Recent Scenes in the Affective Life of Gentrification," 313.

20 Norimitsu Onishifeb, "A Mayor in the Middle of Two San Franciscos," *New York Times*, February 24, 2014.

21 "Mayor Lee Touts Twitter Tax Break at Tenderloin Museum Event," *Bay City News*, April 21, 2014.

22 Kirshenblatt-Gimblett, *Destination Culture*, 7.

23 Gallian, "Evolution of Arts and Cultural Districts," 130.

24 Joe Rosato Jr., "Vintage Ads Get New Life in Tenderloin: Artists Restore Vintage Wall Advertisements in San Francisco's Tenderloin," *NBC Bay Area*, August 23, 2011.

25 Randy Shaw, "The Tenderloin at Night," *Beyond Chron*, August 25, 2014.

26 C. W. Nevius, "Blighted Area Holds High Hopes for Tenderloin Museum," SF Gate, April 22, 2014, https://www.sfgate.com/bayarea/nevius/article/Blighted -area-holds-high-hopes-for-Tenderloin-5419179.php.

27 Cory Weinberg, "New Projects Poised to Finally Reshape San Francisco's Gritty Tenderloin Neighborhood," *San Francisco Business Times*, August 6, 2015.

28 Rosato, "Vintage Ads Get New Life in Tenderloin."

29 John Ferrannini, "SF Transgender District Drops Cafeteria Owner's Name," *BAR*, March 20, 2020.

30 Brooks and Kushner, "Cultural Districts and Urban Development," 4.

31 Kenny Williams Jr., "Three Black Trans Women Are Turning What Was Once Called a 'Gay Ghetto' into America's First Flourishing Transgender District," *Blavity*, July 27, 2020.

32 Donna J. Graves and Shayne E. Watson, "Citywide Historic Context Statement for LGBTQ History in San Francisco," prepared for the City and County of San Francisco, October 2015, https://default.sfplanning.org/Preservation/lgbt _HCS/LGBTQ_HCS_October2015.pdf.

33 Shayne Watson and Graves, "San Francisco," 219.

34 Letter from Compton's Historic District Committee to San Francisco Planning Commission, November 14, 2016, provided to the author by Shayne Watson.

35 Raquel Willis, "Black Trans Women Created the World's First Trans Cultural District," *Out Magazine*, February 18, 2019.

36 Willis, "Black Trans Women Created the World's First Trans Cultural District."

37 Willis, "Black Trans Women Created the World's First Trans Cultural District."

38 Lindsay Nieman, "The Compton's Transgender Cultural District," January 2019, in *No Small Stories*, produced by Kelly Wilson, American Planning Association podcast, https://www.planning.org/podcast/comptons -transgender-cultural-district/.

39 J. K. Dineen, "Mid-Market Project a Step Closer with Transgender District Deal," SF Gate, January 30, 2017, https://www.sfgate.com/bayarea/article /Mid-market-project-step-closer-with-transgender-10895410.php.

40 Willis, "Black Trans Women Created the World's First Trans Cultural District."

41 "About the District," Transgender District, accessed May 12, 2020, https:// www.transgenderdistrictsf.com/about.

42 Susan Stryker, "Resisting Carceral Power: On the Intersections of Trans Resistance, Black Lives Mattering, and Police and Prison Abolitionism at the Crossroads of Turk and Taylor Streets in San Francisco's Tenderloin District," *Medium*, June 16, 2020.

BIBLIOGRAPHY

Archival Sources

Beinecke Rare Book and Manuscript Library, New Haven, CT
Living Theatre Records

*Gay, Lesbian, Bisexual, Transgender Historical Society (GLBTHS),
San Francisco, CA*
Broshears (Raymond) Papers
GLBT Historical Society Oral History Collection (GLBT-OH)
"Groups" Ephemera Collection
Hansen (Ed) Papers
Lucas (Donald Stewart) Papers
Lyon (Phyllis) and Del Martin Papers
Marinissen (Jan) Collection
Polk Street Project Collection
Sarria (José) Papers
Toby Marotta collection of Prospero Project records
Tavern Guild of San Francisco Records

Kinsey Institute, Indiana University, Bloomington, IN
Alice Fields Collection
Thomas N. Painter Collection

Labor Archives and Research Center (LARC), San Francisco State University, San Francisco, CA
San Francisco Labor Council Records

National Archives at College Park (NACP), College Park, MD
John F. Kennedy Assassination Records Collection, Papers of Jim Garrison, 1965–1992, Broshears, Reverend Raymond files

New York Public Library (NYPL), Manuscripts and Archives Division, New York, NY
Barbara Gittings and Kay Tobin Lahusen gay history papers and photographs
Martin B. Duberman Papers
International Gay Information Center collection
International Gay Information Center collection audiovisual materials
Old Catholic Church records

ONE National Gay and Lesbian Archives (ONE), University of Southern California Libraries, Los Angeles, CA
First Church of One Brotherhood Collection, 1956–1976
Itkin (Mikhail) Papers
ONE Incorporated records
Reed L. Erickson papers
Social Service Division and Satellite Offices Records

Pacific School of Religion Archives, Berkeley, CA
Moore, John V. Collection

San Francisco History Center (SFHC), San Francisco Public Library, CA
"Market Street" vertical file
"Polk Street" vertical file

Special Collections Research Center (SCRC), University of Chicago Library, Chicago, IL
Ernest Watson Burgess Papers, 1886–1966

United Methodist Archives and History Center (UMAH), Madison, NJ
Administrative records of the General Board of Discipleship, 1890–2005
Records of the General Council on Ministries, 1934–1990

Organizational Records
Hospitality House records, Hospitality House, San Francisco, CA
San Francisco Night Ministry (SFNM) records, San Francisco, CA

Newspapers and Periodicals

Baltimore Sun
Bay Area Reporter (*BAR*)

Berkeley Barb
Citizens News
Cruise News & World Report
Gay Crusader
Grecian Guild Pictorial
L.C.E. News
Life
Light of Understanding
Los Angeles Times
The News
New York Times
ONE Magazine
Salute: The Picture Magazine for Men
San Francisco Chronicle
San Francisco Examiner
San Francisco News
SDS Regional Newsletter
SF Weekly
Time
Vanguard Magazine
Vanguard Revisited Magazine
Vector Magazine
Wall Street Journal

Moving Image Sources

Kasino, Michael, dir. *Pay It No Mind: The Life and Times of Marsha P. Johnson*. New York: Redux Pictures, 2012.

Stryker, Susan, and Victor Silverman, dirs. *Screaming Queens: The Riot at Compton's Cafeteria*. San Francisco: Independent Television Service/KQED-TV, 2005.

Zagone, Robert, dir. *Drugs in the Tenderloin*. KQED-TV, San Francisco, under the auspices of the Central City Multiservice Center of San Francisco, 1967.

Secondary Sources

Abrams, Lynn. *Oral History Theory*. New York: Routledge, 2016.

Achilles, Nancy. "The Development of the Homosexual Bar as an Institution." In *Social Perspectives on Lesbian and Gay Studies*, edited by Peter M. Nardi and Beth E. Schneider, 175–82. New York: Routledge, 1998.

Acosta, Katie. "'How Could You Do This to Me?': How Lesbian, Bisexual, and Queer Latinas Negotiate Sexual Identity with Their Families." *Black Women, Gender + Families* 4, no. 1 (Spring 2010): 63–85.

Agamben, Giorgio. *Homo Sacer: Sovereign Power and Bare Life*. Stanford, CA: Stanford University Press, 1998.

Agee, Christopher Lowen. *The Streets of San Francisco: Policing and the Creation of a Cosmopolitan Liberal Politics, 1950–1972*. Chicago: University of Chicago Press, 2014.

Andereck, Mary. "Irish Travelers." In *Encyclopedia of World Cultures*, vol. 1, *North America*, 162–64. New York: Macmillan References, 1996.

Anderson, Nels. *On Hobos and Homelessness*. Chicago: University of Chicago Press, 1999.

Anson, Peter. *Bishops At Large*. London: Faber and Faber, 1964.

Armstrong, Elizabeth A. *Forging Gay Identities: Organizing Sexuality in San Francisco, 1950–1994*. Chicago: University of Chicago Press, 2002.

Arondekar, Anjali, Ann Cvetkovich, Christina B. Hanhardt, Regina Kunzel, Tavia Nyong'o, Juana María Rodríguez, Susan Stryker, Daniel Marshall, Kevin P. Murphy, and Zeb Tortorici. "Queering Archives: A Roundtable Discussion." *Radical History Review*, no. 122 (2015): 211–31.

Atack, Jeremy. "Transportation in American Economic History." In *The Oxford Handbook of American Economy*, vol. 2, edited by Louis P. Cain, 23–50. Oxford: Oxford University Press, 2018.

Austin, J. L. "How to Do Things with Words." In *The Performance Studies Reader*, edited by Henry Bial and Sara Brady, 177–83. New York: Routledge, 2007.

Averbach, Alvin. "San Francisco's South of Market District, 1850–1950: The Emergence of a Skid Row." *California Historical Quarterly* 52, no. 3 (Fall 1973): 197–223.

Baker, Blanche M. Introduction to *Gay Bar*, by Helen Branson, 7–16. San Francisco: Pan-Graphic Press, 1957.

Barnet, Miguel. "The Religious System of Santería." In *Sacred Possessions: Vodou, Santería, Obeah, and the Caribbean*, edited by Margarite Fernández Olmos and Lizabeth Paravisini-Gebert, 79–100. New Brunswick, NJ: Rutgers University Press, 1997.

Barthes, Roland. "Semiology and the Urban." In *The City and the Sign: An Introduction to Urban Semiotics*, edited by Mark Gottdiener and Alexandros Lagopoulos, 87–98. New York: Colombia University Press, 1986.

Bauman, Robert. *Race and the War on Poverty: From Watts to East L.A.* Tulsa: University of Oklahoma Press, 2008.

Beam, Myrl. *Gay, Inc.: The Nonprofitization of Queer Politics*. Minneapolis: University of Minnesota Press, 2018.

Beckett, Katherine, and Stephen Herbert. *Banished: The New Social Control in Urban America*. Oxford: Oxford University Press, 2011.

Belshaw, Cyril S. *Traditional Exchange and Modern Markets*. Englewood Cliffs, NJ: Prentice-Hall, 1965.

Benjamin, Harry, and R. E. L. Masters. *Prostitution and Morality*. New York: Julian Press, 1964.

Benjamin, Walter. "Theses on the Philosophy of History" (1940). In *Illuminations: Essays and Reflections*, edited by Hannah Arendt, 255–66. London: Fontana/Collins, 1973.

Bennett, Jane. *Vibrant Matter: A Political Ecology of Things*. Durham, NC: Duke University Press, 2010.

Berlant, Lauren, and Michael Warner. "Sex in Public." *Critical Inquiry* 24, no. 2 (Winter 1998): 547–66.

Bernstein, Robin. *Racial Innocence: Performing American Childhood and Race from Slavery to Civil Rights*. New York: New York University Press, 2012.

Bérubé, Allan. *Coming Out under Fire: The History of Gay Men and Women in World War Two*. New York: Free Press, 1990.

Boag, Peter. *Same-Sex Affairs: Constructing and Controlling Homosexuality in the Pacific Northwest*. Berkeley: University of California Press, 2003.

Boyd, Nan Alamilla. "Who Is the Subject? Queer Theory Meets Oral History." *Journal of the History of Sexuality* 17, no. 2 (May 2008): 177–89.

Boyd, Nan Alamilla. *Wide-Open Town: A History of Queer San Francisco to 1965*. Berkeley: University of California Press, 2003.

Boyd, Nan Alamilla, and Horacio N. Roque Ramírez. *Bodies of Evidence: The Practice of Queer Oral History*. New York: Oxford University Press, 2012.

Brooks, Arthur C., and Roland J. Kushner. "Cultural Districts and Urban Development." *International Journal of Arts Management* 3, no. 2 (Winter 2001): 4–15.

Bush, William S. *Who Gets a Childhood? Race and Juvenile Justice in Twentieth-Century Texas*. Athens: University of Georgia Press, 2010.

Butler, Judith. *Excitable Speech: A Politics of the Performative*. New York: Routledge, 1997.

Butler, Judith. "Performative Acts and Gender Constitution: An Essay in Phenomenology and Feminist Theory." *Theatre Journal* 40, no. 4 (December 1988): 519–31.

Byrne, Julie. *The Other Catholics: Remaking America's Largest Religion*. New York: Columbia University Press, 2016.

Califia, Pat. "The City of Desire: Its Anatomy and Destiny." *Invert* 2, no. 4 (1991): 13–16.

Canaday, Margot. *The Straight State: Sexuality and Citizenship in Twentieth-Century America*. Princeton, NJ: Princeton University Press, 2011.

Caplovitz, David. *The Poor Pay More: Consumer Practices of Low-Income Families*. New York: Free Press, 1963.

Capó, Julio, Jr. *Welcome to Fairyland: Queer Miami before 1940*. Chapel Hill: University of North Carolina Press, 2017.

Carter, David. *Stonewall: The Riots That Sparked the Gay Revolution*. New York: St. Martin's, 2004.

Chanfrault-Duchet, Marie-Françoise. "Narrative Structures, Social Models, and Symbolic Representation in the Life Story." In *Women's Words: The Feminist Practice of Oral History*, edited by Sherna Berger Gluck and Daphne Patai, 77–92. New York: Routledge, 1991.

Chauncey, George. *Gay New York: Gender, Urban Culture and the Making of the Gay Male World, 1890–1940*. 1994. New York: Basic Books, 2019.

Chauncey, George. "The Policed: Gay Men's Strategies of Everyday Resistance." In *Inventing Times Square: Commerce and Culture at the Crossroads of the World*, edited by William R. Taylor, 315–28. Baltimore, MD: Johns Hopkins University Press, 1996.

Clayson, William. "The Barrios and the Ghettos Have Organized! Community Action, Political Acrimony, and the War on Poverty in San Antonio." *Journal of Urban History* 28, no. 2 (January 2002): 158–83.

Cohen, Cathy J. "Punks, Bulldaggers, and Welfare Queens: The Radical Potential of Queer Politics?" *GLQ: A Journal of Lesbian and Gay Studies* 3, no. 4 (1997): 437–65.

Cohen, Lizabeth. *A Consumers' Republic: The Politics of Mass Consumption in Postwar America*. New York: Knopf Doubleday, 2003.

Cohen, Stephan. *The Gay Liberation Youth Movement in New York: An Army of Lovers Cannot Fail*. New York: Routledge, 2008.

Conquergood, Dwight. *Cultural Struggles: Performance, Ethnography, Praxis*. Ann Arbor: University of Michigan Press, 2013.

Crysdale, Stewart. *Churches Where the Action Is! Churches and People in Canadian Situations*. Toronto: Division of Congregational Life and Work, by Board of Evangelism and Social Service, United Church of Canada, 1966.

Cvetkovich, Ann. *An Archive of Feelings: Trauma, Sexuality, and Lesbian Public Cultures*. Durham, NC: Duke University Press, 2015.

Dear, Michael J., and Jennifer R. Wolch. *Landscapes of Despair: From Deinstitutionalization to Homelessness*. Princeton, NJ: Princeton University Press, 1987.

D'Emilio, John. "Capitalism and Gay Identity." In *Powers of Desire: The Politics of Sexuality*, edited by Ann Snitow, Christine Stansell, and Sharon Thompson, 100–113. New York: Monthly Review Press, 1983.

D'Emilio, John. *Sexual Politics, Sexual Communities: The Making of a Homosexual Minority in the United States, 1940–1970*. Chicago: University of Chicago Press, 1983.

DePastino, Todd. *Citizen Hobo: How a Century of Homelessness Shaped America*. Chicago: University of Chicago Press, 2003.

Dinshaw, Carolyn, Lee Edelman, Roderick A. Ferguson, Carla Freccero, Elizabeth Freeman, Jack Halberstam, Annamarie Jagose, Christopher Nealon, Nguyen Tan Hoang. "Theorizing Queer Temporalities: A Roundtable Discussion." *GLQ: A Journal of Lesbian and Gay Studies* 13, nos. 2–3 (2007): 177–95.

Douglas, Mary. *Purity and Danger: An Analysis of Concepts of Pollution and Taboo*. New York: Praeger, 1966.

Drew, Dennis, and Jonathan Drake. *Boys for Sale: A Sociological Study of Boy Prostitution*. New York: Brown, 1969.

Duberman, Martin. *Stonewall*. New York: Plume, 1994.

Dudley, Kathryn. *Debt and Dispossession: Farm Loss in America's Heartland*. Chicago: University of Chicago Press, 2000.

Duggan, Lisa. *The Twilight of Equality: Neoliberalism, Cultural Politics, and the Attack on Democracy*. Boston: Beacon, 2003.

Durkheim, Émile. *The Elementary Forms of Religious Life*. Mansfield Centre, CT: Martino, 2012.

Ellison, Joy, and Nicholas Hoffman. "The Afterward: Sylvia Rivera and Marsha P. Johnson in the Medieval Imaginary." *Medieval Feminist Forum: A Journal of Gender and Sexuality* 55, no. 1 (2019): 267–94.

Enroth, Ronald M. *The Gay Church*. Grand Rapids, MI: Eerdmans, 1974.

Estes, Jeri. *Stilettos and Steel*. Studio City, CA: WordSmith Productions, 2013.

Faderman, Lillian, and Stuart Timmons. *Gay L.A.: A History of Sexual Outlaws, Power Politics, and Lipstick Lesbians*. New York: Basic Books, 2006.

Floyd, Kevin. "Closing the (Heterosexual) Frontier: 'Midnight Cowboy' as National Allegory." *Science and Society* 65, no. 1 (Spring 2001): 99–130.

Foucault, Michel. "Of Other Spaces." Translated by Jay Miskowiec. *Diacritics* 16, no. 1 (Spring 1986): 22–27.

Fraser, Nancy. "Rethinking the Public Sphere: A Contribution to the Critique of Actually Existing Democracy." *Social Text*, nos. 25–26 (1990): 56–80.

Freeman, Elizabeth. *Time Binds: Queer Temporalities, Queer Histories*. Durham, NC: Duke University Press, 2011.

Freund, Alexander. "Under Storytelling's Spell? Oral History in a Neoliberal Age." *Oral History Review* 42, no. 1 (2015): 96–132.

Gallian, Ann M. "The Evolution of Arts and Cultural Districts." In *Understanding the Arts and Creative Sector in the United States*, edited by Joni Maya Cherbo, Ruth Ann Stewart, and Margaret Jane Wyszomirski, 129–42. New Brunswick, NJ: Rutgers University Press, 2008.

Garland, David. "What Is a 'History of the Present'? On Foucault's Genealogies and Their Critical Preconditions." *Punishment and Society* 16, no. 4 (2014): 365–84.

Genet, Jean. *The Thief's Journal*. New York: Grove, 1994.

Gibson, Kristina E. *Street Kids: Homeless Youth, Outreach, and Policing New York's Streets*. New York: New York University Press, 2011.

Gilbert, James. *A Cycle of Outrage: America's Reaction to the Juvenile Delinquent in the 1950s*. New York: Oxford University Press, 1986.

Gilfoyle, Timothy. *City of Eros: New York City, Prostitution, and the Commercialization of Sex, 1790–1920*. New York: Norton, 1987.

Gilfoyle, Timothy. "Policing of Sexuality." In *Inventing Times Square: Commerce and Culture at the Crossroads of the World*, edited by William R. Taylor, 297–314. Baltimore, MD: Johns Hopkins University Press, 1996.

Goffman, Erving. *The Presentation of Self in Everyday Life*. New York: Anchor, 1959.

Goffman, Erving. *Stigma: Notes on the Management of Spoiled Identity*. New York: Penguin Books, 1990.

Gould, Deborah. *Moving Politics: Emotion and ACT UP's Fight against AIDS*. Chicago: University of Chicago Press, 2009.

Gouldner, Alvin. "The Norm of Reciprocity: A Preliminary Statement." *American Sociological Review* 25, no. 2 (1960): 161–78.

Groth, Paul. *Living Downtown: The History of Residential Hotels in the United States*. Berkeley: University of California Press, 1994.

Hacking, Ian. *Rewriting the Soul: Multiple Personality and the Sciences of Memory*. Princeton, NJ: Princeton University Press, 1998.

Hackworth, Jason. *The Neoliberal City: Governance, Ideology, and Development in American Urbanism*. Ithaca, NY: Cornell University Press, 2006.

Halberstam, Jack. *Female Masculinity*. Durham, NC: Duke University Press, 1998.

Halberstam, Jack. *In a Queer Time and Place: Transgender Bodies, Subcultural Lives*. New York: New York University Press, 2005.

Halberstam, Jack. "Shame and White Gay Masculinity." *Social Text* 23, nos. 3–4 (84–85) (Fall–Winter 2005): 219–33.

Halperin, David. *What Do Gay Men Want?* Ann Arbor: University of Michigan Press, 2009.

Halperin, David, and Valerie Traub, eds. *Gay Shame*. Chicago: University of Chicago Press, 2009.

Hammer, Langdon. *O My Land, My Friends: The Selected Letters of Hart Crane*. New York: Four Walls Eight Windows, 1997.

Hanhardt, Christina. *Safe Space: Gay Neighborhood History and the Politics of Violence*. Durham, NC: Duke University Press, 2013.

Hartman, Chester. *City for Sale: The Transformation of San Francisco*. Berkeley: University of California Press, 2002.

Hartman, Chester. *Yerba Buena: Land Grab and Community Resistance*. San Francisco: Glide, 1974.

Hartman, Saidiya. *Lose Your Mother: A Journey along the Atlantic Slave Route*. New York: Farrar, Straus and Giroux, 2008.

Hartman, Saidiya. *Wayward Lives, Beautiful Experiments: Intimate Histories of Riotous Black Girls, Troublesome Women and Queer Radicals*. New York: Norton, 2020.

Hauser, Richard. *The Homosexual Society*. London: Mayflower Books, 1962.

Heap, Chad. "The City as a Sexual Laboratory: The Queer Heritage of the Chicago School." *Qualitative Sociology* 26, no. 4 (2003): 457–87.

Heap, Chad. *Slumming: Sexual and Racial Encounters in American Nightlife, 1885–1940*. Chicago: University of Chicago Press, 2010.

Heise, Thomas. *Urban Underworlds: A Geography of Twentieth-Century American Literature and Culture*. New Brunswick, NJ: Rutgers University Press, 2011.

Henry, George. *Sex Variants: A Study of Homosexual Patterns with Sections Contributed by Specialists in Particular Fields*. New York: Hoeber, 1941.

Hirsch, Marianne, and Leo Spitzer. "The Witness in the Archive: Holocaust Studies / Memory Studies." *Memory Studies* 2, no. 2 (2009): 151–70.

Holmes, Kwame. "The End of Queer Urban History?" In *The Routledge History of Queer America*, edited by Don Romesburg, 160–74. New York: Routledge, 2018.

Hood, Ralph. *The Psychology of Religious Fundamentalism*. New York: Guilford, 2005.

Howard, John. *Men Like That: A Southern Queer History*. Chicago: University of Chicago Press, 1999.

Hyde, George Augustine. *Genesis of the Orthodox Catholic Church of America*. Edited by Gordon Fischer. Indianapolis: Orthodox Catholic Church of America, 1993.

Jackson, Shannon. *Lines of Activity: Performance, Historiography, Hull-House Domesticity*. Ann Arbor: University of Michigan Press, 2001.

James, Jennifer. "Mobility as an Adaptive Strategy." *Urban Anthropology* 4, no. 4 (Winter 1975): 349–64.

Johnson, David K. *Buying Gay: How Physique Entrepreneurs Sparked a Movement.* New York: Columbia University Press, 2019.

Johnson, David K. "The Kids of Fairytown: Gay Male Culture on Chicago's Near North Side in the 1930s." In *Creating a Place for Ourselves: Lesbian, Gay, and Bisexual Community Histories,* edited by Brett Beemyn, 97–118. New York: Routledge, 1997.

Johnson, David K. *The Lavender Scare: The Cold War Persecution of Gays and Lesbians in the Federal Government.* Chicago: University of Chicago Press, 2004.

Johnson, E. Patrick. *Sweet Tea: Black Gay Men of the South.* Chapel Hill: University of North Carolina Press, 2011.

Jones, Karen R., and John Wills. *The American West: Competing Visions.* Edinburgh: Edinburgh University Press, 2009.

Kamel, Levi. "Downtown Street Hustlers: The Role of Dramaturgical Imaging Practices." PhD diss., University of California, San Diego, 1983.

Kaye, Kerwin. "Male Prostitution in the Twentieth Century: Pseudohomosexuals, Hoodlum Homosexuals, and Exploited Teens." *Journal of Homosexuality* 46, nos. 1–2 (2003): 1–77.

Keire, M. L. *For Business and Pleasure: Red-Light Districts and the Regulation of Vice in the United States, 1890–1933.* Baltimore, MD: Johns Hopkins University Press, 2010.

Keller, Karl. "Walt Whitman Camping." In *Camp Grounds: Style and Homosexuality,* edited by David Bergman, 113–20. Amherst: University of Massachusetts Press, 1993.

Kennedy, Elizabeth Lapovsky. "Telling Tales: Oral History and the Construction of Pre-Stonewall Lesbian History." *Radical History Review,* no. 62 (1995): 58–79.

Kennedy, Elizabeth Lapovsky, and Madeline D. Davis. *Boots of Leather, Slippers of Gold: The History of a Lesbian Community.* New York: Routledge, 1993.

Kerr, Daniel. "'We Know What the Problem Is': Using Oral History to Develop a Collaborative Analysis of Homelessness from the Bottom Up." *Oral History Review* 30, no. 1 (2003): 27–45.

Kett, Joseph F. *Rites of Passage: Adolescence in America, 1790–Present.* New York: Basic Books, 1977.

Kirshenblatt-Gimblett, Barbara. *Destination Culture: Tourism, Museums, and Heritage.* Berkeley: University of California Press, 1998.

Knobel, Dale T. *Paddy and the Republic: Ethnicity and Nationality in Antebellum America.* Middletown, CT: Wesleyan University Press, 1986.

Kramer, Ralph. *Participation of the Poor: Comparative Community Case Studies in the War on Poverty.* Englewood Cliffs, NJ: Prentice-Hall, 1969.

Kunzel, Regina. *Criminal Intimacy: Prison and the Uneven History of Modern American Sexuality.* Chicago: University of Chicago Press, 2010.

LaFleur, Greta. *The Natural History of Sexuality in Early America.* Baltimore, MD: Johns Hopkins University Press, 2018.

La Fountain-Stokes, Lawrence. "Gay Shame, Latina- and Latino-Style: A Critique of White Queer Performativity." In *Gay Latino Studies: A Critical Reader,* edited by

Michael Hames-García and Ernesto Javier Martínez, 55–80. Durham, NC: Duke University Press, 2011.

Laqueur, Thomas W. "The Deep Time of the Dead." *Social Research: An International Quarterly* 78, no. 3 (Fall 2011): 799–820.

Lewis, James. *Peculiar Prophets: Biographical Dictionary of New Religions*. New York: Paragon House, 1999.

Lewis, Oscar. *La Vida: A Puerto Rican Family in the Culture of Poverty—San Juan and New York*. New York: Random House, 1966.

Libertoff, Ken. "The Runaway Child in America: A Social History." *Journal of Family Issues* 1, no. 2 (June 1980): 151–64.

Lipschutz, Mark R. "Runaways in History." *Crime and Delinquency* 23, no. 3 (July 1977): 321–32.

Lipsitz, George. "The Possessive Investment in Whiteness: Racialized Social Democracy and the 'White' Problem in American Studies." *American Quarterly* 47, no. 3 (September 1995): 369–87.

Littauer, Amanda H. "Sexual Minorities at the Apex of Heteronormativity (1940s–1965)." In *The Routledge History of Queer America*, edited by Don Romesburg, 67–81. New York: Routledge, 2018.

Lloyd, Robin. *For Money or Love: Boy Prostitution in America*. New York: Ballantine Books, 1977.

Love, Heather. *Feeling Backward: Loss and the Politics of Queer History*. Cambridge, MA: Harvard University Press, 2007.

Malinowski, Bronislaw. *Crime and Custom in Savage Society*. London: Paul, Trench, Trubner, 1932.

Manalansan, Martin F. "Race, Violence, and Neoliberal Spatial Politics in the Global City." *Social Text* 23, nos. 3–4 (84–85) (Fall–Winter 2005): 141–55.

Martin, Bradford. *The Theater Is in the Streets: Politics and Public Performance in Sixties America*. Amherst: University of Massachusetts Press, 2004.

Matusow, Allen. *The Unraveling of America: A History of Liberalism in the 1960s*. New York: Harper and Row, 1984.

Mauss, Marcel. *The Gift: Forms and Functions of Exchange in Archaic Societies*. Glencoe, IL: Free Press, 1954.

McHugh, Siobhan. "The Affective Power of Sound: Oral History on Radio." *Oral History Review* 39, no. 2 (2012): 187–206.

McNamara, Robert P. *The Times Square Hustler: Male Prostitution in New York City*. Westport, CT: Praeger, 1995.

Meeker, Martin. "Behind the Mask of Respectability: The Mattachine Society and Male Homophile Practice, 1950s–1960s." *Journal of the History of Sexuality* 10, no. 1 (April 2001): 78–116.

Meeker, Martin. *Contacts Desired: Gay and Lesbian Communications and Community, 1940s–1970s*. Chicago: University of Chicago Press, 2006.

Meeker, Martin. "The Queerly Disadvantaged and the Making of San Francisco's War on Poverty, 1964–1967." *Pacific Historical Review* 81, no. 1 (2012): 21–59.

Members of the Gay and Lesbian Historical Society of Northern California [Susan Stryker]. "MTF Transgender Activism in the Tenderloin and Beyond, 1966–1975: Commentary and Interview with Elliot Blackstone." *GLQ: A Journal of Lesbian and Gay Studies* 4, no. 2 (1998): 349–72.

Mitchell, Don. "The Annihilation of Space by Law: The Roots and Implications of Anti-homeless Laws in the United States." *Antipode* 29, no. 3 (1997): 303–35.

Moran, Jeffrey. *Teaching Sex: The Shaping of Adolescence in the 20th Century*. Cambridge, MA: Harvard University Press, 2002.

Murphy, Kevin P., Jennifer L. Pierce, and Jason Ruiz. "What Makes Queer Oral History Different." *Oral History Review* 43, no. 1 (Winter/Spring 2016): 1–24.

Myers, John. "A Short History of Child Protection in America." *Family Law Quarterly* 42, no. 3 (Fall 2008): 449–63.

Negrón-Muntaner, Frances. *Boricua Pop: Puerto Ricans and the Latinization of American Culture*. New York: New York University Press, 2004.

Nelson, Alondra. *Body and Soul: The Black Panther Party and the Fight against Medical Discrimination*. Minneapolis: University of Minnesota Press, 2013.

Nestle, Joan. "Flamboyance and Fortitude: An Introduction." In *The Persistent Desire: A Femme-Butch Reader*, edited by Joan Nestle, 13–22. Boston: Alyson, 1992.

Newton, Esther. "The 'Drag Queens': A Study in Urban Anthropology." PhD diss, University of Chicago, 1968.

Newton, Esther. *Mother Camp: Female Impersonators in America*. Englewood Cliffs, NJ: Prentice-Hall, 1972.

Nietzsche, Friedrich. *On the Genealogy of Morals*. New York: Vintage Books, 1969.

Nora, Pierre. "Between Memory and History: Les Lieux de Mémoire." *Representations*, no. 26 (Spring 1989): 7–24.

Paulson, Don. *An Evening at the Garden of Allah: A Gay Cabaret in Seattle*. New York: Columbia University Press, 1996.

Pehl, Matthew. "'Apostles of Fascism,' 'Communist Clergy,' and the UAW: Political Ideology and Working-Class Religion in Detroit, 1919–1945." *Journal of American History* 99, no. 2 (September 2012): 440–65.

Pérez, Hiram. *A Taste for Brown Bodies: Gay Modernity and Cosmopolitan Desire*. New York: New York University Press, 2015.

Platt, Anthony M. *The Child Savers: The Invention of Delinquency*. 2nd ed. Chicago: University of Chicago Press, 1977.

Platt, Warren C. "The African Orthodox Church: An Analysis of Its First Decade." *Church History* 58, no. 4 (December 1989): 474–88.

Povinelli, Elizabeth. *Economies of Abandonment: Social Belonging and Endurance in Late Liberalism*. Durham, NC: Duke University Press, 2011.

Povinelli, Elizabeth. *The Empire of Love: Toward a Theory of Intimacy, Genealogy, and Carnality*. Durham, NC: Duke University Press, 2006.

Povinelli, Elizabeth, and George Chauncey. "Thinking Sex Transnationally: An Introduction." *GLQ: A Journal of Lesbian and Gay Studies* 5, no. 4 (1999): 439–50.

Pruter, Karl. *Old Catholic Sourcebook*. New York: Garland, 1983.

Ravarour, Adrian. "Energy Flow Dance: The Congruity of Continuum Patterns, Axial Transpositions and Momentum Movements: A Choreographic Theory." MA thesis, California State University, Los Angeles, 1992.

Ravarour, Adrian. *Keys to Spiritual Being: Energy Meditation and Synchronization Exercises*. New York: iUniverse, 2007.

Reay, Barry. *New York Hustlers: Masculinity and Sex in Modern America*. Manchester: Manchester University Press, 2010.

Rechy, John. *City of Night*. New York: Grove, 1963.

Rivera, Sylvia. "Queens in Exile, the Forgotten Ones." In *GenderQueer: Voices from Beyond the Sexual Binary*, edited by Joan Nestle, Clare Howell, and Riki Wilchins, 67–85. New York: Alyson Books, 2002.

Roach, Joseph. *Cities of the Dead: Circum-Atlantic Performance*. New York: Columbia University Press, 1996.

Roach, Joseph. "Mardi Gras Indians and Others: Genealogies of American Performance." *Theatre Journal* 44, no. 4 (December 1992): 461–83.

Roebuck, Christopher William. "'Workin' It': Trans* Lives in the Age of Epidemic." PhD diss., University of California, San Francisco, 2013.

Roediger, David R. *Working toward Whiteness: How America's Immigrants Became White*. New York: Basic Books, 2005.

Roediger, David R., and James Barrett. "In Between Peoples: Race, Nationality and the 'New Immigrant' Working Class." *Journal of American Ethnic History* 16, no. 3 (Spring 1997): 3–44.

Rosen, Ruth. *The Lost Sisterhood: Prostitution in America, 1900–1918*. Baltimore, MD: Johns Hopkins University Press, 1982.

Rosenthal, Gregory Samantha. "Make Roanoke Queer Again: Community History and Urban Change in a Southern City." *Public Historian* 39, no. 1 (February 2017): 35–60.

Roszak, Theodore. *The Making of a Counter Culture: Reflections on the Technocratic Society and Its Youthful Opposition*. Berkeley: University of California Press, 1995.

Said, Edward W. *Culture and Imperialism*. New York: Vintage Books, 1993.

Sandberg, Joakim. "Moral Economy and Normative Ethics." *Journal of Global Ethics* 11, no. 2 (2015): 176–87.

Sanders, Andrew. *Inside the IRA: Dissident Republicans and the War for Legitimacy*. Edinburgh: Edinburgh University Press, 2011.

Schechner, Richard. *The Future of Ritual: Writings on Culture and Performance*. London: Routledge, 1993.

Schlossman, Steven, Gail Zellman, Richard Shavelson, Michael Sedlak, and Jane Cobb. *Delinquency Prevention in South Chicago: A Fifty-Year Assessment of the Chicago Area Project*. Santa Monica, CA: RAND Corporation, 1984.

Schryer, Stephen. "'A Culture of Violence and Foodsmells': Amiri Baraka's *The System of Dante's Hell* and the War on Poverty." *Arizona Quarterly: A Journal of American Literature, Culture, and Theory* 66, no. 1 (Spring 2010): 145–64.

Schulman, Sarah. *The Gentrification of the Mind: Witness to a Lost Imagination*. Berkeley: University of California Press, 2013.

Scott, Damon, and Trushna Parekh. "Three Recent Scenes in the Affective Life of Gentrification in San Francisco's Polk Gulch." *Cultural Geographies* 28, no. 2 (2021): 301–17.

Scott, Darieck. *Extravagant Abjection: Blackness, Power, and Sexuality in the African American Literary Imagination*. New York: New York University Press, 2010.

Scott, James. *The Moral Economy of the Peasant: Rebellion and Subsistence in Southeast Asia*. New Haven, CT: Yale University Press, 2006.

Sears, Clare. *Arresting Dress: Cross-Dressing, Law, and Fascination in Nineteenth-Century San Francisco*. Durham, NC: Duke University Press, 2015.

Sedgwick, Eve Kosofsky. "Queer Performativity: Henry James's *The Art of the Novel*." *GLQ: A Journal of Lesbian and Gay Studies* 1 (1993): 1–16.

Sedgwick, Eve Kosofsky. *Touching Feeling: Affect, Pedagogy, Performativity*. Durham, NC: Duke University Press, 2003.

Shah, Nayan. "Between 'Oriental Depravity' and 'Natural Degenerates': Spatial Borderlands and the Making of Ordinary Americans." *American Quarterly* 57, no. 3 (September 2005): 703–25.

Shah, Nayan. *Contagious Divides: Epidemics and Race in San Francisco's Chinatown*. Berkeley: University of California Press, 2001.

Shah, Nayan. *Stranger Intimacy: Contesting Race, Sexuality, and the Law in the North American West*. Berkeley: University of California Press, 2011.

Shopes, Linda. "Commentary: Sharing Authority." *Oral History Review* 30, no. 1 (Winter–Spring 2003): 103–10.

Shumsky, Neil Larry, and Larry M. Springer. "San Francisco's Zone of Prostitution, 1880–1934." *Journal of Historical Geography* 7, no. 1 (1981): 71–89.

Sides, Josh. "Excavating the Postwar Sex District in San Francisco." *Journal of Urban History* 32, no. 3 (2006): 355–79.

Smith, Neil. *The New Urban Frontier: Gentrification and the Revanchist City*. New York: Routledge, 1996.

Smyth, Ted. "Irish American Organizations and the Northern Ireland Conflict in the 1980s: Heightened Political Agency and Ethnic Vitality." *Journal of Ethnic History* 39, no. 2 (Winter 2020): 36–61.

Somerville, Siobahn. "Queer." In *Keywords for American Cultural Studies*, edited by Bruce Burgett and Glenn Hendler, 187–91. New York: New York University Press, 2007.

Sonenschein, David. *Some Homosexual Men*. Austin, TX: n.p., 1983.

Spade, Dean. *Mutual Aid: Building Solidarity during This Crisis (and the Next)*. London: Verso, 2020.

Stack, Carol. *All Our Kin: Strategies for Survival in a Black Community*. New York: Basic Books, 1997.

Steidel, Angel G. Lugo, and Josefina M. Contreras. "A New Familism Scale for Use with Latino Populations." *Hispanic Journal of Behavioral Sciences* 25, no. 3 (2003): 312–30.

Stein, Marc. *City of Sisterly and Brotherly Loves: Lesbian and Gay Philadelphia, 1945–1972*. Chicago: University of Chicago Press, 2000.

Stout, Noelle. "When a Yuma Meets Mama: Commodified Kin and the Affective Economies of Queer Tourism in Cuba." *Anthropological Quarterly* 88, no. 3 (2015): 665–91.

Stryker, Susan. "(De)Subjugated Knowledges: An Introduction to Transgender Studies." In *The Transgender Studies Reader*, edited by Susan Stryker and Stephen Whittle, 1–17. New York: Routledge, 2006.

Stryker, Susan, and Jim Buskirk. *Gay by the Bay: A History of Queer Culture in the San Francisco Bay Area*. San Francisco: Chronicle Books, 1996.

Sullivan, Mark A. *Radical Bishop and Gay Consciousness: The Passion of Mikhail Itkin*. Brooklyn, NY: Autonomedia, 2014.

Susman, Warren. *Culture as History: The Transformation of American Society in the Twentieth Century*. Washington, DC: Smithsonian Institution Press, 2003.

Sweet, Roxanna. "Political and Social Action in Homophile Organizations." PhD diss., University of California, Berkeley, 1968.

Symanski, Richard. *The Immoral Landscape: Female Prostitution in Western Societies*. Toronto: Butterworths, 1981.

Syrett, Nicholas. "A Busman's Holiday in the Not-So-Lonely Crowd: Business Culture, Epistolary Networks, and Itinerant Homosexuality in Mid-Twentieth-Century America." *Journal of the History of Sexuality* 21, no. 1 (2012): 121–40.

Talley, Jodie. "A Queer Miracle in Georgia: The Origins of Gay-Affirming Religion in the South." PhD diss., Georgia State University, 2006.

Taussig, Michael. *I Swear I Saw This: Drawings in Fieldwork Notebooks, Namely My Own*. Chicago: University of Chicago Press, 2011.

Taylor, Diana. *The Archive and the Repertoire: Performing Cultural Memory in the Americas*. Durham, NC: Duke University Press, 2007.

Taylor, William. *In Pursuit of Gotham: Culture and Commerce in New York*. New York: Oxford University Press, 1992.

Thompson, E. P. *Customs in Common: Studies in Traditional Popular Culture*. New York: New Press, 1993.

Thompson, E. P. "The Moral Economy of the English Crowd in the Eighteenth Century." *Past and Present*, no. 50 (1971): 76–136.

Thompson, Paul. *The Voice of the Past: Oral History*. With Joanna Bornat. New York: Oxford University Press, 2017.

Thumma, Scott, and Edward R. Gray. *Gay Religion*. Walnut Creek, CA: Altamira, 2004.

Tompkins, Kyla Wazana. "Intersections of Race, Gender, and Sexuality: Queer of Color Critique." In *The Cambridge Companion to American Gay and Lesbian Literature*, edited by Scott Herring, 173–89. Cambridge: Cambridge University Press, 2015.

Valentine, David. *Imagining Transgender: An Ethnography of a Category*. Durham, NC: Duke University Press, 2007.

Villafañe, Eldin. *The Liberating Spirit: Toward an Hispanic American Pentecostal Social Ethic*. Grand Rapids, MI: Eerdmanns, 1993.

Wacker, Grant. *Heaven Below: Early Pentecostals and American Culture*. Cambridge, MA: Harvard University Press, 2003.

Walsh, Arlene M. Sánchez. *Latino Pentecostal Identity: Evangelical Faith, Self, and Society*. New York: Columbia University Press, 2003.

Ward, Gary L., ed. *Independent Bishops: An Independent Directory*. Detroit, MI: Apogee Books, 1990.

Warner, Sara. *Acts of Gaiety: LGBT Performance and the Politics of Pleasure*. Ann Arbor: University of Michigan Press, 2013.

Watson, Shayne, and Donna Graves. "San Francisco: Placing LGBTQ Histories in the City by the Bay." In *LGBTQ America: A Theme Study of Lesbian, Gay, Bisexual, Transgender, and Queer History*, edited by Megan E. Springate, 215–54. Washington, DC: National Park Service, Department of the Interior, 2016.

Watson, Steven. *The Birth of the Beat Generation: Visionaries, Rebels, and Hipsters*. New York: Pantheon Books, 1998.

Weiss, Margot. "Queer Politics in Neoliberal Times (1970–2010s)." In *The Routledge History of Queer America*, edited by Don Romesburg, 107–19. New York: Routledge, 2018.

Werther, Ralph. *The Female-Impersonators: A Sequel to the Autobiography of an Androgyne*. New York: Medico-Legal Journal, 1922.

Werther, Ralph, and Scott Herring. *Autobiography of an Androgyne*. New Brunswick, NJ: Rutgers University Press, 2008.

Weston, Kath. "Get Thee to a Big City: Sexual Imaginary and the Great Gay Migration." In *Long Slow Burn: Sexuality and Social Science*, 29–56. New York: Rutledge, 1998.

White, Heather. "Proclaiming Liberation: The Historical Roots of LGBT Religious Organizing, 1946–1976." *Nova Religio: The Journal of Alternative and Emergent Religions* 11, no. 4 (May 2008): 102–19.

White, Heather. *Reforming Sodom: Protestants and the Rise of Gay Rights*. Chapel Hill: University of North Carolina Press, 2017.

Wild, Mark. "Red Light Kaleidoscope: Prostitution and Ethnoracial Relations in Los Angeles, 1880–1940." *Journal of Urban History* 28, no. 6 (September 2002): 720–42.

Williams, Cecil, and Janice Mirikitani. *Beyond the Possible: 50 Years of Creating Radical Change at a Community Called Glide*. New York: HarperCollins, 2013.

Williams, Tennessee. *One Arm and Other Stories*. New York: New Directions, 1970.

Wilson, Ara. *The Intimate Economies of Bangkok: Tomboys, Tycoons, and Avon Ladies in the Global City*. Berkeley: University of California Press, 2004.

Woodlawn, Holly, and Jeff Copeland. *A Low Life in High Heels: The Holly Woodlawn Story*. New York: Perennial, 1991.

Young, John Phillip. *San Francisco: A History of the Pacific Coast Metropolis*. Vol. 2. San Francisco: S. J. Clarke, 1912.

Note: Page numbers in italics refer to illustrations.

business associations, 2, 36, 62, 118, 176, 181, 185, 201–2, 211, 243. *See also* gentrification

Business Improvement Districts, 226

butch/femme, 12–13, 19, 31, 113, 133

Butler, Judith, 297n103

Cabello, Anthony, 208, 253–55

cafeterias, 61–62, 66

Campos, David, 284

Caplovitz, David, 140

caregivers, 1, 3–4, 6, 10–11, 33, 35, 102–3, 106, 176–77, 197, 200–202

Casciato, Al, 214

Case, Ron, 227–29, 260–61, 266, *270*, 281–82

Case+Abst Architects, 227

Castro district, 155–56, 170–72, 188, 205, 252

Catholicism, 30, 69, 72–75, 107, 124, 177, 254. *See also* Old Catholics

Catholic Worker movement, 69, 110, 126

"Central City: Profile of Despair" (Forrester), 164

Central City Target Area, 111, 132, 147, *161*

Chanfrault-Duchet, Marie-Françoise, 29

Chauncey, George, 52–53, 61

Chicago Area Project, 115

Chicano movement, 103

child protection, 177–78

child savers movement, 43

Chinatown, 21, 121

Ching, Tamara, 11, 22, 140, 183, 224

Chiu, David, 267

christening, 9, 103

Christianity, 110, 124, 165. *See also* ministers; religion (and queerness); *specific denominations and organizations*

Chung, Cecilia, 18–19, 270–71, *272*

Church of Antioch, 72

Church of God, 86

Church of the Beloved Disciple, 74

Citizens News, *136*

City of Night (Rechy), 6, 24, 202

civil liberties, 134, 139–42, 146, 164

civil rights movement, 66, 109–11, 126, 139–41. *See also* African Americans; race

Clare, Keith St., 111, 146–47, 150, *151*, 152

class, 13, 50–51, 54, 56, 111, 132, 135. *See also* social status

Clay, Charles, 146

cleanliness, 243

Clement, Robert, 74

Cloud Seven Bar, 182

coffee shops, 10, 61–62, 66, 114, 117, 119, 121–22, 134–37, 146, 249

Cohen, Lizabeth, 13, 140

coming-out narrative, 29–30

Commando Queens, 49

communion, 9, 70, 75

Community Action Program, 120–21

Community Boards, 260

Community Leadership Alliance, 281–82

Community of Jesus Our Brother, 150

"Community of the Love of Christ," 101

Compton's Cafeteria, 66, 141–42, 165, 284–85, 287

Compton's Transgender Cultural District, 280, 285–88

Congress for Racial Equality, 121

Conquergood, Dwight, 7

Cooper, Ms. Billy, 288

Cornell, Steve, 188, 201–2

Council on Religion and the Homosexual (CRH), 116–17, 119–20, 129–30

countermemories, 23, 156, *157*, 158, *158*, 159–63, 166, 168, 171–72

counternarratives, 259

covert homosexuals, 56–57, 64

Crane, Hart, 52

creative arts, 95, 97, 100, 147, 162, 283, 285

criminal intimacies, 14–15

criminal justice system, 43, 113, 119, 214–15, 271

homophile groups, 93, 112–17, 121–22, 131–36

homophobia, 17, 74, 79, 118, 121, 123, 137, 158, 165, 204, 230

Honoring Individual Power and Strength (HIPS), 274

Hospitality House, 146, 153, 160

hotels, 10, 47, 62, 234, 250, 253–54, 256, 285

housing, collective, 8, 13, 37, 47–48, 110, 288

Housing Act of 1949, 65–66

Howard, John, 29

"How to Do Things with Words" (Austin), 296n93

Huberman, Ron, 189, 192

Human Rights Commission, 237

Hunters Point, 121

hustlers, *191*; background on, 25; and bars, 190–92, 194, 247; black, 39; and clients, 191–92, 206–7, 246; and identity, 200; and "masculine glamor," 58–61; and meat markets, 39–40, 63; and migratory circuits, 45–46; and moral values, 51–52, 63; and policing, 43, 63–64; and riots, 141–42; and the scene, 6, 117–18; and status, 48, 60; and Times Square, 39. *See also* police; Polk Street; sex work

Hyde, George, 73–74, 96

identity: and abuse, 9, 187; age, 10–11; claiming, 35, 177, 259; and disenfranchisement, 160–61; homosexual (overt/covert), 56–57; nonnormative gender, 12–14, 17, 31, 43, 53, 67, 172–73, 243; and power, 52–53; and renaming, 48; and scholarship, 46; sexual, 12–13, 17, 29, 31, 79, 133, 227, 234, 253; social, 21; spoiled, 187

immorality, 38–39, 180

Imperial Court, 181–82, 233, 239–40, 268–69, 278

imperialism, 258–59

incest, 14–15

interdisciplinary methods, 5, 7, 10, 22, 26, 36–37, 71, 86. *See also* methodologies (of this book)

intergenerational sex, 75

Intersection for the Arts, 121, 128, 147

intimate economies, 21

inverted glamour, 25, 52–54

Irish immigrant, 175, 177, 186–87, 190, 194–95

Irish Mick, 195–98

Irish Republican Army, 186, 190

Itkin, Michael, 71, 95–101, 150

Jackson, Shannon, 23–24

Jenkins, Miss Joyce, 131

Jesus Christ, 88, 98, 165. *See also* Bible; religion (and queerness)

Johnson, David K., 63

Johnson, E. Patrick, 28

Johnson, Janetta, 286–87

Johnson, Lyndon, 120

Johnson, Marsha P., 102–4, 106

Juanita MORE!, 224

judging, 240

June, Jennie, 54–55

juvenile detention centers, 40, 43, 119–20

Kapp, David, 230–33

Keire, Mara L., 39, 62

Kennedy, Elizabeth Lapovsky, 28

Kepner, Jim, 113

Kerr, Daniel, 273

kids, 10–11. *See also* abuse; caregivers; homelessness; hustlers; queens; runaway youth; self-worth; sex work; social trauma; survival; working class

kids on the street, 10–12, 17–18

Kim, Jane, 284

Kimo's, 221, 244–45

Kinsey, Alfred, 11, 40

kinship networks. *See* street families

Kirshenblatt-Gimblett, Barbara, 280, 283

Knobel, Dale, 196

labor, 92

Lanigan-Schmidt, Thomas, 42

Larkin Street Youth, 160–61

Latin Americans, 221, 224, 238–40, 254, 260–61

Lavender Panthers, 85, 93, *94*

Lee, Ed, 279, 283

leftism, 96–97, 104, 114

le Grand, Toto (a.k.a. Lou Rand Hogan), 55

Lettermen Club, 131

Lewis, John, 140

Lewis, Oscar, 120–21

Light of Understanding, 150

Lind, Earl, 54–55

Lipsitz, George, 227, 325n10

listening parties, 258, 267–68

literature, 7

Living Theatre, 96–97

Lobo, Kevin "Kiko," 49, 207, 234–36, *269*

loneliness, 162–64, 199, 203–4

"Loneliness in the Tenderloin" (Broshears), 162

Longseeker, Corey, 32, 175, 199–205, 207–19, 296n87

love, 198, 247–48, 253

Love, Heather, 17–18, 173

Lovell, Kristen, 106–7

Lower Polk Community Court, 226

Lower Polk Neighbors, 211, 220–21, 226–29, 236, 243, 281–82

low-income consumer, 30, 140–41

Low Life in High Heels, A (Woodlawn), 47

Lucas, Don, 114, 132

Lundy, David Royal, Jr. *See* Longseeker, Corey

Lush Lounge, 236–37

Luster, Orville, 116

Lyon, Phyllis, 115, 136

Machado, Agosto, 103

Mahogany, Honey, 286

Malina, Judith, 96–98

Mamiya, Larry, 134, 136–37, 140, 150–51, 153

Manalansan, Martin, 159

Marat, Jean-Paul, 134, 137, *138*, 139, 141–42, *161*

Mardi Gras, 45, 60

Market Street (San Francisco), *9*, 55, 62, 109–10, 113, 118, 126, 142, 152, 183–84

Marlane, Vicki, 284

Marotta, Toby, 205, 207, 296n87

Martin, Bradford, 97

Martin, Del, 116

masculinity, 25, 58–59, 63, 168–69, 175, 189–90, 202

masquerade, 8, 60, 175, 189–90, 198. *See also* personas

Mattachine Society, 112–14, 122, 132–33

Maxwell, Levi, 288

Mayor's Office of Economic and Workforce Development, 226, 260, 267–68, 281, 286

McCleve, David, 211

McHugh, Siobhan, 272

McIlvenna, Ted, 115–16, 121

meat racks, *9*, 39–40, *41*, 44, 50, 59–67, 90, 113–17, 139–41, 152, 184. *See also* hustlers; sex work

medallion project, 282

mediated dialogues, 259–63, 271–72

mental health, 18, 80–81, 214–15, 235–36, 253

Merchants of Upper Market, 155

methamphetamines, 16, 175, 205–8

methodologies (of this book), 6–10, 18, 22–32, 36–37, 71, 110–11, 175, 221, 263. *See also* interdisciplinary methods

Metropolitan Community Church of New York, 101, 105–6

Michaels, Kelly, 33, *34*, 35–36, 68, 80

Michaels, Lucky, 106

"Mid-Market Vibrancy and Safety Plan," 279–80

Shelley, John, 118–19, 121
ships, 277
Shopes, Linda, 259
Sims, River, 1–2, 10, 68–71, 75–83, *84*, 85, 159
single-room occupancy (SRO) apartments, 1–3, 216–17, 250, 253–54, 256
sinvergüencería, 16
sit-ins, 66–67
sit/lie ordinance, 155–56, 159, 171, 319n4. *See also* homelessness
skid row, 113–14, 122, 126
snowball method, 263
social history, 27
social justice movements, 112, 121
social norms, 20–21, 31, 37, 64, 113, 205, 223
social status, 54, 57, 153. *See also* class
social trauma, 5, 9–10, 16, 23, 30, 110–12, 162, 187, 202–4, 257, 297n103. *See also* abuse
social truth, 27–28, 195
social workers, 11, 115–16, 135
Society for Individual Rights (SIR), 73, 122, 131, 136–37
sociological studies, 27, 37, 48, 61, 75, 120, 122
soldiers, 59
Spade, Dean, 15, 135
speech act theory, 97
speed. *See* methamphetamines
spiritualism, 104–6, 127–28
spoiled identity, 187
Stack, Carol, 14
status offenses, 43–44
stereotyping, 17, 20, 29, 113–14, 195–96, 247
Stonewall riots, 29, 101, 103–4
storytelling, 5, 8, 26–28, 85–86, 126, 179, 195, 270, 277–79. *See also* audio portraits; multimedia exhibits; narratives
storytelling phenomenon, 264
Stout, Noelle, 21

Strait, Guy, 43, 46, 63, 118, 123, *136*, 139, 152, 180
stranger intimacies, 46
street churches, 4–5, 15, 71, 110, 149–51. *See also* ministers; religion (and queerness)
street families: and abandonment, 80, 102, 109; background on, 4–5; collapse of, 67–68; and drugs, 205; and fleeing abuse, 79–80; as legitimizers of street life, 50; methods of examining, 36; and Polk Street, 179, 235–36; and pooling resources, 14, 35–36, 49–50; and religion, 103; and survival, 109, 174. *See also* reciprocity
street kids. *See* abuse; caregivers; homelessness; hustlers; queens; reciprocity; runaway youth; self-worth; sex work; sit/lie ordinance; social trauma; survival; working class
street names, 48, 102–3, 109, 202
Street Prophets, 153
street queens. *See* fairies; hair fairies; queens
Street Transvestite Action Revolutionaries (STAR), 101, 104
street workers, 130–31
Streicher, Rikki, 183
structural inequality, 15, 110
Stryker, Susan, 165, 288
Student Nonviolent Coordinating Committee, 121, 140, 150
suicide, 109, 124, 168
surrogation, 24–25
survival: and caregivers, 11, 102; and gentrification, 36; and housing, 254, 256; and kids, 3, 6, 13, 79–80, 109, 246; and kinship, 14, 20, 50, 58, 109, 128, 159; and narratives, 7, 53, 112; and reciprocity, 4–5, 13–15, 20, 32, 134; and sex work, 1, 22, 26, 79; strategies, 6, 9, 23, 26, 53, 158, 288; and Vanguard, 110, 135. *See also* reciprocity